Building & Remodeling for Energy Savings

By
James D. Higson

Craftsman Book Company, 542 Stevens Avenue, Solana Beach, CA 92075

Library of Congress Cataloging in Publication Data

Higson, James D.
   Building and remodeling for energy savings.

   Includes index.
   1.   Dwellings--Energy conservation. I. Title.
TJ163.5.D86H53   696   77-15079
ISBN 0-910460-56-6

Contents

4

Construction Contracting and the Energy Problem 1

Our Nation's energy problem was triggered into an "energy crisis" in October 1973, when an oil embargo was imposed by the Arab oil producing countries. The embargo resulted in a condition where total energy supplies fell 14 percent short of expected consumption. Simultaneously, the price of Middle East oil jumped from $3 to $11 per barrel.

The short-term effects of the "energy crisis" were dramatic. Estimated GNP dropped between 10 and 20 billion dollars. Unemployment rose by 500,000 people, and approximately one-third of a 9.8 percent annual increase in consumer prices was attributed to the "energy crisis". The long term effects are influencing every aspect of our lives and our economy.

Some people believe that the energy crisis is over. Some believe that fuel shortages and gasoline lines were contrived either by big Government or big oil companies or both to raise prices. However, the fact is that *until at least 1990, our energy demands — even at a reduced growth rate — will increase faster than our supply.* Thus, if nothing is done, the shortage will become worse.

The United States of America is an energy intensive country. We have only 6 percent of the world's population, but we account for 35 percent of the world's energy consumption.

- Our consumption of energy is still increasing but at a lesser rate than formerly.

- Domestic oil production peaked in about 1970 and is steadily declining — 4 percent per year since 1973.

- Imports of foreign oil continue at a high volume even at very high prices.

- We imported 6.5 Million Barrels of Oil per Day (MMBD) in 1974. Without new actions, this would double to about 12.7 MMBD by 1985.

- Our balance of payments deficits, due to the continued importation of foreign oil at high prices, have serious implications for employment and the economy.

- Natural gas consumption has been exceeding new discoveries since 1968.

- Natural gas shortages are forcing curtailment to many industrial and residential customers. This causes unemployment, reduction in the production of fertilizer needed to increase food supplies and increases demand for other fuels, mostly imported oil.

Much has been written about solar energy, use of coal, oil shale, and, of course, nuclear energy. Let us look briefly at these alternatives to crude oil as sources of power to determine why energy conservation is the only clear solution for the next twenty years or more.

Solar Energy

The sun's rays have long been known to be a source of energy. Homes have been heated with solar heat as have swimming pools, offices, and other spaces. However, to capture solar energy

5

on a mass basis we would have to commit huge areas of land and almost all building tops to the purpose of actually gathering and absorbing the needed rays. Then, if we could set aside our feelings about environmental protection, or if science and technology could somehow appease these feelings by magically "designing around them" we would still be faced with the fantastic cost of building the solar gathering plants and equipment, and these costs might well prove unacceptable.

More feasible are rooftop installations on individual residences and office buildings. Not much additional technology is required to achieve these. However, it remains for a substantial budget of $100 million to be committed, according to N.A.S.A., the national science foundation, and for half a decade to elapse before production of even the heat-producing cycle of solar equipment could be ready for mass marketing. Solar-produced air conditioning would take from six to ten years to develop.

The theory of capturing solar energy from space stations above the earth's atmosphere — obtainable there in a more concentrated, pure form — and retransmitting it to earth is an exciting subject for speculation and possible future development. Unfortunately, the technique, cost, and lead-off time involved in such a project rule it out as offering any energy contribution in the near future.

Coal

This fossil fuel used to be relied upon to a much greater degree in the United States than it is at present. Now coal supplies less than 20 percent of our power needs, while at the turn of the century it supplied almost three-quarters. However, development of improved techniques for extracting coal have not been forthcoming, and thus the related toll in human lives, health, and environment have assisted in its decline as a high priority fuel. Add to this the formidable base established by the environmentalists — with no flexibility built into their militant standards of safeguarding the earth — and it is apparent that the expansion of coal production faces a stormy and uncertain future.

The most accessible one-tenth of our coal deposits could in theory keep our whole economic system going at an accelerated rate for two generations. Then the best deposits alone could provide a long breathing spell in which to develop new energy sources — solar, geothermal, or nuclear fusion — before we would have to turn to thinner and deeper seams.

A fifth to a third of our best coal deposits lie within one hundred feet or so of the surface, within reach of machines that can remove the dirt and rock "overburden" to expose the seam. Mines can be opened faster, fewer labor problems develop, and conditions are generally safer at these depths. It is possible to get 80 to 90 percent of the coal, whereas in underground mines half of the coal is typically left behind to prevent cave-ins.

And if this were not sufficient inducement to exploit this forgotten resource, realize that production per man hour is three times higher in surface than in underground coal mining. The millions of dollars worth of coal beneath the thirty acres needed to support one cow will continue to make a strong case for digging.

In spite of the potential, coal production is today only about what it was in the 1940's and is not likely to be increased very much in the next few years.

Oil Shale

There are vast deposits of this shale lying at or just below the surface of the ground in Colorado and Western North and South Dakota. Even a portion of these deposits is capable of contributing major support to our imperiled energy supplies. However, uttering the words "strip mining" to an environmentalist is like yelling "sic 'em!" to a slavering attack dog. When the klaxon bleat of the ardent conservationist is added to the already moribund state of general strip mining technology, the prospects for even enlightened use of this procedure are not bright.

By "enlightened" is meant the process of contouring or reconstructing the land to relieve the blighted appearance commonly associated with strip mining. This process of reconstruction attempts, if not to restore the land to its pristine state, at least to mold and to sculpt it into a socially acceptable form. This would seem to satisfy most people, but we live now in an age of heightened ecology consciousness.

Much legislation has been enacted to escalate the environmentalists' cause. Some of it is no doubt meritorious, but along with that has flourished a spate of restrictive prohibitions and procedures that can only have the net effect of thwarting reasonable industrial progress.

Other Sources

Other exotic means of fuel procurement exist, such as taking it from the hot inner core of the earth in the form of heat transmitted to the surface. Great expense, great technical pioneering, and great periods of time are inherent in such theories. They are certainly not part of the short-term energy supply scene.

Nuclear Power

In the long run, it is likely that it will be possible to meet a large portion of our fuel requirements by imaginative use of nuclear energy. This source is probably inexhaustible. Given sufficient time to develop it and to solve the problems of waste, heat, safety, and cost, its use could relieve the pressure on our irreplaceable natural resources such as oil and coal. Having such an unfailing source of power would further be valuable so that our precious resources could be utilized at a slower rate in other areas, like the manufacture of plastics and chemicals.

It is the timing of the availability of adequate nuclear power that is the problem, though. Estimates run from thirty to fifty years as the length of time it will take to have nuclear technology and physical development reach the point where it could be largely responsible for the majority of our energy needs.

Most everyone agrees that there isn't going to be a breakthrough that will let us go back to the cheap energy days of the 1960's and early 1970's. If anything, the problem is only going to get worse.

What Can We Do About It?

The shock of the "energy crisis" has stimulated the search for solutions. Only two basic courses of action are available. The first involves *increasing energy supplies*, including expanded exploration efforts for oil and gas, stepped up coal mining activities, building more nuclear plants and intensified efforts to develop major new sources like solar, geothermal and shale oil. These are long range solutions.

The second involves *energy conservation* to reduce demand. This is our only short term option and is achieved by, for example, reducing speed limits, setting back thermostats, cutting off some lighting and energy conservation in housing, buildings and industry. The first three are examples of curtailment. On the other hand, energy conservation in housing and buildings is

a matter of improvement of efficiency of utilization.

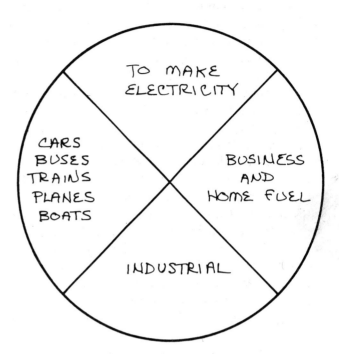

Distribution of Energy Uses

Where the Builder Comes In

About a fourth of all energy sources goes into fuel for heating and cooling homes and businesses. About a fourth of all energy goes into making electricity, another fourth into modes of transportation, and about a fourth into industrial use for manufacturing. Thus the home builder relates directly to energy used in the home through the use of pure electrical power, the use of fuel, and by means of location and transportation decisions; and he relates indirectly by some product decisions as they are tied to industrial production.

The last enters the picture when building or remodeling a home. Just as there have been dramatic shortages at various times of lumber, plumbing fixtures, copper wire, reinforcing steel, and insulation in the past few years, new and unexpected shortages could occur due more than previously to fuel insufficiencies.

So far, this might appear to be a book of negatives, all don'ts and no do's. Happily that is not actually the case. As the steps of building and remodeling unfold, the many facets of energy savings will be woven into the naturally stimulating and creative process of house involvement.

7

Meantime, the concern here is that the builder should not wind up with a house resembling a beached whale, marginally useful at best because the cost of heating, cooling, lighting and using it would nearly be large as the mortgage payment. The idea of heating the home without waste, watching your initial decisions on window placement and shrubs and trees work miracles of weather control, and seeing everywhere the maturation of critical judgments as opposed to haphazard guesswork should excite any creative builder. The fact that money and resources are saved is the materialistic gain. The fact that your approach to home building has been professionalized is a subjective gain of incalculable value and satisfaction.

Until October of 1973 nearly everyone, including the home builders of this country, had naively and blissfully assumed that there would be a ceaseless and increasing outpouring of domestic and foreign oil with which to satiate increasing demand. To inhibit or stifle this growth was considered difficult at best and perhaps foolish if not dangerous. Increasing energy consumption was felt to be a measure of our prosperity. The more energy we used, the better off we all were. Only during an economic recession did energy consumption slow slightly. Energy waste created some problems, but it changed our way of life and most people liked the change. We liked the freedom of driving large cars long distances when it seemed appropriate. We liked having our homes and offices heated or cooled to precisely 72 degrees regardless of the weather and fuel required.

Since energy was cheap, the construction industry built residences, offices, warehouses, and commercial buildings that depended on cheap fuel for light and heat. Urban sprawl was accepted by home owners as inevitable if not desirable. Builders gave little thought to planning for energy savings. And why should they? Gasoline sold for 30 cents a gallon and most homes could be heated and air conditioned for $10 to $20 per month. Why pay for special design features, extra insulation and energy conservation measures when they cost more than they saved? If home buyers wouldn't buy energy-efficient homes, there was no reason to build them. But now we know that the cost of our most useful fuel, crude oil, increased 600% between 1973 and 1977. Other fuels recorded similar but perhaps less spectacular increases.

Worse yet, the cost of energy is expected to increase at about 10% a year even disregarding the effects of inflation. This means that a homeowner who is paying $500 a year for heating and electricity in 1978 will pay $1,000 to $1,200 a year within a decade, even if the value of the dollar does not change. Over the next decade or two the home owner is going to have to live with nearly unbelievable fuel bills unless he becomes committed to conservation. Home buyers and owners wanting to remodel are going to be very serious about energy savings. Every builder and remodeler who wants to sell to the energy conscious buyer or owner must be aware of what can and should be done to cut home energy consumption.

Energy efficient dwellings were built for many years in this country. Many experienced builders will remember homes designed for cross or updraft ventilation, built to take advantage of shade and sun and furnished with small heat sources in every room so the entire house didn't have to be heated to the same thermostatically controlled temperature. Some builders may even remember that most homes in many parts of the country had solar water heaters in the early 1900's. Many more will remember the desirability of building near the streetcar line or within walking distance of stores. To the builder of the 1930's a window that wouldn't open was a waste. In the 1960's we assumed that windows in many buildings would never have to be opened, unless of course the power failed. Times have changed. But from the viewpoint of the 1990's we may realize that the energy binge that began in the 1920's accelerated during the 1950's and ended abruptly in October 1973 was a very unusual period. It is almost inevitable that we will go back to building energy efficient homes and planning to live with less energy at our disposal.

The construction contractor, especially the home builder, is in a sensitive position in this continuing energy problem. Most homes are not built or remodeled under the supervision of an architect. The home builder has much more discretion about what goes into the homes he builds or remodels than the builder putting up office buildings and warehouses. The custom or speculative home builder has the opportunity to keep his homes from becoming functionally obsolete as the energy needed to heat and light homes becomes more expensive. Home buyers want reassurance that what you sell will save them money. Most buyers are willing to pay for these future savings. Don't let what you build fail to meet the challenge of changing availability of energy. Don't fail yourself to stay informed of what you could and should be doing to build energy savings into your homes. Your clients and buyers rely on you to give them the best of what is possible and desirable in energy saving measures.

This book is intended to show what you could and should be building into the new homes and remodeling jobs you will have in the next ten years. Many of the chapters deal with design features that improve the energy efficiency of homes. Others deal with materials and equipment that may not be familiar to you but which every energy conscious builder should be aware of. Some chapters point out new areas of opportunity for construction contractors. Other chapters are intended to stimulate your thinking about the business decisions you make from day to day. Taken as a whole, this book should make it easier for you to meet the needs of energy conscious buyers of the 1980's.

Location of the House 2

Whether a home is in the city or in the suburbs, there are some locations that cause more energy problems than others.

Excessive Noise

If a home is situated near a flight pattern of an airport it can be easy to buy and very hard to sell. A location near a highway or road, particularly where there is a grade causing a frequent use of lower gears or a bus stop can cause windows to be closed more than would be normal. This drives up the need for air conditioning in warmer weather and thus increases energy costs. Beware also of a sports arena, meeting halls, or bowling alley — any facility that draws crowds and their automobiles.

Excessive Wind

Acquaint yourself with the direction of the prevailing wind, its strength, and the house's orientation to it. This natural phenomenon will enter our discussion in many areas — orientation, fenestration, landscaping, pool heating, etc. Generally speaking, if the home is situated where it is vulnerable to a lot of steady wind, the fuel bills are going to be unavoidably high in cold weather.

Wind has the effect of decreasing the insulating blanket of still air that usually surrounds a building. Wind carries the solar heat away from the building and evaporates any moisture that may have collected on the roof or wall surface, thus decreasing the surface temperature below the air temperature. This would be desirable in the cooling season but undesirable in the heating season.

Homes and apartment buildings should have their most vulnerable portions, which include entrance and glazed areas, oriented away from the prevailing winds to reduce air leakage around doors, windows, and any other openings. In the northern hemisphere, the north and west sides of a building are usually exposed to wind the most. If there must be an entrance on the north or west, it should be shielded. A combination of high winds and low temperatures in winter increases the need for wind protection to reduce infiltration.

Saving Transportation Costs

In choosing the location of a home, transportation costs are as certain a fixed cost as are electricity, taxes, and the mortgage payments on the house itself. It is true that some costs of mobility are optional, like ski trips, frivolous shopping, and extraneous social calls, but transportation expense associated with earning a living, going to school, obtaining services, and mandatory shopping can extort a high ransom indeed in terms of wasted time, energy, and money.

Vehicular transportation extracts a very human toll in wasted time that is seldom talked about.

Our periodicals are rife with figures that take the kilowattage of, say, a large commercial building that stays entirely lighted but empty all night and show that the identical kilowattage could provide the total electrical needs of the nice folks in Milpitas, California (population 25,000), for a full week — all from one night's wasted power. To those who have become jaded by such comparisons, the following set of figures should yet prove arresting:

Saga of a 40-Mile Commuter

¾ hour	extra time spent commuting to work each way
1½ hours	extra time each day
33 hours	extra each month
386 hours	extra each year
16 days	lost annually, figuring full 24 hours
21 days	lost annually, if 8 hours sleep excluded

Three full weeks of otherwise controllable free time, a whole second annual vacation period, is lost by commuting in an automobile fifty miles instead of ten.

A Move to the City

Many factors point the way to a rejuvenation and revitalization of our cities. For one thing, a major cutback in development of large remote tracts of land is almost certain. Another is renewed emphasis on mass transit. For example, B.A.R.T. in San Francisco, after a delayed and shaky start, is off and working following its initial growing pains. Fuel shortages and expenses will dictate continued expansion of public transportation. Cultural values of the city are too valuable to foresake: witness the expansion in recent years of theater, art, and music facilities in Los Angeles, Milwaukee, and Dallas.

Often the choice in deciding on a city home or a suburban home is between the convenience and fuel savings of the city home, previously set forth, and the advantage of more square footage, a larger lot, and the newness of the suburban home. In view of the energy squeeze and the human and cultural values inherent in the city location, we will be gazing with a more critical eye on the seeming attributes of suburbia. The city home or the home near work, and the value of cultural and recreational proximity are better both for convenience and for future investment appreciation.

Homer Hoyt of Homer Hoyt Associates states that assessing the impact of a gasoline shortage on real estate values is difficult because of other strong influences, namely, "inflation and a sharply declining birth rate." But he is certain that "the impact of the energy crisis is going to be different for varying types of properties and different locations."

In outlining basic differences for varying types of real estate, Hoyt stresses location as a prime factor in determining value with the most positive outlook for residential and commercial properties *near transportation and shopping*. He reports a probable decline in value for distant resort areas, and urban sites for residential use at a distance from metropolitan centers.

On the positive side of the ledger, Mr. Hoyt includes:

Single-family homes — These will rise in price where they exist in areas close to industry in the suburbs or on rail lines.

Apartments and condominiums — there will be increased building of high rise apartments catering to couples without school-aged children.

Mr. Hoyt cautions smaller investors from purchasing on city outskirts. "The return from buying vacant land on the outskirts of metropolitan areas for future building can often be realized by a professional real estate developer, often a giant corporation, but likely not by the smaller investor."

Other Nearby Facilities and Services

In *The Higson Home-Buyer's Guide* a list is included of facilities and services that are desirable to have within bicycling or walking distance of the home. It is as follows:

1. School	9. Club, town square
2. Police and fire station	10. Drugstore
3. Hospital and medical services	11. Bookstore
	12. Laundry and cleaner
4. Mass transit stop	13. Church
5. Market	14. Bank
6. Playground, tennis	15. Restaurants
7. Library	16. Barber, beauty parlor
	17. Motion picture theatre
8. Service station (with mechanic)	18. Specialty shops

Here the facilities and services are numbered in an order of approximate priority. From the standpoint of ideal logistics in ease of house

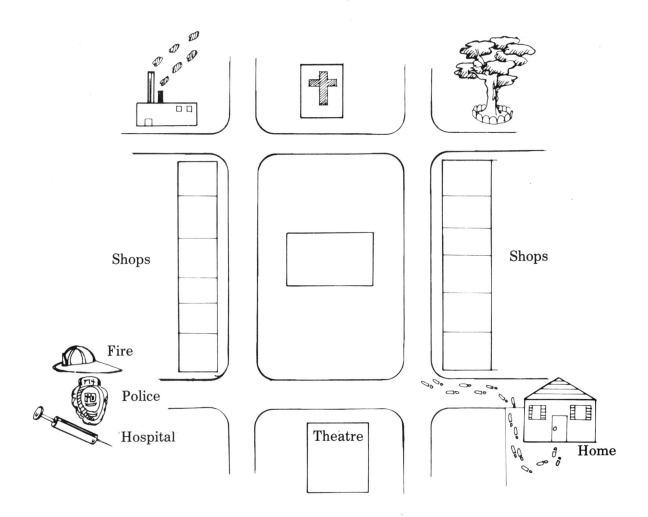

Shops

Shops

Fire

Police

Hospital

Theatre

Home

Ideal Village Plan

operation, one might envision a utopian village, where work, play and twenty or more of the facilities indicated were situated as their counterparts might have been in a self-sufficient medium to small town or township within a larger city.

The New Era of Recreation and Home, Sweet Home

Life is not all work, and it is imperative to maintain some balance between making a livelihood and planning for the increased time and enjoyment of it. Location remains the major factor in reducing wasteful transportation commitments with regard to leisure as well as work.

Professor James Flink of the University of Caifornia states flatly that the automobile has stopped being an historically progressive force in American culture, and that its domination of American civilization is coming to an end. Dr.

Flink predicted a return of the middle classes to the cities, greatly improved non-automobile transit systems, and a drastic alteration in our view of the automobile, which he has intepreted in the past to be symbolic of individualism, privatism, materialism, and escapism. He sees the new culture value as a "communitarian ethic" where people develop an awareness of their community and its concerns.

High energy costs favor those developers who recognize the need for relating community planning to fuel conservation by creating master-planned, self-contained villages. Mr. Frank E. Hughes of the Irvine Company of Newport Beach says, "Personally, I feel that developers of totally planned communities will be in a far better position than builders of isolated housing tracts to weather the effects of the energy crisis. In the Irvine Company's distinct villages a major objective is to locate schools, shopping, and recreational facilities close to residential areas.''

High energy costs also favor smaller builders who can develop single lots or small tracts of close-in land. The development cost should be much lower because curbs, streets and utilities are probably already in. Buyers recognize the value of good location and know that higher fuel costs make most close-in building sites much more attractive.

This point cannot be driven home too strongly: the selection of a home location should not contain a prison sentence of three weeks each year to be spent in solitary, nonproductive, nonrecreational time encapsulized within a metal box on wheels—commuting. Do, then, seek locations near places of work or at least near public transportation, where a portion of travel time can be recaptured in the form of reading and other resourceful leisure-time pursuits. Give preference to close-in lots and assign a dollars and hours-of-commuting saved value to these sites. In many cases the in-city lot may be worth more in the long run and you can sell these advantages to your clients.

An established neighborhood has a reputation — all neighborhoods do. It is important to know that it is a good one, that the schools are highly regarded, crime rate negligible, and most of the checkpoints of convenience, necessity, and pleasure covered to some reasonable degree. Apart from what real estate brokers tell you, get direct information from a loan officer at the nearest savings and loan or one of their appraisers. The loan officer of the nearest bank also has information and opinions on this. City offices, chambers of commerce, and even retail establishments can also be helpful. The more objective you are about determining the validity of investing heavily in the property, the more sound that investment will be and the faster it will grow.

You are selling housing to people who probably recognize that they spend the majority of their leisure hours in their home or in the immediate vicinity. This is especially true of people of modest income who are restricted by high transportation costs. It also affects older, less flexible people who are pretty much stuck in the house when fuel becomes scarce or expensive.

Consider as well the impact on fuel conservation of mounting experimentation with the four-day workweek, now a reality in many businesses. There is also the self-programmed workweek, where the employee, within limits, specifies his or her own floating work schedule. Most drastic, of course, was the three-day forced workweek imposed on Great Britain by the energy crisis and coal strike. And consider also the statement made by the French architect and planner Pierre Dufan that the home of the future will be playing a much larger role than it does at present. He reasons that the home will become more important as the world moves away from a factory-oriented to a paper-oriented society — much more work will be done in the home.

In this expanded and increasingly dualistic role, the location and function of the home as a recreation center and workplace achieves formidable significance. ''Location is everything'' may sound like a boring truism, but it has a very real meaning here. *If* the home has a potential for enjoyable use in increased leisure time hours, *if* some recreational facilities such as a park, golf course, library, tennis courts, or riding stables are within an easy bicycle ride, and *if* the home is near a stop for rapid transit line or train that *could* link it with more far-flung recreational pursuits, it surely has the transportation bugaboo defeated.

The Site

Knowing the approximate size of the house you intend to build, be sure that it will not be larger or more elaborate than its companion houses. The best house in a block suffers by comparison at the time of resale, but the more modest home in the company of impressive adjacent houses rides on the investment coattails of its more illustrious neighbors. This can be your gain as well, if you are the one who builds the more modest home.

Difficult building sites like hillsides or some canyon properties, while already deemed ill-advised because of energy-related transportation problems, often cause lending institutions to be negative as well. Those attractive views and snug canyons may be all very well for the romantically and nostalgically inclined, but the lender's gimlet eye sees them in a sweat of anxiety about improper cutting and filling above or below the property, poor fire protection, landslides, mudslides, slow resale in case of repossession, high insurance rates, and limited utility choices. Actually, people do not like negotiating many steps and different levels, plus there are higher building and maintenance costs in these locations. The possibility of a garage situated at a great distance and several levels away from the house is sheer hell in rainy weather.

If this were not reciting sufficient reason for giving pause to thoughts of hillsides and canyon sites, this even more cardinal investment-building rule is often violated on difficult sites: *do not put a high percentage of construction funds into the ground!* Call it the "Iceberg Theory," if you will. You are no doubt familiar with the threadbare analogy of the floating iceberg with 80 percent of its mass under the water and only 20 percent showing above the water. By keeping this principle in mind, your construction dollars will be saved from a grave of unseen reinforcing steel and concrete caissons, and wind up where they should be, in the visible, decorative, and humanly useful elements of the house.

Finally, be watchful for future changes in the area for the better or for the worse. Ask yourself if the nearby commercial district you are relying on is healthy and prospering. Stores for rent are an indication that it is not. Be certain that schools are good. Check to see that recreational facilities are kept up. Recheck the area for *noise pollution.*

The Economics of Land and Building

A national survey of land prices over the past several years shows the proportion of land to building to be about 20 percent to 80 percent. Therefore, working against a $100,000 total project cost, the land would be about $20,000 and the building about $80,000.

Expensive? Yes. Yet if construction is inhibited for the near future, which appears to be the case, and half of the homes that are built are built as condominiums, and if prices continue to rise 7 to 9 percent a year, the comparatively few new homes that are built with energy conservation in mind and in good locations will likely turn out to be very fine investments.

Planning the Site

In planning of the site or "plot," it helps to arrange the elements of design on a scale drawing of the property. The various building masses can be cut out of cardboard in 1/8-inch or ¼-inch scale and temporarily positioned on a plot plan of the same scale. Thus you can begin to get a feel of the general relationship of these elements as they relate to one another and to roads, setbacks, utilities, existing landscaping, and existing structures. You can sketch out the contour lines as described in *The Higson Home-Builder's Guide;* after that, sketch on the probable "flow lines" of surface water drainage, noting where all water will leave the property.

This visualization of the total site in almost three dimensional perspective is invaluable when the building program moves ahead. As the builder, your most useful tool will be the perception of the plans in space and time. You should endeavor constantly to "see" the drawings as occupying space and to acquire a sense of the production steps as they ultimately unfold in the building of the house.

Initial Steps

Obtain the exact dimensions of the lot from the real estate broker or the title company. Arrange a drawing of it in 1/8-inch scale. Check the title policy or preliminary title report for any easements. Confer with the following city or county offices for the information about the site:

Planning Department
> front, rear, and sideyard setbacks
> building height limit
> garage and parking requirements
> any special use permits or variances required
> correct house numbers and address assigned

Building Department
> fees for plan check and building permit
> any special charges like "sanitary district," or grading, demolition
> approximate length of time to process plans
> obtain permit forms

Engineering Department or Public Works
> arrange for cutting the curb and driveway approach
> location and fee for sewer plus *depth* of sewer
> location and fee for water service and water meter
> discuss any sidewalk replacement or requirements

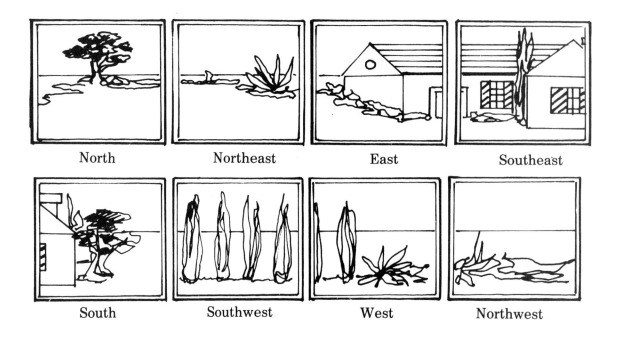

| North | Northeast | East | Southeast |
| South | Southwest | West | Northwest |

Building Site Photographs

A very effective method of studying your site at your leisure is to take eight camera shots of the compass points North, Northeast, East, Southeast, South, Southwest, West, and Northwest from some central point on the lot shooting *away* from the approximate house site. When developed, arrange them in correct sequence like the old panorama group photographs. This photographic record will provide a constant verification source for views and vistas as the planning of the site and home progresses.

The Characteristics of the Soil

Be satisfied that soil conditions are not burdensome and are adaptable to your building and landscaping objectives. By way of illustration, a little known fact is that the halcyon slopes of the most sought-after portion of the French Riviera near Nice — St. Paul de Vence, Vence, Cagnes — are composed of rock. This unhappy reality necessitates blasting with dynamite for all roads, house pads and footings, new trees of any size, basements, septic tanks, terraces, and swimming pools. Because there are nearby houses already in existence, many small charges of powder must be set off in order to build — anywhere from 200 to 400. For example, a swimming pool that would cost $6,000 in this country would cost $20,000 in France given those soil conditions. Needless to say, all building costs are astronomically high and time

schedules lengthy. Prices of houses are very high, since the houses are but tips of icebergs with much of their building cost buried beneath the ground where you cannot see it.

Clay soil presents problems in drainage and moisture absorption. Special precautions have to be undertaken to prevent dampness from entering a home built over such soil, particularly if a concrete slab floor is desired. In landscaping a clay soil lot, it is essential that areas be sloped and not level, for the hard pan beneath the topsoil will otherwise cause the water to stand, and ground cover and lawns will rot.

Adjacent neighbors can be a good source of information on soils, as is the building inspector who is responsible for the foundation inspections. A landscape architect also knows his soils and will be able to help you. If it looks like the soil is somewhat out of the ordinary, a soils engineer should be brought in for advice.

Utilities and Services

Consult with the electric, natural gas, telephone company, and Television Community Antenna System to find out how they will enter your property to service the residence. Ideally these utilities will enter underground so as not to sully the environment with ugly poles, wires, and exposed meters — the ultimate ecological insult.

16

The Importance of Good Drainage. Every professional builder should build roofs, decks, and balconies that drain well. A well thought out water disposal system for roof and other surface water should be built into your original thinking about the house and overall site. Most cities prohibit you from draining such water into the sewer system. Moreover, the law will not let you drain water onto another person's property unless it has historically flowed onto it, just as you cannot interrupt the flow of drainage water that has habitually drained from another lot over your property. Therefore, you must make plans to drain every bit of water into the street or public storm drain or stream. Take note that some lots may require extensive grading or undergound drainage pipes and catch basins in order to accomplish this.

A Word About Sewer Depth. All utilities except the sewer operate by pressure or conduction. The sewer and entire waste drainage system operate by gravity. A minimum "fall" of ¼ inch to the foot in the direction of the sewer connection where it enters the property is essential. This affects the height of the first floor of the house. So it is vital in situating the house to know the depth of the sewer. It is possible to place the house lower than the sewer, but the disadvantages are numerous. A sewer pump has to be installed, and it needs constant inspections and maintenance, and even then is not perfect. Since it requires an electric motor to be in operation whenever the drains are being used, it is utterly inconsistent with an energy wise house.

Building Materials and Your Site

There are many approaches to indigenous house construction. Scott Nearing, considered a flaming liberal in the thirties and forties and now a mellowed vital man in his seventies, and his wife Helen wrote, in *Living the Good Life: How to Live Sanely and Simply in a Troubled World* about building his house in Vermont entirely out of rock rubble which he piled up in a double wooden form into which he poured concrete to solidify the loose rocks. This was an excellent idea. It certainly produced a rugged, indigenous looking house and at a cost considerably less than building walls up one stone at a time.

This subject of building material will be covered in greater detail as we approach the matter of style in a later chapter. In connection with the purchasing of a lot though, we are looking broadly at the idea of versatility of materials selections and at design objectives that are energy saving and cost saving. Some sites assist in this; others frustrate it. Be alert to flexibility in your choice of materials and in the use of materials inherent in various sites. Scott Nearing had loose rocks readily available, so they were a natural material for him to use.

Be wary if either site or layout dictates or inhibits the use of any materials. For example, the process of delivering supplies up or down slopes is difficult and expensive. Most bulky materials such as masonry, lumber, lath, and sheetrock are delivered to the job by means of large trucks that dump them as close as they can get to the house site. Job site work roads in damp or rainy climates will not serve these massive delivery trucks. Make certain that material deliveries will not be a problem or become a large extra expense for you.

Consider using materials that are consistent and homogeneous with the site. Also demand of them that they be energy conserving. It is a gross conceit to enter a neighborhood or even rugged terrain and defy the nearby structures, their ecological reality, and their materials of construction. Such willfulness displays an environmental irresponsibility that is callous beyond comprehension. Plan to have your house flow out of and in consonance with surrounding topography and structures as if you were part of a total landscape and not in business for yourself. Similarly, direct your efforts to the use of materials that are in maximum harmony with the surroundings.

Utilities and Your Project 3

The Basic Utilities

    Sewer

    Water service

    Electricity

    Natural gas

    Telephone

These are the basic utilities, that is services usually provided by a large municipal or private company to which the house is connected. In many ways these vital umbilicals are taken for granted by most of us, but our challenge here is to ease the homeowner's burden of energy consumption and, while doing so, attempt to exercise cost savings. Therefore, let us tackle these primary sources and prevent them from getting in the way of our objective.

Local conditions vary to a great degree. But just as no wise buyer is going to involve himself with a house without knowing the very real costs of transportation, neither will he saddle himself with a utility gobbler whose monthly operating costs rival the mortgage payment in size.

Sewer

This is by far the most convenient and thrifty means of waste disposal and can harbor only two areas of continuing expense. Find out if there is a bond or construction or connection charge as yet unsatisfied or a sanitary district fee that might be levied on an annual basis. Septic tanks and cesspools are a necessary headache in many areas. Even so, there is no reason to avoid the issue of maintenance. Consider this additional cost when you buy the property. If the cost is reasonable, have these figures ready for your buyer's inspection.

Water Service

In addition to being watchful about the cost of this vital service, there are some further facts that you will want to know:

    Degree of hardness

    Quality of taste

    Pressure

If the water is extra hard, a water softener will likely be required if it is not already present. The cost of rock salt will easily become lost in the grocery budget, but if monthly service is required, that is one more secondary utility expense to be reckoned with.

Some water may be perfectly safe for drinking but may not taste pleasant. You will then need bottled water or a charcoal water purifier for drinking water — another monthly charge.

Lack of sufficient pressure will be treated later as it applies to the plumbing *within the house*. However, the neighborhood may not be getting enough pressure delivered to the lots. While not strictly an energy or cost problem, it

TO FIND YOUR DAILY CONSUMPTION OF ELECTRICITY...

Southern California Edison Company SCE

| SERVICE | READINGS | KWH | AMOUNT |

04 02 06 02 1386 2370 **984** 32 10

Divide this by this

YOUR CURRENT BILL IS FOR **60** DAYS ELECTRIC SERVICE

Please return this stub with remittance payable to Southern California Edison Company, P.O. Box 2691, Long Beach, California 90801

16.4 = Average Daily
60)984.0 KWH Usage

Amount now due

Daily Consumption of Electricity

ENERGY USED TO OPERATE SOME TYPICAL APPLIANCES

Remember, one kilowatt-hour is 1,000 watts of electricity used for one hour, or 100 watts—such as a 100-watt light bulb—used for 10 hours.

100-watt light bulb	1/10 KWH per hour
40-watt light bulb	1/25 KWH per hour
Clothes Dryer (Electric)	3-1/3 KWH per load
Clothes Washer	1/3 KWH per load
Food Waste Disposer	1/100 KWH per load
Dishwasher (rinse, wash & dry)	1 KWH per load
Food Waste Compactor	1/5 KWH per load
Food Freezer—Frost Free	
16 cu. ft.	5 KWH per day
20 cu. ft.	5-1/4 KWH per day
24 cu. ft.	5-1/2 KWH per day
Refrigerator Freezer—Manual defrost	
16 cu. ft.	3-2/3 KWH per day
20 cu. ft.	5-1/3 KWH per day
24 cu. ft.	7 KWH per day
Refrigerator—Frost Free	
16 cu. ft.	5 KWH per day

Appliance Energy Usage

---

could be a very real problem to the homeowner if the lot is of good size with a fair amount of planting on it. If investigation reveals that neighbors have acceptable pressure and the specific property does not, it may have a faulty service line leading into it or a faulty meter, either of which should be remedied by the city or district at their expense. Also, the meter size could be too small. A 5/8-inch size is too small for most tract-sized lots of 50 by 90 feet or more, and even a 3/4-inch size is not enough for a larger home with an ample lot.

Electricity

Utility rates for electricity vary in different areas, but one common denominator for comparison is the number of kilowatt hours used. This figure normally can be found on the invoice. If not, the power company can supply it. Its value lies in being able to make a direct comparison in monthly hourly consumption between one home and another. Take the bill and do the following:

A very crude rule of thumb is that between 250 and 350 kilowatts is fairly standard as

20

average monthly usage for a three to four bedroom home in a mild winter. Here is a description of kilowatt usage in more detail.

This is what the prestigious Rand Corporation said in a report to the California Assembly in 1972: "Electricity is more efficient than gas at the point of end use, but the process of generating electricity by burning gas under a boiler at a steam-electric generating plant is so inefficient that the overall process of generation, transmission, and end use in almost every case requires more energy than if gas were burned directly in the household to achieve the same end use."

Moreover, the electric utility companies have run into still more environmental agencies, laws, and militant groups that have stalled the building and expansion of the needed generating plants. The handwriting should be clearly on the wall: "Strive for a balance in utility sources!"

Natural Gas

Where alternative fuel sources like natural gas are available, take advantage of them. There may be an initial cost for running the gas line to the property, but the gas company will normally pay for part of that expenditure. The dividend that will result is a saving in buying cheaper appliances, quicker and more efficient application of heat to the water heater, space heaters, boilers, and lower monthly operating costs.

Another attribute of natural gas is its superiority for range-top cooking. Julia Child says, "Gas is certainly the most supple heat source." Why is this? One reason is that the chef in a busy kitchen can visually regard the flame and adjust the heat instantaneously. He can react to it and the contents of the vessel on it in one single visual/mental process. This is important when you consider the problem of operating, say, four, six, or eight burners simultaneously. Electricity is fine for both self-cleaning and microwave or electronic ovens, but the point here is to emphasize versatility. It is just fundamentally good business to have two or three arrows in your quiver.

Telephone

The telephone can represent a chilling addition to your utility cost structure if the home is in one of those gerrymandered districts where most "local" calls become long distance calls because your sphere of calling interest lies in another telephone company's district.

Be on guard against this type of situation or your buyer's telephone bills will spiral out of sight. If he lives in District 1 and makes most of his calls to District 2, he could be charged for each telephone call at long distance rates.

Television Cable Systems

These Community Antenna Television Systems (C.A.T.V.) are optional for the subscriber. Where the cost is reasonable, they are a pleasant alternative to the regular home television choices. They add more stations to the dial, plus some locally originated material, and most systems provide FM antenna service right along with the television.

Alternative and Secondary Utilities

In these days of threatened energy shortages and electrifying cost hikes, why not investigate alternative fuel sources?

Is there a good source of firewood nearby?

How much does a cord of wood cost delivered and stacked?

Is there good trash collection service?

Is there a monthly charge for trash service? How much?

Is the house dependent on coal or oil for heating?

Is the home storage facility adequate for keeping enough of this fuel for, say, one or two months ahead?

Is enough natural light being used to cut down electricity costs?

What about using trees to minimize air conditioning costs?

Later on we will explore more exotic fuel sources such as butane, kerosene, alcohol, home-generated electricity, even candles. Suffice it to say for the present that utilities are the lifeblood of the home. Our total dependence on them makes it mandatory that you seek a home with a balanced, versatile, and economical utility repertoire.

Concentrate on cost comparisons and diversification. Know what it will cost to operate the house, and seek as high a degree of versatility as you can.

Reconciling Style With Energy Savings 4

As an art form, architecture is generally conceded to be socially and politically oriented. That is, because of its physical immensity, it is usually controlled by factors other than the artist's will. Some styles are even identified by names of the monarchs who reigned during the time the style flourished, such as Elizabethan, Queen Anne, Georgian, Victorian. The distinguishing features of these houses, although somewhat eroded by modification, improvisation, and revivalist restyling over the years, continue in some measure through duplication of these styles today.

Similarly, broader spans of history stamp the passport of other styles, such as Greek or Classical, Federal, Colonial, and Neoclassic. Then we come to an even broader designation that relates more to vast geographical regions than to eras or personalities, with names such as Alpine, Tyrolean, Spanish, Mediterranean, Florintine, Mexican, and possibly such words as "townhouse," "villa," "country," and "farmhouse."

Most architects worth their salt refuse to discuss their design work in terms of these simplistic word handles. After all, if houses are to be more or less duplicated from past eras, who needs a skilled, creative artist to design them? Any competent draftsman with a background in art or architectural history can paraphrase existing styles with a room arrangement modified to suit his client. Yet we must have some language for discussing what you as a home builder desire in house style without the necessity of having the architect's creative

pallet at hand. Moreover, we have the additional objective of incorporating energy savings into whatever style is selected.

Indigenous Houses

The key word in style selectivity is "indigenous." A style should be natural or native to the environment for which it is intended. By and large those styles which bear names of *regions* and are not named for individuals or bracketed in time periods or eras hold the key to indigenous housing in some countries. On the one hand, describing a house as a "French house" says nothing, because of France's diverse ecology and clutter of historical styles, whereas Spanish does denote a certain indigenous kind of architecture due to the relative homogeneity of climate, language, culture, building materials, etc. The same might be said of Alpine or Mexican.

Also, in discussing indigenous styling it is wise to eliminate from consideration state buildings, schools, monumental architecture of any kind, since buildings created on such a grand scale can hardly be called indigenous. The design of large buildings can leap across national barriers, jump backward or ahead in time, and do whatever it wants as long as there is money to pay for it. It holds no clue for our quest.

In *The Decline of the West, Part II*, Oswald Spengler writes:

"Like the shell of the nautilus, the hive of the bee, the nest of the bird, it (the house) has

English Cottage   Italian Villa

an innate self-evidentness, and every trait of original custom and form of being, of marriage, of family life, and of tribal order is reflected in the place and in the room organization of parterre, hall, wigwam, atrium, court, chamber, and gynaeceum. One need only compare the lay-out of the old Saxon and that of the Roman house to feel that the soul of the men and the soul of the house were in each case identical.''

A study of France's housing sheds solid light on the influence of local ecology on architectural style in a country no larger than Texas.

Weather plays a strong role in this influence. Obviously in climates of heavy rainfall and snowfall, a steep roof, even though badly built, or of poor materials or in need of repair, wards off the elements like putting a peaked newspaper over your head in a rainstorm. Moreover, the arrangement of the house mass on a vertical rather than a horizontal plane suggests a heat preservation problem. In addition, there is an abundance of the long timbers for construction of beams, corner posts, studs and joists and rafters.

Conversely, the warmer temperate climates promote a more relaxed roof form. Less timber and a limitless supply of stone, whether cut or used in crude form, points the way to a more rambling house form arranged on the horizontal rather than the vertical plane. Heat entrapment and protection from rain and snow, though considerations, are less important than protection from the sun. This last is accomplished by the thick stone walls and self-insulating roof tiles. Often there are generous overhangs, porches and terraces used liberally with the style.

Why an indigenous residence? In terms of saving energy, the answer is simple. The closer those style elements of roof, fenestration (door

and window design and placement), house mass, and materials out of which it is built come to being compatible with the natural elements in which it is situated, the more functional and comfortable the house will be. Furthermore, it will be less costly to build and less costly to operate. It will also last longer. For these reasons plus that of aesthetics, it should appreciate well over the years and provide a good investment as well.

In *Poetry of Architecture*, John Ruskin points out the indigenous peculiarities of the more steeply pitched roof of the English cottage and the flattish roof of the Italian villa and how these features validate their own uniqueness.

''The first remarkable point of the building is the roof. It generally consists of tiles of very deep curvature, which rib it into distinct vertical lines, giving it a far more agreeable surface than that of our flatter tiling. . .We have in these roofs an excellent example of what should always be kept in mind, that *everything will be found beautiful, which climate or situation render useful*. The strong and constant heat of the Italian sun would be intolerable if admitted at the windows, and, therefore, the edges of the roof project far over the walls, and throw long shadows downwards, so as to keep the upper windows constantly cool.''

In selecting a neighborhood in which a major visual asset is the consistency of its architecture, however, it is necessary to part company with the objective of indigenousness.

There is always the renegade who will throw up a Bauhaus Modern house in a neighborhood dominated by brick Tudor replicas. He is the exception that should prove the rule: a neighborhood of harmonious, traditionally styled houses should not be jarred by such an inconsistent element. Under certain circum-

Keep in Harmony with the Neighborhood
Architecture

stances a skilled architect can modify a traditional styling to achieve some more realistic environmental ends and still keep a balance with the historical alliances surrounding the house. He will usually work willingly on a problem such as consistency or blending, where he is not arbitrarily being required by a client to compromise his professional integrity and become chauvinistic.

The strong economic reason follows that the speculative builder who builds an inconsistent house in an otherwise harmonious neighborhood, may run the risk of having his investment stagnate.

Modern architecture *can* create truly unique, indigenous houses, but our now ended ability to squander energy tended to shift the architects' attention from indigenousness to modern stylistic conceits that virtually flaunted energy profligacy. The most creative modern architects have reveled in the flat roof forms, the walls of floor-to-ceiling glass, the indoor-outdoor living and viewing concept, high clerestory panels of glass, slab floors, experimental fireplace forms with minimum radiation, conversation pits, open floor plans, even open baths and toilets. They have pursued these fascinating design frontiers with one magnificent assumption that can no longer be made: an unlimited source of cheap energy.

There have been proposals by various columnists and commentators that all designers of buildings, and this would include *all* buildings, be restrained *by federal law* from designing structures that have nonopenable windows and nonswitchable lights. There could certainly be developed some simple criteria that would not impose any significant inhibitions on the scope of design, yet would fetter the spendthrift wizard who perpetuates a ceaseless, clawing, ever burgeoning drain on our energy supplies.

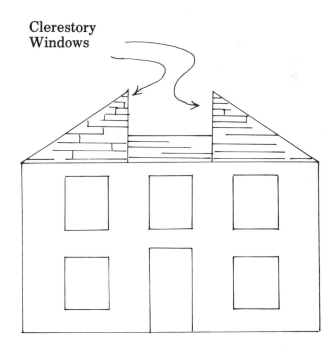

Clerestory Windows

Mine Shaft Modern

Illinois Farmhouse

Undoubtedly, modern architects will turn more attention to the energy problem. Certain design conventions of recent modern styles, such as the flat roof, glass walls, and open floor plan, will of necessity become less popular, if in truth, they ever were. The style nicknamed, "mineshaft," will probably receive more attention than it is getting right now.

With its aborted roof shapes, clerestory windows, and woody cut-up barn look, it has plenty of modern appeal and a high degree of functionalism besides. It may even be indigenous, but associated more with the lean-to-shed roofs over mine shafts or of the feeding troughs built up against larger barns, rather than with classically indigenous forms, whose ecological practicability was built up over centuries.

What Style Should You Select?

You should select a style out of those available to you that is the most indigenous to your area. It should take into consideration the climate, topography, existing houses, materials, and subcontractors able to work with those materials. It should be one that maximizes the use of the total environment, that wholly fits, that "reads."

Ruskin says in his introduction to *The Seven Lamps of Architecture:* "Know what you have to do, and do it. . .failure is less frequently attributable to either insufficiency of means or impatience of labor, than to a confused understanding of the thing actually to be done...''

Where not dictated by a neighborhood ethic, get yourself some principles and stick with them. Begin by comparing the ecological character of your local area with that of other areas of the world, then to other areas within the United States.

The rain forests of the Pacific Northwest are certainly comparable to the Black Forest area of Germany. Southern California can be likened to the French Riviera. Northern California resembles parts of Northern Italy and France; New Mexico and other parts of the southwest, parts of Mexico and Spain. There is some similarity between parts of the Caribbean and Greece, Florida and the Italian Riviera. New England resembles portions of mother England, Flanders, and Alsace in France.

Although these references are obviously imperfect and quite broad, their importance can be seen in studying this picture of a lovely farmhouse in Illinois in the heart of the Midwest.

Now the Midwest ecology approximates some areas in Europe of high climatic change. Yet the architectural pedigree of the house in the drawing is representative of a breed of substantial farmhouses in large areas of the states of Missouri, Illinois, Indiana, and Ohio that came under southern influence in the nineteenth century. It is Georgian at the core, but evinces neoclassical elements with the addition of the portico and columns — definitely not an indigenous style for the Midwest.

The roof is flattish for the amount of snow

26

and rainfall, and the portico on the little-used nonentrance elevation we see here suggests ante-bellum Southern pretension and the influence of an aristocratic feudal society, rather than the more northernly utilitarianism more aptly expressed in early New England Colonial houses. If a transplant from Europe were desired, the French style of farmhouse seen in Normandy and Brittany or the English Cotswolds would have been more adaptable and does in fact relate to the New England houses.

One of the trademarks of a good indigenous house is lack of ornamentation. The house should not be pretentious in any way. It should be built from predominantly local materials. It should fit comfortably into its environment. Its roof should perform the sheltering job it was intended to do. Its overhangs and eaves should do their job of shading and sun protection to the degree necessary. The window and door openings should express a visual rhythm and balance, at the same time accomplishing their functional admittance of light, air, and human beings.

High utility costs and maintenance costs should be avoided. A bi-annual coat of heavy paint on smooth boards is a needless shackle for the homeowner. Use natural materials, use rough or resawed materials, use stains and washes. Only commit yourself to a little bit of trim and metal painting, and you will guarantee a happier and wealthier owner.

Second only to location, style is everything, but keep it in a style indigenous to the surroundings.

Once you have a rough idea of the style best suited to the site and your client (if this is to be a custom home) you will want to have a sketch made by whoever draws your plans.

Sir Henry Wotton wrote in *The Elements of Architecture,* ". . .get some ingenious gentleman. . .to do it for you, and to give you a design of it on paper, *though but roughly drawn. . .*" (The italics are added.) This idea of a roughly drawn sketch or study should be your first objective with the architect or designer. If someone outside your office is going to make this sketch, your understanding should be that for a certain fixed fee of, say $200 to $400, he would furnish some studies — to see if his ideas are what you or your client want. If not, you should have the option to conclude the arrangement after paying up the partial design

bill — with no strings attached. Incidentally, as is only fair, design time is charged for at a much higher rate than straight drafting time, usually twice as much or more.

Introduce your concern for utility diversification, energy conservation, and low-cost maintenance into the initial design phase. That can influence the house mass and the materials of construction, elements that are often incorporated in the studies.

Beware of several architect-type syndromes that can spell death to your energywise intentions before the vellums get off the drafting table: the open-floor plans, all glass walls modern Swedish fireplaces with minimum radiation, and flat roof design.

The Schedule for the Drawings

Each architect or designer's office has its own production method, but once having agreed upon a particular architect or designer, make clear *your* intended schedule or need for the drawings by certain dates. Once the design concept is agreed upon, you will require this approximate work from the designer:

First, you need a few prints of *preliminary floor plans* for help in making initial decisions with special sub-trades, decorator, landscaper, and for your own use.

Second, you will need fairly complete *floor plans, elevations,* and *rough specifications* for the lender. He will usually not need cabinet and structural details to process your loan application.

Third, you will need the *structural sections, foundation* and *fireplace plans* for the engineer if the architect feels that one is needed.

Most architects and building designers can figure the beam sizes and footing sizes required for a residence and can even work out the more complicated calculations for earthquake (seismic) and wind resistance of horizontal forces. However, the more sophisticated remodeling jobs and complicated new homes may call for the services of an engineer. Discuss the necessity of this service with the designer and your desire for a firm fee quotation, otherwise this expenditure can sometimes get out of control. After all, $200 to $400 can buy a lot of engineering time with relation to residential work on a site that is both level and stable.

Fourth, the final working drawings, including all *details, connections, door, window,* and *finish schedules* will be needed for your submission to the building department.

Other Professionals

The Decorator. Decoration is not a luxury; it is a necessity. If you did nothing but leave a house or room addition bare of drapes and furniture and sashayed about in a toga and ate and slept on tatami mats, the place would still have to be decorated. The answers to questions about types of brick, counter-top selections, cabinet facing and style selections, floor covering, tile choices, paint colors, light fixtures, concrete finishes or colors and hardware knobs and locks, and many other decisions that have to be made for the subcontractors, are part of decoration.

Whether you do it or have it done, do realize that decorative planning and coordination are demanded at every step of the way in a remodeling or building project. At this early stage it is sufficient that your file set of floor plans be converted to this purpose by drawing in the furniture to scale and picturing it as it will be when the house is finished. Draperies should be shown in their open position by little wiggly lines. This can be checked as the design is refined, and you will have a running record to help avoid conflicts in window placement, light switches, and other awkward design errors. All tables, lamps, large musical instruments, game tables, chairs, desks, in short everything, should be drawn in to help in this visualization.

The Landscaper. The other professional, or "professional function" if you do it yourself, which should be introduced at this early planning stage, is landscaping. A whole chapter is devoted both to it and decoration later on, but here I want to alert you to the fact that at the first hint of a plot plan and a floor plan it is none too soon to begin an orchestration of exterior planting aimed not only at beautifying the property but at making its contribution to privacy, noise reduction, and energy savings.

Some hedges can trap as much sound, wind, and driving rain as a wood wall or fence. Certain trees can shield windows and French doors from glaring sun and its heat in summer and admit welcome solar radiation in winter. Some trees and plants can even supply food and accomplish all of these other things at the same time, besides looking attractive for good measure.

Remember, the byword is "early" when thinking of decorating and landscaping. The first glimpse of floor plans emerging from the designer's office should be your clue to start working hard in these areas.

Planning the Exterior 5

It should be apparent from the first moment your energy conscious client looked at your house or plans that environmentally indigenous design, and resultant low-cost heat and air conditioning, was a major consideration. The steeper the roof pitch, the more spacious the attic, the more gracious the eaves and overhangs, the more indication of good insulation, the more Mother Nature will be working in the house's favor when either cold or extreme heat sets in.

The exterior material of the building, the presence of storm windows and doors or insulated glass, the essential insulation of walls and ceilings, the quality of weatherstripping, the quantity and amplitude of fireplaces, topnotch mechanical equipment, diversified zone thermostat controls — all bespeak a thorough approach to basic energy conscious construction.

Planning the Site

The entire lot should be planned as a single entity. Landscaping stands in equal importance to the house as being worthy of thorough design, even if the ultimate plan is not completed all at one time. Morever, any kind of grading, hauling, filling, movement of earth affects the landscaping plan.

When the site of the home is established, there is a tendency to "cut" the level pad for the foundations of the house along with the driveway without any clear idea of whether any soil removed would be valuable later on in the landscaping plan, as if landscaping merely consisted of bushing up what ruined portions of the lot were left over after the seemingly more prestigious house was completed. This tendency must not prevail. See that landscape plans and their attendant grading plan are integrated with the house plans from the very start.

Think South

The house is best situated when it takes the maximum advantage of any privacy the site might afford. Orientation of the main rooms used for living such as the family room, kitchen, and living room, should not only enjoy protection from the public view but from the prevailing wind as well. As to the sun, it should be guarded against in summer and invited inside in the winter. Pietro Aretino, writing in 1537, says, "Nor does the winter sun ever rise without entering my bed, my study, my kitchen, my other apartments, and my drawing room." So let the house attract the sun in those windows and at that time of day when it will be most beneficial. Do keep in mind in house orientation that north light may be wonderful for artists and people living in the southern hemisphere, but it is useless as a source of warming sun, as any self-respecting cat will tell you from its vantage point on a south-facing window sill.

An ideal orientation is shown in this drawing:

This plan has been naively idealized simply to illustrate these ultimate objectives:

1. Maximize privacy by minimizing the number of rooms discernible from the public street or walks.

2. Entreat the morning sun into bedrooms

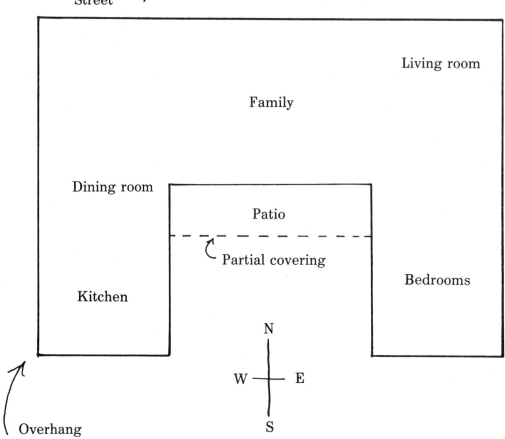

Street ↑

Living room

Family

Dining room

Patio

Partial covering

Kitchen

Bedrooms

N

W — E

S

Overhang

Ideal Building Orientation

and breakfast room in a manner that would put a smile on Signor Aretino's face.

3. Strive for complete privacy in the patio and shelter from prevailing winds, which come from the northeast in this example.

4. Control by an overhang the western sun that would otherwise enter the kitchen and family room the latter part of the day.

5. Partially roof over the patio for protection in hot weather and rain, yet still let the sun come in.

6. Provide an integrated landscaping plan for the finishing touches on this close approximation of an indigenous house layout.

Designing to Beat the Heat

An Energy Conservation Ordinance project in Davis, California where Central Valley temperature goes well over 100 degrees reported that: "Properly designed wood frame buildings require no summer air conditioning in the Davis-Central Valley Climate. Tests showed that well-oriented dwellings with adequate overhead insulation seldom get warmer than 75° Fahrenheit, while identical dwellings with inadequate overhead insulation and improper window orientation often got warmer than 100 degrees Fahrenheit."

They also verified that roofs should not be dark-colored. "Dwellings with north-south window orientation," continued the report, "used from 50 to 88 percent less electrical energy for cooling than the worst cases with large, unshaded east and west windows and inadequately insulated, *dark*-colored roofs."

At least 30 percent of the energy used for heating and cooling can be saved simply by using good design principles at no extra cost to the consumer.

The ideal dwelling would have: 1. north-south facing, 2. good insulation, 3. a light-colored roof, and 4. good shading with deciduous trees.

Designing the House

Architects and planners Brent, Goldman, Robbins and Bown, Inc., of Santa Monica, California, are exploring the different shapes, sizes, locations, and configurations of buildings relative to their effect on energy conservation.

"Indigenous architecture has always been responsive to weather conditions," says one of the partners. "Many urban design projects geared to technological advances and the assumption of abundant energy have moved away from these basics.

"There is a range of design elements which can reduce monthly consumption of heat, lighting, and air conditioning."

In the final stages of design by the firm is a residential building in Long Beach, California, which orients south and to the ocean. The architects are currently reviewing window placements, using shading devices, and adjusting fenestration angles to reduce the need for air conditioning.

A commitment to a rigid style of architecture will somewhat reduce the flexibility afforded by placing house and overhang masses where they are most effective environmentally. Seemingly regimented styles like Federal and Regency can appear in books and magazines as very "buttoned-up," pristine case studies of elegance and balance with no quarter given to an extra extended eave, protruding overhang, balconies, porches, and other projections and appendages that can make a house function better in its environment. However, it was mentioned earlier that certain neighborhoods dictated a definite style and in these cases an imaginative designer can often modify the style in a manner that will achieve the functional goals without sacrificing stylistic conformance.

Building Height and Shape

A two story building has a smaller surface area exposed to the elements than a single story building with the same square foot area. However, a two story building will usually be subjected to greater wind velocity which increases air infiltration and heat loss. A taller building is less likely to be shaded or protected from winds by surrounding buildings and trees. More important, the "stack effect" in a two or three story building makes controlling warm and cool air at all levels more difficult and makes infiltration of outside air much more of a problem. A square building has a smaller surface area than the other shapes with the same floor area and a spherical or round building would have the smallest surface of all.

Ceiling Height

Greater ceiling heights are an advantage in the summertime because they allow warm air to rise. However, greater ceiling heights increase the perimeter areas, thus increasing heat transmissions through the walls. Reduced ceiling heights reduce the exposed exterior wall surface area and the enclosed volume. A reduced ceiling height can also increase illumination effectiveness. If you increase the ceiling height, increase only the wall surface, not the window area. This way the effect on energy consumption will be small if the wall is well insulated.

Building Forms

Buildings that are elevated on columns or have overhanging upper floors will have a larger heat loss and heat gain due to the extra exposed floor surfaces. While this may be of slight advantage all year in the southern regions, or anywhere in the summertime, it presents a serious increased heat loss in colder climates.

Zig-zag shapes in east and west walls provide self-shading to reduce summer solar loads, provide natural wind breakers, and permit low rays to penetrate into the building in the winter to supplement the heating system if the windows in the zig-zag are facing south. Face the windows in the zig-zag to the north in a hot climate all year. This way in both summer and winter natural lighting is available at both east and west facades without the penalty of increased summer heat gains. The energy requirements due to the additional wall surface for the zig-zag form must be weighed against the other energy benefits. The zig-zag configuration is only one example of manipulating form to get the maximum energy benefits.

A sloping roof facing south receives more solar radiation in any climate in the United States than a roof facing north or even east or west. Therefore, select a building configuration to give minimum south roof and wall exposure to reduce cooling load where cooling is important.

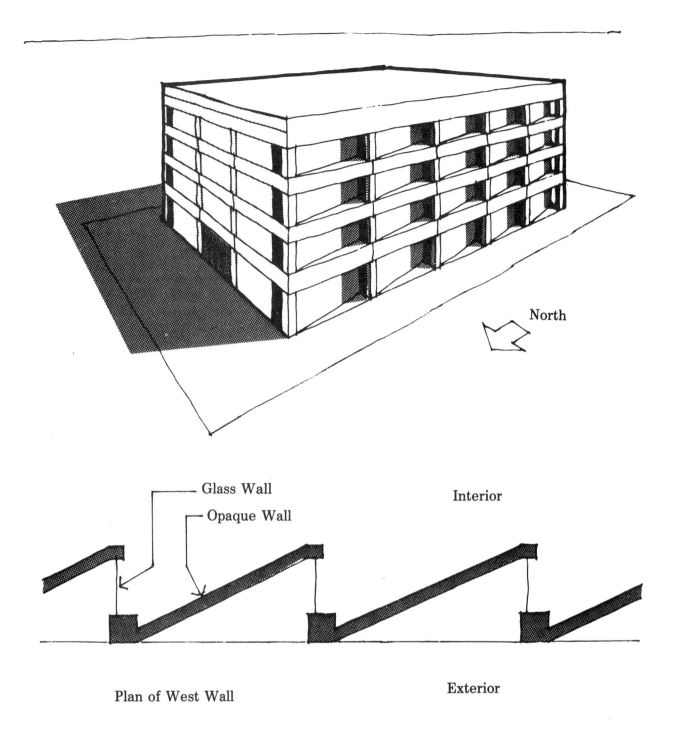

Glass Wall

Opaque Wall

Interior

Plan of West Wall

Exterior

Energy-Saving Building Form

Similarly, select a building with a minimum north wall exposure to reduce heat losses where heating is most important.

Why the Roof First?

The hierarchy of the exterior design of dwellings is led by the roof form. The house mass under it is generally a single rectangular form, or a grouping of rectangular forms, growing, usually at some odds with nature, out of the earth. Its one opportunity to make peace with its environment is by the aptness of its roof design — its crowning glory, so to speak. A great roof can be truly inspirational.

Drawn by a master architect of the old school, this New England-styled modified gambrel roof is indeed a thing of beauty. This is not intended to limit the concept of roof beauty

Modified Gambrel Roof

to quaint, steeply pitched roofs of colder climates. In Spanish, southern French, and Southern California homes with lower pitched roofs over houses of more horizontal, rambling form, a different kind of roof beauty emerges that just as aptly reflects its environmental influences. The Trulli houses of Alberobello in southern Italy with their unusual roofs are likewise uniquely attractive and quite indigenous to this locale, as are the sculptured Antonio Gaudi roofs of Spain.

Gaudi Roof

Fine-tune your sensibilities to respond to attractive roofs, and you will actually experience an almost physical sensation of enthrallment when gazing upon a great roof. The same feeling will grip you when seeing an inspired drawing of a roof. Do not spare imagination and expense to obtain a decent roof, and if the designer's first attempt at the roof in his initial sketches does not act as a heady stimulus to build it straightaway, take the warning of your muse to heart and ask him to try again. Keep after it!

The major function of the roof, of course, is to provide shelter, and protect the house. This consists of protection from water and sun in a relationship that varies in importance depending on climate.

The natural water-shedding qualities of a roof increase with its steepness. Conversely, the flatter it is, the more watertight it has to be, down to the point where a flattish roof must be as absolutely waterproof and watertight as a shower pan or it will leak.

As an interesting bench mark, most roofs with a pitch of less than four-in-twelve require extra waterproof protection *and* heavier structural members, whereas pitches of four-in-twelve on up to steeper pitches shed water more easily and require lighter support due to the trussing

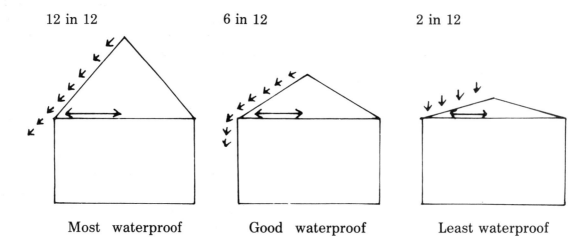

12 in 12   6 in 12   2 in 12

Most waterproof   Good waterproof   Least waterproof

Roof Water-Shedding Efficiency

or tying effect gained by the rafters standing more upright and their not being subject to the same gravitational forces as low-pitched roof rafters.

In his *Lectures on Architecture,* John Ruskin writes: "I am sure that all of you must readily acknowledge the charm which is imparted to any landscape by the presence of cottages; . . . Has it ever occurred to you to ask the question, what effect the cottage would have upon your feelings if it had *no roof, no* visible roof. . .if instead of the thatched slope. . .or the rough shelter of its mountain shales. . .there were nothing but a flat leaden top to it, making it look like a large packing-case with windows in it? . . . If you think over the matter you find that you actually do owe a great part of your pleasure in all cottage scenery. . .to the conspicuousness of the cottage roof — to the subordination of the cottage itself to its covering. . .The very soul of the cottage — the essence and meaning ot it — is in its roof; that is that, mainly, wherein consists its shelter.

"Now, do you suppose that which is so all-important in a cottage can be of small importance in your own dwelling-house? . . . whatever external splendour you may give your houses, you will always feel there is something wanting, unless you see their roofs plainly."

From an energy-saving standpoint, the most effective roofs happen to be the most beautiful — a rare occurrence. Tile and slate roofs are the most attractive, provide the greatest safety from fire, have the longest life, and require the least maintenance. They are also the most expensive.

Along with wood shakes and shingles, they are the most decorative.

In remodeling roofs and ceilings do not sacrifice attic spaces needlessly unless you do not wish to take advantage of one of the greatest natural insulating barriers. Even when fully insulated, the air space between roof and ceilings below is additionally valuable in stamping out the last vestige of unwanted heat and cold, just as is the crawl space underneath conventional foundations as opposed to the modern slab foundation.

Chimney and Eaves

Before leaving the roof part of the exterior, do not neglect the closely related chimney and eaves — those other very vital parts of an indigenous roof. Chimneys should be neither too skimpy and narrow nor too short. If the home style is historically derivative, the chimney should be in keeping with that style, which is fairly simple to verify from texts and photographs. It is imperative that its scale be in proportion to the roof.

Eaves cannot always be generous, even though that would be desirable from an energy standpoint. It depends on the style. But eaves should look purposeful, bold, and rich. They should border the roof the way a good mat and frame border a fine painting; and the way the right amount of white shirt cuff shows at the sleeves of a man's suit jacket. Do not look on unquestioningly at the designer's first sketch of the eaves and chimneys and nod in weak assent.

Wait for that thrill of delight to grip you, as surely it will, when the roof, eaves, and chimney are dramatically compelling. If you do not experience that tug of ecstasy, ask the designer, "Do you feel happy with such and such?" or "Shouldn't this be bolder?" or "How do *you* feel about this? Shouldn't there be more molding?" or, best of all, "Why don't you sketch two or three alternatives?"

Fenestration

To borrow some expressions from music, if the roof is the overall phrase that the design expresses, the windows and doors are the rhythmic parts within that phrase. The roof and fenestration express themselves in this manner within the context of a house design. This is not to say that symmetry is always essential, but balance and good rhythmic form is.

Fenestration Symmetry

Even though the windows of the house below are larger than the door, they are balanced by a strong horizontal affinity. Not only is the height of both openings the same, but the over-door fan light is balanced by the panels underneath the windows.

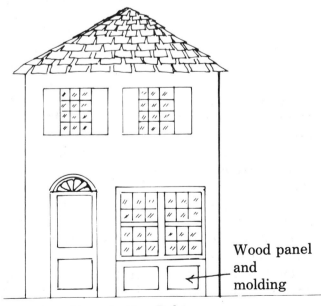

Wood panel and molding

Fenestration Balance

This analogy can, of course, be pushed to absurdity. Lest it become didactic, it is sufficient to state that openings in a wall for doors and windows should not merely be punched out as if the builder were wielding a gaint cookie cutter with reckless abandon. The exterior appearance of these openings should have a rhythmic relationship that is pleasing and satisfying to the eye.

Some general rules for this relationship are that windows and doors should be the same height at the top. For shorter windows with their sills higher off the floor, it is desirable if the sill heights match each other.

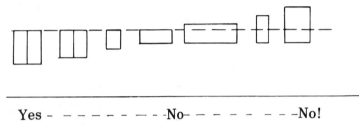

Yes - – – – – – – –No– – – – – – –No!

Window-Door Height Levels

A disparity in window width where they serve small rooms is sometimes unavoidable, but unless a design excuse can be found for it, the heights should remain uniform. Also it helps, even in width, if a "module" can be established where there is some spacing relationship between both window placement and window size. In traditional house styles two types of windows prevail, double hung and casement windows. Both are adaptable to insulated glass or storm sash for weather protection.

A technical note on window sizes is in order here. Most building codes require the builder to provide one-eighth of the floor area of a room in windows. Thus a room 15 feet by 22 feet, or 330 square feet, needs 40 square feet of window areas (330 ÷ 8 = 40). This would mean that it should have two windows about 4 by 5 feet in size.

These window requirements are minimal, especially where the direction of exposure is north, northeast, or northwest, or anywhere that overhangs project out over the openings. In planning an exterior of a house, be conscious of adequate openings to provide plenty of light or the house will become cavernous.

Energy Efficient Doors and Windows

Heat loss per unit area through windows and exterior doors is much greater than through most wall materials. A single pane of glass resists heat transfer on the order of one unit compared to 10 units for an insulated wall. Ordinary double-glazed windows have a resistance of about two units and some heat reflecting double-glazed windows have over three units of resistance. Due to solar heat gain, a double-glazed window on the south wall of a building as far north as Canada can have about the same net heat loss over a full heating season as an equal area of insulated wall.

Often windows are encased in an aluminum frame. Twenty-five per cent of heat lost through such a metal framed window occurs through the frame where only 13% is lost through a wood frame. A 10 square foot aluminum framed window facing south (the best of orientations) can lose as much as 425 BTU per day in winter.

In most parts of the country, the solar load in the summer on each 100 square feet of east or west side windows requires approximately a ton of cooling capacity. Windows on the north of a building (excluding winter) and in all cases the south side of the building (if windows are shaded) are most desirable. If a rectangular building, 2½ times longer than it is wide and oriented east-west with 50% glass, is turned 90°, the cooling load is reduced by 30%. This is only 50% more load than if the building had no windows at all. An additional 25% savings can be obtained if shade trees surround the building.

Windows of any appreciable size in east, west and south walls must be shaded. Glass can be tilted out at the top. Glass tilted at 78° reflects 45% of radiation compared with 23% when the glass is vertical. For an 8 foot piece of glass, this tilt has the same effect as a 16 inch shade projected above the window.

From mid-March to mid-September a south facing window can be completely shaded by an overhead projection just a little shorter than the height of the window. Such a window facing only 30° from south toward either the east or west would require an overhead projection more than twice the height of the window to be shaded. Venetian blinds provide the same shade effect as a building projection. However, since the blind is often on the interior of the building, the heat absorbed remains inside. For example, a light-colored Venetian blind set at a 20% slant absorbs about half of the direct solar radiation falling on it, transmitting this heat to the interior, and reflects only about 35% to the outside. The amount of heat reflected to the exterior depends on the blind color. A blind with one dark side could absorb heat in the winter and be reversed to a light side in summer to reflect more light and heat.

The Windowless House?

Many otherwise well-informed builders and designers have assumed that the most energy efficient home would be a windowless home or at least a home with a minimum of window area. The "Arkansas Home" was an early (1974) attempt by H.U.D. and Arkansas Power and Light to develop an extremely energy efficient home. The Arkansas house used a glass area limited to 8% of the square footage of living area. The California Administrative Code, Title XXV, Chapter I, Article 5 limits single glazed window area to 16% of the heated floor area "with no distinction of window orientation." A study by the American Physical Society sponsored by the Federal Energy Agency (PB-243-117) has now demonstrated that in most U.S. climate areas well located windows are more effective in saving energy than the best insulated wall, even considering the added cooling load if the building is air conditioned. Refer to the New York — Dallas table listing energy gains and losses for various window types at each of the four principal compass directions.

Note the three columns under *South* for both New York (top of the chart) and Dallas (bottom). The figures under *W* show the energy saving + per square foot of glass during the winter heating season. This indicates that with the exception of glass coated with aluminized mylar, each window gained more energy by trapping sunlight than it lost by radiating heat to the outside. The *S* column under *South* shows that all the windows resulted in an undesirable heat gain (-) in the summer, thus requiring air conditioning to cool the interior. The plus figures in the *Total* column under *South* show the energy saving per square foot of glass when both summer losses and winter gains are considered. For window and orientation combinations with a plus sign in the total column, the larger the window the more energy is saved.

New York City

	North			East			South			West		
	W	S	Total	W	S	Total	W	S	Total	W	S	Total
Standard 1/8" glass	-84	-43	-127	-38	-76	-114	+29	-59	-30	-38	-81	-119
Solar control glass	-43	-39	-82	-2	-68	-70	+58	-53	+5	-2	-73	-75
Aluminized mylar on 1/8" glass	-105	-11	-116	-93	-19	-112	-76	-15	-91	-93	-20	-113
1/8" glass with window blind or shade	-84	-15	-99	-38	-26	-64	+29	-20	+9	-38	-28	-66
Solar glass and shade	-43	-13	-56	-2	-24	-26	+58	-18	+40	-2	-25	-37
Storm window	-25	-37	-62	+14	-65	-51	+71	-51	+21	+14	-69	-55
Solar glass and storm window	-5	-33	-38	+30	-59	-29	+82	-45	+37	+30	-62	-32
Insulated solar glass	-5	-17	-22	+30	-30	0	+82	-24	+58	+30	-32	-2
Aluminum mylar on insulated glass	-31	-9	-40	-22	-15	-37	-8	-12	-20	-22	-16	-38
Storm window with window blind or shade	-25	-13	-38	+14	-23	-9	+71	-18	+53	+14	-24	-10

Dallas - Fort Worth

	North			East			South			West		
	W	S	Total	W	S	Total	W	S	Total	W	S	Total
Standard 1/8" glass	-24	-95	-119	+26	-156	-130	+102	-118	-16	+26	-185	-159
Solar control glass	-7	-80	-87	+38	-135	-97	+107	-101	+6	+38	-161	-123
Aluminized mylar on 1/8" glass	-46	-41	-87	-33	-56	-89	-14	-46	-60	-33	-63	-96
1/8" glass with window blind or shade	-24	-49	-73	+26	-70	-44	+102	-57	+45	+26	-80	-54
Solar glass and shade	-7	-39	-46	+17	-57	-40	+86	-46	+40	+17	-66	-49
Storm window	+1	-73	-72	+44	-124	-80	+109	-92	+17	+44	-149	-105
Solar glass and storm window	+9	-62	-53	+48	-109	-61	+107	-80	+27	+48	-131	-83
Aluminized mylar on insulated glass	-12	-22	-34	-2	-34	-36	+14	-27	-14	-2	-40	-42
Storm window with blind or shade	+9	-34	-25	+48	-52	-4	+107	-41	+66	+48	-61	-13

Energy gain (+) or loss (-) in winter (W) and summer (S) for various window types at each compass heading in two cities (in thousands of BTU's per square foot per season).

Sample energy saving computation based on heating oil at 60 cents per gallon and electricity for cooling at 3.75 cents per K.W.H.: 1 S.F. of window rated at +100 saves 69 cents in heating in winter. 1 S.F. of -100 window costs 53 cents in cooling energy in summer

Note: All values assume that the window is adequately weatherstripped or sealed.

New York — Dallas Windows

You will notice that only south facing windows have a plus sign. Does this mean that the energy efficient home can have large windows but only on the south side? Not at all! Plenty of glass area on the south is an important part of energy saving, but the table assumes that the building is fully air conditioned, not shaded in any way from the outside and that no effort is made to manage solar heat gain during the summer. This will not always be the case. With a little planning, many east and west facing windows can become significant energy savers along with south facing windows.

Builders have used overhanging roof lines for years to shade windows. This is especially useful on the south side where an overhang about equal to the height of the window will shade a south facing window in the summer because the sun is more nearly overhead during the summer months. The winter sun is lower on the horizon, allowing the sunlight to fall fully on the window. Such an overhang would reduce the undesirable summer heat gain to nearly zero, causing the net energy saving to equal the winter saving benefit. An overhang-protected, south-facing window is going to save energy almost anywhere in the U.S., regardless of the type of glass or frame. The larger the window, the more is saved. An east or west facing window benefits less from a large overhang because most heating occurs when the sun is rising or setting and below most any reasonably broad overhang. However, deciduous trees could be used to shade the window in summer. In winter the tree would be bare of leaves, allowing full exposure to the sun. In the Dallas chart most east and west windows save energy in the winter. Thus an east or west facing window that was fully shaded in the cooling season would be an energy saver in Dallas and similar climates.

The New York — Dallas table also assumes that the home is air conditioned during the hottest part of the year. Many homes are not air conditioned. Opening the window to allow air circulation will lower room temperature to near outside temperatures, thus making summer heat gain through the window less important. For well ventilated homes without air conditioning, the winter saving is the key consideration. In the Dallas climate most east, south and west windows are energy savers in the winter.

The New York — Dallas table can be used to calculate the dollar savings of the various windows. Assume that oil heat is used at a cost of 60 cents per gallon. At a furnace efficiency of 67% it would take oil worth $6.90 to produce 1,000,000 BTU's of heat. Each 100,000 BTU's saved would save 69 cents. Thus each square foot of south facing storm window in Dallas — Fort Worth in the winter (rated at + 109 in the Table) would save 109,000 BTU's or 75.2 cents (1.09 x $.69). If that window measured three feet by four feet (12 square feet) the saving would be $9.03 for the winter.

Electric air conditioning with a typical cooling efficiency of 7 BTU's per watt hour will cost about $5.36 per million BTU of cooling when electricity costs 3.75 cents per K.W.H. Thus one square foot of south facing standard 1/8'' glass in New York in the summer (rated -59 in the table) would require an expenditure of 31.6 cents in cooling energy.

Notice that in the New York — Dallas table, solar control glass (usually sold as ''heat absorbing glass'' is effective in cutting down heat gain in summer but in every case is not as effective as standard storm windows. Morover, storm windows cost less and provide a big

advantage over solar control glass when the heat gain in winter is included.

Aluminized mylar can be applied after the window is installed and makes the exterior highly reflective (mirror-like) from the exterior. The benefit provided by this coating is very small when compared to standard 1/8'' glass and even wastes energy when used on a south facing window. The table shows that storm windows are a good choice over standard 1/8'' glass, especially in a climate similar to New York City. But notice that most of the benefit from storm windows in Dallas comes from the advantage during the summer cooling season! A simple white roll down shade or venetian blind would provide nearly the same benefit as a storm window in New York and actually be significantly better than a storm window on the east, south or west side of a building in Dallas. The shade has no effect on solar heating in the winter when compared to standard 1/8'' glass and thus could be pulled down or left up depending on what was needed at the time.

Windows in Northern Cities

Even in northern climates where the heating season may be 9 months long the orientation of windows is more important than the window type. Contrary to what many builders and designers believe, windows in cold climates can help cut heating costs. At higher latitudes the sun is lower on the horizon during the winter and strikes windows more nearly at a right angle, thus increasing solar gain. Any snow on the ground would also add to the radiation received through the window. Most important, summer cooling is unnecessary in most northern states. The result is that winter gain is maximized and summer excess heating nonexistent.

The Sault Sainte Marie, Michigan — Seattle, Washington table gives window heating gain or loss figures for cities that are representative of the northern area of the U.S. Only winter heating is considered. Notice that storm windows on the south, east and west side save energy. The larger the window the more energy is saved. Only north side windows radiate more heat than they capture. Even standard 1/8'' glass windows on the south side are only slight energy consumers rather than energy savers in Sault Sainte Marie.

The energy efficient home is not necessarily

	Sault Sainte Marie, Michigan			Seattle, Washington		
	North	East or West	South	North	East or West	South
Standard 1/8" glass	-173	-94	-8	-63	-23	18
Solar control glass	-98	-28	50	-30	7	43
Storm window	-62	5	79	-14	21	56
Insulated solar glass	-25	35	102	2	33	65
Reflective insulated glass	-60	-45	-27	-25	-17	-9
Aluminized mylar on 1/8" glass	-196	-177	-155	-88	-78	-68

Energy gain or loss (-) for the heating season for various window types at each of four compass headings in two northern U.S. cities (in thousands of BTU's per square foot per season).

Sault Sainte Marie — Seattle Windows

a windowless home. Just remember to emphasize south facing windows whenever possible, and keep the overhang about equal to the window height on the south side in areas where the cooling load is a significant energy cost consideration. The Small-Homes Council - Building Research Council of the University of Illinois at Urbana — Champaign (One East Street Mary's Road, Champaign, Illinois 61820) offers an eight page brochure which explains the solar mechanics of window orientation and illustrates how various floor plans are compatible with south facing windows. Ask for publication C2.3 "Illinois Lo - Cal House." The cost is 25 cents.

Another major heat loss is from air infiltration around doors and windows. Properly fitted windows can be the biggest single energy saver. A poor fitting window without weatherstripping, for example, can allow 5½ times as much air infiltration as an average fitting window that is weatherstripped. Weatherstripping can significantly cut down on air infiltration even with a poorly fitted window, but the place to begin is still with a quality window, properly fitted.

Thermal break type windows reduce heat loss. These window frames are basically metal with some less conductive material (like vinyl) sandwiched in between the outside and inside metal frame units to cut down on the amount of cold transmitted through the metal. Wood window frames conduct less heat than metal, and arc now made with vinyl facings which reduce the likelihood of warpage over a period of time. Authorities disagree on the amount of heat conducted through the metal sash compared to wood sash, but in any event the thermal break type does reduce heat loss by close to 25% and

can cut down condensation about the same amount.

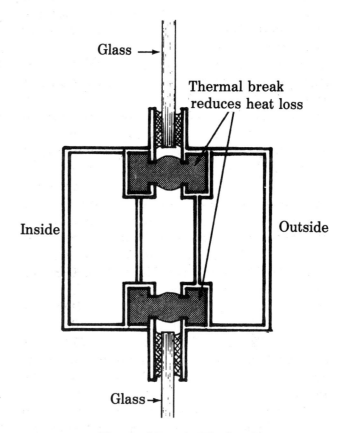

Thermal Break Windows

Sliding glass doors with large glass areas should be avoided. They are thermally inefficient and have large areas subject to possible air infiltration. In those cases where sliding glass doors must be used, make sure that a thermal break type, double glazed door is used. Properly weatherstripped and installed, they are much more energy efficient than standard sliding glass doors.

The storm sash is the common, more economical answer to winter cold. Some types are not satisfactory in summer because they do not provide adequate ventilation. There is a more-or-less permanent operable storm window that is more costly; it consists of movable sash and screen that can be opened in warm weather without being removed. The cleaning and maintenance of poorly designed storm windows can be an expensive and recurring chore. However, installing storm windows and doors will reduce air infiltration significantly and cut down transfer of heat through the exposed surface by 50 percent.

Storm windows and doors vary widely in basic design, durability, and cost. Storm windows range from single glass panels, that must be put in place each fall and removed each spring to triple track assemblies, which include sliding upper and lower windows and a screen. These latter windows can be used both during heating and cooling periods and can be opened for natural ventilation at other times. Because they are left in place permanently, wear and tear and the chance of breakage is minimized.

You should be aware that it is not the storm window itself that keeps the warmth inside in winter and outside in summer. It is actually the dead air space—at least ¾ inch—between the two windows that saves energy.

The size of the storm window is determined by the size of the window frame and not by the glass area. Storm windows should be properly installed and fit tightly to do the most good. To assure a tight fit, permanent storm windows should be sealed to the outer window frame with caulking compound or other sealing material. Storm window frames should have a tiny opening at the bottom to allow water vapor to escape. Storm windows are generally more economical than double pane windows in existing houses, because they usually cost less to install and they reduce infiltration of air around the window sash.

Storm doors may not always be economical when considered for winter heating savings alone unless the doorways are frequently used. However, they may still be a good investment, since they can be used as a screen door in the summer months if they have interchangeable glass and screen inserts. If the house already has a screen door, it generally will not pay to replace it with a storm door. Storm doors over doors with inset glass areas save more energy than those over solid doors.

Adding storm windows can be an expensive improvement to an existing house. The installed cost will exceed two dollars per square foot and may be much more if standard size units can not be used. But storm windows are a practical addition in warm as well as cold climates where electric heating and cooling are used. In general, any home built in an area with more than 4500 winter degree days should have either double glazed windows or storm windows. A "Degree Day Table" for several hundred U.S. cities appears on page 261 and the following five pages.

Insulating Glass

Factory-sealed *double glass* is the next best means of retaining heat within the house in winter and keeping it out in the summer. These windows must be sealed *at the factory* where air within the panes is completely dried and the glass perfectly sealed. Obviously, this insulated double sash is more expensive than regular sash, and it is not available in all sizes. Therefore, the factory-insulated glass has to be considered right along with the design of the house or remodeling project. But once installed, we are talking about years of energy saving and added comfort, not to mention easier cleaning because of the absence of condensation and dirt on the inside surfaces such as occurs with storm windows.

Understanding Sunshine

Daylight is composed of sunlight and diffused light. The two are quite different. Sunlight is essentially parallel rays and can therefore be manipulated by optical devices. With diffused light, on the other hand, the weaker rays are coming from any direction and cannot be as effectively manipulated by optical means such as lenses and mirrors. Diffused light is present along with sunlight on clear days and is also present on overcast days when sunlight is not. Sunlight is better for lighting deep inside a room because it is more intense and will provide reflected light over a larger area. However, sunlight can create heat problems, increase the cooling capacity needed, tends to fade or age woods, plastics and fabrics and moves relative to the sun's position at the time of day and season.

Sunlight can be converted to more diffused

light by obscure glass. Also, some of the more harmful components, such as ultraviolet radiation, can be removed or reduced with sun screens or any number of patented coatings that are available for glass. Tinted glass reduces light levels and glare. However, it absorbs solar energy, making it a radiant heating panel when it is exposed to the sun. Reflective and heat-absorbing glass rejects solar energy and does not become hot. It intercepts up to 80% of the radiant energy, which is very helpful for cooling in summer, but results in a loss of useful heat in winter. Natural light is lost when tinted or reflective glass is used.

How to Use Windows

Extensive research has been conducted on the introduction of daylight through windows. Some very good work was done early in the century on industrial applications where light was needed for critical tasks inside factory buildings. Daylight was a normal design requirement in most buildings prior to the introduction of fluorescent lighting in the late 30's and 40's. Thereafter it became less and less critical as high level artificial illumination became more ''practical''. Nevertheless, studies and analysis continued on daylighting, particularly in relation to school classrooms — probably because their moderate room sizes and predominant occupancy during daylight hours continued to make it practical to consider the use of daylight.

The proportion of wall area that is occupied by windows influences the volume of light that it is possible to introduce. The upper limit, of course, is the complete window wall. This provides maximum light volume in a given situation but may well create other problems such as over-illumination, over-heating and psychological problems such as exposure and insecurity. At the other end of the range are the suggested minimum window areas. Building standards and codes such as the FHA Minimum Property Standards set limits such as 10% of the room floor area. Other minimum standards have been suggested, such as 20% of the wall area, based on the psychological value of a view. Light and view are both important in deciding where and how large a window should be.

The position of the window in the exterior wall has an effect on the penetration of sunlight and, to a lesser extent, diffused daylight as well.

A window located high on the wall will allow the deepest penetration of sunlight. A low sill height allows the floor surface to play an important role in light reflection. A window located adjacent to a side wall improves illumination by reflection from the adjacent wall.

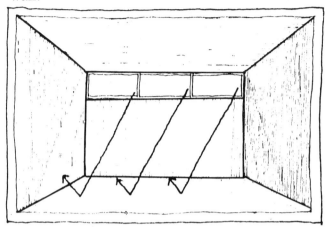

A high window allows
deep penetration

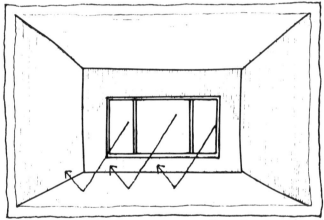

Low sill placement can allow floor reflected light to help balance near ceiling and wall areas

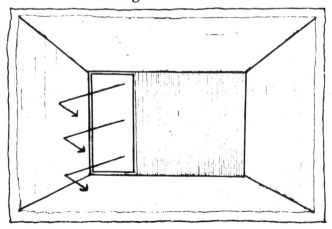

Windows near a wall emphasizes
side reflected light

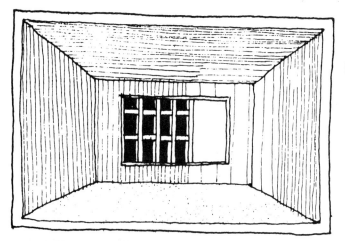

Adjacent surfaces can obstruct portions of the sky and reduce the amount of sunlight

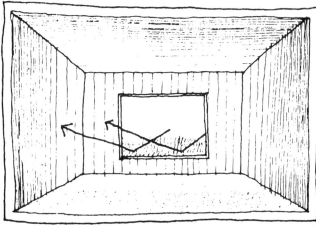

Adjacent surface can reflect light into windows and increase the amount of daylight

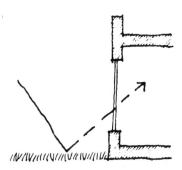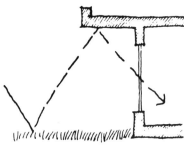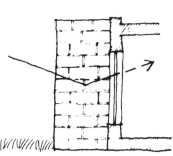

Some examples of adjacent surface reflective action

The position of the window relative to external surfaces influences the amount of light that can be admitted by the window. The light reflected from light colored ground surfaces, roof or soffit or adjacent walls, can increase the amount of daylight that enters windows. Obstructions outside the window can decrease the heat and sunlight entering a room while increasing the amount of diffused light. Remember that the view through the window will also be affected by any obstructions.

Rooms are much more pleasant in which windows are arranged on more than one wall. This is not only because of better control of ventilation through use of cross-ventilation, but to achieve better distribution of light than if all light comes from the same direction.

Windows on two opposing walls give bi-directional light, and a space twice as wide can be illuminated. Windows on several sides of a room can accommodate the movement of the sun and allow good illumination over a large portion of the day.

See that window placement permits proper arrangement of furniture. Your sketch or set of plans can come in handy here. Check out all draperies, shades, and shutters to see that they pull completely on top of or to the sides of windows to enable a maximum amount of light and air to enter.

Windows are expensive to alter in an existing house or in one you are building *after* the covering of the wall is complete. So evaluate all openings carefully in terms of the rooms they are serving before construction begins. Give special attention to rooms facing north with only one wall having windows: you should probably insist on *doubling* the minimum requirement, 10% of the floor space in windows, to achieve proper light. Otherwise the owner may have to resort to supplementing natural with artificial light.

Light Diffusing Materials

Diffusing panels offer a range of lighting possibilities. In a very fine grained diffusing panel, such as transluscent plexiglass, light which enters the panel will be diffused over a wide area. This converts incident sunlight into a distribution similar to diffused light and provides a more uniform distribution throughout the day. Because they distort visible rays, these panels offer increased privacy and visual screening. Glare can be a problem, particularly when in direct sunlight.

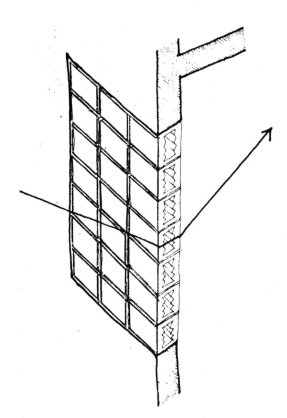

Prismatic glass block can re-direct light

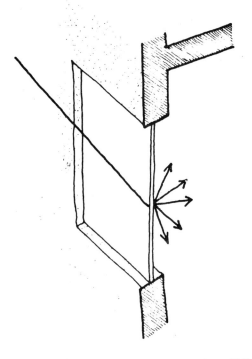

Panels of diffusing glass or plastic give diffused light on the inside. Double layers can provide thermal insulation

Prismatic glass block can provide unusual properties. When constructed with rows of louvers cast into the two internal faces of the block, sunlight can actually be directed deep into the room. Roof mounted block can be designed to transmit the low angle winter sun, block summer sun above 45°, and admit all north light. These directional properties are most effective with sunlight, as diffused light can only be partially directed by the louvers. Since the internal surfaces consist of continuous small louvers, these units obscure vision and provide visual privacy.

Skylights
The way to rid the house of any pockets of darkness and reduce electric bills at the time of

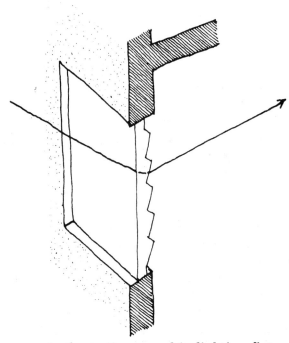

Lenses similar to those used in lighting fixtures can angle daylight deeper into buildings than a normal ray pattern would allow

remodeling is by adding a skylight, that is if the inclusion of one or more is not too destructive to the aesthetics of the roof. Skylights can bring

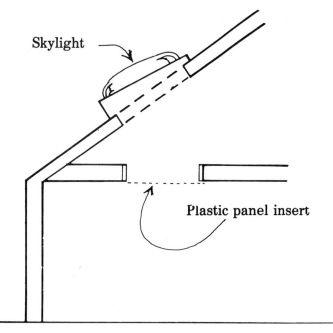

Skylight

Plastic panel insert

Attic Skylight

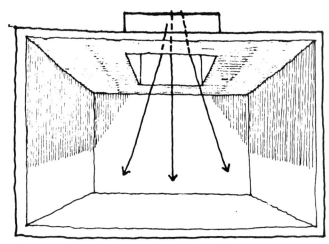

Direct downlight skylights depend on the reflectivity of room surfaces (particularly the floor) for dispersion

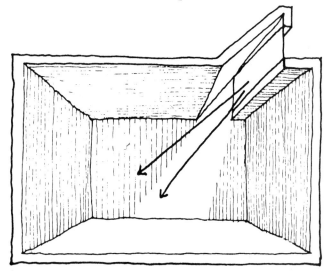

Single side skylights or clerestories give monodirectional light unless the room surface reflect well

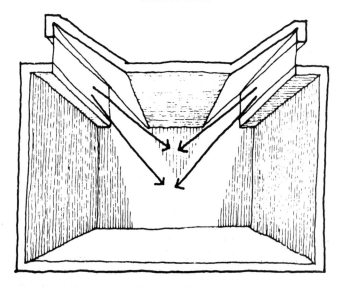

Opposite side skylight give two-directional light

light into those dark areas of the house for all the years of the future.

The attic space poses no problem: the skylight is simply installed over the area where light is desired in the living space below. Then one or more translucent panels of plastic are installed in the ceiling. The plastic is easily removable by hand and often can be worked in as an attic access cover, thus killing two birds with one stone. Even a third and fourth bird can be plucked off by installing a cheap porcelain socket at the concealed edge of the plastic cover which can then light the hall below and the attic above and cause the plastic to serve as a light fixture when artificial light is required.

Single and double side skylights and clerestories handle light like windows located at an elevated position. They are frequently subject to obstruction of some portions of the sky which illuminate them. Opposite side skylights or clerestories, when oriented to east and west, allow the introduction of sunlight (at varying levels) through almost the entire day or a balanced bi-directional diffused light which gives greater uniformity of room illumination.

Reflective skylights, monitors and clerestories offer added light control. By their configuration they can introduce light into spaces that might otherwise be difficult to illuminate with daylight. Shape design can give selective admission or cut-off of sunlight. Color treatment of the reflective surfaces can change the nature of the reflected light, cooling or warming to meet your requirements.

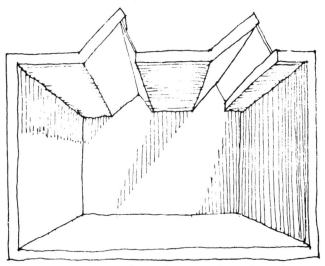

Sawtooth skylights or clerestories give mono-directional light unless the room surfaces reflect well

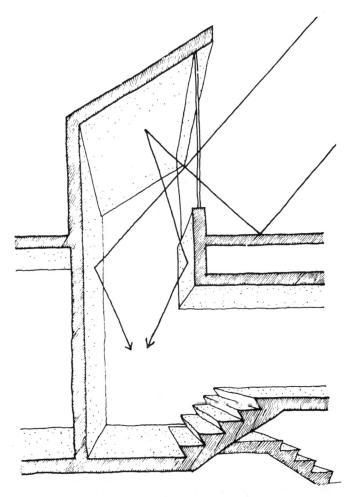

Monitors can gather light into spaces otherwise difficult to illuminate. Lighting depends on the reflectivity of surfaces

Added screens and louvers can provide very precise control as in the Kimball Art Museum installation where a reflector of perforated reflective metal produces almost totally uniform illumination of the curved ceiling.

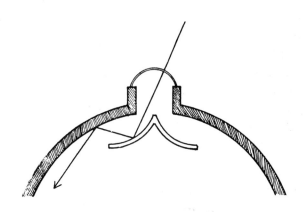

Kimball Art Museum

Reflectors

Reflective surfaces can be used very effectively to direct daylight through windows and deep into a room. Mirror-like reflective surfaces can direct a very controlled beam into the room. They are effective with sunlight and work well with diffused light also. Light matte surfaces are less effective but provide a diffused reflected light from incident sunlight or diffused light. Simply providing light colored surfaces on those building elements in front of a window will increase the level of reflective light. But specifically designed reflectors are more effective because they can be formed to direct light where it is needed in the interior. Keeping the reflectors clean is necessary if they are to be effective. They should be easy to clean or self cleaning by rainfall.

An interesting study of reflected sunlight is being researched by a group at the University of California, Lawrence Radiation Laboratory. In this system, narrow reflecting blinds are located at the window to direct light deep into the room. These are adjustable and can be set to give maximum light penetration for a given angle of sunlight. They can be moved to follow the motion of the sun, direct light to various portions of the room or control the amount of light entering. The blinds are used in conjunction with a highly reflective ceiling surface to extend the depth of light penetration by additional reflection. The reflecting blinds may be used on east, south, or west walls but

45

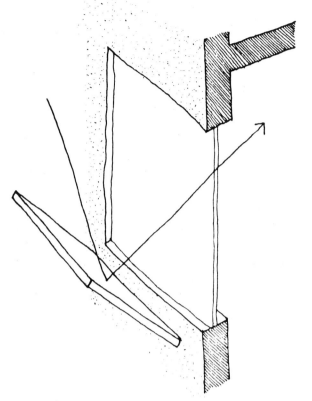

Reflecting surfaces can direct daylight into the upper levels of a room and thus to greater depths

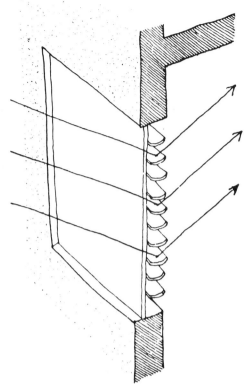

Multiple reflector surfaces can be movable blinds to allow adjustment to track the sun or control the amount of daylight entering

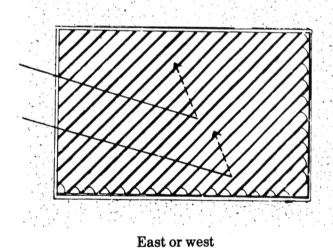

East or west

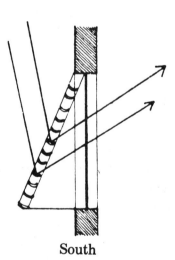

South

Louvered Collection System

different configurations provide the best performance in each case. For east or west walls the louver system is rotated up to 45° in the plane of the window.

On the south wall light can be collected through a much longer portion of the day if the louver system is tilted out at its base up to 20° to intercept more vertical rays. As the sun reaches higher noon positions in the summer months, the amount of sunlight striking a vertical window is reduced. If the louver system is tilted outward at the base, it can intercept an appreciably larger portion of this incident light and reflect it back into the room. Unfortunately, this configuration introduces practical design and maintenance problems.

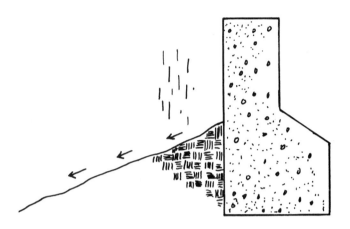

Proper Drainage

Drainage and Foundations

It is cheaper to build on a slab than to build on conventional foundation "stems." It is also then more difficult to establish property drainage away from the house. Also many people react negatively to walking about on concrete floors even when the floors are thickly padded and carpeted. They complain of a degree of dampness and a hardness that is apparent when comparing concrete floors with the slight yielding springiness of regular joisted floors with a crawl space or basement underneath.

Given proper insulation, a conventional wood-joisted floor will retain heat better than will a slab floor. Moreover, with a conventional foundation the maintenance of under-house mechanical parts, pipes, ducts, etc., is greatly simplified, inasmuch as they are accessible.

The concern for a good roof and surface water drainage ties directly into the landscaping design and should be an integral part of it. Your plot plan should show the drainage layout clearly. Little arrows should point the direction of the flow lines of drainage water and where it eventually finds its way off of the property.

All roof water and surface water should be made to drain away from the house. This should be a cardinal objective in the fine-grading that is done near the end of the job.

In the event that you are careless about this, the house will attract moisture into the crawl space or basement or slab, and a dehumidifier will have to be installed.

Failure to grade the soil properly brings the soil into dangerous contact with stucco and wood. The correction of this involves either the adjustment of the grade so the earth is well below—preferably six inches below—the top of the foundation or concrete slab, or, if this is impossible due to the way the drainage works, building a concrete "cheek wall" as a barrier for protection against infestation. This problem of soil being in potential contact with the wood frame of the house is one of the most common items recommended for correction on a termite inspector's report and can involve considerable trouble and expense to rectify.

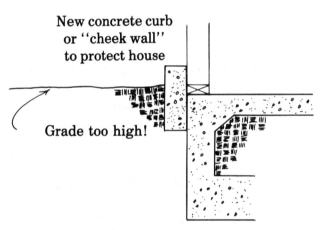

New concrete curb or "cheek wall" to protect house

Grade too high!

Original foundation & slab

Building Foundation

The bottoms of downspouts should have a "kicker," or short dog-legged pipe that directs the water two feet or so away from the foundation of the house; concrete "splash blocks" can accomplish the same purpose. Either device can be removed or shifted for mowing lawns or maintaining foundation planting, but keeping excessive water away from the foundation is essential.

Gutters should be slightly pitched to encourage the water to travel to the downspout locations. If downspouts have a tinny dripping sound, you can soften the sound by gluing a scrap of old sponge onto the inside of the bottom horizontal surface where it turns out away from the house, sometime when the spouts are dry. Exterior drains should be flushed with a hose every so often.

In the case of basement dampness, check any light wells to see that they are waterproof. Also check the ground around the basement wall or around any slab to see that it is four to six inches below the bottom or "sill plate" of the wall and that it *slopes away from the building*. This is as important as the diversion of the downspout water, for the sloping ground adjacent to the foundation is needed to drain off any water that falls directly on the surface of the ground.

Good Exterior Materials

Houses of masonry construction or masonry veneer construction are generally better heat preservers than standard stud and stucco or stud and siding or shingle houses. However, good insulation will make the walls of the simplest tract house about as protective as a five-inch thickness of masonry veneer.

Glass, on the other hand, unless it is double thickness, is not a good exterior wall material in excessive quantities, simply because it so easily conducts heat to the outside and cold to the inside. To bring it up to the protective level of the structural wall, it needs to be double thickness or it is little better than an open hole in the wall.

Landscaping as an Energy Saver 6

There are very precise styles of landscaping just as there are styles of residential architecture. In the Japanese style, which is unique, the basic plan is meticulously maintained as a dynamic slow-motion scenario, sometimes for centuries. Often it is distinguished by the painstaking raking of white sand around the plantings. The Italians and French, probably because of their warm summer climate and abundance of lush planting, developed gardens that were virtual rooms without roofs. The English were noted for their profusion of planting, their woodsy settings, their love of a multitude of plants that de-emphasizes formality. In describing English landscaping, the term ''the English garden'' came to mean a paradisiacal palette of super-lush multicolored flowers, shrubs, and trees.

In the United States, in which the average homeowner has greater space and there is a reliance on outdoor recreation and do-it-yourself activities and a dependence on the automobile, landscaping is regarded as a means of tying the disparate elements of a lot together in a harmonious relationship. The house, the driveway, the garage, the swimming pool, cabana, shuffleboard pad, toolshed, and shop all need some sort of resolution. So instead of rejoicing in the planting itself, the average American tends to treat it more as a functional part of his property. He tends to create a windbreak here, put some shade over the air conditioner there, screen the toolshed and woodpile here, anchor the house in its surroundings there, and plant a ground cover everywhere.

That is one approach to landscaping. Let us

recognize it. Let us further recognize that we will be striving to add one more utilitarian nuance to the role of the landscaping, that of energy saving. But above all else, let us recognize that inherent in all landscape design should be the overriding ideal of beauty, not function. In landscaping, function is second; it is something we should attempt to include on the way to beauty.

Trees and grass absorb sunlight and convert a large portion of heat into other forms of energy. For comparison, temperatures taken over asphalt in sunlight were 125° Fahrenheit and over a nearby shaded area of grass 98° Fahrenheit. Shaded grass areas adjacent to buildings rather than asphalt drives and parking lots would reduce heat gain. Glare, dust and noise would also be reduced.

A shelter belt of trees can reduce wind velocities by 50% and has been demonstrated to reduce heating fuel consumption in exposed houses in lee of the trees by 30%. Wind breaks, whether natural or manmade, should be considered an essential tool of thermal design.

How To Proceed

In the past in planning a country property, the landscaping might be planned first and the house fitted in wherever it could be, almost as an afterthought. This is pointed out to emphasize that the landscaping should, at the very least, be designed at the same time the house is being planned for the lot. That is the exact time a professional would wish to be thought into the picture, and if you are going to attempt to do the landscape design yourself,

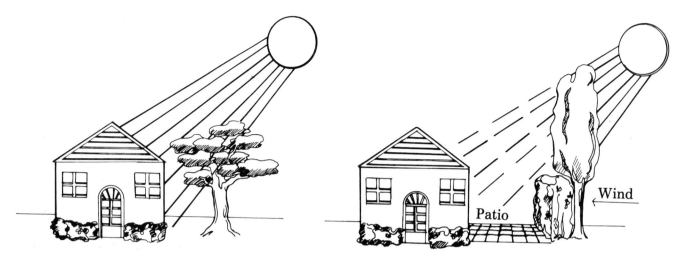

Utilizing Landscaping for Efficient Sun and Wind Screen

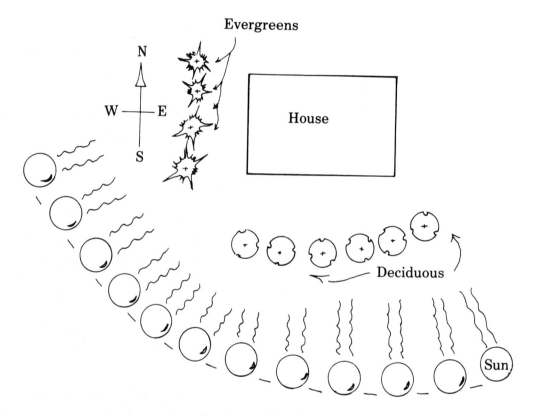

Landscape Design

that is the time to organize the landscape plan.

Next, a schedule of landscape production needs to be established at the time production of the house is started. You can see that as certain earth is cut, filled, hauled, leveled, or piled, it relates to the ultimate plan. If a driveway or swimming pool is to be excavated, for example, the earth from that excavation might be invaluable in some other part of the lot for a windbreak type of planting mound or spread over an area of poorer soil as topsoil. Not a spade of earth should be turned without knowing if it is needed in the future landscape plan.

Finally, you come to the actual planting, the stage that is most enjoyable. It can also be the most frustrating and unrewarding if the preplanning has not been done. However, armed with the complete plan, you can set about making lists of trees, shrubs, ground cover, plants, and flower requirements with some confidence that you are working toward a creative whole.

A Tree For All Seasons

André Lenôtre, the famous French landscape artist in the time of Louis XIV, advised all of his clients that trees placed near the house should be kept at the same distance from the house as the height of the house. This was probably a good design maxim and still may be. Keeping in mind Lenôtre's rule, you might plant some trees at a distance of about twenty feet from the house to accomplish the objective of windbreak in winter and shading in summer. However, there could be conflict, since the windbreak needs to operate all year round and must, therefore, be evergreen, whereas during the winter you need to let as much of the sun's solar heating effect get through as you can. This can be resolved by planting a combination of evergreen and deciduous trees. First determine the direction of the prevailing wind and on which side the trees should be evergreen; on the remaining sunny sides, you can plant deciduous trees.

Architect Richard Cramer, Chairman of the Art Department at the University of California at Davis, says: "Deciduous trees are a natural. They are a God-given solution to about half of the (heat) problems. They are covered with leaves in the summer when you need the shade, and they lose their leaves in the winter so the sun shine through the branches and help heat a house."

Indicate the location of air conditioning compressors on the landscape plan, and be certain that they receive shade in the summer. They should be open on three sides with air free to flow all around them.

Another forceful argument for Lenôtre's distancing of trees far enough from the house is that it avoids the problem of leaves filling the gutters and downspouts. Where trees are planted less than ten feet away from the house the gutters become clogged and high ladder work is required in order to free them, creating an arduous chore in the winter and spring.

The swimming pool area is another spot where either deciduous or very dirty trees are a terrible nuisance. Even in an age when the cleaning of the pool can be automated, it seems the height of foolishness to tolerate or to create an automatic source for dirtying it.

What About Vegetables and Herbs?

Says Russell Page in *The Education of a Gardener*, "Gardens whose purpose is to raise crops of vegetables. . .should be firmly enclosed in formal limits whether of hedge or fence or wall." He was opposed to *indecision* reflected in a sort of merging of flowers into vegetables, vegetables into shrubbery, etc. These productive areas of vegetables need to be defined and protected, yet left open to the sky.

An herb garden, too, is a valuable asset to any conscientious cook. Herbs are attractive, as opposed to most vegetables, which generally look like fetching weeds. And herbs can blend fairly well with other planting. For convenience, therefore, they should be planted near the kitchen door.

A Fine Point in Planting Hedges

A well-planted hedge is often a better windbreak than a wall since an enclosing fence or wall can cause the wind to swirl around in vicious eddies. The benefits of a stout boundary hedge surrounding delicate garden planting such as unestablished shrubs and roses are incalculable, for most of the damage created by totally obstructing walls occurs on the windward side of the wall. A hedge, while breaking the main force of the wind will allow a gentle stream of air to filter through to provide a healthy circulation of air at the base of the hedge. Box, eugenia, and ligustrum hedges are generally the most effective for this job depending on how well they do in your part of the country.

Keeping the Lot Clean During Construction

Very early in the course of construction, starting with the pouring of the foundation footings, the various subcontractors seem to enter into a plot to thwart any later attempt you might make to grow even a sprig of grass on the property. The prelude to this plot is when the ready-mix concrete trucks do their washing out, usually in the future site of a bank of deep-rooted flowering shrubs that will sorely need deep, clean topsoil. As finish work on the slab or basement floor get underway, more washings out and dumpings of wet concrete take place. In a few weeks, the mason begins his cement-mixer washouts and dumpings of hunks and pieces of unused mortar and saw cuttings or fine brick dust.

The plot thickens during plastering or walling when fine gypsum is either blown or wasned over much of the property, and if the exterior walls are to receive masonry veneer or stucco, the assault to the entire perimeter of the house is intensified with a vengeance.

Have an understanding with the tradesmen where the washouts are to take place. Post signs if necessary. Try to avoid this unneeded problem.

Landscaping Lighting

Some exterior lighting is desirable in your landscape plan both for beauty and for safety. However, if you added up the amperage required to illuminate or even highlight a few areas on a good sized lot, the total might be staggering. Consider the 12-volt system available at most garden and hardware stores. It is sold in ready-made units of a set number of lights already to go, or groups of lights can be put together on a modular basis as you like.

In designing a new house or in remodeling, it is convenient if an outlet for the transformer is provided, or two — for the front and back yards — if the property is good-sized.

Water Conservation, Mulching, and Irrigation

A program of heavy mulching not only reduces the need for as much water in warm weather, but it reduces the number of weeds as well. A great variety of materials can be used for making mulches: leaf mold, sawdust, compost, redwood bark chips, buckwheat hulls, and even certain new products on the market that use recycled rubber.

It is a tremendous saving in personal energy to have a plan of irrigation worked out right from the start. With plastic water pipe of all sizes available, a rather extensive system is relatively easy to install. However, one word of advice is in order. Be sure that the plumber furnishes a "T" of an inch diameter for sprinklers near the hose bibs at the front and at the back of the house. This will cut down on the expensive sprinkler valves required to turn water on and off. Larger originating pipes and fewer valves not only cut down on initial expenses, they reduce both replacement cost and, most important, time in tending to the watering. Obviously, if you can only run four or six sprinkler heads off one small valve, you will need many valves and much time to do your watering.

An added dividend for having very few valves is that the whole irrigating system can be automated and put on a time clock at a much lower cost than if there are many valves to operate. Moreover, a time clock enables a large property to be watered in the very early morning when there is little other demand for water and pressure is high. Also in those cool early hours the water will do the most good as there is the least evaporation.

What to Do With an Oversized Lot

Developers experience a running battle with city planners over the minimum allowable size of lots. In some areas, the planners try to force the developer into creating half and full-acre lots. This may be fine for certain mature farmlike terrain with grown trees and shrubs, but in fairly raw level situations, the commitment to land and maintenance can be ruinous to the builder's house sales, for no homeowner wants to buy a house with a built-in maintenance headache.

One answer for the individual attempting to keep up with a large property is to screen off a portion of the lot, much as a restauranteur does with an unused portion of his dining room. The "undeveloped" portion can be planted in such things as eucalyptus or fruit trees and spaced in an orderly manner. Or the ground can be kept clear and maintained on a minimal basis.

Planning the Interior 7

Most developed neighborhoods are dominated by a certain style of home. It could be that one or two-story houses prevail. Once you have selected the location, it is sound practice to go with the trend in the area.

In those cases where you have a freedom of choice in design, given a minimum-sized house of, say sixteen-hundred square feet, the most efficient arrangement for temperature control is a two-story house plan with separate thermostats and mechanical systems upstairs and down and a traditional room arrangement where rooms not in use can be closed off.

Early Colonial houses took this form with the second story actually comprising the large attic space under the steep-pitched roof. Warmth in the house was maintained by a large central chimney mass near which the stairs were constructed. Natural light and air in moderate weather was admitted to this floor by dormer windows that also had the advantage of lending aesthetic relief to the broad expanse of roof. This style can be traced back to the country cottages of England — the Cotswold and Elizabethan types are good examples — and also the Normandy farmhouses in France.

However, if you pay rapt attention to roof and eave design overhangs, window placement, and planting, the one-story house can be made about as efficient as the two-story. However, it must just be remembered that you cannot enjoy the natural phenomenon of rising heat in heating and cooling, and, of course, the one-story house will lack the insulation of the second story and attic. One-story houses have to be temperature-zoned along the horizontal plane rather than the vertical plane.

Although one-story houses are more costly to build because of the larger roof and foundations, there are more buyers seeking them, which is persuasive argument.

Split-level houses are most suitable to the sloping sites for which they were originally designed. In tract offerings they enable the builder to offer more square footage on a small lot without having to build two-story homes to which there could be some sales resistance. When split-levels are placed on level lots they look strangely out of place. Stair climbing is a necessity even to circulate within the "ground-floor" living areas, since the family room and living room are frequently at different levels. Costs of construction are higher because different horizontal levels have to be combined. Energy conservation and mechanical problems are not simple to cope with because of the three and sometimes four varied levels.

Remodeling is particularly costly when it involves adding a second story to a house or adding onto a second story. If the remodeling can be accomplished on level ground adjacent to the house, the cost is much more reasonable, not far above that of new construction. In ground-floor remodeling you are putting most of your client's dollars where the results can be seen and appreciated, which is not the case in second-floor additions. The original foundations of the house were no doubt intended only for one-story construction, and footings will have to be widened and deepened to support the added second-story loads. Moreover, the problem of roof support is a major design concern, not to mention the problem of working soil and drain lines from any added plumbing fixtures into ceilings and walls on the first floor.

The Basic Rooms Required

The room requirements of most homeowners are usually based on present customary usage *plus* some added room or space need. In the case of older people, there is often a shrinkage in room and space requirements. To this is often added a desire for increased privacy or, at least, a special work, hobby, intellectual, artistic, or recreational fulfillment which requires some separation.

From the viewpoint of a nation that has gone through an energy shortage period linked with strong government pressure to reduce fuel consumption, there are some new criteria in room requirements which doubtless have emerged. If thermostats were kept down to the mid-sixties, for example, it would be highly desirable if the living room or family room, provided it had a fireplace, could be closed off and warmed separately with a wood fire.

Furthermore, the presence of an attractive secondary eating area in the kitchen could be of value under any circumstances, and particularly in reducing the need for heat in other larger rooms.

This is not to say that visual flow or a feeling of spaciousness need be sacrificed, for that is usually one of the major incentives for new or remodeled housing. Actually, the ideal of Andrea Palladio, the sixteenth-century Italian architect whose ideas were imitated so much throughout western Europe, was to have a series of internconnecting rooms whose high and wide double-leaf doors revealed one grand chamber after another — but these rooms still could be closed off. They had separate fireplaces, and the large doors were thick and protective. The idea of corridors for circulation within a house is a very late invention; in the finest Jacobean mansions, the rooms are entered one from another. Hallways to circulate traffic separately to the individual rooms may have developed as an extension of the foyer.

Room for Privacy

The desire for privacy is usually another underlying goal in buying or building a home. Sociologically we are entering a totally new era. Amid discussions of and experiments with the four-day workweek, forced use in Britain in 1974 of the three-day workweek, change from a manufacturing to a paper-oriented society, higher living standards for much of the population, it stands to reason that people will depend upon the home itself to a greater extent for recreational, creative, and business activities.

Consider incorporating a private den, study, or office into the floor plan. Consider, also, having this room placed away from the normal flow of house traffic. If sufficient light is available during the day, its location near the master bedroom is particularly desirable just because it utilizes that part of the house which in most floor plans would have the fewest distractions during the day and early evening. Conversely, the proximity of such a den to the kitchen, family room, hobbies, activities, and television could defeat the purpose of such a sanctum.

Do not overlook porches, balconies, and terraces as great contributors to this same privacy objective in warmer weather. If access and use of such supplementary areas can be confined to one or two inside rooms like the master bedroom and adjacent study or office, plus another bedroom or two with their own porch or terrace, many hours of useful enjoyment and productivity will be added to the use of your house.

The shaded rooms are ones that would be most desirable to depend on as specific living areas in cold weather, with little fuel requirements except for fireplaces and for cooking.

The Master Bedroom in its Expanding Role

Louise Klots, Senior Vice President of Habitational Design, Inc., says, "Since families will be spending more time together in the future. . .master bedroom *retreats* (should) be treated so that parents can have greater opportunity for isolation from children in the home."

In an interview concerning his work habits while writing books, British best-selling author and veterinarian James Harriot, who wrote *All Creatures Great and Small,* said that he worked best in the bosom of his large, active family with the "telly" going full blast. His book was marvelously readable, but few of us could write down a recipe for scrambled eggs in such a setting. An example probably more applicable

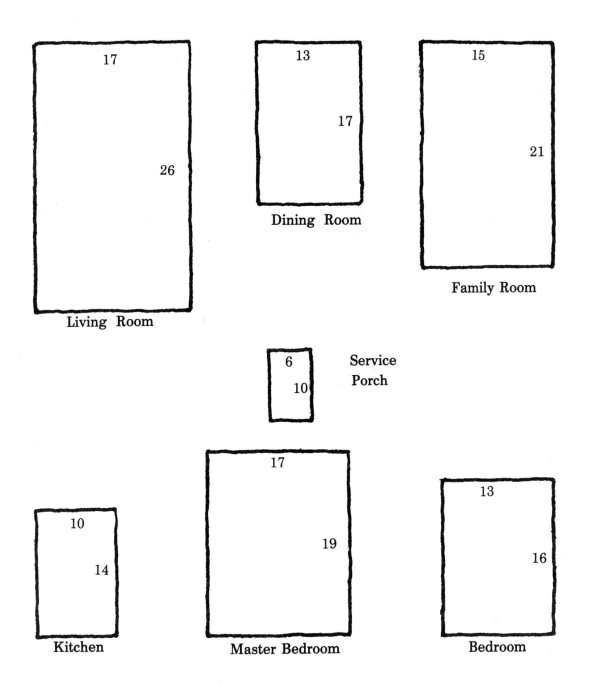

Ideal Room Dimensions

to our harried homeowner in search of quiet would be that of Machiavelli, who, after a day with rustics in the open air, put on court dress and retired to his library to read the ancients and write. So, for yourself, determine to include a bit of built-in privacy.

Rooms for Dining

One condominium model in the Coronado Shores Towers development in San Diego demonstrated the feasibility of numerous dining locations by actually setting up four diverse dining areas in the same medium-sized apart-ment: one was in a separate dining area adjacent to the living room, another for snacks and breakfast was in the kitchen, another was for outside dining on a balcony, and another was an intimate area for only two in the living room near the fireplace and television.

Eating is a repetitive activity and can in some homes become monotonous. The attempt here is to lend variety by providing a number of attractive locations all conveniently set up and ready to perform the same ritual in diverse settings.

Floor Plans in General

Be advised against that architect's delight, the open or free-form plan. There is no way to compartmentalize portions of the house for separate heating and cooling. In addition, you will find that potential buyers do not tend to form lengthy lines seeking to buy the house from you. One buyer in ten will consider a free-form experimental type of plan over a traditional floor plan. It is with some amusement that one notes, when these plans are photographed in magazines and newspaper home supplements they are more frequently than not the homes of the architects themselves.

Entry Hall, Stairs, and Powder Room

Much as good shade trees and a superior roof design help to "anchor" the house in its exterior surroundings, an entry hall or foyer can provide such an anchor — that is, a sense of visual and sensual orientation — on the inside. A proper entry hall can also provide a buttress, both real and psychological, between the intimacy of the home and the sometimes hostile elements of nature.

The ideal entry is itself a room, preferably two stories in height, at least able to reveal a glimpse of the second-floor spaces at the head of the stairs. It also provides a partial but not necessarily direct view of the living room, which gives this same introductory feeling of expectation and interest.

From an energy standpoint, the entry hall or foyer consumes a minimum amount of fuel. It can be lit by very low wattage bulbs. If there is a heating register in the entry it can be closed off, and, provided the thermostat is not located there, this closure will not affect the heat control of the other first-floor rooms. Often some of the return air grills for the heating and air-conditioning system are located in first and second-floor hallways; even this does not cause a problem by reintroducing relatively colder air back into the equipment, since these grills are usually placed high up on the walls and convey the warmer air that accumulates there back into the equipment.

A large entry hall enhances a feeling of spaciousness as it relates to the adjacent living spaces. For zone control of temperature, it is helpful if doors of either the recessed pocket type or the large double leaf type can close off the entry when heating and cooling require-

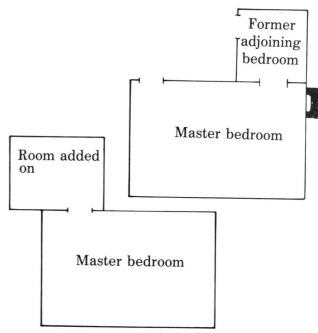

Bedrooms and Adjoining Rooms

ments are maximal. However, much of the time they will not have to be in the closed position.

One thing to check is that the entry has plenty of natural light, thus not requiring any artificial light in the daytime. Some entries can be greatly improved by adding a larger window or a skylight. In original planning and remodeling, particularly, see that there is plenty of light, with special attention given to north-facing entries.

In any original planning or remodeling note also that a closet for coats is a must, and that to have less than four feet of hanging space is niggardly.

As to this buffering effect of an entry as it relates to smaller houses, note that even a tiny vestibule can accomplish its insulating purpose against the out-of-doors if that is all that is possible. Apart from the disagreeable aspect of walking directly into a living room from the outside, an entry area protects the room from the direct assault of cold or warm air, wind, rain, or snow, plus furnishing a place for guests to remove wet or muddy rainwear and leave umbrellas.

A small entry like the one shown does not need to be heated. It merely serves as a neutral chamber between the interior and exterior of the house, much as a mud room or back porch might do at the rear of the house, or for that matter, a grand revolving door in a hotel or office building.

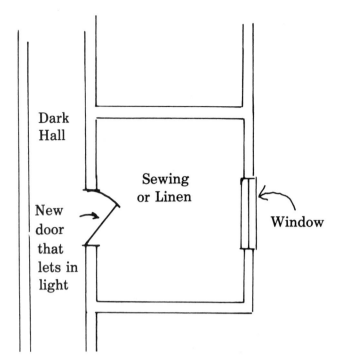

Lighting a Hall

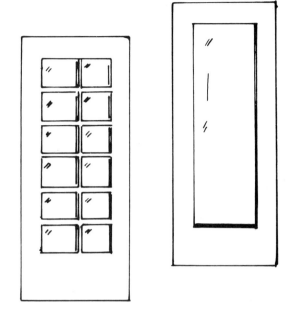

French Door with Glass or Plastic

Stairs: A Blot or a Glory

There are several checkpoints for utility and beauty that apply to stairways:

1. The step itself is the "tread" and should be no less than ten inches deep.

2. The distance up of each step is the "rise" and should be no more than 7½ inches.

3. The width of steps from side to side should be no less than three feet, and preferably 3½ feet or more in width.

4. The overall shape of the stairs should embody at least one landing and not be a straight run. This is not only desirable aesthetically but might spare someone a fall down a full flight of stairs.

5. No glass should be near enough to where you could fall through it, either head-on at a landing or stair bottom or to the side by losing balance.

6. Ideally, a source of light should emanate from the second as well as the first floor so you *neither* ascend nor descend into darkness during the daylight hours.

7. Naturally, there should be protective and decorative hand railings, balusters, and attractive trim at the edges and sides of the stairs.

Halls that are Welcoming

Halls that are narrower than three feet six inches have a confined feeling. A hall should be four feet wide or more in order to impart a feeling of graciousness. The practical reason for this is that you will have the sense that two people could pass one another going in opposite directions in such a hall and that it is not a one-way street.

While halls should be well-lighted for safety, assure yourself that they do not require artificial lighting in the daytime. The use of skylights to solve this problem was suggested previously. There is another method of admitting natural light that is available where an outside room lies between the hall and its natural source of light; by using a French door with obscure (frosted) glass panes or a single pane of translucent plastic, the hall can be changed from a shadowy cavern into a cheerful passageway even when the French door is closed.

The Powder Room

The powder room ought to be arranged so that when its door is open its toilet fixture is not in clear view from the entry hall. The best

57

design is to have a tiny foyer for coats that separates the powder room from the main hall areas. This arrangement enjoys the added advantage of being a sound insulation barrier that helps discourage the fastidious guest from resorting to the custom of running water in the lavatory aimlessly for the full time he is in the powder room.

All powder rooms should have exhaust fans. True, they are not required by building codes in rooms that have openable windows, but consider that powder room windows are rarely opened, especially when they are near the main entrance door, which they frequently are. The fan is, therefore, essential.

What Should You See From the Entry Hall?
What is visible to a person standing in the entry foyer of a house is what conveys that first lasting impression. In a traditional Victorian home, the library all neatly lined with books would be the next room where a guest would be admitted. These days the living room would likely be the logical second step, but with some room layouts, much else can be in view as well. Shiny fixtures can peep from the powder room, kitchen appliances and laundry equipment can show their gleaming faces, and sometimes uncleared dining tables can feed the curious eyes of a first-time guest or stranger. Reserve these evidences of mechanical and personal functioning for friends and family. They are too interwoven with the intimate life of the occupants of the house to warrant such display.

Things to See	Things Not to See
The sweep of ascending stairs	Powder room fixtures
Partial glimpse of second floor	Dining room
Partial view of living room	Service hallway
Door for coat closet	Kitchen
Door for powder room	Laundry

Living Room, Family Room, and Dining Room
What were their historical uses? The parlor, or what the living room would have been in the old days, was the room for ultimately receiving and talking to guests once they had progressed through the foyer and library. Here were found the fussy Victorian chairs and davenports with their antimacassar coverings, the curio cabinets, the small table for holding the tea and smaller ones for cups, frequently an organ or a piano. This was the formal room, one in which the householder put his best foot forward. Invariably there was a fireplace, often some needlework in progress, and the best painting and artwork.

The earliest room for informal family living grew out of a combination of the large family kitchen with its informal dining area and an area such as a basement rumpus room. The family room, which was often larger than the parlor, became a place where the family lived informally, played games, sometimes ate, watched television, tried to read, and, in short, spent most of its time.

Dining rooms were and are for family dining and have held their own, although sometimes in combination with the living room, as an "L" or portion of it, and sometimes with the family room, but rarely these days with the kitchen. These combinations usually occur in small homes or where the feeling of openness can only be achieved by connecting spaces.

The Dining Room: A Late Starter. This room that is now so commonplace, was not really popularized in the bourgeois home until near the end of the nineteenth century. Charles Edward Hooper, writing in 1906, said that, "the exclusive dining room is a comparatively new thing (then). The demand for a separate room is due to different conditions of social intercourse." In fact, this demand continues to this day when a majority of home buyers desire a separate dining room for the sentiment of formality that it expresses and the convenience of closing it off if necessary.

The separate dining room adds its own reason for control of heat and cool air. If used once a day or less frequently, its registers can be closed most of the time. Moreover, a separate dining room is very sparing of electricity consumption. It is not necessary to illuminate a room you do not see, whereas darkening a portion of the living room such as the dining "L" can be depressing. The separate dining room can be lit with a few candles or one simple chandelier on a rheostat or dimmer.

Breakfast Room
Although the breakfast area may be a part of the kitchen and sometimes a separate room usually in larger homes, this quotation from Oliver Coleman, writing in *Successful Houses* in 1899, serves as a good reminder as to orientation: "The dreariest of the meals, the

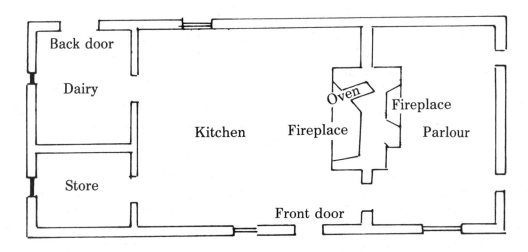

Energy Saving Room Arrangement

breakfast, should have the fullest benefit of the morning sun. In the winter this is good, of course, while in the summer the early morning is often the only time of the day worth living.''

The Best Arrangement for Saving Energy

Large, broadly connected rooms bordering on the open plan are hard to zone separately for heating and cooling. To control heating and cooling, generally speaking, it is best if rooms for general living purposes can be closed off and if they boast that secondary source of heat, a fireplace.

Often limited to constructing one fireplace in a home, the builder will tend to allow this important decorative and functional element to migrate to the family room. In most homes, and in particular the split-level plans, this pattern can virtually sound the death knell of the fireless, isolated living room, turning it into one of those soulless formal spaces that nobody uses. There it will sit, full of pretentious, never-used furniture, a complete waste except for callers to whom you do not wish to appear too friendly.

Ideally the family room would have its own fireplace and, if not adjacent to the kitchen, could also be closed off. If it is part of the kitchen, the family room is easy to warm, with cooking appliances nearby and its own fireplace. Such a room combination makes, of course, the ideal place for the family to spend most of its time. The way such a room was used in the past can be seen from this drawing of an actual house, the Barton House, in the time of Queen Elizabeth in the sixteenth century.

Incidentally, it was expressed at the time (1554) that the house should run east to west so the early sun would light the bedrooms and get people up early, and the setting sun would light the living room and kitchen so that work could be continued as long as possible into the early evening. Not many windows were placed in a true south-facing wall as we would like them for a heavy dose of midday sun, because of the fear the sun would fade hangings and clothing, warm the house too much, and spoil all the food in summer. We do not share such fears today because of faster colors, overhangs designed as part of the house to protect against sun, window coverings of every possible description, insulated glass, and refrigeration.

It would be best, then, if both living and family rooms were separable and each had its own fireplace or had one serving both rooms if there happened to be a common wall between the two. However, this look-through type of fireplace is inferior from the standpoint of providing good radiation. Outside doors leading directly into living or family rooms should be protected against intrusion of cold by storm doors in winter or, in the case of sliding patio doors, by insulated glass.

Fireplace damper blades should be operable, and if they are stuck, these are not difficult for a mason to fix. Except when there is a fire in the fireplace, the damper blades should be in the closed position to keep wind and cold air out and warmer air in.

The Bedroom's Other Role

The bedroom suffers by an incomplete

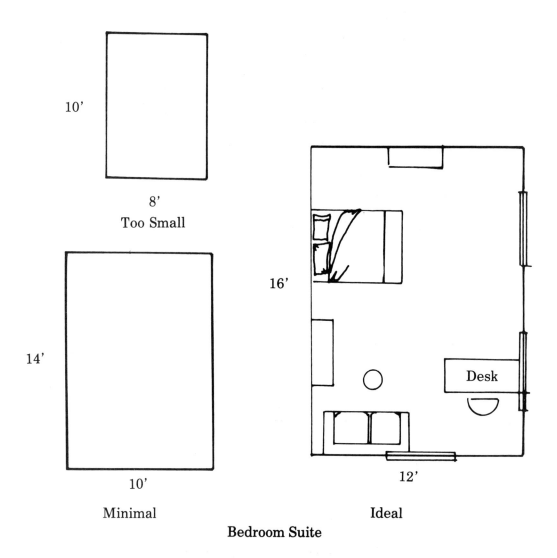

10'

8'

Too Small

14'

10'

Minimal

16'

Desk

12'

Ideal

Bedroom Suite

analysis of its dual rather than its single role in most people's lives. Its name suggests a single purpose — that of a sleeping chamber. In fact, the F.H.A. and most city building codes specify a minimum size for a bedroom of something like eight by ten feet. A typical roughly sketched floor plan of such a cubicle shows a big rectangle where the bed is to be placed, two little rectangles for nightstands on each side of the bed, and a medium-sized rectangle for a bureau, and a small chair or two. There you have a minimal bedroom and its furnishings.

The fact is that in addition to the third of our lives that is spent in bed sleeping, there is a tremendous amount of additional time apt to be spent in a bedroom if it is decent sized: dressing, reading, letter writing, music listening, napping, studying, practicing, and small scale hobbies. All these other activities are liable to take place in the bedroom of any human being who is out of swaddling clothes.

First of all, then, the bedroom should be of sufficient size to accommodate a desk, easy chair, decent light for reading, and whatever other objects and furnishings are pertinent to study, hobbies, music, and other nonsleeping activities — even entertaining guests as in the case of an unmarried son or daughter.

The minimum size for any bedroom that is to be anything but a sleeping chamber is 10 by 14 feet, or 140 to 150 square feet.

The key to successful bedroom use is often the width — the space between the end of the bed and other furniture or the wall. Too narrow a room can cause real problems in furniture arrangement. This is why it is important for you to draw in the furniture carefully to scale on your early floor plan, even in the minor bedrooms. Once having done so, there should be a 1½ foot to 3 foot passageway between major pieces of furniture.

The Bedroom Suite — or Combined Study
As mentioned previously, the demand for an

60

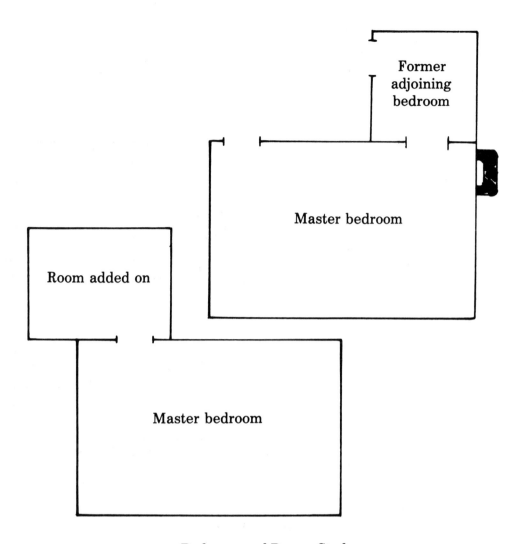

Bedroom and Den or Study

isolated study or den will be growing in future years. Because of increased leisure time, more work being done at home, the need for areas for reading, study, listening, thinking — privacy! — is expanding.

By the nature of its location away from the heavy family traffic pattern, the master bedroom generally offers a good locale for this private den. In one case shown, the den is merely an adjoining bedroom that can be opened to the master bedroom by the installation of a pair of recessed pocket doors. The den in the second example is a room added onto the master bedroom.

The addition of a room on the ground-floor level of the house is one of the least expensive forms of remodeling. Even the small fireplace shown is relatively cheap if the chimney is only one story high, thus needing only a minimum amount of scaffolding to be constructed. This is a case of getting a tremendous amount for your money. Such an addition should not exceed $3,500 including the fireplace and some bookshelves, but excluding floor covering.

If the study or den idea is not feasible, at least set aside a portion of the bedroom for a desk and comfortable easy chair for reading (with good natural light) so that a corner of the bedroom is decorated like a den. Another decorating thought is to *demote* the bed itself, perhaps building out small wardrobe closets on either side with attractive molded doors, perhaps furring down the ceiling over the headboard. The effect here is to sort of subtract the quality of dominant *bedness* in the room, thus producing more of a sitting-room effect.

How to Achieve Privacy and Quiet

Bedrooms function most ideally when they are situated on the least noisy portion of the lot. However, if traffic noise is unavoidable, the first effort should be to screen the room by a wall and

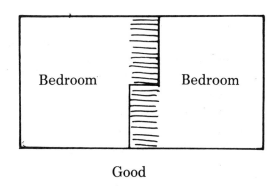

Good

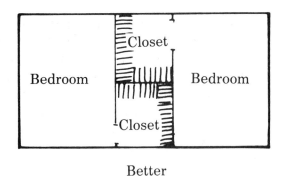

Better

Bedroom Floor Plans

planting. On a particularly noisy site, a foreground sound can be created within the protected wall area beside the bedroom by installing an inexpensive fountain of the sort where water would drop from a decorative source on the wall down into a small pond below. This has the effect of setting up an intermediate sound buffer, which more or less screens out the more objectionable sounds.

The next step is to install insulated glass in the windows and thick, opaque-lined window coverings as draperies. Since we are much more susceptible to noise at night than in the daytime, quiet is of maximum concern in sleeping areas.

Inside the house the isolation of one sleeping quarter from another is handled easily if there are closets or wardrobes separating adjoining bedrooms. The double set of walls and doors plus the clothing inside the closet act as a good built-in sound barrier.

However, in existing older homes not so much attention was paid to this feature, and often adjoining bedrooms are separated by only a single uninsulated wall. A fairly effective means of soundproofing is to install a decorative soundboard of a half-inch thickness on each side of the common wall using spacers of about a half-inch to hold the board out from the wall on each side.

In new construction or in remodeling, where separating closets just cannot be arranged, the wall can be doubled up so interior wall covering, such as plaster or sheetrock, is nailed to only one side of the thick wall. Insulation can be woven between the staggered studs, and the soundboard can be installed on both sides as well.

The Energy-Dependent Bedroom

In becoming aware of the many uses to which the bedroom can and may be put, we should emphasize some features that make a bedroom less dependent on energy in order to be enjoyed.

The double bed is an obvious energy saver simply because of its utilization of body heat. In fact, the Nazis in World War II conducted a number of unsavory and brutal "scientific" experiments for the purpose of finding the most effective method of resuscitating pilots downed in frigid waters. The result was that one way the almost frozen victim was revived was by simply being put in bed with another human being.

Queen and king-sized beds are not as effective. It is amusing to note that in older hotels and inns in Western Europe (just as that useful fixture, the bidet, can universally be counted on), a large percentage of bedrooms come with their version of the double bed: the four-poster bed in England, the *grand lit* in France, and the *matrimoniale* in Italy. The double bed is insisted upon by many sensible travelers who carry their heritage of self-reliance with them.

Thomas Jefferson was intrigued with the boxed-in beds of northern Europe but deplored the difficulty of making them up. So he designed one for Monticello that could be raised and lowered and was, in fact, *between* two rooms — a marvelous space enlarger when raised. Built-in boxed beds of northern Europe are certainly snug but are doubtless too hard to make up and too stifling in summer. Canopied double beds hold a partial answer, but these were aimed at privacy *within* the bedroom and reduction of drafts, neither of which is of overriding concern here.

Extra blankets, a quilt, or comforter should be found within the bedroom — either on a closet shelf or in a blanket chest within easy reach of the bed — not in a distant hall closet.

Specific light for reading should be available without having to depend on overall room lighting. The small tensor lights are adequate for a person with normal eyesight. They can be bought on small adjustable stands or clipped onto the headboard. Their brightness is the equivalent of about a forty-watt incandescent light bulb.

While on the subject of light, be sure there is good natural light for reading in both the bedroom and study. This will eliminate use of any artificial lighting during the daytime.

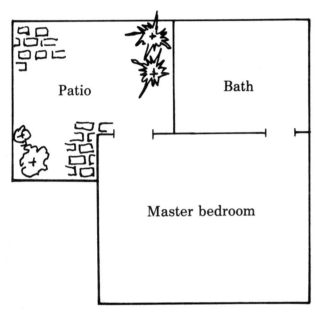

The Patio - A Bedroom Amenity

Other Bedroom Amenities

As a private sanctum, there are other amenities that can make the bedroom more enjoyable. One is a built-in bookcase so the bedroom can have its own source of reading material, another is a source of music. A small hot plate or means of warming coffee or broth is also a welcome addition.

In designing a new house it is good to have some controls for outside lighting in the bedroom in case of suspicious sounds at night.

In the case of a one-story house, the bedroom can be greatly enhanced by its own private patio. Not only is isolation desirable inside the house but outside as well. A precious secret garden can be a haven on warm days when the home owner has work or reading to do but wants to be out-of-doors and needs to

concentrate. If traffic noise is a problem, create a foreground sound by installing a fountain or an outside speaker for music. These sound buffers will protect both the patio and the bedroom. They function like a fire-fighting team using a back fire to fight a forest fire.

If the wardrobes or closets open directly into the bedroom and dressing is done in that room, a trick in heating is to position two or three "flush heat light" fixtures as nearly over the dressing areas as possible. With infrared bulbs in them, these "heat lamps" can be switched on for dressing only and will provide instant, radiant heat right where it is most needed and only for the time that it is needed, without firing up the whole heating system.

Bathrooms

In the nineteenth-century home, bathrooms were fewer and larger, sometimes sybaritically palatial rooms with mahogany cabinet enclosures and elaborate hardware. Near the end of the century, the fetish for cleanliness and functionalism forced the gleaming pipes back into the open and expelled the cabinets in favor of free-standing claw-footed tubs and gigantic lavatories. The wall-hung toilet of today is an outgrowth of the desire to get at every square inch of floor space with a mop and pail with no obstructions in the way.

With less domestic help and more bathrooms, the trend grew for smaller rooms, with less floor space and fewer pipes to clean. Back to the built-ins. The apron in front of the tub was a great stride in that direction, since it closed off that champion cleaning challenge under the base of the four-footed tub. Lavatory "pullmans" did their job of enclosure, and the deed was done. We had come full circle back to the furniturelike bathroom.

The minimum size of a three-fixture bathroom can sensibly be shrunk down to is a space five feet wide (the length of a tub) and eight feet long, which is space enough for three fixtures arranged beside each other along one wall. Certainly, master baths, variations on the three-fixture theme, and baths having access from more than one doorway require more space.

When building or remodeling, realize that 90 percent of the house buyers want a stall shower in the master bedroom. About 50 percent want a tub as well, but most of these will accept the

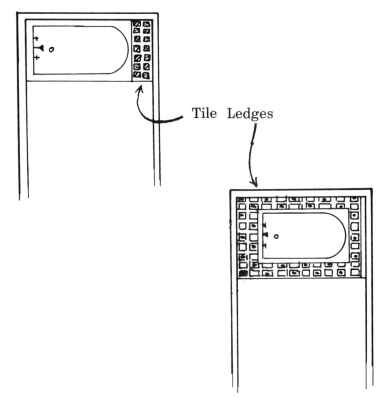

Tile Ledges

Baths

house if there is a tub in one of the other bathrooms that is not too distant. In the master bath, a shower over the tub will not satisfy the stall shower requirement.

Stall shower design should call for the shower being as open as possible. More light and less expense will result if the end wall of a shower is kept open. The glass panel, sometimes called an "in-line" panel, is cheaper than a stud wall with plaster on one side and tile on the other and the tile doorway is expensive. With the panel more light will be gained and a separate shower light can likely be avoided, depending on the size of the room and what natural and artificial light is available.

Take note in planning of the convenience in operating the shower. See that the door swings in such a way that you can reach the valves while standing outside the shower and that you can also reach the shower head to test the temperature of the water without getting inside. Shower doors should be made of safety glass and have a bar on them for towels. Normal shower ceiling height is 7 to 7½ feet, slightly lower than the 8-foot ceiling height of the typical room. Higher ceilings than this make the shower feel strangely elongated.

Bathtubs now come with slip-proof bottoms, and they are ordered right or left-handed, depending on the valve location. The standard tub size is five feet long by thirty-two inches wide by sixteen inches high. The plumber can get you a tub that is six inches longer than that at a slightly higher price.

In designing a bathroom with a tub, you can make its actual length and width appear much greater by installing a ledge the same height as the tub at one end or along the side or both, and then tiling this ledge to match the walls. Where space permits, this will give the tub a much larger appearance along with providing a convenient place for soaps, shampoo bottle, and the like.

Some builders and designers are promoting very eyecatching tiled "Roman" tubs of gigantic size. The trouble with these is an energy-conscious house is the enormous quantity of water required to fill them, not to mention the time wasted waiting around while the filling takes place. It is possible to design a tiled Roman tub without making the bathing cavity so large that you need to drain a hundred-gallon water heater just to fill it. Shallowness, steps, seats, and shape of the deepest body cavity determine the ultimate number of gallons needed and in no case should this exceed one hundred gallons or 13 cubic feet of combined hot and cold water.

Toilets and Water Conservation

About 40 percent of all water used in the house is used for flushing toilets, and for most of these flushes, nowhere near the full tank amount of water is required. A good investment is the half-tank flush valve obtainable at most hardware stores. It will cut the usual six to ten gallons of flushing water in half.

Lavatories and Bidets: A Better Way to Go

A second lavatory in a bathroom presupposes that the double usage is a constant enough pattern to justify this extra fixture. If this is not the case, or even if it is, the bidet represents a much finer investment. The fixture itself is more expensive than a lavatory, but the cost to plumb it with water and drain is about the same. In addition to the hygienic function for which it was intended, it is an extremely versatile fixture, which performs admirably an abundant variety of other operations:

1. A miniature sitz-bath for man or woman.

2. A foot washer par excellence (In the 1870's they actually manufactured such a fixture.)

3. A perfect vessel for soaking lingerie.

4. A water-saving urinal *for either sex* (no more than a quart of water is needed to rinse out the fixture!)

5. A bathtub for small pets.

The Placement of Fixtures

In building or remodeling, check with the plumber if you want to have decorative colored fixtures. The price differential is not so great as it once was, but some items are difficult to get, and you do not want any work held up because of back-ordered fixtures. Just as with clothing, one becomes bored and exasperated with faddish colors that do not stand the test of time, a maxim people tend to forget. (Remember the black, pink, and green fixtures of the immediate pre- and postwar years?) Keep color selections in the subtle shades like sand, beige, gray, etc.

Decorative faucets and spouts have gone up astronomically in price due primarily to the rising cost of choice metals such as brass. When you face the fact that fancy bathroom fittings utilize stock manufactured valves inside, the expense seems hardly worth it. In presenting tract models and custom spec houses, the builder is constrained from omitting second lavatories and decorative fittings because of his belief that the mass buyer of his product expects them at least in the master bath and, in the case of the hardware, in the powder room. But when you think that these three sets of decorative lavatory valves and spigots will cost between $200 and $500 more than the standard lavatory sets, as an owner who can direct his own decisions, you are well advised to put your money elsewhere into a more deserving category of expense. After all, these hardware items can always be added later if your buyer develops an overpowering remorse about not having them and feels unable to survive without 24-karat gold dolphins on a $25 basin. The smart home builder would prefer that his money go for better quality structural and mechanical features.

Lighting and Heating the Bathroom

Bathrooms require more light than the minimum building code provides. Natural light is always a problem in a bathroom because of two classic handicaps these rooms suffer:

1. Designers usually provide windows that are too small.

2. The mirror area above the lavatory is usually backlit by whatever natural light is available, in most cases.

These handicaps can be overcome by confirming that you have at least eight square feet of window area (a two foot by four foot window at the very least) in a small bath and twelve square feet of window area or more in a large bath. Here is where a skylight can be extremely helpful in eliminating both handicaps. It adds light without subtracting privacy, and it can add it in the right place: near the mirror and window areas so that light comes from the *side* rather than the back.

Heat lights are modest sources of radiant heat, they are instant, and they are specific in

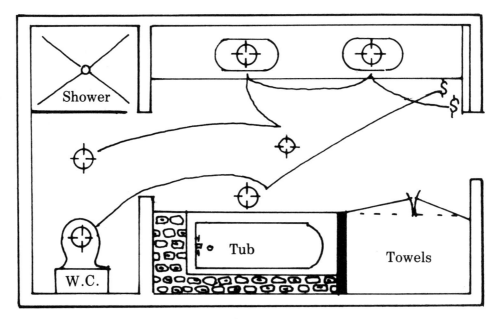

Compartmentalizing the Bathroom

what they heat. Thus they are helpful in bathroom heating. Here are several tips for installing them for greatest efficiency.

1. They are most effective on furred-down (lowered) ceilings, such as 7 to 7½ feet high rather than 8 feet.

2. Two are better than one; three are better than two.

3. They function best when *grouped* over the area where you will be coldest when drying from a shower or tub bath. Since they do not warm the air, only *you*, there is no point in neatly stringing them out for overall space heating.

An economic consideration in their installation is to use them for at least a portion of the regular bathroom lighting. Have one or two fixtures or flush lights for normal bath lighting plus a separate switch for the heat lights, which can be turned on when extra lighting and temporary, instant heat are needed.

This discussion of heat lights does not alter the fact that all baths should also be included in the house's mechanical heating system. A builder who does not tie in the bathrooms to the general heating scheme has taken a shortcut in order to save a few dollars and has made the house less livable and downright uncomfortable in cold weather.

The heat register for the bathroom should not merely be the back side of the bedroom's register cut through both sides of the wall. This produces nothing but a continual sound transmission problem and is another hallmark of cheap-jack building.

Compartmentalizing the Bathroom

If a second lavatory is needed on the basis of bathroom congestion and usage, a stronger campaign could be mounted for closeting the toilet or combined toilet and shower in a separate small room off the bathroom so the lavatory can be used without the whole bathroom being monopolized. Also a secondary vanity mirror in some alternate dressing area of the bedroom could relieve some pressure on the lavatory area. The "room within a bath" idea also makes the closing of a second door possible, as in the case of the compartmentalized powder room, so that the use of the toilet or shower area is not apt to disturb someone who is in the bedroom.

Other Bathroom Amenities

Thorough bathroom planning would also include a consideration of the following:

Medicine cabinets	Towel storage
Intercom	Telephone outlet
Solid wood door(s)	Seat in shower

| Niche for shampoo | Ledge around tub |
| Oversized mirrors | Exhaust fan (near toilet) |

Flooring the Bath

The old traditional tile floor and tile base is often a good investment if there are any number of young people using the bathroom. Second choice would be vinyl flooring with coved base for easy cleaning. However, for adult use, the carpeted bathroom is hard to beat. It has three distinct attributes:

1. It feels warmer and seems to reduce the need for heat that you almost instinctively yearn for the moment your feet touch a tile floor.

2. It deadens sound — having the opposite effect of tile, which maximizes it.

3. It creates a decorative flow of color from adjacent rooms that takes the curse off of an otherwise cut-up smallish area.

The Kitchen as an Energy Saver

As was shown in the humble Elizabethan farmhouse, the kitchen served as family room and dining room as well as much else. Being large and well heated, with its constantly tended fire for baking bread and cooking aromatic dishes, it must have been a truly enjoyable place to while away the time.

As the bourgeoisie developed so did its house style, which included domestic help. This meant that the mistress of the house could stay as far away as possible from the scene of scullery toil, as she tended to do more often than not. The kitchen in the basement was the epitome of this house-mistress detachment. If today one visits the house of Thomas Carlisle near Cheyne Walk in London, it is possible to see a well-preserved example of a modest city household's kitchen belowstairs, in this case with a cozy informal dining room attached. The television series ''Upstairs, Downstairs'' depicted this arrangement most graphically escalated to a very much grander house of the upper middle class.

In all of the thousands of old flats throughout London and all other cities that developed in the nineteenth century, these kitchens have found

their way upstairs, and, in most instances, the basement has been remodeled into a complete basement apartment or, in some cases, two apartments, since there were usually ample servants' rooms and related storage rooms to warrant the renovation into additional units.

With the kitchen's migration back upstairs, and the hand-in-hand diminution of domestic help came a desire for compaction and handiness. Writing in 1906, an architect said: ''Keep the kitchen as small as your fittings will allow without cramping. If the cook should be able to stand in the centre of the room and by revolving on her heels perform her duties, both time, space, and the cook may be saved. The principal trouble with the average kitchen lies in the fact that there is an unlimited amount of travel involved.''

The miniaturization of the kitchen does not refer to an eating area in the same room, or to the various related storage areas, laundry equipment, freezers, barbecue, or fireplace. It refers to the hard-core area of the working kitchen where the cooking is done. In fact, in the interest of energy-saving, and because of its inherent warmth and nearness to food and potential companionship, the kitchen is an ideal room in which to have an attractive secondary dining area and even some comfortable chairs and a television set; and, best of all, a fireplace will not only make breakfast more pleasurable but will enhance some of the other meals in cold weather.

Good Kitchen Planning

Kitchen shapes fit into four general categories: the one wall, the ''L'', the ''U,'' or the corridor.

Usually the shape is determined by the room shape, doors, windows, and where the kitchen is to be located with respect to other rooms.

Within the kitchen shape are four basic work centers: refrigerator, sink, mixing, and range/serve. The Small Homes Council of the University of Illinois at Urbana-Champaign, Illinois (61801), publishes a very comprehensive *Kitchen Planning Guide* along with other informative housing publications. One of its important planning tools to save labor and time in the kitchen is to plot a ''work triangle.'' You can do this on your preliminary floor plan. Draw a line from the sink to the refrigerator to the cook top, leaving out the mixing area because of

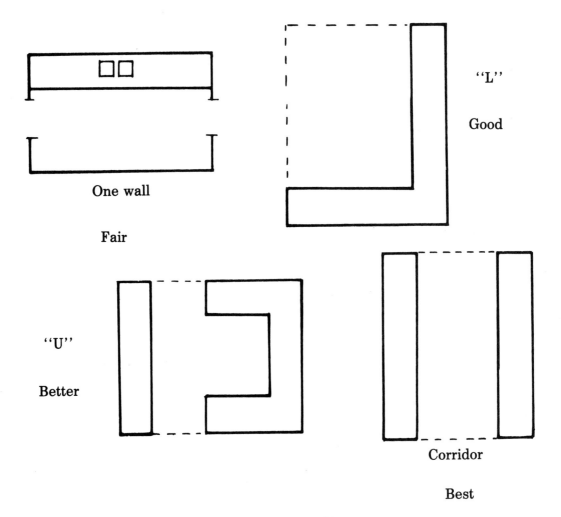

"L"

Good

One wall

Fair

"U"

Better

Corridor

Best

Common Kitchen Shapes

its lesser use. The sides of the triangle should total less than twenty-three feet but never more than twenty-six feet if work steps are to approach the ideal minimum.

For simplicity of determining the most traveled paths, the separate oven location is also disregarded, since oven use comprises an average of just about 5 percent of all kitchen preparation chores. One caution: tall appliances should be located so as to avoid blocking the flow of work from one counter to another. Furthermore, foot traffic *through* a work triangle by people circulating from one room to another should be avoided.

Selection of Appliances

In a recent tract of high quality homes in the Bretton Woods neighborhood of Buena Park, California, the twenty-five hundred square foot homes that included microwave ovens and trash compactors in the models evoked the most outstanding response from buyers. The anticipation of cooking food in a fraction of the accustomed time and at a fraction of the previous electrical cost generated a high degree of enthusiasm. The microwave oven conserves on electricity by accomplishing a comparable task with about half the electricity of the

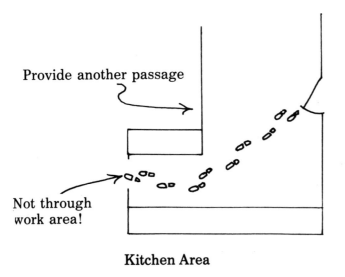

Provide another passage

Not through work area!

Kitchen Area

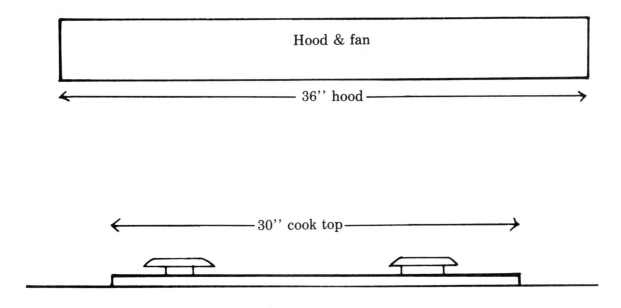

3 feet x 100 C.F.M. = 300 C.F.M.

Cook Top and Hood

traditional oven. The oven setup used in the homes referred to was a single self-cleaning oven with the electronic oven installed above it as an option.

Gas cook tops or full ranges are the ones that appeal to professional chefs, experienced amateur chefs, and homeowners skilled in the preparation of quality food. Most builders do not put them in because they fear losing buyers who do not like the darkened cooking utensils or the occasional odor of gas.

The Aga stove, a marvelous stove used in Great Britain, Scotland, and Ireland, has not yet reached our shores. If it does, the massive appearance and gargantuan burners will not cause the Board of Directors of Corning to tremble. However, its use of peat coal, its room-warming and water-warming qualities, and its versatility and cheapness are outstanding.

Exhaust fans over ranges are excellent, but these should have enough air-moving ability (referred to as "C F M's") to overpower moisture and smoke and expel it. It is thought that one hundred C F M's (or Cubic Feet per Minute) per lineal foot of hood length is necessary to do a good job of this. In the following example, the drawing shows a three-foot hood. Applying this formula, or three times one hundred, we arrive at three hundred C.F.M. as the hood rating required.

Double-compartment sinks with garbage disposals and adjacent dishwashers are more or less standard. A thought on energy saving is to have good rinsing materials right at hand at the sink so that barely used dishes and glasses can be soaped and hosed off quickly and left to dry in the dishwasher racks. They can be put away later after they have dried. This will reduce the need for so many dishwasher loads and lead to substantial energy saving on the dishes and glasses handled in this fashion.

Three-compartment sinks with the garbage disposal located in a small center well are a designer's dream and a homeowner's nightmare. They are not only more expensive than regular two-compartment sinks, but they force you to avoid the garbage at the drop of a hat, for they will hold only a minimum amount of food waste before overflowing into the adjacent compartments. These abominations were clearly designed by callow industrial designers whose only acquaintance with dishwashing was the mother, wife, or restaurant owner who did the dishes for them.

Refrigerators and freezers can be checked from time to time for normal temperature settings. Refrigerators should usually be set at 45-50° and freezers at 0°. Most refrigerators are right-handed with hinges on the right side, but be certain when ordering that this does not elongate the work triangle and create an

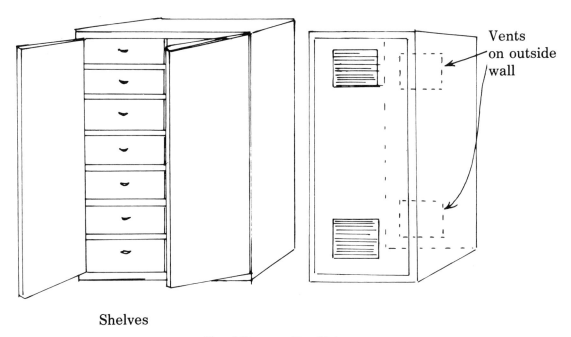

Vents on outside wall

Shelves

Food Storage Facilities

awkward situation. It goes without saying that the less you open the refrigerator and freezer, the less will be their use of energy. Some of the most popular refrigerator models now have water and ice cubes available from an outside aperture in the door, which reduces the need to open the door every time anyone wants a drink.

Another argument in favor of running gas to the kitchen is the feasibility of having a gas-fired barbecue. The convenience of having this appliance indoors and located near the cook top as part of the vital work triangle relieves the cook top or oven broiler from the job of preparing many fish and meat dishes, and enables the barbecue to carry its share of inexpensively prepared entrees.

Most trash mashers are about the same price as a barbecue — $150 — and all operate on similar screw-type compaction principals. They take amazingly little power to operate because of the wizardry employed in the mechanical design. Ecologically they help preserve the environment by reducing solids in areas where trash is dumped, and along the way they minimize trash handling around the home.

Garbage disposals, even at best, produce annoying sounds, but cheaper models deteriorate more quickly than better ones and suffer from lack of sound-insulating materials. So buy the better, more soundproof model, and do not ruin the valuable secondary eating area with annoying motor noise.

A Fireplace in the Kitchen

Nothing can stamp the seating area of the kitchen as warm and inviting so well as a fireplace. A gilding of the lily would be to have a rich brick floor as well. Obviously the inclusion of a fireplace makes the kitchen truly independent of the basic heating system. In one fell swoop this combination room can become virtually self-sufficient.

Storage, Pantries, and Coolers

Machiavelli said, "Every fortress should be victualed for a year." While a year may be overdoing it, and while hoarding is a demeaning concept, it has to be a part of any conscientious fuel-saving program to eliminate unnecessary shopping trips. The cost of operating a car for short runs for staples and supplies has to be enormous when applied to the units purchased.

Storage closets and pantries, and full-height wall storage cabinets are worth their weight in gold.

While on the subject of food storage, one wonders what happened to the old-fashioned vegetable coolers, where long-lasting fruits, vegetables, and grains could be kept in almost ideal temperature balance. Such a closet or cupboard required only proximity to an outside wall and the installation of louvered grills both high and low. The wall should be in shade and on the exterior, and would, ideally, receive some breeze. Otherwise, a little fan could help to

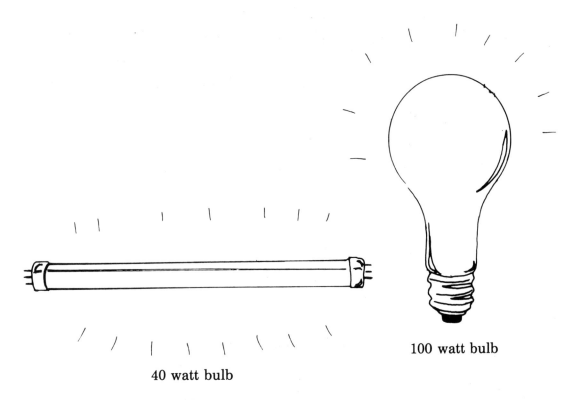

100 watt bulb

40 watt bulb

Kitchen Lighting

circulate the air in hot weather.

Lighting the Kitchen

Much like the bathroom, a kitchen needs to receive more than a minimum amount of light. A window over the sink should be generous, say five feet wide by four feet high, especially if it is the only source of light. It should be placed as high in the wall as possible to cause the light to penetrate deeply into the room, since there is usually only this one outside light source in the hard-core working part of the kitchen. If this window is on the west side, it needs some shade planting on the exterior for protection in summer. Be sure that the kitchen window is easy to open without having to climb up on the sink to obtain leverage.

The secondary portion of the kitchen, used for eating and other family purposes, should have its own window or French doors, and as Oliver Coleman was quoted earlier ". . .the breakfast should have the fullest benefit of the morning sun."

The kitchen calls for both general overall lighting and specific lighting over sink, mixing area, range top, etc. Although generally conceded to be rather cold looking and able to petrify the most charitable of interior decora-

tors, fluorescent light, nevertheless, produces far more candlepower — between two and four times more — for the same amount of wattage than incandescent light.

The kitchen provides a good opportunity for the designer to conceal fluorescent tubes with attractive soffits, skirt boards below upper cabinets for counter lighting, panels in the ceiling surrounded by rich moldings, and any other way he can take the curse off these utilitarian energy sources.

Even the most adamant decorator can abide the fluorescent tube (concealed, of course) in kitchens, baths, laundry rooms, basements, garages, storage rooms, attics, etc. The electrical savings are enormous.

Reducing the power drawn by lights has a double effect: energy for air conditioning and for operating the lights is reduced. Waste heat is a by-product of illumination; that is, a 100-watt light bulb produces 100 watts of heat. In a space with 100 footcandles illumination (that recommended for reading tasks of average printing on poor paper) waste heat can account for 37% of the summer cooling load. If the illumination is raised to 400 foot-candles, the factor will rise to 70% of the summer cooling load. Less than ½ of the heat produced by fluorescent lamps is

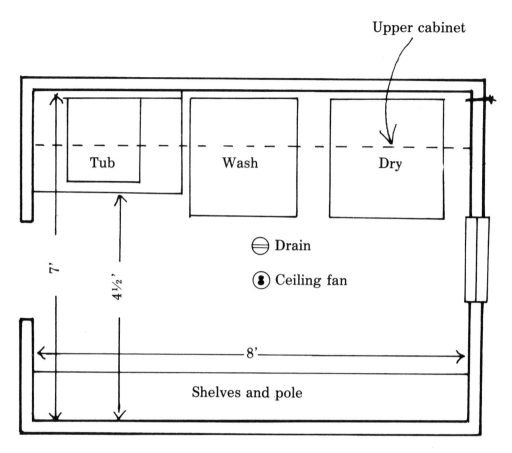

The Laundry

radiant whereas ¾ from incandescent or filament lamps is radiant. Since fluorescent bulbs provide two to four times as much light per watt of electricity as incandescent bulbs, radiant heat of fluorescent lamps, for equal illimination, is approximately 1/5 that of incandescent — a big advantage in a kitchen where heat is usually a problem anyhow.

Other sources of light are the high-intensity discharge lamps: mercury, metal halide and high pressure sodium. Because of the high intensity from a point source and noisy ballasts, these lamps are not used for home interior lighting.

The efficiency of lamps in terms of lumens per watt is as follows:

Incandescent	8-22 lumens/watt
Fluorescent	79 lumens/watt
Mercury	30-65 lumens/watt
Metal halide	70-95 lumens/watt
High pressure sodium	110 lumens/watt

Without a change in lighting, light-colored reflecting surfaces such as walls, ceilings and floors can increase illumination as much as 30 foot-candles, as compared to dark surfaces.

Heating and Food Warming in the Kitchen

There should be a heating register provided in the kitchen in any high-quality mechanical system. If this register is too near the originating equipment, it might need a damper blade to suppress noise and excess heat. Kitchens can overheat, particularly as preparation for an important meal hits full stride. At such times an overall exhaust fan is often the more pressing requirement.

A good feature is a food warmer. It can be accomplished either by the warming drawer appliance made for the purpose or by the installation of two or three infrared bulbs underneath the upper cabinets near where the food is exited to the dining area.

The Final Amenity

Some planning should be done to facilitate serving food to the exterior of the house — to an adjacent patio, a poolside area, a nearby terrace. If there are no French doors giving onto such an area, there should be some easy means of passage, or a counter-ledge at the kitchen window. This latter is easy to install, inexpensive, and totally able to accomplish the purpose of graceful movement of food.

The Location of the Laundry

The first choice for the laundry location should be the opposite of where it has often been lo, these many years. It should be nearest the bedrooms for obvious ease in picking up and returning bed linens, towels, and clothing. Second choice is on the first floor near the kitchen, and next choice is the classic basement location. The least popular and the least functional location is in the garage.

In addition to convenience, the choice should be partially governed by access to natural light. However, if a dark location like the basement is preordained, try somehow to work in a large well-window or two. Failing all else, be certain of adequate artificial lighting by providing the equivalent of at least 150 watts of incandescent lighting.

Spaces in the Laundry

The washer-dryer, laundry tub, drip-dry area, and ironing spaces are all elements of a well-equipped laundry room and take approximately this much space:

Washer-Dryer 5 feet 6 inches by 2 feet 6 inches (plus 3 feet 6 inches work space in front of appliances).

Laundry Tub 2 feet 6 inches by 2 feet 6 inches.

Drip Dry 2 feet 6 inches by 2 feet 6 inches.

Ironing Space 6 feet by 4 feet 6 inches (includes board).

If you combine the drip-dry area and the laundry tub, as suggested below, and use the work area required in front of the appliances for ironing space, the following will result:

More space than this is, of course, desirable, particularly for folding and stacking, also for operating appliances and ironing at the same time. However, space may be limited near the bedroom area, and this locational convenience may be worth a little crowding.

Where Can Energy be Saved?

Drying. Try to have a gas line available for the dryer. A gas dryer is cheaper to operate than an electric dryer and is apt to remain relatively even more so. Gas dryers even cost less at the time of original purchase. It is obvious that drying loads should be saved up so the dryer only runs when full.

The development of drip-dry materials has only just begun and they have proved to be great time and energy savers, especially if there is an efficient arrangement for drying them in quantity. These clothes can either be hung out over a tile area sloped into a floor drain (resembling the base of a stall shower without any enclosure) which allows very long clothing to hang without a fold, or as shown in the drawing above, hung on a clothes pole suspended over a standard laundry tub. This latter arrangement is least expensive and saves space as well. Moreover, it preserves that stalwart of olden days, the laundry tub, from falling on increasingly hard times due to builders' persistent cost cutting.

Supplement these methods with alternative open-air drying areas both inside and outside the house so that for a few items it is not always necessary to run power-consuming drying equipment.

Be sure that the dryer is vented to the outside. For this reason it is desirable to plan its location for an outside wall.

Washing. In addition to the washing machine, consider this same laundry tub as a handy fixture not only for collecting water from the drip-dry fabrics, but for light washings of lingerie, barely soiled items, and other things that scarcely need twenty minutes of tumbling about in a regular washer load and twenty more minutes in a regular drying load.

Laundry appliances make noise, and you must think about insulation of walls and floor if the units are on the second floor, or on the first floor, for that matter. It is desirable to have a drain on the floor to receive the overflow if there should be any spillage from the appliances. An exhaust fan in the ceiling or wall is valuable for expelling the moisture generated by the dryer. It is a good idea to install a large wall cabinet over the equipment for storage of washing supplies. On first floor or basement installa-

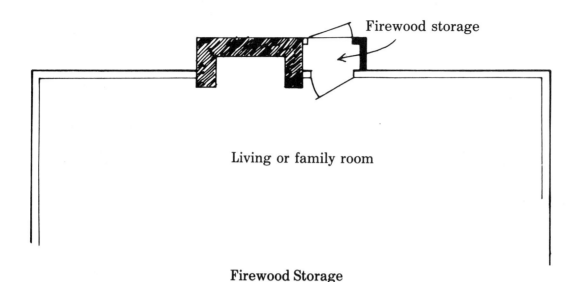

Firewood storage

Living or family room

Firewood Storage

tions, a laundry chute down from the floor above can be quite an asset; it can be designed to terminate in the storage cabinet above the equipment for easy transferal of the articles to the machines.

Remember these checkpoints for a good laundry:

Convenient location	Adequate spaces
Good natural and artificial light	Floor drain
Availability of gas	Laundry tub
Drip-dry provisions	Soundproofing
Folding counter	Laundry chute
Storage cabinet	Exhaust fan

Storage

Most builders and designers have a written or mental list of minimal storage requirements that includes so much clotheshanging space (about eight to ten feet per person), linen storage, coat closet, closet for brooms and vacuum, and kitchen-related storage for food and utensils. They literally run out of gas beyond that point. Yet for energy conservation there is much other storage space that is wanted

For one thing, wood storage space is essential if the fireplaces are to be enjoyed. The best facility for this is a low cabinet that can be reached from both inside and outside the house.

Even better would be to have some storage

near each fireplace. In upper floors this can either be a built-in cupboard or a free-standing coffer. The space can be filled once a week with wood, and this supply will ordinarily last through the week without refilling.

Space for wine storage is given little, if any, thought in this country but is considered an indigenous part of the design in much of western Europe. The ideal location is underground, in a portion of the basement that has no water- or space-heating equipment, yet is not vulnerable to freezing. The single most important feature in wine storage is not coolness for its own sake, but an *even* temperature with little variation from hour to hour, day to day, week to week, and that preferably does not rise much above the low sixties or fall below the mid-fifties during the year.

Basement

Try to arrange for some natural light in the basement. If it is used for anything except storage, see that its walls and any windows are insulated. If it is used only for storage, insulate the floor above it well, and see that the basement door to the house is weatherstripped. The inexpensive rubber or plastic kind available in rolls at the hardware store is adequate.

Garage

Every garage should have a window to admit natural light. A good builder will provide one. This can be of obscure glass so prowlers cannot see if a car is there or not. In northern states, the garage needs to be heated at least above

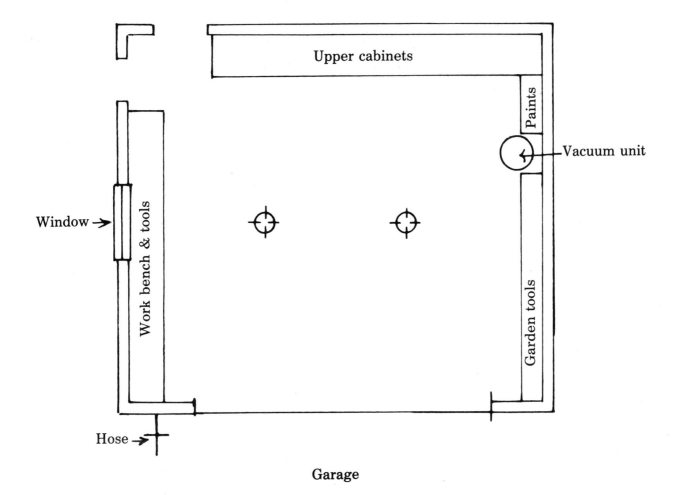

Garage

freezing. If attached to the house, the shared wall should be well insulated and the connecting door weatherstripped. An important and often neglected item is weatherstripping the bottom of the large overhang garage door. This can be done with a rubber, plastic, or felt blade that will prevent wind and leaves and dirt from entering when the door is supposed to be closed.

Additionally, the garage floor should slope to the outside or to the drain. The walls should rest on concrete curbs about four inches in height to thwart dampness and make for easy, sanitary hosing of the floor. Water and extra electrical outlets for tools and vacuum should be available.

In figuring the square footage cost of housing, the garage can sometimes be as expensive to build as the rest of the house. This is true when the house is of masonry materials or when the garage is under a second floor thus requiring complete plastering. In such an instance, where garage costs are high anyway, analyze this area as a truly functional storage and utility space with an eye to totally equipping

it so that clients really get their money's worth. The cost of natural light, good artificial light, drainage, water, power, storage cabinets with doors on them, temperature control through minimum heat and ventilation are not that great that one should forgo developing this highly usable room to its highest potential. Furthermore, an energy-conscious home owner will no doubt be keeping his car longer and maintaining it better than the average person; and this improved garage facility will aid him.

Garages need to be vented in two places near the floor in order to insure dilution with sufficient outside air of any gasoline fumes that might collect. Most important of all in the consideration of safety is the proper installation of any natural gas appliance or fixture, such as a water heater, space heater, or gas dryer. In the garage area these units must be placed on two-foot-high raised platforms. This keeps their pilots and burners up off the floor where gasoline fumes could collect. In fact, just the pilot igniting the burners can cause an explosion that could send the garage roof up about fifty feet in the air.

Plumbing and Electricity 8

General Planning of the Plumbing

It is often brought up in the context of economic construction that plumbing fixtures should be grouped in clusters: that is, that baths should be placed back-to-back, washer-dryer appliances set up near the kitchen, and second-floor baths positioned over first-floor baths and so on. To some extent this is valid. Some labor and materials are saved by toilets feeding into a common soil line and vent. However, there are other ways to save money like placing toilets near outside walls, reducing needlessly long sewer runs by keeping baths nearer the main sewer line, and seeing to it that not too many joists have to be cut to get soil and waste lines down into the sewer system. The desirability of good traffic planning and control of noise by having closets adjacent to baths and compartmentalizing within the bathrooms far outweighs the small saving made by grouping, except in mass-produced or extremely tight-budgeted housing.

In addition to reducing the length of pipe runs to the sewer, a good planning practice is to attempt to place the fixtures on one wall rather than on two or three walls of a bathroom. But here again, only do this if there is no lessening of living convenience and deadening of sound.

Water-Supply System

In much of the United States where temperatures vary greatly, water pipes should be insulated, both hot and cold. Insulating the hot water pipes prevents heat loss in winter and insulating the cold, stops freezing in the winter and moisture condensation in the summer months. In areas of very moderate climate where temperature variation is not extreme, this is not necessary.

When water piping is being installed, keep an eye on the insulation padding used where pipes are secured by clips to wood members or where they pass through holes drilled in the framing. This padding should make the pipe fit snugly and securely or else it may vibrate with the flow of water traveling under pressure. Hose bibs, shower heads, and valves should all be substantially backed with wood so they do not wiggle in and out when they are touched.

The Drainage System and Vents

The drainage system is that conglomeration of soil lines (toilet drains) and waste lines (other drains) that feeds into the sewage disposal system. During construction these are installed in two phases: the groundwork, which is mainly below the first floor and below ground; and the rough plumbing, which includes the "top out" where soil lines, waste lines, traps, cleanouts, and vents are completed and run up through the roof. It is tested by filling the whole drainage and vent system with water. Any leaks at the joints are checked and corrected at that time.

This testing of the drainage system, conducted by putting the system under pressure and completely full of water, is an exaggerated condition, inasmuch as when it is functioning normally it operates by gravity and natural fall rather than pressure. Therefore, if it successfully passes the test at top-out, the drainage system seldom causes a problem unless there is a shifting of the building or settling that

77

somehow dislodges a joint connection or splits a pipe, which is highly unlikely. Leaks more typically stem from the water supply system, the connections where fixtures join the water and drainage systems, and from faulty waterproofing around or above fixtures or showers.

In checking out an existing house, see that the drains are able to clear rapidly by filling lavatories and bathtubs with water and seeing how quickly they empty. Wad up bits of paper, drop them into the toilets and flush them. While running water to check pressure and drainage, note any rusty color in the water; this signals a rusting or corrosion in the water-supply system.

Fixtures and Valves

Try the various valves several times. Be sure that they operate easily and do not drip. Toilet tanks should be checked also. Dripping valves and leaky toilet tanks can account for much lost water over a period of time. However, the saving grace of a faulty valve or leaky fixture is that it can be replaced without replumbing the whole house. Usually the deficient valve or fixture just needs to be disconnected and a new part or the whole unit be replaced.

In new work, buying the cheapest fixtures is not a good idea. But avoid decorative hardware, unproven designs, gimcrackery of any kind. Specify what plumbers and supply men have confidence in. Invest in quality in order to reduce maintenance, waste, and worry.

Know these quality differences:

Toilets

Materials are all the same: vitreous china. Where space permits use large or "elongated" models that project about 29 inches from wall. The siphon-jet is the best and quietest. The reverse-trap is second best on both counts. From there on, design is by choice and pocketbook.

Bathtubs

Material can be cast iron or pressed steel: insist on cast iron. Steel "gives" when you put your weight on it; steel is quick to chip and has a tiny ring.

Lavatories

Materials are the same as the bathtub. Cast iron is best. Wide spread (8- to 12-inch) faucet separation is best; counter installation best. Design is up to you; oval is popular now. Close spacing of faucets chafes your knuckles.

Shortages During Construction or Remodeling

Several years ago there was a scarcity of toilets and some other fixtures. Color selections were erratic. Curiously some more expensive models and some miscellaneous color choices were available. To complete a house on schedule often saves more money than delaying things for a budgeted item. Therefore, in overall planning, set aside a part of your contingency money for what can only be called "expediting" — just to cover some occasional banditry on the part of subs and suppliers.

So as not to disrupt the decoration plan if you are forced into a color fixture, borrow a toilet tank lid because it is easy to carry, and arrange for matching or complementary tile and wallpaper. Make a silk purse out of a sow's ear, unless, of course, all the supply house has is turkey red or lavendar.

Water Heaters

In choosing among electric, oil, gas, coil-type, automatic, and instant water heaters you can no doubt make this decision from knowledge of what use is prevalent in the area. Where natural gas is available, it is likely to be the most efficient means of heating water. Electric heaters are slower to heat up the water again or "recover," and will need a larger storage tank because of this failing. Bear in mind these typical usages:

Electrical dishwasher load	4 to 5 gallons
Normal shower (10 to 15 minutes)	9 to 12 gallons
Tub bath	10 to 15 gallons
Washer with full load of clothes	25 to 40 gallons!

You can see from these approximations that *capacity* and *recovery* are the two vital factors involved. A fifty-gallon water heater is satisfactory for most medium-sized houses of four bedrooms and two baths. Moreover, the fifty-gallon size is the largest made that can be called a high-production item, which enables it to be sold at a competitive price. However, seventy, eighty, ninety, one hundred, and larger gallonage heaters are also available and really have to be judged in relation to the house's

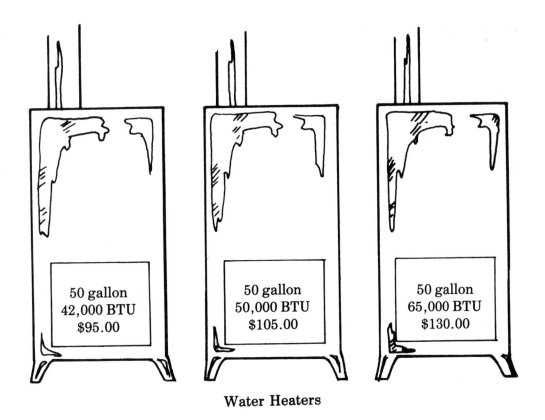

Water Heaters

requirements and whether you are going to combine space heating with water heating, for this requires substantially greater gallonage than even those listed above.

A major unsung factor in *all* heater selection, not just electric heaters, is *high recovery*. This feature does not alter tank size. Rather, it makes whatever size you decide upon that much more efficient for very little more in initial cost. Two ordinary fifty-gallon gas water heaters that appear similar on the outside can have radically different recovery or reheating capabilities:

The tank on the right heats water at a rate *50 percent faster* than the one on the left. It has larger gas burners underneath the tank, and the difference in cost is about $30.

Water Softener

These devices are useful in areas noted for hardness of water. The customary installation is to connect the softener tank to the hot water supply system only. The chemical salts used to soften the water are harmful to toilets and bad for garden irrigation and are not known for producing good drinking water. Therefore, by limiting the soft water to the hot water side of the system, most of the water used for washing dishes, clothes, hair, and humans get softened without incurring any bad effects.

Electricty: General Wiring and Energy Conservation

Much like the "shut-off valve" of the water supply system, the electrical system must have its principal turn-off mechanism or service switch, called simply "the main" or the main breaker. It is a means of disconnecting all circuits in the house at one fell swoop. It is usually located in or near the main service panel. Be sure that this service panel is of adequate size for future electrical uses or enlargement of the home. The electrician or the utility company's service man can advise you about this.

Typical residential service sizes are 100, 125, 150, 175, and 200 ampere size. The 125 or 150 ampere sizes are usually optimum for most homes without electric heating or air conditioning. The 175 or 200 ampere sizes are needed for houses having all-electric heating. Typical branch circuits supplying lights and plug receptacles (also called "duplex outlets") are 15 or 20 amperes each and have a safety feature of either fuses or circuit breakers. In the event of any overloading, the fuse or circuit breakers will give way before the wire can overheat and cause a fire somewhere in the unseen part of the house. This phenomenon is akin to a hemorrhage in the human circulatory system due to

79

high blood pressure; in the case of the electrical system the weak point is controlled at the point where fuses or breakers are located.

This brings us to the point of cautioning about overloaded circuits. This can be wasteful of energy and costly besides, for, apart from the safety factors involved, as the load on a circuit is doubled the power loss along that circuit is quadrupled. The cost of this wastage will more than offset the cost of another circuit or larger wire in the existing circuit.

The common signs that indicate an overloaded circuit are:

Motors running slowly

Unusually small television picture

Fuses blown or breakers reset often

Jamb switch

Indicates on in attic or basement

Energy Saving Switches

In an existing house, the problem of overloading circuits can often be solved by somehow relieving the suspected circuit of some of its burden. Certain appliances, particularly those that produce heat, like toasters and irons, can be plugged into alternate circuits instead of the one causing trouble. Light wattages can be lowered and lamps can be shifted to substitute plug receptacles.

Saving by Using Low-Voltage Wiring and Switching

There is a method of wiring that goes by trade names like Remcon, Bryant, G.E., or Touch Plate Remote-Control Wiring. It utilizes normal 110-voltage wiring to plug receptacles, fixtures, and appliances, but all switching is done by thin low-voltage "bell wire." While no electricity is really saved by the wiring system itself, the low-voltage method enables a rambling, spread-out or very large house or property to have its lighting and plugs switches from various locations at relatively low installation cost. Thus, remote lights can be controlled from innumerable locations such as the master bedroom or a faraway playroom or garage so that lights that might tend to be left on because of localized switching controls can be more conveniently controlled from great distances.

Designing for Low Power Consumption

The greatest amount of electrical power is used when it is heating water and space.

Whenever possible, if electricity is already in use in a house, remember that insulation is the key to keeping this utility cost down — that, and zone control, so that heat is reduced in unused rooms.

Too many lights controlled from one switching circuit represents a shortcut in the electrical wiring design, which is sometimes passed off as a convenience. This "convenience" can cause your client a lot of extra power use. Special wall-washers, decorative flush lights, art lights, aisle lights, all kinds of filler and back-lights plus exterior lights that are beyond what is needed for safety — all should have controls set aside separately from those required for minimal acceptable lighting for normal house and garden use. Otherwise, you are stuck with an unnecessary number of lights being used all of the time.

Closets that require the turning on and off of lights can be equipped with a jamb switch. This will turn on the light only when the door is open, like the refrigerator or automobile light. Also, in remote areas like basements or attics, a switch can be used that embodies a small red pilot light indicating whether the remote light is on or not.

The low cost of fluorescent lighting was mentioned earlier, and its use should be considered in any area where decorative appearance is not a major concern, especially in any location where the fixture is apt to remain on for long periods of time.

Basement window wells can be lightened by

painting them white or lining them with aluminum foil or mirror in order to conserve lighting energy. The garage should have a window and, ideally, the attic should have a dormer or two or a skylight for natural light.

Dimmer switches or rheostats are a help in areas like entry halls or dining rooms, where intensified illumination may be desired for a brief time. This way, a fixture of six 40-watt bulbs burning a total of 240 watts can be regulated to use only half of that wattage a majority of the time it is on.

Time clocks are a good investment for regulating necessary outdoor safety lighting. By controlling entry lights and other front and backyard lighting with clocks, lights will always be on when and where they are most needed, but will never be left on in error for long periods of time.

Good electrical planning and wiring is a superb investment. It lasts forever and is virtually service free once it has been correctly installed. How often does one have a power leak or a stopped up wire or a switch in need of oiling or grills needing to be vacuumed? Just keep this valuable utility in balance with other sources of power and you will not be shanghaied by lack of availability or outlandish price increases.

Steer Clear of Aluminum Wiring

In houses built after 1965 there is a possibility that aluminum wiring was used; there are over 2 million such houses in the United States. Among the suspected metallurgical problems of aluminum wiring are its brittleness and tendency to break, and, if this were not sufficiently unnerving, it has a coy habit of creeping away from pressure points where it has been fastened. As it ages it clothes itself in aluminum oxide, and this corrosion further increases resistance conditions.

Manufacturers have been struggling to upgrade aluminum wiring by changing alloys and making other alterations to improve it. However, a building and safety official in a major Southern California city said: "It's only 60 percent as effective as copper in carrying electrical current. Brittleness is what causes failure through breakage. It's inefficient and will cause fires. We'd be much happier if it weren't used."

The signs of aluminum wiring are flickering lights, sizzling light switches, hot plug receptacles, hot cords and plugs, red glowing switch plates in the dark, the smell of smoke, and so-called "wiring fires."

Better the seller than the buyer be of such a house.

Adding Electrical and Plumbing Systems

The first step, after the design direction of any remodeling job is established, is to have the electrical and mechanical services evaluated to see if the project can be accomplished at a minimum expense utilizing existing services. After all, the *dormant* part of the house (which is most of it) can be added onto by simply applying *more* concrete, more wood, more bricks; however, oftentimes the electrical and mechanical parts cannot simply be added onto. Unfortunately, it may be necessary to change or enlarge the old services and equipment altogether, often at great expense.

The concern with the electrical system is that the existing "service," referring to the panel box, should be of sufficient size to accommodate added circuits for wall plugs, fixture outlets, heating, and appliances. Adding an electric heater to a new room can be an expensive way of heating that space, though it is still sometimes less expensive than enlarging the existing system, if that is the only alternative.

The addition of a 150-square foot room (10 by 15 feet) usually requires a 15 or 20 ampere supplementary circuit, and this rule of thumb can be followed on other additions:

	20-ampere circuits
Major appliances (like dishwasher)	1 for each
150-square-foot bedroom (den study)	1
350-square-foot (15 by 23 feet) living room (or rec room)	1 or 2
Bath with electric heater	2
Laundry room (with electric dryer)	2 or 3
Hobby room (with outlets for saws, etc.)	2 or 3
Swimming pool (with gas heater)	2
Garage	1 or 2

Attic addition of 2 bedrooms, 1 bath   1 or 2

Kitchen remodeling (add built-ins)   5 or 6

If the new electrical demand means that the service has to be changed, the cost for a larger panel or subpanel plus bigger wires being pulled into the new box could run to several hundred dollars. That would be the type of remodeling expense that is extremely unrewarding for there is nothing visible to show for it. In general, be governed by what minimum electrical circuits have to be added for required plugs and lighting, and attempt to keep additions in line with what will fit with the existing service.

At the time of checking out the adequacy of the electrical service, it is wise to look into the idea of skylights in any dark areas of the house. These have to be added structurally and involve the carpenter and roofer and sometimes the plasterer to do some patching on the ceiling below. If they can be worked in, they will save on electricity and make the house more pleasant to live in long after the cost of the skylight is forgotten.

Adding to The Plumbing System

This trade's work breaks down into five parts: the sewer connections and the main house sewer line, the soil and drain lines and vents, the water supply system, bathroom and kitchen fixtures, and the natural gas supply. Sewer connections and the main house sewer line leading to it are more or less uniform. However, when a bath is involved, the large soil and drain lines leading from the major fixtures are a sizable consideration in remodeling. The problem in bathroom remodeling is always how and where to join the main sewer line without demolishing the whole house. Once that problem is solved, one tackles the large bend under the toilet (on second floor remodeling), and after that the vents that have to be run up through the roof.

Installing water and gas lines is not too difficult inasmuch as the pipes are small in diameter. When water pipes run exposed in an attic or crawl space, where freezing is apt to occur, they should be wrapped.

Conventional Heating and Air-Conditioning Units 9

The ideal house to heat would be like a heat-retention oven, where a very small amount of heat such as, say, a single fire in the living room, could by radiation heat the entire house. This would work much as the single large chimney did in Colonial houses, the chimney that was located absolutely centrally to all of the rooms.

This kind of house could be heated for very little if it approached being airtight, which it seldom did. Now, however, it is possible to build a house nearly airtight, with little warm air getting out and a minimum of the cold penetrating the walls, ceiling, doors and windows.

Before proceeding further to thoroughly understand this subject of heat and cold, you should know something about the three different types of heat:

1. *Conduction.* This is heat transferred through matter as through a soldering iron, a wire, or a boiler plate.

2. *Convection.* This is heat carried by the motion of masses of material, such as hot water or steam.

3. *Radiation.* This is heat transferred from the heated body by vibrations in the air and reconverted into heat when it encounters any obstacle capable of absorbing it. This is the phenomenon that occurs with the suns ''rays,'' a fire in the fireplace, a radiator, or an infrared electric bulb.

With the exception of "forced air," which reaches us as pure convection heat, much household heat actually gets to us in the form of radiated heat. The fireplace, the radiator, the heat lamp, the floor, ceiling or walls warmed with electric wires send their ultimate heat message out in the form of radiated heat. Radiant heat methods and combinations of these methods, like steam and water combined with radiators, are the most costly to install and, in the case of electric radiant heat, also the most costly to operate. More about this later.

What Heating System to Select

Some of the most important considerations in deciding on what kind of heating system is best for your customers are the following:

regional weather characteristics

type of house

initial cost

cost of operation

There are three basic categories of heating methods: forced air, hot water, and electricity. In the first two of these methods there is a choice of what sort of fuel is used to heat the air chamber or boiler. It can be natural gas, bottled gas, solar radiation, oil, coal, or electricity. Keep in mind that a system such as forced air, because of existing duct work and return-air provisions, may be adaptable to air conditioning at a later date. This versatility is precluded in

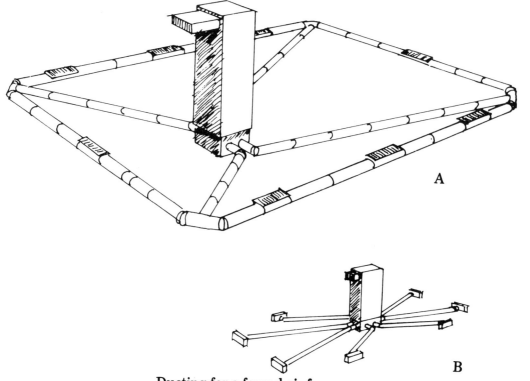

Ducting for a forced air furnace
A; perimeter loop
B; individual register ducts

hot-water and cable-electric systems. Here we will have a look at the basic heating methods along with some of their good and bad points.

This chapter will review what you should know about saving fuel with conventional heating systems. Solar heating is an important subject in the fuel savings picture and is treated at length in the next chapter.

Forced-Air Systems

Forced air is generated by heating air in a chamber. When that air reaches a certain temperature it is forced from the chamber by means of a fan through duct work, preferably under the house, to the various rooms to be served.

There is a little more expense for duct work installed in a *perimeter-loop*. But in colder northern climates having the ducts circulate air around the entire perimeter of the house, accompanied by good insulation of the slab or crawl space and outside walls, should produce a very snug environment. Here is a case in which a small additional expenditure at the time of installation can result in greater saving in heating effort and in increased comfort for years

to come, in fact for the entire life of the house. For even if the mechanical part of the heating system wears out and has to be replaced, the duct portion lasts and lasts.

Forced air has one capability not shared with other systems: speed. While hot water and electrical systems have some other attributes, forced-air systems take air that can be heated in a little less than two minutes and move it rapidly throughout the house. This is valuable in temperate climates where there is not an immense prolonged demand for heating, but where temperature fluctuations require minor thrusts of heat, and where the heat is wanted more or less instantly. These systems are easily adaptable to air conditioning which, happily, has a similar requirement for speed in those same temperate climates.

Here are the hallmarks of a good forced-air installation:

1. Locate equipment centrally in the floor plan in order to balance the runs of duct work so none is extremely long, bearing in mind that equipment makes noise and should preferably be in a basement or on

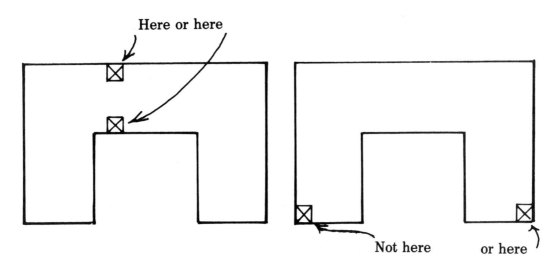

Here or here

Not here   or here

Preferred furnace locations

an outside wall.

2. Equipment space should be large enough to accept added components required for air conditioning. These include the fan coil, air cleaner, and some way to drain off condensed water, if only to a little dry well in the side yard.

3. Ducting should be large enough for air conditioning, which requires larger ducts than those needed for minimal heat ducting. Return air provisions should also be generous and able to draw air back to the equipment from more than one source.

4. Thermostats should be installed at about light-switch height in important well-used rooms, like a living room, and should not be on an outside wall or behind a drape or in the path of direct sunlight.

5. The plenum, which is the large air-disbursing chamber underneath or on top of the furnace, and the return-air duct should be lined with sound insulation in order to kill the noise of the large amounts of air that rush into and out of this equipment.

6. Where air conditioning is planned there must be a way to run the refrigeration lines from the forced-air equipment in the house to a condenser unit outside the house. This run should be a distance of not much more than fifty feet. In new construction it is best to anticipate this future need and (for $100 to $200) either install these lines or arrange a "chase" or runway where access will be possible later without tearing the whole house apart.

7. Make sure the unit is properly sized for the home. Added insulation, better weatherstripping and more efficient use of windows will lower the heating requirement. Oversizing of the furnace leads to reduced furnace efficiency because of the increased cycling and pilot light losses. Note the table "Gas Furnace Efficiency Economics." An adequate and double sized furnace is shown for each of four cities. The double sized gas furnace uses both more gas and electricity to produce the same amount of heat.

8. In the normal gas furnace cycle the blower is turned off when the furnace bonnet temperature drops below 100°F. If the bonnet thermostat is set to turn the blower off only after the temperature reaches 5 degrees above room temperature, there will be an energy saving of about 1 to 2%. The blower will run longer and may "cycle" on and off occasionally, but will still end up saving fuel. The table

City	Furnace size in 1000 BTU's/Hr.	Gas use in Therms/Yr. (Furnace)	Electric use in KWH/Yr. (Blower)	Utility total cost in $/Year
San Diego	35	221	49	328.50
	70	246	51	331.93
Atlanta	80	623	164	398.72
	160	723	173	411.01
Philadelphia	60	675	185	617.17
	120	789	196	641.23
Minneapolis	80	1,168	334	522.39
	160	1,392	361	553.57

Gas Furnace Efficiency Economics
(Blower shut-off at 100° F.)

City	Gas use in Therms/Yr. (Furnace)	Electric use in KWH/Yr. (Blower)	Utility total cost in $/Year	Percent savings over 100° shut-off
San Diego	200	93	326.73	.5
	209	115	328.62	1.0
Atlanta	540	322	393.69	1.3
	587	399	401.81	2.2
Philadelphia	593	347	607.07	1.6
	646	438	621.89	3.0
Minneapolis	1,036	603	512.49	1.9
	1,146	780	532.94	3.7

Blower shut-off at
5°F. over room temperature

"Blower Shut-off at 5°F. over Room Temperature" shows the saving for four cities with adequate and double adequate furnaces.

9. An automatic setback thermostat is a good investment. It automatically reduces the heating or cooling during sleeping hours and will save many a night of careless fuel consumption when the equipment is left on by mistake. The table shows how much energy a 6 degree setback can save. Notice that the percentage saving is the greatest in milder climates but the dollar saving is greatest in colder climates.

10. Avoid locating registers directly under or over windows. A register at the window will help ensure a more even temperature throughout the room but results in unnecessary heating or cooling of the window and wasted energy. Below or above the window is a favorate location for air registers and most warm water or steam radiators are placed under windows. This is probably because home owners and designers want to avoid putting furniture near a heat source and under the window may be about the only place where there won't be any furniture. Several studies point out that a heat source under the window "bathes" the glass and frame area in a steady flow of warm currents, ideal conditions for both infiltration and convection losses.

City	Reduction in heating fuel use (%)	Heating fuel cost reduction in 1977 dollars		
		Gas	Resistance	Heat pump
Atlanta	34.4	$51.20	$196.70	$96.20
Boston	27.4	111.10	235.90	115.20
Cheyenne	25.2	31.10	136.00	77.60
Chicago	23.9	60.80	131.60	70.30
Dallas	38.2	33.60	117.10	52.90
Kansas City	27.0	28.10	81.10	38.30
Knoxville	30.4	73.20	126.10	63.00
Minneapolis	20.6	54.60	149.50	87.30
Philadelphia	28.8	75.80	198.80	94.30
Phoenix	49.8	53.90	167.40	67.80
San Diego	64.4	69.70	250.00	93.20
Seattle	34.1	72.50	93.10	33.24
Washington, D.C.	28.2	95.60	269.90	132.30

Estimated savings by lowering thermostat
heat setting from 74 to 68°F.

11. Consider using outlet diffusers in critical rooms. In most warm-air and central air-conditioning systems, registers are used over the supply outlets in each room. A register simply admits warm or cool air to the room, and does nothing to distribute or mix the air that normal convection does not accomplish. A diffuser installed at each supply outlet instead of a register or grill will actually mix the room air with conditioned air from the furnace or central A/C unit. This makes temperatures in a room more even and reduces drafts. By increasing comfort, diffusers can encourage more economical thermostat settings.

12. Some heating and cooling systems can be *zoned* economically so that they are warmer or cooler than the remainder of the house. The remaining rooms can be heated or cooled to the degree of comfort required. There are two basic ways to "zone off" areas of the house, that is, to keep some at lower levels of energy consumption than others. The first is to add a separate wall thermostat for each area for which separate control is desired. This may be a room (as with electric baseboard heat), or a series of rooms:

Hot water systems. Depending on room layout and the type of system, one or more valves controlled by a thermostat can zone an area.

Forced-air systems [*heating or cooling*]. A thermostat here can control a damper that regulates the flow of conditioned air to the area that needs zoning.

The second way to achieve zoning in a house is more local. With this technique, rather than a wall thermostat controlling a zone, control is placed at the distribution unit:

Steam radiators. Usually valves on steam radiators are all-on or all-off. Valves are now available that automatically shut off at a particular temperature.

Forced-air heating or cooling. Many registers and diffusers are adjustable, and some control can be achieved through trial and error here, but this method is not automatic.

Hot water radiators. In either baseboard hydronic or radiator systems, individual control can be achieved, as long as each radiator is on its own loop. Valves actuated by self-contained thermostats are available for the purpose.

Except in houses heated by electric baseboards, any zoning method will affect the balance of the heating or cooling system; that is, as less heating or cooling is delivered to some areas, more will be delivered to the rest. Unless the balance of the system is adjusted at the time the whole system is zoned, some of the areas of the house may be overcooled or overheated.

The air for forced-air units can be warmed by a variety of fuels as mentioned, but if natural gas is available to be piped into the house, it will eliminate fuel storage problems.

Above all, encourage your client to include heating and forced-air equipment, or any other equipment for that matter, in a maintenance program involving care for motors, belts, filters, and grills. Thus heat is not lost nor energy nor money wasted in heating up all the dust in the ducts and clinging to the grills as the fan tries vainly to force the air through a clogged system.

The Hot-Water System:
A Conduction-Radiation Combination

Fundamentally, a hot water or steam system uses a boiler, small pipes to circulate the hot water, and radiators to heat the individual rooms. It has tremendous advantages where the climate calls for prolonged periods of space heating. It is remarkably efficient and astonishingly simple. In European homes where hot water heating is used extensively—as it was until recently in this country—it is almost uncanny the way a couple of smallish radiators underneath huge windows or at the sides of French doors can heat a cavernous room in the dead of winter. Once the hot water has conducted the heat to the radiator, radiation transmits it to the objects that the warm air waves encounter, and it is most effective.

Instead of having an air chamber, the hot water originates in a boiler, which heats it, then circulates it by means of a pump (except in some rare gravity or thermal-syphon systems) through the labyrinth of various pipes and radiators whence the water eventually returns to the boiler at the end of the line for reheating. Hot water for bathing and washing can be obtained from water circulating through a coil within the boiler, thus killing two birds with one stone. However, there needs to be a separate storage when this is done, since the boiler operates only spasmodically in warm weather.

Hot water systems are noiseless. Operating costs are as low as any. Moreover, in certain types of construction, as in the south of France or in some areas of the southwest United States where completely masonry houses are built of stone or brick, duct work is impracticable and hot water piping is the most feasible solution.

On the minus side, cost of installation is generally higher than forced air because of the higher cost of the boiler, copper piping, and the type of skilled labor involved. The system is not adaptable for air conditioning, which would have to be separate. It is not a quick system for heating, though not as slow as some forms of electric heating. Finally, the radiator becomes a decorator's *bête noir*. In new construction you can, with some imagination, compose little wall niches and other tricks of grillwork and diversion that can remove a bit of their offensiveness. In spite of this, radiators are still ugly. However, where heating demands are great and cooling by air conditioning not essential, such as in the Northeastern states, you may wish to consider this system with its higher initial cost as a fair trade for economical lifetime operation, lack of noise, and constant uniform heat.

Electric Heating

The cost of heating homes with electricity is often the lowest from an installation standpoint and the highest from a monthly operation standpoint. Homes with electric heat may use $300 or $400 worth of electricity in cold months, even when reasonably well insulated. During the 1960's electricity producers promoted the "All Electric Home" and offered incentives to builders who put up high electric consumption units. Today we realize that electric resistance heating (passing electricity through an element designed to resist electric flow and thus give off heat in the process) is a fairly inefficient use of electrical energy. The modern heat pump is a much more satisfactory solution and may be the only practical answer where oil, coal or natural gas are unavailable. As fossil fuels increase in price, we can expect the heat pump to become more competitive with gas, coal and oil furnaces because much of the cost of electricity to the homeowner reflects the cost of existing generating and distribution facilities. Most experts anticipate that electricity will increase in price, but at a lower rate than coal, oil or gas.

The heat pump is the most efficient way

currently available to heat homes with electricity. In fact, it is about twice as efficient as a resistance heater. That is, it produces heat at about one-half the cost of a resistance heater of the same capacity. Heat pumps use the same principle that a refrigerator or air conditioner uses to capture warm air and move it to another surface. Coils gather heat available from the outside even on a cold day and transfers it through a compressor which concentrates the heat on indoor furnace coils to heat the home. In summer the process is reversed and the unit becomes an efficient air conditioner to cool the home. There are some notable disadvantages however. Heat pumps cost about twice as much to buy and install as a conventional oil or gas furnace. The cost is competitive only if both heating and air conditioning are planned. Heat pumps had a reputation for unreliability in the 1950's but today should be about as maintenance free as an oil or gas furnace. Like any furnace heating system, the filters must be cleaned or replaced occasionally. The biggest drawback is that in very cold weather even an appropriately sized unit can not extract enough heat from the outside air to produce the required amount of heat. During these peak load periods the resistance coil heater built into most heat pumps is required to maintain the temperature required, thus lowering the unit efficiency and raising the operating cost. Resistance heating is not needed if the unit is able to draw on a stored heat source when the air temperature is very low. For example, the heat pump could draw heat from a tank of warm water during the coldest days. The water could be warmed by a solar heating system. Several experimental systems use a heat pump to turn water to ice in an insulated tank in the winter while giving off heat for the home. In the summer the heat pump is reversed to use the ice for cooling the home while reheating the water in the tank. This is referred to as an annual cycle energy system (A.C.E.S.) and would be most effective where annual cooling and heating requirements are about in balance. Costs are still much too high for routine application. However, it is a very promising application for the heat pump.

Key Points to Remember About Heat Pumps

Heat pumps have become much more reliable since the 1960's but only the better units can be expected to have a compressor failure rate less than 5% per year. Some manufacturers have produced units that are little more than standard air conditioning units with reversing valves. A heat pump has to operate two to eight times longer per year than an air conditioner under conditions that subject the compressor to high stress and wear. If the compressor is not well adapted to the unit and the load the installation will be much less than effective from a service standpoint. Failure rates of up to 10% per year are not uncommon for some models of heat pumps. Most heat pumps are sold with a one year materials and labor warranty and five years parts warranty on the compressor. Some units are now available with a full parts and service contract for five years or more. A contract of this type will help your client limit his repair expense to a known figure. In addition, manufacturers of the more reliable units are more willing to provide extended warranty or service contract agreements.

Heat pumps are only slightly more difficult to install but are much less tolerant than more conventional equipment to improper installation and servicing. Installing good equipment under the wrong conditions will be as disastrous as selecting the wrong equipment. Since the output of the heat pump, unlike that of a gas or oil furnace or electric resistance heat, decreases as the outdoor temperature drops, proper sizing of the heat pump requires more sophisticated load calculation and duct design than the other systems do. This presents a problem as not all manufacturers of heat pump equipment provide the training to dealer personnel and the detailed guidelines that are required. The table summarizes frequent installation mistakes and the probable result.

The major heat pump manufacturers have accepted their responsibility for insuring proper application and installation of their equipment by providing the necessary training to qualify their dealer personnel. This is not necessarily true of the manufacturers who offer a heat pump product as something "to sell up to" or "round out their air conditioner line." The result of this attitude is not only inferior equipment, but inadequate application guidelines and training. To the extent that some manufacturers fail to provide adequate training and technical guidelines and instructions to installing and servicing dealers, and to the extent that some manufacturers have not exercised proper care in assuring themselves of the qualifications of the local dealers of their products, equipment

Type of Misapplication	Result
1. Oversized equipment	1. Frequent cycling, high wear, loss of temperature and humidity control
2. Inadequate sized ductwork	2. Low indoor air flow, high compressor suction and discharge pressure, high pumping rates and compressor failure
3. Undersized power wiring, especially for strip heat	3. Frequent fuse failure, fire safety hazard
4. Oversized liquid refrigerant tubing	4. Liquid slugging, compressor mechanical failure

Typical Results of Heat Pump Misapplication

City	Heat Pump	Gas Furnace and Central Air Conditioning	Electric Furnace and Central Air Conditioning	Oil Furnace and Central Air Conditioning	Baseboard Resistance Heater and Room* Air Conditioning
Houston, TX	688.80	544.80	574.04	685.72	410.21
Birmingham, AL	697.66	572.54	684.88	767.00	499.72
Atlanta, GA	700.78	560.57	656.74	743.77	482.98
Tulsa, OK	744.42	598.23	735.74	811.59	538.89
Philadelphia, PA	885.89	743.09	944.61	935.28	728.23
Seattle, WA	477.29	518.30	473.23	684.70	312.83
Columbus, OH	876.61	701.70	946.10	964.60	757.86
Cleveland, OH	943.29	637.59	1071.75	954.83	823.81
Concord, NH	1044.92	667.69	1219.93	928.32	1024.90

*Individual room cooling equivalent to 57-89% of full cooling load.

Annual Owning and Operating Costs For Alternative
Heating and Cooling Systems (Dollars)

problems will continue to be compounded by poor field practices. Make sure that the dealer or subcontractor who provides your equipment is well qualified in heat pump system design.

The table "Annual Owning and Operating Costs" shows that the heat pump is competitive in cost with only certain systems in some cities. The table was produced for the Federal Energy Administration and is based on 1976 installed costs, normal life expectancies, local fuel costs and climates, and typical service requirements. Notice that each system in the comparison has air conditioning. Heat pumps are only cost competitive when your customer is planning to include air conditioning. Also notice that where natural gas is available, gas is almost always the first choice. About 50% of the new homes built today are built in areas where electricity is the only inexpensive energy source. In 1980 this percentage will be much closer to 60%. It is in these areas where only electricity is available and where air conditioning is nearly universally used that heat pumps will be widely accepted. Fuel prices will have to more than double their 1977 levels before a heat pump is the best choice for most homes.

Converting an existing furnace to the heat pump requires an air distribution system which is adequate to carry the air flow of the pump. Although non-ducted systems can be converted, it requires extensive alteration of the house and as a result is very costly. The types of systems most likely for conversion are basically gas, oil, or electric forced air furnaces. Most natural gas heating systems are forced air furnaces, and these could be converted. However, many of these systems are likely to have inadequate ductwork, especially if there was no plan for future installation of central air conditioning at the time of construction. Most fuel oil systems in older housing are hot water or steam systems. These are not likely prospects for conversion either. In 1970, only some 600,000 housing units were heated by electric forced air furnaces. The other 4,358,500 electrically heated units were non-ducted systems and thus not easily converted to the heat pump. Systems using bottled gas are also unlikely to be ducted.

At current prices the only systems which are likely to be converted to the heat pump are electric forced air furnaces in cases in which the furnace is at replacement age and the homeowner wants central air conditioning or has a central air conditioner which is also ready to be replaced. Obviously this is a modest market.

In some cases it may be possible to add a heat pump to an existing ducted furnace heating system. A remote heat pump conditioning coil can be fitted into the supply air duct of a forced air gas or oil furnace. Such a system, in addition to providing cooling in the summer, would be able to use the high heating efficiency of the heat pump cycle in milder weather, but rely on the combustion of fuel during the very coldest weather when the full capacity of the furnace is needed. Most important, this system could be retrofitted to an existing home, provided the forced air ducts were the right size for air conditioning. Several manufacturers have equipment on the market for this purpose.

Cable Electric Systems

Heating by convection through wires in the ceiling (sometimes called either ceiling heat or cable electric heat) is a clean, noiseless, and fairly efficient method. Individual rooms do have their own thermostats, a seeming plus, since this represents the zenith of zoned control of heat. However, the tendency of the user is not to close down a sufficient number of rooms to make significant cost savings. Therefore, it can be costly to operate.

Moreover, cable heat needs extensive insulation to keep rooms separately zoned and to keep heat from the first floor from rising uninvited to the second. It is not adaptable to air conditioning and is a screaming pain in the case of repairs to the house, remodeling, or placing light fixtures or hooks in the ceiling. Any disruption of the intricate fabric of wires imbedded there is like burning a hole in an electric blanket: the heat-producing current is broken. Some building codes and regulations now prohibit or severely restrict these cable heating systems.

Getting Efficient Equipment

Many advances have been made in the efficiency of modern heating and cooling equipment. Most any heating or cooling system you install will use many times the original purchase price in gas, coal, oil or electricity. A small improvement in efficiency will mean a big saving in fuel costs over the years. Most furnaces and air conditioners are rated for efficiency and the rating is stamped on the date plate. This figure is usually unrealistic in that the unit in actual use will seldom or never be that efficient. However, it will provide a useful index to compare units of various manufacturers.

The most important consideration in buying a window air conditioner is the EER - Energy Efficiency Ratio. The higher the EER number, the less electricity the unit will use to cool the same amount of air. EER's will range between 6 and 12. Don't buy a unit with an EER of less than 9. You'll pay more for the units with higher EER's, but the electricity savings will be worth it. A window unit with an EER of 12 cools 50% more air for a dollar's worth of electricity than a unit with an EER of 8.

The Association of Home Appliance Manufacturers (AHAM) publishes a directory listing all certified window and through-the-wall air conditioning units as well as their capabilities and EER's. This directory also lists the range of EER's available for a given capacity. If, for example, you wish to purchase a conditioner with a 10,000 to 11,000 BTU per hour capacity, you can see that 115-volt window models with this capacity are available with EER's ranging from 6.2 to 12.0, and that higher-voltage window models have EER's of 5.0 to 8.0, while through-the-wall models have EER ranges of 6.2 to 12.0, and 5.5 to 8.0, for lower and higher voltage models, respectively.

This AHAM directory is available at most dealers and you should ask to see it when purchasing an air conditioner. If you know the room size, the directory has a simple procedure for determining how large an air conditioner you need. If you're midway between two sizes, get the smaller of the two. An air conditioner that's too big will shut off before it removes enough humidity from the air to make the room comfortable.

Air economizers are now used on many air conditioners to further reduce fuel consumption. Sometimes known as an outside air enthalpy cycle, an air economizer is used with a central air conditioning system. Sensing the moment that outside air enthalpy (temperature and humidity) drops below the enthalpy of the inside air (some varieties sense only dry bulb temperature), an air economizer shuts off the compressor and diverts outside air into the house. This is a particularly useful feature in

City	Hrs. Saved Yearly in Compressor Operation	% Savings	For 2-ton Unit: Approx. $ Savings (Kwh = 3 cents)
Akron, OH	272 hours	32.9%	$33
Albany, NY	224	30.0	27
Augusta, GA	302	18.6	36
Chicago, IL	220	27.3	26
Columbus, OH	272	26.7	33
Dallas, TX	219	11.5	26
Denver, CO	180	22.0	22
Des Moines, IA	218	22.8	26
Detroit, MI	244	32.1	30
Kansas City, MO	196	15.2	24
Los Angeles, CA	491	57.3	59
Louisville, KY	251	20.0	30
Madison, WI	209	26.7	25
Miami, FL	510	14.6	61
Minneapolis, MN	212	27.1	25
New Orleans, LA	377	15.9	45
Omaha, NB	214	22.1	26
Pittsburgh, PA	273	32.0	33
Portland, OR	158	37.0	19
Roanoke, VA	281	24.2	34
Salt Lake City, UT	189	19.9	23
San Francisco, CA	219	41.6	26
Seattle, WA	127	57.1	15
Syracuse, NY	243	30.7	29
Washington, DC	277	26.0	33

Estimated Savings of Compressor Operation

climates where the temperature at night drops considerably from its daytime highs. In short, an air economizer relieves the compressor of the job of removing heat that had accumulated in the structure of the house during the day. Above is a table of estimated savings based on location.

High-speed flame retention oil burners are available for both new and existing oil fired furnaces.

This term and variations on it refer to a new, more efficient type of oil burner presently marketed by several manufacturers. If an oil burner is in need of replacement, consider this option, as it can result in a 10% reduction of consumption over more traditional models.

Fireplaces

This eulogy to fireplaces by Scott Nearing is very persuasive: "We enjoy open fires, so we planned fireplaces for every room. Even in mild weather there is something indescribably attractive and satisfying about the flickering glow of a wood fire. The heat thrown off may be negligible, but the live coals vitalize the atmosphere and the leaping flames enliven the surroundings. In cold weather, open fires contribute the tangy perfume of burning wood as well as welcome warmth. Thoreau considered his fire a friend: 'My house was not empty though I was gone. It was as if I had left a cheerful housekeeper behind.' A room without an open fire in winter is almost as desolate as a room without windows."

Rooms already heated to maximum by the house's mechanical or electrical space-heating equipment do not benefit from the fireplace being used. It would be better if the fireplaces's damper were closed to stem the outflow of warm air. In fact, a fire burning in a well-heated room will actually draw the heat from the room by sending it up the chimney.

The only effective plan for a conventional fireplace, and that which was no doubt the Nearings' objective, is to keep the thermostat at a minimum temperature like sixty to sixty-three degrees—just enough to take the cold edge off the room—dress warmly, and then use the area around the lighted fire for added warmth and comfort. Though the air temperature is low, you will be warmed by the radiant glow of the fire.

Though the conventional fireplace is nearly useless from an energy conservation standpoint, the fireplace can become a very useful part of the home heating plan. Manufactured metal fireplace forms are available that produce more heat than they waste. These are insulated metal shells the shape of the fire box and are sold under names like Heatolator, Heatform, Fireolator, Octa-Form or Econoform. The form is built into a wall or corner of either a new or existing home and covered with masonry or conventional wall finish materials. Heat circulation is provided by inlet and outlet vents which collect cool room air at the floor level, warm it in air coils built into the bonnet of the unit, and then distribute the heated air through ducts to as many as three rooms. Some of the units are available with a fan to improve the air flow. A separate duct to the exterior draws cool exterior air into the fire area for combustion, thus reducing the amount of warm room air that is sucked up the chimney. A glass closure screen on the front of the fire box will make the fireplace even more efficient. Units rated at over 40,000 BTU's per hour are available to supplement or even replace conventional furnaces, especially where electricity is used for heating. Make a point of considering a heat circulating fireplace with an outside combustion air duct whenever you plan a fireplace. The additional investment is inconsequential when amortized over the life of the house and buys a unit that costs little or nothing to operate and maintain. In a power emergency in cold weather, the fireplace could make an otherwise uninhabitable house very warm and comfortable.

Decorative metal firebricks increase the radiation properties of the firebricks with which the fireplace cavity may be lined. They are also attractive. An antique dealer can be most helpful in getting you these items.

Artificial gas logs, though sometimes attractive and obviously labor-saving, provide very little in the way of heat. Besides, there is frequently an incomplete combustion of the gas that operates them, thus they tend to give off a gassy smell over prolonged use. They are not much of an asset in energy conservation and are mainly a decorative luxury.

Iron Stoves

These attractive old free-standing stoves are still manufactured and can be most decorative and useful in a family room, rumpus room, den, or library. They can be bought by contacting the Portland Stove Foundry Co., Sales Office, Box 59, Sterling Junction, Massachusetts 01565.

Remodeling and the Heating System

Two basic questions await your heating subcontractor:

1. Is the present system capable of heating the expanded remodeled area?

2. Can ducts, pipes, or wires, be connected to the new area without undue cost and inconvenience? Much money and, in this case, fuel energy will be saved if the present system can be made to handle the addition.

The meeting with the heating subcontractor is a good time to review the present heating system in terms of lowering its cost of operation. It may have been some time since it was last "balanced." Some rooms may be receiving too much heat, some too little. Often the adjustable blades in forced air register grills do not close all the way and hot air presses against them and squeezes out under pressure, particularly when they are in smaller rooms at the beginning of a long run of duct work. In these instances, a special damper blade can be installed that restricts the hot air *before* it can attack the register, thus keeping up a better pressure and flow to the needy rooms and causing the thermostat to turn off earlier.

Zoning the added spaces of a remodeled house so that they can operate independently of the existing system is desirable if the spaces are larger enough and cannot be served by the simple addition of an offshoot duct or wiring pattern of the existing mechanical or electrical system. Small apartment-type heating equipment is inexpensive to buy and relatively cheap to operate. Just recognize that any new originating system still requires installation space and venting through the roof, plus combustion air venting to an outside wall. If planning to hook a room addition into an existing air conditioning system, remember that in addition to the cold air supply from the air conditioning equipment, the return air system *to*

93

the equipment is vital to complete a proper circulatory layout.

Humidity—How to Measure and Correct It

When dry air is heated, moisture in the air drops. Humidity can be measured by a "humidistat," a small metering device you can buy in most hardware stores. When it drops below 30 to 40 percent the air to too dry. This can be corrected either by an automatic humidifier in the forced-air furnace or, in the case of other equipment, a mechanical atomizer.

This lack of moisture in the air can produce a nasal and respiratory problem resembling extreme hay fever. In winter, with no pollen in the air to plague the victim, the hay fever symptoms can prove truly mystifying to the sufferer. The phenomenon is actually the drying of the membranes in the nasal passages and the resultant eye-watering, congestion, and related hay-fever symptons. By bundling up in warm clothing, lighting a fire, turning down the thermostat to sixty-two degrees or less, the results could prove startling.

But remember that altering the humidity can waste energy. Just as an evaporative cooler takes heat out of the air as moisture is evaporated, so a humidifier cools the air during winter heating. Running an air conditioner will lower the humidity though this is unnecessary if the humidity is below 65%.

Getting Into the Solar Energy Business 10

Every so often it seems, the American people learn about a totally new product in the marketplace. A few years ago, for instance, the sophisticated hand electronic calculator was but a wink in a scientist's or mathematician's eye. Now, you can walk into almost any retail outlet and for a few dollars buy what would have cost several thousand dollars in the 1960's.

Similarly, it wasn't too long ago when stereo systems first came on the marketplace, and Americans heard a totally new language—woofers, tweeters, anti-static devices, distortion levels, etc. To choose properly, serious audio fans had to learn what these terms meant, and then they had to learn how to compare competing products. Because so many Americans took the time and trouble to learn these essentials, stereo manufacturers by and large fought for the consumer's business by selling quality rather than imagery. Two important results occurred—superior products and satisfied customers.

Will solar evolve, as stereo did, into a widespread, beneficial industry? To a great extent, that answer depends upon the American consumer. The more well-informed professional contractors who install solar devices, the greater the chance that solar power will reach its full potential—providing safe, economical energy to millions of American families.

To be a good installer of solar systems does not mean you have to become a mechanical or an architectural engineer. It does mean that at certain times you may have to call on one of these experts to give you specific advice for a specific home. But before you get to the point of bringing in the expert, there is a lot you can do to decide whether solar is what your client needs and what type of unit is best for him.

Perhaps the best place to start is with knowledge of how solar works, and the various subsystems that make up a solar heating installation: The collector, storage, the distribution network, and controls.

The Solar Collector

The solar collector is the subsystem you probably think about when solar energy is discussed. This is the component whose main function is to capture the sun's energy. There are many types of collectors available: high performance collectors such as the focusing collector which tracks the sun, a vacuum-sealed collector which has very low heat loss, and the more conventional flat plate collector. To understand the principle upon which a collector operates, look at a typical flat plate collector that would be appropriate for residential and commercial purposes. See Figure 10-1.

Beyond the casing and the installation, the flat plate collector has three main elements—the transparent cover or covers, the collector plate known to engineers as the absorber, and the channels in the collector plate.

The transparent cover can be made out of glass or plastic. Glass holds its transparent characteristics well over the years. However, various quality characteristics such as transparency, strength, etc., vary from product to product. The same can be said of plastics. Some contain high transparency characteristics for long periods of time, while others do not. Some

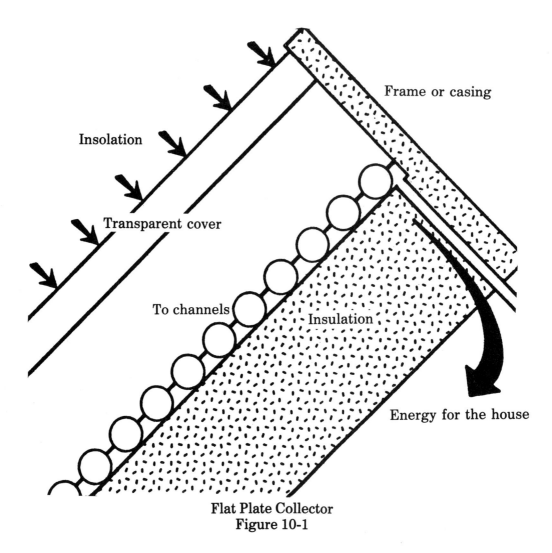

Flat Plate Collector
Figure 10-1

turn yellow, reducing the capability to transmit solar radiation. Some glass and plastic covers are almost vandal-proof, while others can be damaged very easily. These may be important considerations when you are selecting the materials you plan to install. Ask for test reports that show anticipated durability and transparency characteristics. You may need these reports for your engineering consultant.

The transparent cover serves many purposes. It keeps outside air from carrying away the heat that has been trapped. It also keeps out the wind and the elements, protecting the inside components and reducing energy loss by convection. In warm areas, one cover is usually all that is necessary, but in colder climates, two transparent covers or insulated glass are generally considered necessary.

Here is how the typical flat plate collector works. Solar radiation passes through the transparent cover (a small portion is absorbed or reflected off the covers's surfaces) and hits the absorber plate. Most of the radiation is absorbed by the plate and picked up by the fluid (air, water, or other liquids) passing through the channels in or against the plate. Some of the radiation is reflected off the plate back to the cover—how much depends upon the absorbing and reflecting characteristics of the coating on the collector plate. The better the absorbing quality, the more radiation captured, the less reflected back to the cover. Special coatings have been developed which are highly absorptive with low reradiation. Most collector plates are black or a dark color. Dark colors absorb radiation much better than light colors. Conversely, you can't always tell by the color whether the coating has the desired selectivity characteristics.

Some manufacturers offer what are known as ''selective'' surfaces for the collector plate. These are not painted, but rather specially coated metals that appear to be a technical improvement over flat black paint because

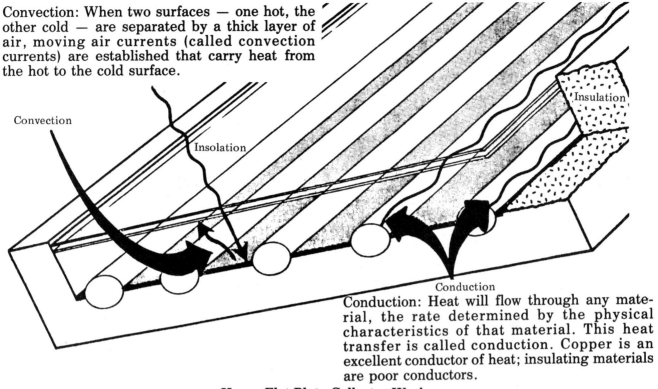

Convection: When two surfaces — one hot, the other cold — are separated by a thick layer of air, moving air currents (called convection currents) are established that carry heat from the hot to the cold surface.

Convection

Insolation

Insulation

Conduction

Conduction: Heat will flow through any material, the rate determined by the physical characteristics of that material. This heat transfer is called conduction. Copper is an excellent conductor of heat; insulating materials are poor conductors.

How a Flat Plate Collector Works
Figure 10-2

reradiation losses are decreased. Selective surfaces cost more initially than flat black paint, and the extra cost must be weighed against the value of increased efficiency and the life expectancy of the coating. No matter what coating or metal is used, some portion of the incoming radiation will be radiated back, and of that portion, the transparent cover either will allow some to pass through or absorb the rest. The reason for two transparent covers in some collectors is to improve the insulation, just as storm windows reduce the loss of heat through the window. More than two covers are not necessary. Still other portions of the collected energy are lost from the collector plate through convection to the air space above and conduction by the metal in the plate, and through the insulation on the back and side. Figure 10-2 shows how the collector works. How much is lost through conduction depends upon overall design of the collector. The net result of all these losses is that only a certain portion is absorbed by the passing fluid. The fewer the losses, the more efficient the collector.

To reduce losses through convection, some collectors have honeycomb material located between the transparent cover and the collector plate. This limits the formation of convection currents which are responsible for some of the loss. See Figure 10-3.

The advantages of honeycomb in reducing convection losses may be offset by the greater expense and by increasing conduction losses if the honeycomb conducts heat from the collector plate to the transparent cover. In addition, the honeycomb should help the collector survive

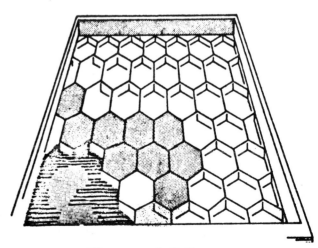

Honeycomb Collector
Figure 10-3

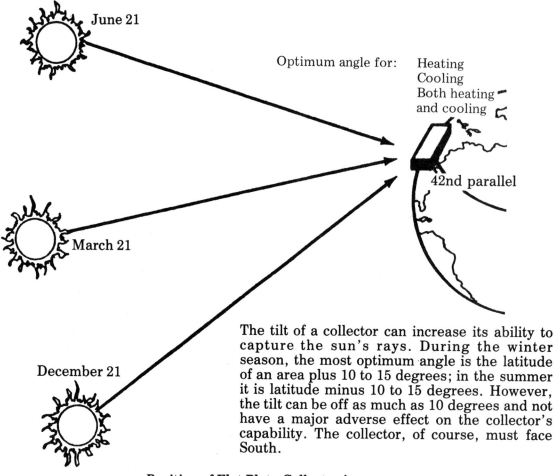

June 21

March 21

December 21

Optimum angle for: Heating
Cooling
Both heating
and cooling

42nd parallel

The tilt of a collector can increase its ability to capture the sun's rays. During the winter season, the most optimum angle is the latitude of an area plus 10 to 15 degrees; in the summer it is latitude minus 10 to 15 degrees. However, the tilt can be off as much as 10 degrees and not have a major adverse effect on the collector's capability. The collector, of course, must face South.

Position of Flat Plate Collector in
Relation to the Sun
Figure 10-4

stagnation temperatures—high temperatures which can occur when the collector is not in use.

A properly designed honeycomb structure can add to the strength of a collector, increasing resistance to hail, and adding to the capability of the collector to replace a portion of the roof.

Angle of Tilt

Depending upon local climatic conditions, an important design factor for a flat plate collector is its position in relation to the sun. If a solar system is designed for heating, the collector surface in most instances should be nearly perpendicular to the sun's rays in the middle of January, generally the coldest days of the year. This is usually an effective position for capturing the sun's rays. (See Figure 10-4). This perpendicular position is the sum of your latitude plus 15 degrees. Most any map of the U.S. will tell you the degrees of latitude in your area. If the solar system is for heating and

cooling, the most optimum angle is the same as the latitude. If the system is for cooling in the summer or heating a pool, you should mount the collector at an angle about 10 to 15 degrees less than the latitude.

Several precautionary notes should be considered on the optimum angle of the collector. If the collector is within 10 to 15 degrees of the optimum, it will not make much difference in the energy recovered by the collector. What all this means is that if you decide to put a flat plate collector on a roof, and the roof has a 45-degree tilt, and the job is in Phoenix (42 degrees of latitude), there's no need to go to the added expense of building in the other 3 degrees on the collector. Similarly, if you design a solar house, don't hesitate to shade a few degrees off here or there to obtain some other desired end result. Further, some solar systems have a mirror or reflective surface next to the collector to augment the radiation reaching the absorber by reflecting extra sunlight into it. This is often done with cooling systems where higher temperatures are needed.

The ideal position of the collector for the greatest annual and seasonal energy recovery is facing due South. However, a variation of as much as 15 degrees in either direction will not significantly reduce the efficiency of the collector.

Concentrating collectors can only collect direct solar radiation, so they aren't much good on cloudy days. Flat plate collectors do not have this limitation and can pick up diffused radiation. The extra cost of the reflector must be weighed against the BTU's on sunny days only.

Beyond the main elements within the collector, it is important to keep in mind that soundness of construction is an important characteristic in obtaining an efficient collector. It must keep out wind, rain, and dust, so good sealants are necessary.

Another important feature of the collector is the insulation under the absorber plate to reduce downward heat losses. Some insulation does not hold up well over a long period of time under the very hot conditions present under the absorber. Fiberglass, 3 to 4 inches thick, holds up well. If you do not install efficient insulation, you will lose much of the heat collected and have an inefficient collector. If the insulation does not hold up, your client could be faced with periodic replacement, and high repair bills.

Collector Efficiency

Manufacturers boast of the efficiency of a collector. By this is meant the ability of the collector to capture the sun's power. For instance, if it is said that a collector has a 50 percent efficiency, that means that under certain conditions, the collector captures 50 percent of the total energy hitting the surface of the collector.

There are many conditions that will affect the efficiency of a collector. Of primary importance is the amount of radiation you can expect in your area for the particular period in which the solar system will be used. For instance, if you plan to install a space heating system, you should know the efficiency of the collector during December, January, and February when your client needs the system the most. How much radiation you can expect will depend upon the amount of sunshine and the

atmosphere where you live. A table later in this chapter gives solar radiation levels by month in various parts of the country.

In some limited areas, there are so many cloudy days and many partially cloudy days that the amount of radiation reaching the collector will usually be found to be so small as to make it unlikely that it would be advantageous for you to install a solar system. Further, the efficiency decreases as the temperature difference between the outdoors and the absorber plate increases. To put it in another way, the colder it gets on the outside, the more inefficient the collector will be. This is because the differences in temperatures cause an increase in energy loss through conduction and reradiation.

To show how efficiency varies among competing collectors in terms of temperature differences, the National Bureau of Standards has developed standards by which efficiency can be measured. An increase in the flow of the fluid through the collector can help to reduce losses. For instance, if there is no movement at all, the fluid will become very hot and lose a great deal of heat. As the fluid starts moving, the temperature is reduce and heat losses are reduced.

Another factor affecting efficiency is the evenness of the flow of the fluid through the channels and the arrangement of the channel system; the more even the flow, the more efficient the system.

The temperature at which heat must be stored also has an effect on a system's efficiency. In some systems, heat must be stored at high temperature (100° to 175°F) to keep the home warm, in this case the collector must produce hotter water or air. The hotter the system operates, the lower the efficiency of the solar system. In other systems, heat is stored at lower temperatures (85° to 125°F) and so the solar collector system operates at higher efficiency. Collector efficiency is only one of several considerations in system performance and quality, so the above comparison does not necessarily indicate that the lower temperature system should be the choice.

Why is Efficiency Important?

First, to make the point that there are a number of engineering factors that have a bearing on how efficient a given collector is. Second, the efficiency of a collector is a major factor in determining a whole system's performance.

Let's say that you are evaluating two competing collectors. Both are estimated to have a 20-year life span and require little maintenance and few repairs. Collector A costs $10 per square foot installed, while Collector B costs $6 per square foot. Both receive on a given day 200 BTU's per square foot per hour. Collector A has a 60 percent efficiency and will deliver 120 BTU's per hour per square foot. Collector B has a 50 percent efficiency and delivers 100 BTU's per hour per square foot. Which collector should you recommend to your client?

If the two collectors are the same in all other aspects, recommend Collector B because it delivers 20 BTU's per dollar while A delivers only 10 BTU's per dollar. But notice that there are other considerations besides first cost and efficiency. The buyer will want to know whether the collector is covered by a warranty, what the warranty covers, and for how long. A warranty is either "full" or "limited." If it is limited, it will only cover certain features, and not the whole product. The following are some major, extremely important considerations:

•Durability of the product. How long is it expected to last? Is it weatherproof and does it shed water?

•Ease of repair. If something goes wrong, how long will it take to fix it, and are repair parts easily obtainable? And what will various repairs cost?

•Susceptibility to either freezing or overheating. There are a number of adequate solutions to both problems, but you should be sure the collector you install has built-in protection for both extremes. You should also have assurances that if the collector is used for hot water purposes, and if antifreeze fluid is used in the collector, it cannot mix with water for domestic use.

Systems using water or "corrosion inhibited" water solutions can be built so that the collector and exposed piping will drain when temperatures drop close to freezing or when the collector is not being used. Alternatively, a nonfreezing fluid can be used in place of water in the collector. Water-antifreeze (meaning ethylene glycol type antifreeze formulations such as those used in automotive cooling systems) are not recommended for use in home solar applications. Exposure of ethylene glycol antifreeze mixtures to high temperatures such as those encountered in most systems in the summertime accelerates the rate at which the ethylene glycol will degrade, forming acids which are corrosive to most metals, including copper and aluminum.

The "nonfreezing" fluid selected should be one which will not degrade at maximum temperatures expected, which can reach 400°F.

Electric warmers can be used to prevent freezing, and they are acceptable in southern areas of the country where freezing temperatures occur infrequently. In colder areas, however, the cost of operating an electric warmer might be prohibitive, and power failures can occur just when severe freezing weather might be encountered. Obviously, any such use of electric energy tends to defeat the purpose of a solar energy system.

Overheating could have a detrimental effect on a solar system, if there are no built-in protective devices in active systems. Active and passive systems are explained later in this chapter. Your client shouldn't have to worry about what will happen to his collector if he goes on a vacation for several weeks during the middle of the summer.

Corrosion and leakage problems must be considered. Metal corrosion can cause irreparable damage to a solar system and shorten a system's life span. More importantly, corrosion can cause serious health problems if the water is used directly by the user.

Suitable protection against corrosion depends upon the system and the metals used. Potable water is the water one uses for drinking and washing. Inhibited water means that chemicals have been added to the water to prevent corrosion. Nonfreezing, nonaqueous heat transfer fluids are various liquids used in a solar system to prevent freezing. Most of these fluids are noncorrosive to the three metals commonly used in solar systems, but are not drinkable.

These three most commonly used metals are copper, steel, and aluminum. Copper is more expensive, but it can be used with most potable waters without inhibitors. Steel and aluminum are more economical, but inhibitors must be

Typical fluid solar system

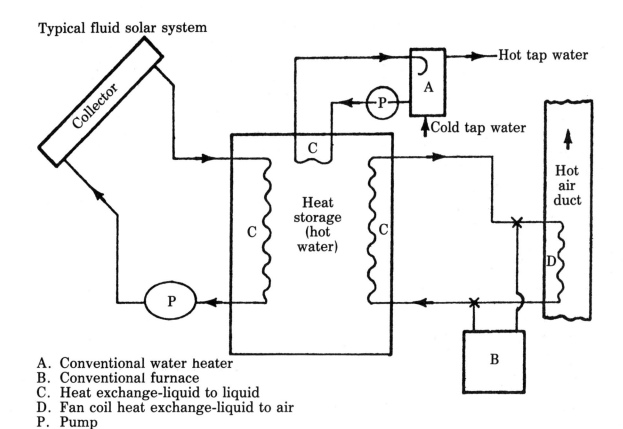

A. Conventional water heater
B. Conventional furnace
C. Heat exchange-liquid to liquid
D. Fan coil heat exchange-liquid to air
P. Pump

Typical air solar system

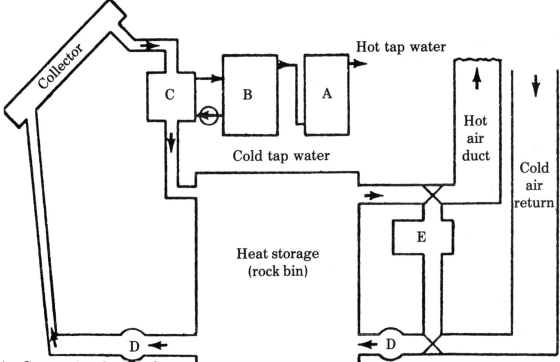

A. Conventional water heater
B. Solar hot water storage
C. Air to liquid heat exchange
D. Blower
E. Conventional furnace

Solar Space Heating and Domestic
Hot Water Systems
Figure 10-5

added to prevent corrosion in most systems. Copper will hold up over a long time without inhibitors, while steel and aluminum will fail quickly unless they have special coatings. In inhibited water, all three will last indefinitely as long as the inhibition is maintained. All three will hold up indefinitely in suitable nonaqueous, nonfreezing, heat transfer fluids.

Steel and aluminum must be electrically isolated from each other and from copper to avoid galvanic corrosion. Isolation is obtained by using insulated rubber or plastic connections to join dissimilar metals.

For leakage, another rule of thumb is that the greater the number of joints, the greater the possibility of leakage. Know what happens if a leak occurs and how it can be fixed. Some liquid collectors with unique channel systems have reduced the need for soldered joints considerably without hurting the efficiency of the collector.

Solar collectors which supply hot air are generally free from problems associated with freezing, corrosion, and boiling. Air leakage in piping and joints between collector sections, although not potentially as damaging as in liquid collectors, can reduce efficiency. If you recommend equipment of this type, be sure that the entire collector array will perform as well as individual sections or modules. Figure 10-5 shows a fluid and an air system to help you compare these two methods of heating.

Before buying a collector you have not used previously, ask whether the collector meets standards of the National Bureau of Standards. If the manufacturer claims such standards are met, you should get that in writing. These standards do provide a degree of assurance, and if a seller claims such standards are met, he is legally accountable for that claim.

The Storage System

Storage facility is the next important subsystem, after the collector, for most solar systems. Basically, the collector captures heat from the sun and transfers it to storage for later use. There are three main methods for storage—water, rocks, and change-of-state storage. Each has its advantages and disadvantages.

Water Storage

Water has the advantages of low cost and high heat capacity (the ability to contain heat effectively within a limited amount of space). Water storage tanks must be protected from freezing if located outside. Tanks must be protected from corrosion, either through use of a corrosion inhibitor in the water or by constructing them with corrosion-resistant material. Storage tanks must be heavily insulated to prevent the stored heat from being lost.

Materials currently used for water storage have both advantages and disadvantages. To insure that steel has a long lifetime, rust and corrosion inhibitors may be added. But, if so, much care must be taken to insure that the water in the system does not mix with the potable water because inhibitors are toxic.

Plastic tanks do not have corrosion problems, but the types of plastic needed to store large quantities of water at high temperatures is rather expensive when compared with steel. Concrete is safe, durable, and economical, but if a leak develops, it is hard to repair. Great care must be taken to make certain that the tank is properly sealed when it is first built and installed. Some experts recommend bladders or diaphragms lining the tank to insure water tightness.

Weight is another important consideration. Two thousand gallons of water weigh about 9 tons. No matter where the storage system is located—in the basement or floor—adequate structural support must be provided.

As discussed earlier, to prevent damage to the collector under freezing conditions, either a nonfreezing fluid must circulate through the collector or the collector must be built so that it drains when temperatures drop close to freezing. Although the amount of fluid needed in the collector itself is small and its cost is not an important factor, it is generally not practical to fill the large storage tank with the nonfreezing fluid. Therefore, a heat exchanger must be used to transfer heat from the fluid in the collector system to the water in storage. A draining system eliminates this heat exchanger and its cost, as well as temperature losses occurring from the exchange. However, a draining system using water or inhibited water as the fluid depends in most instances upon the reliability of the draining mechanism to prevent costly freeze-up. Building reliability into such systems generally costs money.

Despite its limitations, water is at present

the most practical method for storing heat for liquid-type solar collectors. Make sure that the heat storage system is well insulated. Sprayed polyurethane foam, mineral wool insulation, fiberglass, and vermiculite are all excellent insulation materials for the outside of the tank.

Rock Storage

For air-type solar collectors, rocks or pebbles are the most cost-effective way to store the collected heat. Rocks are easily obtainable, economical, and are not subject to problems stemming from corrosion, freezing, or leaking. Further, there is no need for an expensive container. However, rocks and pebbles do have two main disadvantages: they take up a lot of space and are much heavier than water. The space needed for storing heat with rocks is roughly three times the amount needed for water. This can be a major problem for some homes.

Another advantage of rocks is that they can be used to store heat at temperatures about 212°F, while water containers designed to carry temperatures over that point need to be able to withstand pressure and can be costly unless a fluid is used that has a high boiling point. The ability of the rocks to reach higher temperatures is important because such heat will not go wasted if the collector delivers it.

For best results, the rocks or pebbles should be roughly round, of uniform size, and up to 2 inches in diameter. These provide minimum resistance to the air passing through. Other solids can be used but are usually much more expensive.

Change-Of-State Storage

This method of storing solar energy, uses materials or substances that change composition from solid to liquid when heated. The changes permit the storage of more heat per pound than if the material did not change composition. When a material such as Glauber's salts is cooled, and goes from a liquid to solid state, it gives off this extra heat. This method, however, is still in the experimental stage.

The great advantage of change-of-state storage is that it can contain a great amount of heat in a limited space and at limited weight. Let's say that the objective of a storage system is to hold 200,000 BTU's at 100-160°F. Water systems would need 53 cubic feet (3,300

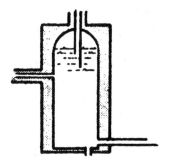

Water storage holds heat well and is economical, but the tank must be protected against corrosion and heat loss. It is the most practical method for storage of liquid systems.

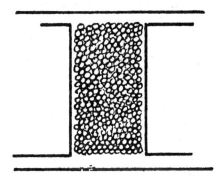

Rocks or pebbles also are economical and retain heat well. No corrosion-proof tank is needed, but more space is required for the same amount of storage that water would provide. It is the most practical method of storage for air systems.

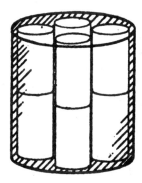

Change of state or salt storage is also economical and uses less space than water or air. But the salts can only go through so many heating and cooling cycles before they lose their capabilities to store heat. They have not been used on a commercial basis yet. Some interesting experiments are being conducted which may prolong the number of cycles.

Types of Storage
Figure 10-6

pounds), rocks would need 175 cubic feet (17,500 pounds), while Glauber's salts would require only 19 cubic feet (1,740 pounds). In addition, such salts are obtainable at relatively reasonable prices.

Salt storage, however, has a number of major limitations. The salts can only go through so many cycles before their natural state is altered to the point where they lose their capacity to successfully store heat. There are some chemical additions which act to prolong the number of cycles considerably, and there are some interesting experiments which, if successful, may prolong the life span.

Second, though salts are economical, present costs for containerization and transportation are fairly expensive. Mass production could bring these costs down dramatically, but there are at present no marketable systems.

Designing Your Systems

The equipment supplier will usually provide at no cost, the engineering assistance needed to calculate the BTU's of storage capacity you should have in the system you are installing. The key is matching the collectors to the heat requirement and then being sure that the storage tank has the ability to absorb the full energy output of the collectors.

Active and Passive Systems

There are two basic ways to distribute solar energy. An active system uses mechanical means such as pumps, valves, and so on, for operating. A passive system uses natural forces such as gravity, convection, and nocturnal radiation, to accomplish the same objective. Both types of systems have their advantages and disadvantages.

Passive systems are more economical to operate. In some cases in certain climatic regions, heating and cooling by solar has for many years been economically competitive with conventional forms of energy. However, these systems are limited by seasonal conditions and architectural restraints. They work well in hot, dry areas, but in cold temperatures or humid areas they are subject to such problems as freezing or excessive humidity. They may not be able to provide uninterrupted comfort levels. In most cases, the requirements of a passive system will dictate the overall design of the structure more so than with active systems. For

instance, one type of passive cooling system requires a water pond on the roof with movable shutters which cool the home off by evaporation and nocturnal radiation. The shutters are closed during the daytime to prevent reheating. This system is most effective in areas of low humidity with clear night skies.

Active systems, properly designed, can work in almost any area. Initial costs for an active system are generally higher than those for a passive system, but costs may be more economical in terms of BTU's delivered per dollar invested. Active systems are not as architecturally restrictive as passive systems.

Some solar manufacturers utilize both passive and active techniques, combining some of the economic values of the passive system with some of the versatilities of the active method. These are referred to as "hybrid" systems.

System Back-Up

A conventional furnace, (oil, gas, electricity) serves as a back-up energy source for most space heating and cooling, hot water, and some swimming pool solar systems. For cost effective reasons, most active solar systems are not designed to handle all the anticipated demand. If, for instance, a solar system were designed to handle 100 percent of the heating load during the middle of the winter, the collector and storage system would have to be large enough to provide energy for extended periods when the sun didn't shine. As these expanded units would only be used during limited periods, the extra cost normally isn't justified by the savings in fuel cost.

Beyond providing heat when the sun doesn't shine, conventional heat sources are often used directly in conjunction with solar heat. For instance, solar energy could be used to bring water up to a temperature of 100°F, and conventional energy used to boost the temperature another 40° for a dishwasher.

Domestic Water Heating

The best known solar method is hot water heating. These units have been in use in many locations since the early 1900's, and have an overall record of acceptable performance when properly constructed and maintained. Because of fuel savings, they can return the original costs or pay for themselves within a reasonable period of time if replacing electricity or high-price fuel. The payback period depends upon the cost of conventional heating, the amount of water used in the household, the insolation rate, and the efficiency of the unit. Generally, these units save 50 to 80 percent of the water heating cost, again depending upon the unit and location.

Be sure that the system you recommend meets local toxicity and potable water standards. These standards have been established to protect against unsafe drinking water.

For hot water systems, the general rule of thumb for the size of the collector is about one square foot for every gallon of water required every day. Not counting dishwashing and washing machines, the average family uses about 60 gallons of hot water per person. With a family of four, a typical hot water installation would be about 60 square feet. This would take care of 50 percent to 80 percent of the total hot water needs, depending upon climate, with the conventional system supplying the remainder. A system could be designed, of course, to handle nearly all hot water needs.

Swimming Pool Systems

Some solar heaters for swimming pools operate on the same basic principle as a hot water system, except that the storage area is not the hot water tank but the swimming pool. A number of experts suggest that solar swimming pool systems be designed so that they could be used to heat domestic hot water.

Some solar swimming pool heaters use unglazed collectors. They can do this since the temperature to which it is desired to heat the pool is only a relatively few degrees above the outside air temperature. Unglazed collectors are very inefficient when operated at high temperatures, and may not be suitable for dual purposes.

One of the most effective and economical ways to heat a swimming pool is by using the pool itself as the solar collector and simply providing an easily removable durable transparent plastic membrane on the water surface. If maintained on the pool when not being used, water temperatures can be kept above 80 degrees for several months without fuel supplements.

If a separate collector is used, it should either be of the draining type or otherwise able to withstand freezing. Even though the night temperature of the air may be 40°F. or more, the collector could go below freezing due to nocturnal radiation. This process, nocturnal radiation, can also be used to cool the pool in summer months if the water becomes uncomfortably warm.

"Hybrid" Solar Systems

Some manufacturers are combining solar systems with heat pumps for the purpose of reducing auxiliary electricity costs. The heat pump has the capacity to extract heat from either cool air or cool liquid and increase the temperature to a useful level for heating. When used for cooling, the pump extracts heat from the house and then raises the temperature high enough to be dumped outside. The Freon extracts the heat from the water by evaporation of this liquid. Then, as the Freon vapor is compressed, its temperature is raised to a temperature range of 100 to 150°F. This hot Freon vapor then flows through a heat exchanger which uses the heat in the Freon to heat water or air. The Freon is cooled and condensed to liquid in the exchanger and, after the liquid leaves the exchanger, it is allowed to expand to a low pressure. At the lower pressure, it evaporates at a low temperature, colder than storage, so it then can pick up more heat from the stored water to begin the cycle all over again.

Needless to say, the warmer the water in storage, the less work the heat pump needs to do to deliver useful heat. It works out, however, that the colder the stored water, the more efficiently the solar collector will function.

The heat which the heat pump delivers is the sum of the heat extracted from storage plus the electric energy delivered to the compressor of the heat pump. The total BTU's delivered by the heat pump to the house divided by the BTU's supplied by electricity is what engineers call the coefficient of performance. Thus, if 3 BTU's were delivered to the house for every BTU equivalent of electricity, the COP would be 3.

A problem with heat pumps, however, is that the colder the source used to evaporate the Freon, the lower the COP. This is where solar comes in. It can be used to heat the air or water, thus reducing the work that the heat pump must do and thereby increasing the COP. As you can see, the higher the COP, the less electrical energy required for a given amount of useful heat delivered to the house.

One key advantage to the utilization of solar with heat pumps is that solar can be allowed to operate more effectively. As stated earlier, the efficiency of a solar system increases as the temperature of the fluid pumped through the collector decreases. Therefore, a solar collector is able to be operated at a lower temperature when used with a heat pump system and thus will collect more of the sun's energy for use than will a nonheat pump system. A properly designed heat pump solar energy system will have its collector working at peak efficiency and its heat pump supplying only the additional heat required of the house. In other words, the higher the average COP, the better.

Another way that a common air-to-air heat pump can be used in a solar heating system is by employing it as a furnace, to increase the temperature of air being supplied from the solar system to the distribution ducts. Outdoor air is used as the heat source for the heat pump, electricity providing the necessary temperature increase in the Freon cycle. Although this system does not have the higher collector efficiency of the design employing solar storage as the heat pump source, it does not suffer from mid-winter depletion of storage to temperatures consistently too low for direct solar heating without electricity supplement. Annual electricity usage in the two systems is not greatly different.

Solar Energy and Air Conditioning

If you live in an area where summer air conditioning is considered essential, a heat pump costs only a little more than a conventional Freon air conditioner. Systems using heat pumps for summer cooling may be able to use the storage system to store ''coolness'' during off peak hours and thus help alleviate the summer peaks that the electrical utilities experience on hot summer afternoons. If your utility system adopts off-peak pricing (costs are higher per kilowatt during periods of high use, lower during periods of low use), this solar-heat pump combination would work even further to your advantage. In the Washington, D.C. area, a house that requires a 4-ton air conditioning system will find that it actually operates only about 25 percent of the time. If water storage were to be used, a 1-ton unit could be used to handle the load by operating 100 percent of the

time or, the 4-ton unit could be used only 6 hours a day at off-peak times.

What Should You Recommend?

To begin with, solar energy is not suitable for everyone's house. You will have to know whether the house or lot can handle a large enough collector and storage system. The collector will have to face a southern direction and receive enough unobstructed sunlight. For the specific area, you will need to know how much usable radiation will fall during the time your client intends to use the solar system. As will be explained later, this figure, the amount of usable radiation along with the system's efficiency and the size of the collector, will allow you to determine how many BTU's the unit will receive.

Here are a few approximate space needs for various systems:

•For hot water systems, the general rule of thumb is 1 square foot of collector area for every gallon of water required per day. In other words, for a family that uses 80 gallons a day, an 80-square foot collector will be needed for the solar heater to furnish about three-fourths of the hot water in a sunny climate.

•For swimming pools, the rough estimate is 1 square foot of collector for every 2 square feet in the pool. If a pool is 600 square feet, you will need about a 300-square foot collector.

•There are many variables to take into consideration to determine the approximate space needs for a solar heating system, but, as a rough calculation, estimate 1 square foot of collector for every 2½ to 4 square feet of house. So if you are working with a well-built, 1,500-square foot house in a cold, sunny climate, about 500 square feet of collector can supply two-thirds to three-fourths of the annual heat requirements. As the efficiencies of collectors increase in the future, the size of the collector necessary will decrease.

•Approximate space needed for storage is as follows: For rock systems, about ½ cubic foot of rock storage for every square foot of collector; for water, about 1 to 2 gallons (0.13 to 0.25 cubic feet) of storage for every square foot of collector; for salt (when commercialized), about 1 cubic foot of storage for every 9 square feet of

Region system size	Solar, pct of hot water	Solar system cost ($)	Pay out time, years (electricity)		
			3 cents/Kwh	3½ cents/Kwh	4 cents/Kwh
East Coast (N.Y., Boston, Washington)					
50 S.F. system	47	900	8.9	8.0	7.2
75	60	1,200	9.2	8.2	7.4
100	72	1,500	9.5	8.5	7.7
South Florida (Miami)					
50 S.F. system	69	900	6.7	5.8	5.3
Upper Midwest (Chicago - Omaha)					
50 S.F. system	54	900	8.1	7.1	6.4
75	69	1,200	8.3	7.4	6.7
100	84	1,500	8.5	7.5	6.8
Lower Midwest (St. Louis - Nashville)					
50 S.F. system	51	900	8.4	7.5	6.7
75	65	1,200	8.7	7.7	7.0
100	79	1,500	8.9	7.9	7.1
Southwest (Dallas)					
50 S.F. system	62	900	7.4	6.4	5.7
75	84	1,200	7.1	6.3	5.7
Desert Southwest					
50 S.F. system	80	900	7.1	6.3	5.7
Southern California (Los Angeles)					
50 S.F. system	62	900	7.4	6.4	5.7
75	84	1,200	7.1	6.3	5.7

Solar Water Heater vs. Electric
Hot Water Heater
Table 10-7

collector. There are a number of factors which will determine the actual size of the system. For example, in winter, the people in Maine do not receive as much sun as those who live in Virginia. Consequently, those who live in Maine will need a larger collector to accomplish the same end results. (Yet the economics of solar heating are much better in Maine than in Miami.) Similarly, you may advise your client for any number of reasons to limit the use of the collector, having it only provide 50 percent of a hot water load, for instance, rather than 80 percent.

In considering whether a solar space heating system will be suitable, an important question concerns insulation.

Don't plan a solar heating system for a poorly insulated home. With improved insulation in the house and with some attention to heat recovery, the collector and storage space needs could be reduced dramatically. It cannot be stressed often enough that the key to conserving conventional fuel and reducing utility bills is to *insulate* then *insolate*.

The reason for this is simply sound economics. The reason your client is buying solar energy is to save money on heating bills. It is more economical to save heat through better insulation than by adding heat through a solar system. Once your client has a soundly insulated house, then you will be able to determine whether the purchase of a solar energy system is worth the investment.

Is Solar a Good Investment?

The question is simple, the answer is complex. When you recommend a solar system, your customer will want to know about initial and lifetime costs. Today some hybrid or passive solar systems are close in price to comparable conventional heating and cooling systems. If these systems function properly, the consumer can expect a very short payback period—that is, the time needed when the savings from using solar energy will pay for the extra costs of the system.

If you are going to recommend an active

Region system size	Solar, pct of hot water	Solar system cost ($)	Pay out time, years (gas) 12.5 cents/Therm	15 cents/Therm	17.5 cents/Therm	20 cents/Therm
East Coast (N.Y., Boston, Washington)						
50 S.F. system	47	900	19.0	17.4	16.1	15.0
75	60	1,200	19.4	17.8	16.5	15.4
100	72	1,500	19.7	18.1	16.8	15.7
South Florida (Miami)						
50 S.F. system	69	900	15.7	14.3	13.1	12.1
Upper Midwest (Chicago - Omaha)						
50 S. F. system	54	900	17.8	16.2	15.0	13.9
75	69	1,200	18.1	16.6	15.3	14.3
100	84	1,500	18.4	16.8	15.5	14.5
Lower Midwest (St. Louis, Nashville)						
50 S.F. system	51	900	18.3	16.7	15.4	14.4
75	65	1,200	18.7	17.1	15.8	14.7
100	79	1,500	18.9	17.3	16.0	15.0
Southwest (Dallas)						
50 S.F. system	62	900	16.6	15.1	13.9	12.9
75	84	1,200	16.5	15.0	13.8	12.8
Desert Southwest						
50 S.F. system	80	900	14.5	13.1	12.0	11.1
Southern California (Los Angeles)						
50 S.F. system	62	900	16.6	15.1	13.9	12.9
75	84	1,200	16.5	15.0	13.8	12.8

Solar Water Heater vs. Gas
Hot Water Heater
Table 10-8

system, however, initial costs will be much larger than the price for a conventional system, and the payback period will be much longer. Your client will in a sense be paying for several years' supply of energy all at once. As with passive systems, your client will have to be concerned about durability. Maintenance and repair costs will add to the time needed to pay back on the system. But when the solar system is paid for, your client knows that he will have free energy coming into his home.

There are times when a solar system is not a smart purchase, when conventional systems are a better buy. You may find that initial costs are prohibitive, or that the time period to pay back the investment is too long, or that some of the unknowns about solar, such as solar rights and property appreciation or depreciation, are too risky.

The easiest and most persuasive way to help your client evaluate the advisability of installing a solar system is to compute the payback period. If the payback period is, say 10 years, and you have a sound, durable product, you can be fairly confident that the system is a good buy for your client. If the payback period is longer, say 20 years, then risks will be appreciably higher.

Tables 10-7 to 10-11 are intended to illustrate the economics of solar systems under "typical" conditions in various part of the United States. Water heater calculations are based on "typical" hot water use by an average family of four. Space heating calculations are based on a 1,500-square-foot single-family residence which is of "typical" construction (varies from one area to another). Electricity, oil, and gas prices used cover the ranges encountered in each area. In calculating future savings, it was forecast that electricity prices would escalate at 7.5 percent per year (5 percent inflation + 2.5 percent). Gas and oil prices were forecast to escalate at 10 percent per year. This is probably conservative. Pay out time is the time required for cumulative savings to equal first cost.

Remember that the overall calculations apply to a general area; they may not apply to a specific location. In other words, your client may live in an area where, because of high costs for

Region	Solar system cost ($)	Pay out time, years			
		*3 cents/kWh **40 cents/Gal	*3½ cents/kWh **43 cents/Gal	*4 cents/kWh **45 cents/Gal	*5 cents/kWh **45 cents/Gal
East Coast - Boston					
40% Solar	4,875	12.1	11.4	10.7	--
50% Solar	6,750	12.6	11.8	11.2	--
East Coast - New York					
40% Solar	4,700	13.0	12.1	11.4	10.5
50% Solar	6,800	14.4	13.5	12.8	11.9
East Coast - Washington					
40% Solar	3,475	10.4	9.6	9.0	--
50% Solar	5,300	12.0	11.2	10.5	--
Upper Midwest (Omaha - Chicago)					
40% Solar	3,200	9.2	8.5	8.0	--
50% Solar	4,825	10.6	9.8	9.3	--
Lower Midwest (St. Louis - Nashville)					
40% Solar	3,275	10.8	10.0	9.3	--
50% Solar	4,825	12.3	11.4	11.0	--
Southwest (Dallas)					
40% Solar	2,200	9.2	8.3	7.7	--
50% Solar	3,000	10.0	9.1	8.5	--
60% Solar	4,875	12.4	11.5	10.8	--
Southern California (Los Angeles)					
50% Solar	1,500	6.7	6.1	5.6	--
60% Solar	2,175	7.8	7.2	6.7	--
70% Solar	3,000	9.0	8.3	7.7	--

*Electricity
**Oil

Solar space heating plus solar hot water heating vs. oil heat plus electric hot water heater
Table 10-9

Region	Solar system cost ($)	Pay out time, years (electricity)			
		3 cents/kWh	3½ cents/kWh	4 cents/kWh	5 cents/kWh
East Coast - Boston					
40% Solar	4,875	10.2	9.1	8.2	--
50% Solar	6,750	10.9	9.8	8.9	--
East Coast - New York					
40% Solar	4,700	11.5	10.3	9.3	7.9
50% Solar	6,800	12.7	11.4	10.4	8.8
East Coast - Washington					
40% Solar	3,475	8.8	7.9	7.1	--
50% Solar	5,300	10.2	9.1	8.3	--
Upper Midwest (Omaha - Chicago)					
40% Solar	3,200	7.6	6.7	6.1	--
50% Solar	4,825	8.8	7.8	7.0	--
Lower Midwest (Nashville - St. Louis)					
40% Solar	3,275	9.5	8.5	7.6	--
50% Solar	4,825	10.7	9.6	8.6	--
Southwest (Dallas)					
40% Solar	2,200	8.2	7.3	6.6	--
50% Solar	3,000	8.7	7.8	7.0	--
60% Solar	4,875	10.9	9.8	7.8	--
Southern California (Los Angeles)					
50% Solar	1,500	5.7	5.0	4.5	--
60% Solar	2,175	6.7	5.9	5.3	--
70% Solar	3,000	7.6	6.7	6.0	--

Solar space heating plus solar hot water heating
Table 10-10

Region	Solar system cost ($)	Pay out time, years (gas)			
		12.5 cents/therm	15 cents/therm	17.5 cents/therm	20 cents/therm
East Coast - Boston					
40% Solar	4,875	20.5	18.9	17.6	16.5
50% Solar	6,750	21.5	19.8	18.5	17.3
East Coast - New York					
40% Solar	4,700	22.1	20.5	19.1	17.9
50% Solar	6,800	23.5	21.8	20.4	19.2
East Coast - Washington					
40% Solar	3,475	18.8	17.3	16.0	14.9
50% Solar	5,300	20.6	19.0	17.6	16.5
Upper Midwest (Omaha - Chicago)					
40% Solar	3,200	17.1	15.6	14.4	13.4
50% Solar	4,825	18.8	17.2	15.9	14.8
Lower Midwest (Nashville - St. Louis)					
40% Solar	3,275	19.7	18.1	16.8	15.7
50% Solar	4,825	21.2	19.5	18.2	17.0
Southwest (Dallas)					
40% Solar	2,200	18.0	16.4	15.2	14.1
50% Solar	3,000	18.7	17.2	15.9	14.8
60% Solar	4,875	21.4	19.8	18.4	17.3
Southern California (Los Angeles)					
50% Solar	1,500	14.2	12.8	11.7	10.8
60% Solar	2,175	15.7	14.3	13.1	12.1
70% Solar	3,000	17.1	15.6	14.4	13.3

Solar space heating plus solar hot water heating
vs. natural gas heat and hot water heater
Table 10-11

conventional fuel and because of the high insolation rate, solar systems appear to be particularly attractive. Yet the particular site of a home—in the shadow of a mountain, for instance—may negate these cost and insolation advantages.

Table 10-12 can be helpful to you in determining the basic advantages of solar in your general area. By finding the insolation rate (low: 250-350 langleys per day, average 300; medium: 350-450, average 400; and high: 450-550, average 500), you can quickly determine the competitiveness of solar in your area.

Installing a Solar Hot Water System

There is nothing highly technical or exotic about solar heating. Most of the components are available from plumbing and electrical supply dealers. Most experienced carpenters, plumbers and electricians will have no trouble installing their respective parts of the system. As a builder you will have to make some basic decisions on where the collectors and water storage are located and how much of the heat load the solar system will carry. It isn't practical to install a solar space heating system that carries 100% of the heat load. All this excess capacity would go to waste for all but a few days a year. And even then, during some periods of cloudy weather, some type of a backup system would be needed. It is better to install a system that supplies 40 to 60 percent of the heating needed and let the conventional furnace carry the remainder of the load. Don't worry about the exact percentage of heating your solar heating system will produce. It will be reducing the home owner's fuel bills by a significant amount and will repay the cost in 10 to 12 years if it is efficient, located correctly and requires little maintenance.

The following pages describe a practical solar space heating system designed and built under the supervision of the National Aeronautics and Space Administration. It can be installed in most any residence. The materials for this system cost about $3,000. The labor cost would be between $1,000 and $2,000 depending on the system location, wage scales and site

States and Stations	Jan	Feb	Mar	Apr	May	June	July	Aug	Sept	Oct	Nov	Dec	Annual
Alaska, Annette	63	115	236	364	437	438	438	341	258	122	59	41	243
Barrow	*	38	180	380	513	528	429	255	115	41	*	*	206
Bethel	38	108	282	444	457	454	376	252	202	115	44	22	233
Fairbanks	16	71	213	376	461	504	434	317	180	82	26	6	224
Matanuska	32	92	242	356	436	462	409	314	198	100	38	15	224
Ariz., Page	300	382	526	618	695	707	680	596	516	402	310	243	498
Phoenix	301	409	526	638	724	739	658	613	566	449	344	281	520
Tucson	315	391	540	655	729	699	626	588	570	442	356	305	518
Ark., Little Rock	188	260	353	446	523	559	556	518	439	343	244	187	385
California, Davis	174	257	390	528	625	694	682	612	493	347	222	148	431
Fresno	184	289	427	552	647	702	682	621	510	376	250	161	450
Inyokern (China Lake)	306	412	562	683	772	819	772	729	635	467	363	300	568
La Jolla	244	302	397	457	506	487	497	464	389	320	277	221	380
Los Angeles WBAS	248	331	470	515	572	596	641	581	503	373	289	241	463
Los Angeles, WBO	243	327	436	483	555	584	651	581	500	362	281	234	436
Riverside	275	367	478	541	623	680	673	618	535	407	319	270	483
Santa Maria	263	346	482	552	635	694	680	613	524	419	313	252	481
Soda Springs	223	316	374	551	615	691	760	681	510	357	248	182	459
Colorado, Boulder	201	268	401	460	460	525	520	439	412	310	222	182	367
Grand Junction	227	324	434	546	615	708	676	595	514	373	260	212	456
Grand Lake (Granby)	212	313	423	512	552	632	600	505	476	361	234	184	417
D.C., Washington (C.O.)	174	266	344	411	551	494	536	446	375	299	211	166	356
American University	158	231	322	398	467	510	496	440	364	278	192	141	333
Silver Hill	177	247	342	438	513	555	511	457	391	293	202	156	357
Florida, Apalachicola	298	367	441	535	603	578	529	511	456	413	332	262	444
Belle Isle	297	330	412	463	483	464	488	461	400	366	313	291	397
Gainesville	267	343	427	517	579	521	488	483	418	347	300	233	410
Miami Airport	349	415	489	540	553	532	532	505	440	384	353	316	451
Tallahassee	274	311	423	499	547	547	521	508	†	†	292	230	---
Tampa	327	391	474	539	596	574	534	494	452	400	356	300	453
Georgia, Atlanta	218	290	380	488	533	562	532	508	416	344	268	211	396
Griffin	234	295	385	522	570	577	556	522	435	368	283	201	413
Hawaii, Honolulu	363	422	516	559	617	615	615	612	573	507	426	371	516
Mauna Loa Obs.	522	576	680	689	727	†	703	642	602	560	504	481	---
Pearl Harbor	359	400	487	529	573	566	598	567	539	466	386	343	484
Idaho, Boise	138	236	342	485	585	636	670	576	460	301	182	124	395
Twin Falls	163	240	355	462	552	592	602	540	432	286	176	131	378
Illinois, Chicago	96	147	227	331	424	458	473	403	313	207	120	76	273
Lemont	170	242	340	402	506	553	540	498	398	275	165	138	352
Indiana, Indianapolis	144	213	316	396	488	543	541	490	405	293	177	132	345
Iowa, Ames	174	253	326	403	480	541	436	460	367	274	187	143	345
Kansas, Dodge City	255	316	418	528	568	650	642	592	493	380	285	234	447
Manhattan	192	264	345	433	527	551	531	526	410	292	227	156	371
Kentucky, Lexington	172	263	357	480	581	628	617	563	494	357	245	174	411
Louisiana, Lake Charles	245	306	397	481	555	591	526	511	449	402	300	250	418
New Orleans	214	259	335	412	449	443	417	416	383	357	278	198	347
Shreveport	232	292	384	446	558	557	578	528	414	354	254	205	400
Maine, Caribou	133	231	364	400	476	470	508	448	336	212	111	107	316
Portland	152	235	352	409	514	539	561	488	383	278	157	137	350
Massachusetts, Amherst	116	†	300	†	431	514	†	---	---	---	152	124	---
Blue Hill	153	228	319	389	469	510	502	449	354	266	162	135	328
Boston	129	194	290	350	445	483	486	411	334	235	136	115	301
Cambridge	153	235	323	400	420	476	482	464	367	253	164	124	322
East Wareham	140	218	305	385	452	508	495	436	365	258	163	140	322
Lynn	118	209	300	394	454	549	528	432	341	241	135	107	317
Michigan, East Lansing	121	210	309	359	483	547	540	466	373	255	136	108	311
Sault Ste. Marie	130	225	356	416	523	557	573	472	322	216	105	96	333
Minnesota, St. Cloud	168	260	368	426	496	535	557	486	366	237	146	124	348
Missouri, Columbia (C.O.)	173	251	340	434	530	574	574	522	453	322	225	158	380
University of Missouri	166	248	324	429	501	560	583	509	417	324	177	146	365

Average Solar Radiation per day in Langleys
Table 10-12

conditions. The system will provide about 40 percent of the heat needed for a typical 1,500 square foot house meeting 1974 F.H.A. insulation standards. The system uses a solar collector, hot-water distribution system, hot-water storage tank, circulating pump, flow controls, and a water-to-air heat exchanger mounted in the return air duct of the existing warm-air furnace. The solar collector on the roof of the home is heated by the sun just as a greenhouse for wintertime gardening is heated. On sunny days, water circulating through the

States and Stations	Jan	Feb	Mar	Apr	May	June	July	Aug	Sept	Oct	Nov	Dec	Annual
Montana, Glasgow	154	258	385	466	568	605	645	531	410	267	154	116	388
Great Falls	140	232	366	434	528	583	639	532	407	264	154	112	366
Summit	122	162	268	414	462	493	560	510	354	216	102	76	312
Nebraska, Lincoln	188	259	350	416	494	544	568	484	396	296	199	159	363
North Omaha	193	299	365	463	516	546	568	519	410	298	204	170	379
Nevada, Ely	236	339	468	563	625	712	647	618	518	394	289	218	469
Las Vegas	277	384	519	621	702	748	675	627	551	429	318	258	509
New Jersey, Seabrook	157	227	318	403	482	527	509	455	385	278	192	140	339
New Hampshire, Mt. Wash.	117	218	238	†	†	†	---	---	†	†	†	96	---
New Mexico, Albuquerque	303	386	511	618	686	726	683	626	554	438	334	276	512
New York, Ithaca	116	194	272	334	440	501	515	453	346	231	120	96	302
N.Y. Central Park	130	199	290	369	432	470	459	389	331	242	147	115	298
Sayville	160	249	335	415	494	565	543	462	385	289	186	142	352
Schenectady	130	200	273	338	413	448	441	397	299	218	128	104	282
Upton	155	232	339	428	502	573	543	475	391	293	182	146	355
North Carolina, Greensboro	200	276	354	469	531	564	544	485	406	322	243	197	383
Hatteras	238	317	426	569	635	652	625	562	471	358	282	214	443
Raleigh	235	302	†	466	494	564	535	476	379	307	235	199	---
North Dakota, Bismarck	157	250	356	447	550	590	617	516	390	272	161	124	369
Ohio, Cleveland	125	183	303	286	502	562	562	494	278	289	141	115	335
Columbus	128	200	297	391	471	562	542	477	422	286	176	129	340
Put-in-Bay	126	204	302	386	468	544	561	487	382	275	144	109	332
Oklahoma, Oklahoma City	251	319	409	494	536	615	610	593	487	377	291	240	436
Stillwater	205	289	390	454	504	600	596	545	455	354	269	209	405
Oregon, Astoria	90	162	270	375	492	469	539	461	354	209	111	79	301
Corvallis	89	†	287	406	517	570	676	558	397	235	144	80	---
Medford	116	215	336	482	592	652	698	605	447	279	149	93	389
Pennsylvania, Pittsburgh	94	169	216	317	429	491	497	409	339	207	118	77	280
State College	133	201	295	380	456	518	511	444	358	256	149	118	318
Rhode Island, Newport	155	232	334	405	477	527	513	455	377	271	176	139	338
South Carolina, Charleston	252	314	388	512	551	564	520	501	404	338	286	225	404
South Dakota, Rapid City	183	277	400	482	532	585	590	541	435	315	204	158	392
Tennessee, Nashville	149	228	322	432	503	551	530	473	403	308	208	150	355
Oak Ridge	161	239	331	450	518	551	526	478	416	318	213	163	364
Texas, Brownsville	297	341	402	456	564	610	627	568	475	411	296	263	442
El Paso	333	430	547	654	714	729	666	640	576	460	372	313	536
Ft. Worth	250	320	427	488	562	651	613	593	503	403	306	245	445
Midland	283	358	476	550	611	617	608	574	522	396	325	275	466
San Antonio	279	347	417	445	541	612	639	585	493	398	295	256	442
Utah, Flaming Gorge	238	298	443	522	565	650	599	538	425	352	262	215	426
Salt Lake City	163	256	354	479	570	621	620	551	446	316	204	146	394
Virginia, Mt. Weather	172	274	338	414	508	525	510	430	375	281	202	168	350
Washington, North Head	†	167	257	432	509	487	486	436	321	205	122	77	---
Friday Harbor	87	157	274	418	514	578	586	507	351	194	102	75	320
Prosser	117	222	351	521	616	680	707	604	458	274	136	100	399
Pullman	121	205	304	462	558	653	699	562	410	245	146	96	372
Univ. of Washington	67	126	245	364	445	461	496	435	299	170	93	59	272
Seattle-Tacoma	75	139	265	403	503	511	566	452	324	188	104	64	300
Spokane	119	204	321	474	563	596	665	556	404	225	131	75	361
Wisconsin, Madison	148	220	313	394	466	514	531	452	348	241	145	115	324
Wyoming, Lander	226	324	452	548	587	678	651	586	472	354	239	196	443
Laramie	216	295	424	508	554	643	606	536	438	324	229	186	408
Island Stations													
Canton Island	588	626	634	604	561	549	550	597	640	651	600	572	597
San Juan, Puerto Rico	404	481	580	622	519	536	639	549	531	460	411	411	512
Swan Island	442	496	615	646	625	544	588	591	535	457	394	382	526
Wake Island	438	518	577	627	642	656	629	623	587	525	482	421	560

† Denotes only one year of data for the month — no means computed.
--- No data for the month (or incomplete data for the year).
* Barrow is in darkness during the winter months.
Langley is the unit used to denote one gram calorie per square centimeter.

Average Solar Radiation per day in Langleys
Table 10-12 (Continued)

collector is used to absorb heat and carry it into the house or to a hot-water storage tank for later use. At night or on cloudy days, heated water from the storage tank is used. The pump circulates water from the storage tank to the collector and then to the heat exchanger in the return air duct of the warm-air furnace and then back to the storage tank as shown in the figure. The hot water in going through the heat exchanger warms up the returning house air

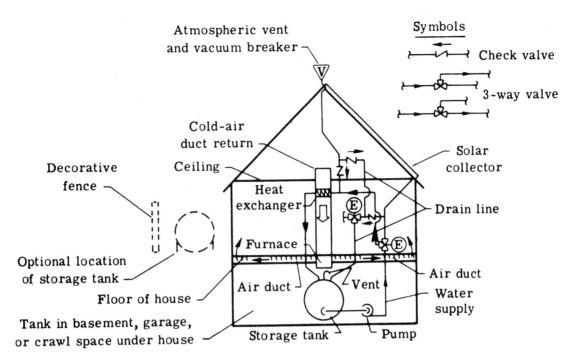

Night or cloudy-day operation

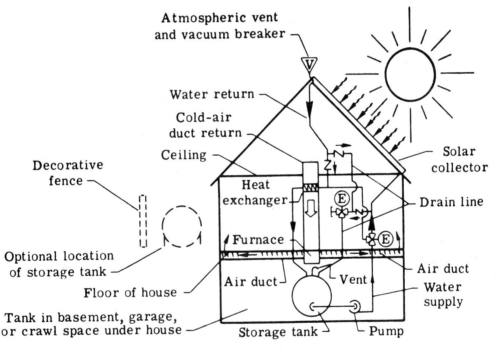

Sunny-day operation

Schematic Flow Diagram of Solar
Heating System
Figure 10-13

before it returns to the furnace for final reheating. In order to regulate the flow of water to the heat exchanger, another thermostat is added to the house and set a few degrees above the existing thermostat. In some cases the air is heated sufficiently by the solar heated water and the existing thermostat does not cut on the burner in the furnace to provide any additional heat. At night or in cloudy weather when hot water is available from the storage tank, the pumped water automatically bypasses the collectors and goes directly to the heat exchanger.

To provide a reasonably large amount of the heat needed, the area of the solar collector system should be approximately one quarter to one-third the floor area of a home. Use the higher figure if the average solar radiation for December, January and February is about 250 langleys per day. Use the lower figure if the December to February average is closer to 300 langleys per day. If the winter average is below 200 langleys, a solar heating system may be practical only in isolated areas where no inexpensive fuel source is available.

Description of the System

The home should have a south-facing roof adequate to provide this required area of collectors. It is not necessary for the roof to face directly south. Deviation from due south by 15° or 20° does not seriously affect overall performance.

The ideal pitch for winter operation is approximately equal to the local latitude plus 15°. However, the improved performance achieved by mounting the collector at this exact pitch does not save enough to pay for the structural system to support it. Such a structure would have to be sturdy enough to meet local building codes and to withstand high winds blowing on the rear of a tilted solar collector which might tend to lift it from the roof. It is much simpler to mount the collectors directly on the existing roof and leave the shingles in place. Roof pitches from 3 in 12 to almost vertical are acceptable. The collector, described here weighs only about 2½ pounds per square foot and would need little if any additional roof support.

The insulated hot-water storage tank, for storage of excess heated water for later use, can be located in the garage, in a tool shed, behind a decorative fence, or buried underground — whichever is most convenient. Plastic pipes carry the hot water to and from the tank. Plastic pipes are low in cost, easily installed, and provide sufficient insulation. To size the storage tank, approximtely 1½ gallons of water storage should be provided for each square foot of solar collector area plus approximately 1 gallon, for expansion, for each 50 gallons of water storage. This allowance must be included for thermal expansion since the water in the tank expands when it is heated. A 1,000-gallon tank, or the next largest convenient size, would be about right for a 500 square foot collector. Figure 10-13 illustrates the major system components.

The most critical part of a solar heating system is the collector. It must have a high collection efficiency and yet be inexpensive since it represents a large part of the initial cost of the total system. It is, therefore, important that the appropriate collector type and size be used for each particular home in order to minimize the cost. By increasing the collector area, the homeowner can save a higher percentage of his heating bill. However, as the cost of the solar system increases, the system becomes less cost effective.

A typical cross-sectional view of a solar collector mounted on a roof is shown in Figure 10-14. Most of the incoming solar rays can penetrate the glass or plastic cover without much energy loss. These solar rays are absorbed by the blackened surface; thus, the surface and the water flowing through the channels in the absorption panel are heated. The heat rays reemitted by the panel are of a longer wave length which cannot get back out through the glass or plastic cover and are trapped in the space between the glass or plastic cover and the panel.

In areas of the United States where hailstorms could cause glass breakage, a plastic cover may be more suitable. A special type plastic of 4 mil thickness, such as Tedlar film, is required for satisfactory performance. If there are any greenhouses in your city, it is not likely that hailstorms are a problem.

A more likely problem may be vandals throwing rocks. If this could be a problem, the glass should be covered with hardware cloth screen wire material with a ¼- to ½-inch mesh size. The hardware cloth will decrease the energy available by approximately 7 percent.

Equally important to efficient operation and minimum cost are the hot-water distribution system, the flow controller, and the hot-water storage tank. The hot-water distribution system can be made from chlorinated polyvinyl chloride (CPVC) plastic pipe and fittings. This type of pipe is not as expensive as steel or copper and is superior to the steel in corrosion resistance. Another advantage of the plastic pipe and plastic fittings is the ease with which they can be fabricated and assembled. No special tools are required to assemble the plastic piping other

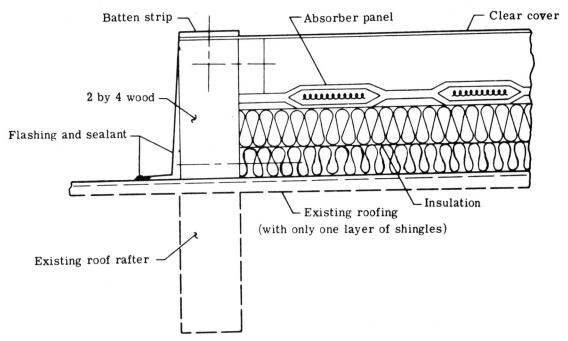

Typical Solar Collector Cross Section
Figure 10-14

than a saw, some sandpaper, and the proper glue. The plastic pipe and fittings are glue welded together. Metal-to-plastic adapters are available and required for plastic pipe connections to the metallic components such as the solar panel, heat exchanger, and valves.

Flow control of the water in the solar heating system described here is accomplished with the differential temperature flow controller (DTFC) and two three-way resistance heater operated valves. The flow controller is of the differential temperature comparator type. Whenever the temperature in the solar collector is 10°F. higher than the temperature of the water in the storage tank, the thermomechanically operated valves will allow the water to flow through the solar collectors. When the temperature in the solar collectors is 5°F. greater than the temperature of the water in the storage tank, the two three-way valves are de-energized and the water flow is diverted from the solar collectors and through the heat exchanger only. Because the water flow is through the solar collector when the two three-way valves are energized, the system is also fail-safe. If the power is lost to the solar heating system, the two three-way valves open and a vacuum breaker automatically opens to allow the solar collectors to drain by gravity.

You will have to use a corrosion inhibitor in the solar heating system water. A water treatment company in your area will recommend the appropriate type, concentration, and frequency of treatment. It is very important to specify the types of metal in the system. The metals described here are aluminum, copper, and steel. Your local water treatment company will probably recommend that sodium dichromate be used with a concentration of 250 parts per million. However, a word of caution: Sodium dichromate is toxic and cannot be connected to the hot or cold water system of the house. The concentration should be periodically checked, especially after additional water is added to the storage tank. This treatment costs only $5 to $10 but is very important to the lifetime of the system. It will extend the life of the aluminum panels from approximately 3 months to many years.

Bill of Materials

The materials needed for the solar heating system described here are listed in Tables 10-15 and 10-16. Manufacturers are listed for most of the materials required. The remaining materials are available at building supply stores.

The Collector

A layout drawing of the solar collectors mounted on the homeowner's roof should be

115

Item	Item Description	Manufacturer (a)

Panel (Site fabricated)	Aluminum roll bond panels:
	  Alloy 1100; thickness, 0.060 in.; with, 33.75 in.; length 96 in.; 20 panels required
	  (Olin Brass Article FS-7767 or equivalent)
		Olin Corp., Olin Brass, East Alton, IL 62024
		
		Tranter, Inc., 705 E. Hazel St., Lansing, MI 48909
		
		Dean Products, Inc., Panel Coil 1025 Dean St., Brooklyn, NY 11238
		
		Fafco, Inc., 5860 Spring St. Redwood City, CA 94063

Panel (Commercial)	Extruded aluminum tube with fins: Outside diameter, ½ in.; wall thickness, 0.035 in., 2 fins; total width, 3 in.; total length, 2000 ft.; total weight, approximately 250 lb.	Brazeway, Inc., 2711 E. Maumee, P.O. Box 546, Adrian, MI 49221 (Many manufacturers make similar panels)

Collector insulation	Fiberglass insulation:
	  Thickness, 1.5 in.; width, 3 ft.; length, 8 ft.; density, 3 lb/ft^3; 20 pieces required.
	  Owens-Corning Fiberglas catalog No. 703 or equivalent)
		Owens-Corning Fiberglass Corp. Fiberglas Tower, Toledo, OH 43659
		
		Johns-Manville Corp., 22 E. 40th St., New York, NY 10016
		
		PPG Industries, Fiber Glass Div., One Gateway Center, Pittsburgh, PA 15222

Cover	Polyvinyl fluoride film:
	  Thickness, 0.004 in.; total width (including overhang), 3.5 ft.; total length (including overhang), 170 ft.; total area, 595 ft^2
	  (Du Pont Tedlar PVF film 400BG20TR or equivalent)
		E.I. Du Pont de Nemours & Co., Inc. Film Dept., 1007 Market St. Wilmington, DE 19898
		
		General Electric Co., Space Products Div. Valley Forge Space Center, P.O. Box 8555 Philadelphia, PA 19101
		
		Filon Div., Vistron Corp., 12333 S. Van Ness at El Segundo Blvd., Hawthorne, CA 90250
		
		ASG Industries, Inc., P. O. Box 929 Kingsport, TN 37662

Water pump	Rotary vane, positive displacement type pump:
	  Capable of pumping 240 gal/hr of water, internal relief valve must be set at 50 psig; 1/3-hp, 120-V; 60-cycle motor
	  (Procon Model No. C02057HFEP or equivalent)
		Procon-Colerain Products, Affiliate of United States Service Equipment Co. Div. of Standex, 910 Ridgely Rd. Murfreesboro, TN 37130
		
		Bell & Gosset, ITT, 8234 Austin Ave. Morton Grove, IL 60053
		
		Aurora Pump Div., General Signal Corp. 800 Airport Rd., N. Aurora, IL 60542
		
		Thrush Products, Inc., W. 8th at N. Jefferson, Box 228, Peru, IN 46970

Water storage tank	Concrete water storage tank:
	  Size, 1000 gal; width, 5 ft; length, 9 ft; depth, 6 ft
	  or
	Steel water storage tank:
	  Size, 1000 gal; diameter, 4 ft; length, 10 ft 8 in.
		Local concrete (septic) tank suppliers
		
		Local tank suppliers

Insulation for storage tank	Standard tank insulation (equivalent to 6 in. of fiberglass insulation): Thickness, 6 in.; width, 23 in.; length, 48 in.; 24 pieces required	Same as for collector insulation
Heat exchanger	Water-to-air heat exchanger: One-row coil; type T; finned width, 18 in.; finned length, 22 in.; without turbulators	Trane Co., 3600 Pammel Creek Rd. La Crosse, WI 54601 General Electric Co., Air Cond. & Heating Appliance Park, Louisville, KY 40225 American Air Filter Co., Inc., 200 Central Ave., Louisville, KY 40208 Young Radiator Co., Dept. T-72, 2825 Four Mile Rd., Racine, WI 53404

Wood	Redwood or treated pine:
	  2 by 4 in.: total length, 320 ft.
	  ¼ by 2 in.: total length, 320 ft.
		Local lumber company

Bill of Materials for Solar Heating System
Table 10-15

Item	Item Description	Manufacturer (a)
Plastic tubing	Chlorinated polyvinyl chloride (CPVC) tubing: ¾ in.: nominal diameter, length as required ½ in.: nominal diameter, length as required Tees and ells, number and size as required	Local plumbing supply stores
Pipe strainer	Pipe strainer for suction side of pump, 1-in.-diameter pipe size, with 100-mesh-size stainless-steel screen	Local plumbing supply stores
Three-way valves	Three-way fan coil valves: ¾ in.: 125 psi; operating temperature, 40°F to 240°F; bronze body; 0.9-A rating; 24 Vac; 60 cycles, 1 required (Taco Product No. 561-3 or equivalent) 1 in.; same information as for ¾-in. valve; 1 required (Taco Product No. 562-3 or equivalent)	Taco, Inc., 1160 Cranston St. Cranston, RI 02920 Automatic Switch Co., 56-A Hanover Rd. Florham Park, NJ 07932 Skinner Electric Valve Div., Skinner Prec. Ind., Inc. 100 Edgewood Ave. New Britain, CT 06050 Bell & Gossett, ITT, 8234 Austin Ave. Morton Grove, IL 60053
Check valve	Bronze swing check valve: ¾ in.: 125 psi; screwed ends; 3 required (Jenkins No. 92-A or equivalent)	Jenkins Bros., 100 Park Ave. New York, NY 10017 Taco, Inc., 1160 Cranston St. Cranston, RI 02920 Automatic Switch, 56-A Hanover Rd. Florham Park, NJ 07932 Bell & Gossett, ITT, 8234 Austin Ave. Morton Grove, IL 60053
Vacuum breaker (antisiphon kit)	Vacuum breaker for ¾-in. pipe	Whirlpool Corp., Administrative Center Benton Harbor, MI 49022 The Johnson Corp., 809 Wood St. Three Rivers, MI 49093 Beacon Valve Co., P. O. Box 478 2 Jackson St., Waltham, MA 02154
Black paint	Enamel flat black paint: 2 gal. needed for required two coats on aluminum (Sherwin-Williams catalog No. F62B50 or equivalent)	Sherwin-Williams Co., 101 Prospect Ave., N.W., Cleveland, OH 44101 PPG Industries, Inc., 10800 S. 13th St. Oak Creek, WI 53154 3M Co., 3M Center, St. Paul, MN 55101
Primer	Zinc chromate primer: 1 gal. needed for required 1 coat (PPG catalog No. 6-204 or equivalent)	PPG Industries, Inc., 10800 S. 13th St. Oak Creek, WI 53154 Sherwin-Williams Co., 101 Prospect Ave., NW., Cleveland, OH 44101 3M Co., 3M Center, St. Paul, MN 55101 Rust-Oleum Corp., 2301 Oakton St. Evanston, IL 60204

Bill of Materials for Solar Heating System
Table 10-15 (Continued)

made before ordering materials. The roof on which the collector is to be mounted must face a generally southern direction, be large enough for the required collector area, and be exposed to the sun during the middle of the day. Measurements of the available roof area are required before selecting the location for the collectors. Working space around and between each collector bay should be adequate for the collector installation and for the water supply and water return pipes. Measurements should be made in the attic as well as on the roof. Four collectors in each bay are described here since this configuration will fit most homes. This configuration can be changed to suit the roof but the water flow through each bay must be the same for best performance. All bays must have the same number of collectors per bay to obtain the same water flow through each bay. More than five collectors per bay are not recommended because a larger pump will be required.

The solar panel recommended is shown in

Component Name	Symbol	Component Description	Manufacturer (a)
Transformer	T1	120 to 24 Vac; 4 A (Type 6K8OVBR or equivalent)	Allied Electronics Corp. 401 E. 8th St. Fort Worth, TX 76102
Transformer	T2	120 to 24 Vac; 1 A (Type 6K113HF or equivalent)	(1976 Engineering Manual and Purchasing Guide No. 760)
Relay	R1	24 Vac; 10 A; double pole double throw (Type KA11AG or equivalent)	Newark Electronics Corp. 500 N. Pulaski Rd. Chicago, IL 60624 Allen-Bradley Co.
Relay	R2	24 Vac; 10 A; double pole double throw (Type KA11AG or equivalent)	Allen-Bradley Co. 1201 S. 2nd St. Milwaukee, WI 53204 Radio Shack Div. 2617 W. 7th St. Fort Worth, TX 76107
Thermostat	T-2	(Chromalox WR-1E30 or equivalent)	Edwin L. Weigand Div. Emerson Electric Co. 7500 Thomas Blvd. Pittsburgh, PA 15208 Honeywell, Inc. 2701 Fourth Ave., S. Minneapolis, MN 55408 General Electric Co. 1 River Rd. Schenectady, NY 12345 Robertshaw Controls Co. Control Systems Div. 1701 Byrd Ave. Richmond, VA 23230
Thermostat switch	T-1	Bimetallic operating temperature 40° F to 200° F; single pole single throw; 115 Vac; 10-A rated; well included (Mercoid type FM437-3-3516 or equivalent)	The Mercoid Corp. 4201 Belmont Ave. Chicago, IL 60641 PSG Industries, Inc. 910 Ridge Ave. Perkasie, PA 18944 United Electric Controls Co. 80 School St. Watertown, MA 02172 American Thermostat Corp. Box 60 South Cairo, NY 12482
Differential temperature flow controller	DTFC	120 Vac; 10° F turn-on differential; 5°F turn-off differential; two thermistors included; 300° F maximum sensor temperature (DEKO-LABS Model TC-3 or equivalent)	DEKO-LABS Box 12841 Gainesville, FL 32602 Rho Sigma 5108 Melvin Ave. Tarzana, CA 91356 Jack S. Scovel 4220 Berritt St. Fairfax, VA 22030

Bill of Materials for Electrical Supplies
Table 10-16

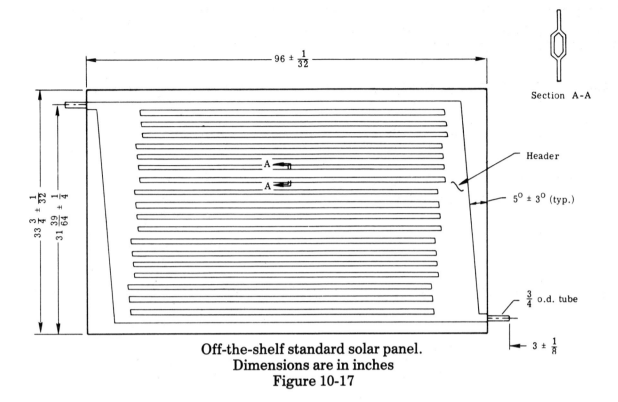

Off-the-shelf standard solar panel.
Dimensions are in inches
Figure 10-17

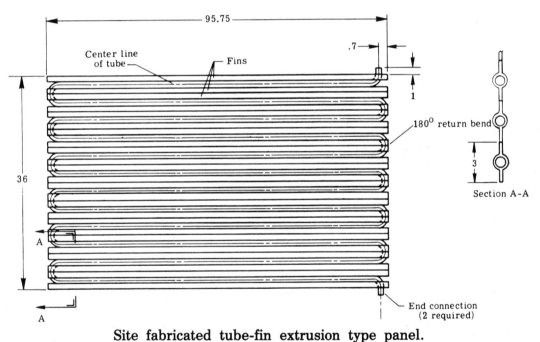

Site fabricated tube-fin extrusion type panel.
Linear dimensions are in inches
Figure 10-18

Figure 10-17. The water flow path of the panel allows complete draining of all water from the panel to prevent freezing problems. Hose connections from one panel to the next are described later in this chapter. This panel is available commercially and is similar to panels produced by several manufacturers.

Most builders would prefer to work with panels that are available through supply houses. However, an efficient solar collector can be built from extruded aluminum tubing as shown in Figure 10-18. The tube must be bent in 180°

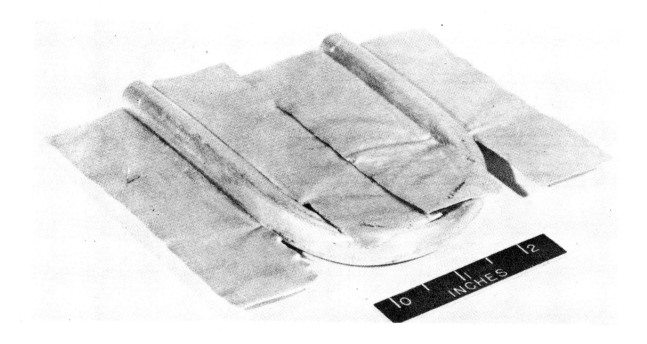

180° Bend
Figure 10-19

turns as illustrated. A photograph of one 180° turn is shown in Figure 10-19. Start by cutting the fins away from the tube to make the panel water inlet as shown in Figure 10-20. After the water inlet bend is made, unroll another 8 feet of the extrusion section to make the first 180° return bend as shown in Figure 10-21. After making each turn, unwind another 8-foot length to the next turn. This operation should be done on a flat surface in order to bend the turns all in the same plane. A total of 11 turns will be required for each panel plus the two 90° end turns. The panel will be flexible as the last turns are made so it is advisable to attach it to a 3- by 8-foot piece of plywood which can be rotated with the panel to aid in making the turns. The outline of the panel should be drawn on the plywood and small nails should be used at each turn to hold the tubing in the proper location after the bends have been made. The water must drain out of the panels to prevent freezing during cold weather. This drainage can be accomplished by making the tubes and fins between bends parallel during panel assembly and installing the panels level on the roof. A check should be made when the first panel is made to see if the water will drain out. The final panel will look like the panel shown in Figure 10-18. Twenty panels will be required for a total of 480 square feet.

It is very important to prevent the tube from collapsing while being bent. Wood blocks which minimize the distortion of the tube and fins should be of a hard wood such as maple or birch. (See Figure 10-22.) Details of the groove are also given. Slots and cutouts are to allow room for the fins. A block with a groove is used to minimize the distortion while cutting the fins. The thin aluminum fins can be easily cut with any type of sharp tool. Be careful not to damage the tube. The assembly of these wood blocks is shown in Figure 10-23; this is very similar to a standard tube bender which would damage the fins. The difference between the standard tube bender and this one is that the finned tube bender has slots for the fins. Practice making several bends before starting a 3- by 8-foot panel. Buy extra material when ordering the tube fin extrusion. If 2000 linear feet of material were ordered, this would include 80 extra feet.

The solar collector panels in this system are housed in frames made from pine 2 by 4's. The inside openings in the framing should not be less than 3 by 8 feet as shown in Figure 10-24. Notches and holes for inlet and outlet tubes on panels should be laid out and fabricated on an individual basis because of the tolerances used by the manufacturer of the panels. The panels and the openings in the frame should be numbered with matching numbers. Each panel

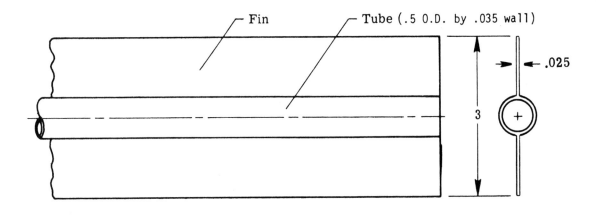

Fin   Tube (.5 O.D. by .035 wall)

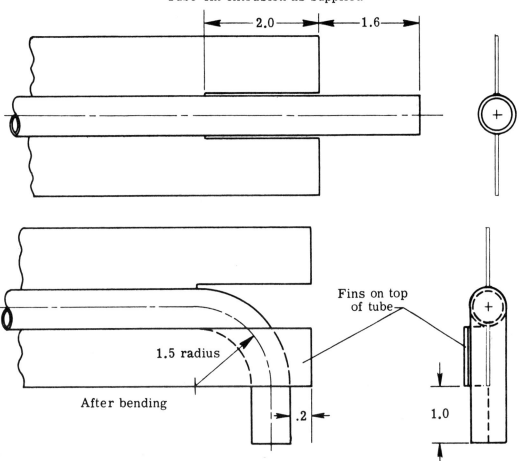

Tube-fin extrusion as supplied

Fins on top of tube

Typical end connection of panel. Linear
dimensions are in inches
Figure 10-20

should be measured and the corresponding opening in the collector frame laid out for drilling and notching as shown in Figure 10-24. The holes for the inlet and outlet tubes may be drilled at this time, but the notches should not be cut until the frame has been installed on the roof. The openings in the framing for the site

fabricated tube fin extrusion type panels are shown in Figure 10-25. The solar heating collector is made up of five groups, or bays. Each bay contains four panels. The bays should be spaced approximately 2 feet apart and 2 feet from the edge of the house roof to provide accessibility to each bay during installation and

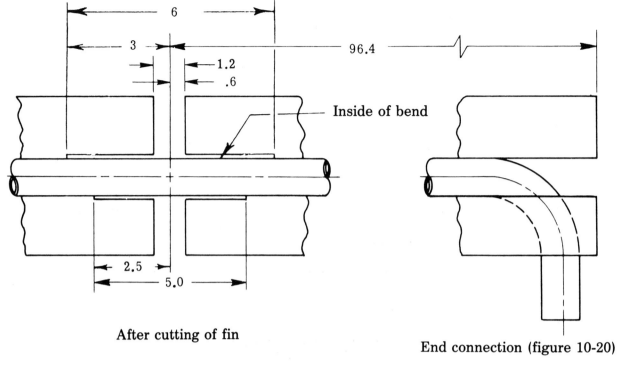

After cutting of fin

Inside of bend

End connection (figure 10-20)

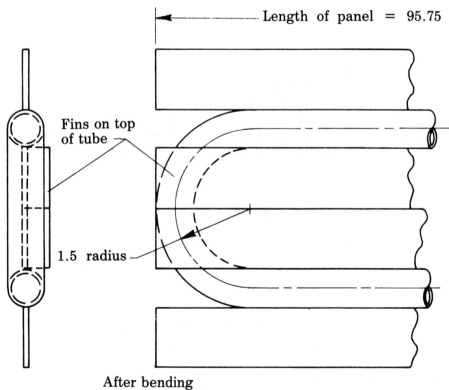

Length of panel = 95.75

Fins on top of tube

1.5 radius

After bending

Typical 180° return bend
Figure 10-21

later when maintenance is required.

The frames should be made up on a flat surface such as a patio or garage floor. The framing for the solar collector should be nailed together by using sixteen-penny nails. A typical plan view of a completed frame for one bay of the solar collector is shown in Figure 10-24. For durability and to meet some local building codes, the 2 by 4's should be treated lumber.

The panel size can be changed as long as all

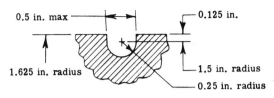

0.5 in. max — 0.125 in.

1.625 in. radius — 1.5 in. radius

0.25 in. radius

Groove details

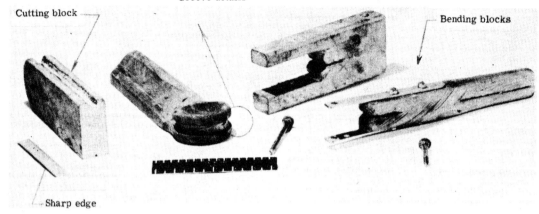

Cutting block

Bending blocks

Sharp edge

Cutting block and bending tool
Figure 10-22

Cutting block and assembled bending tool
Figure 10-23

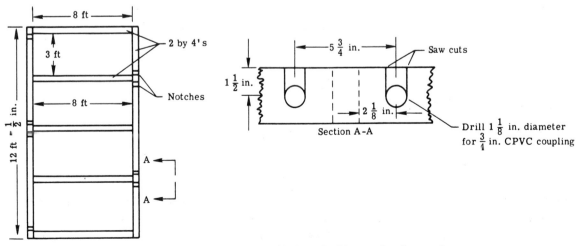

8 ft

3 ft

2 by 4's

8 ft

Notches

$12 ft \pm \frac{1}{2}$ in.

A

A

$5\frac{3}{4}$ in.

Saw cuts

$1\frac{1}{2}$ in.

$2\frac{1}{8}$ in.

Section A-A

Drill $1\frac{1}{8}$ in. diameter
for $\frac{3}{4}$ in. CPVC coupling

Typical bay for off-the-shelf standard panel
Figure 10-24

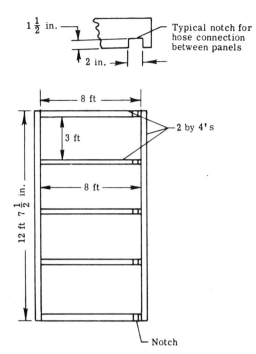

1½ in.

Typical notch for hose connection between panels

2 in.

8 ft

2 by 4's

3 ft

8 ft

12 ft 7½ in.

Notch

Typical bay for a site fabricated panel
Figure 10-25

panels are the same size, but is not recommended because it will increase the cost of having the panels fabricated. Of course, the number of panels per bay can be changed to make it easier to install the hot-water distribution system described later in this chapter. The bottom end of the bay should not come down too close to the intersection of the roof and the eaves. Enough space must be allowed to install the hot-water piping. (See Figure 10-26.) This space will be

largely determined by the pitch and size of the roof as well as the style of the house.

After the solar collector panel framing for each bay has been nailed together, the location on the roof should be properly laid out by measuring equal distances from the crown of the roof. As each bay frame is moved into position it should be secured in accordance with local building codes. The frame should be slant nailed on both the inside and outside periphery at intervals not greater than 1½ feet with ten-penny nails. See Figure 10-27.

Cut notches by making two saw cuts 1½ inches deep at layout marks as shown in Figure 10-24, and by tapping the 2 by 4 near the bottom of and between the saw cuts with a hammer. Usually, this procedure will cause the wood between the saw cuts to split away from the 2 by 4 neatly at the bottom of the two cuts; thus, a rectangular notch is formed. The blocks removed in forming the notches should be saved and given a number corresponding to each notch. The blocks are to be used for support of the battens that are installed later.

Prior to further installation, cut the insulation to fit inside the frame, paint the panels with one coat of zinc chromate primer and two coats of flat black enamel, and cut the polyvinyl fluoride cover for one bay.

Flashing

Aluminum roof flashing should be installed around the outer edge of the collector frame bay, except at the notches for inlet and outlet tubing of the solar panels, prior to installation of insulation, panels, and polyvinyl fluoride cover. The notches should not be covered with flashing

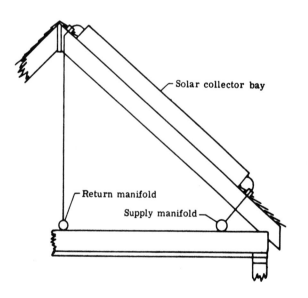

Solar collector bay

Return manifold

Supply manifold

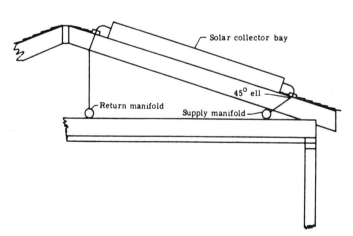

Solar collector bay

45° ell

Return manifold

Supply manifold

Piping for roof
Figure 10-26

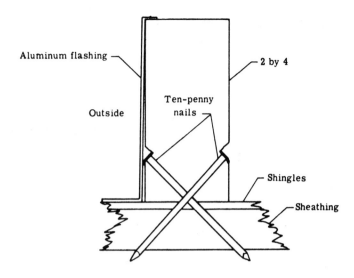

Cross section of collector bay frame member
Figure 10-27

until the insulation, solar panels, and polyvinyl fluoride covers have been installed. The flashing to seal the joint between the collector frame bay and the roof shingles should be installed starting at the bottom outside edge of each collector frame bay. Cut the flashing in pieces as long as practicable for bending. This will minimize the number of joints requiring sealing with the roof cement and the number of places for water to leak through.

The part of the flashing that covers the outer edge of the upper surface of the collector frame should be 1/2 to 5/8 inch wide, no more than 5/8 inch, because enough space must be allowed to staple the polyvinyl fluoride cover on. The flashing should be lapped to reduce the possibility of water getting inside the collector frame. From the bottom and each lower corner

of the collector bay frame, work horizontally to the center of the bay; then from each lower corner, work up the sides of the bay overlapping the flashing over each previously installed piece. Special corner pieces of flashing are shown in Figure 10-28. The last piece on the bottom edge of the collector frame should overlap the two previously installed pieces of flashing. On each side of the collector frame, work from the bottom of each side until the top edge of the frame is reached. At the top edge, the special corner pieces of flashing are installed before the top piece. (See Figure 10-29.) The remaining flashing is installed on the top edge of the collector frame in a manner similar to the way the flashing was installed on the bottom edge of the collector frame. This flashing, at the top edge of the collector frame, should be slipped under the shingles above it. After the roof flashing has been installed, all edges and lap joints should be covered with roofing cement spread with a putty knife.

Completing The Roof Insulation

The thermistor to monitor the temperature of the solar panels should be attached to the back of one of the upper panels of the collector bay as shown in Figures 10-30 and 10-31. For additional details on the thermistors, see Table 10-16. Drill a small hole, 1/8 to 1/4 inch, through the roof inside an upper panel receptacle at a place close to where the thermistor will be after the solar panel has been installed, to allow the wires from the thermistor to go through the roof.

The insulation, panels, and polyvinyl fluoride cover should be installed in warm dry

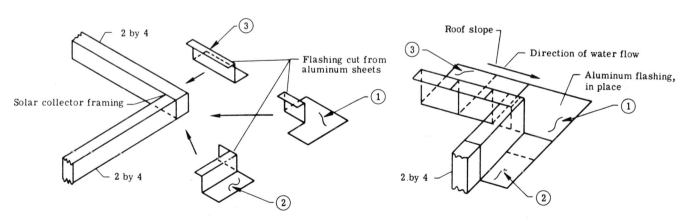

Bottom corner of flashing. Install in order of
numbers shown in circles
Figure 10-28

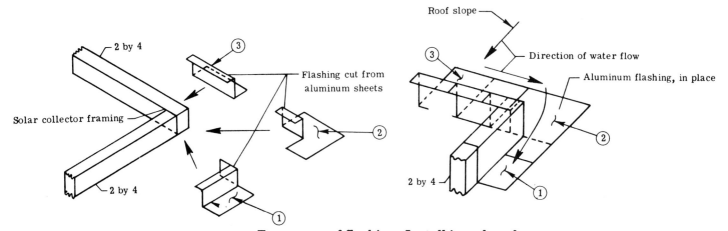

**Top corner of flashing. Install in order of
numbers shown in circles
Figure 10-29**

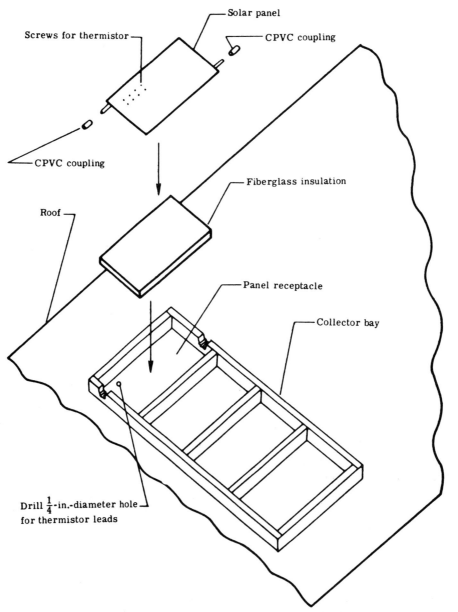

**Exploded view of solar collector bay
Figure 10-30**

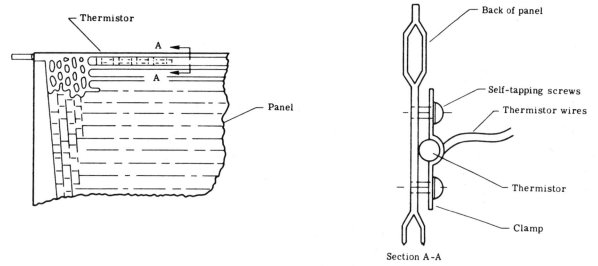

Thermistor installation
Figure 10-31

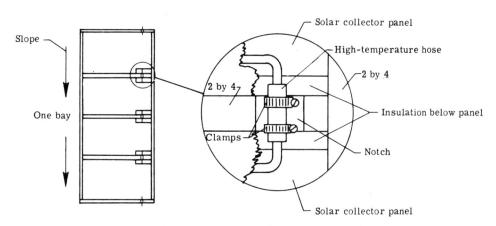

Typical connection between site
fabricated panels
Figure 10-32

weather because the insulation must not get wet. The polyvinyl fluoride film should be installed when air temperature is at least 70°. This film will sag in warm temperatures if installed when air temperatures are low. First, the 1.5-inch-thick fiberglass insulation is placed inside each panel receptacle on top of the shingles; then the solar collector panels are placed on top of the insulation, seating the inlet and outlet tubing in the cylindrical groove, as shown in Figure 10-32 and 10-33, depending on the panel used. Lift the solar panel to which the thermistor is attached at the upper edge and thread the wires from the thermistor down through the fiberglass insulation, through the hole that was drilled in the roof. The wires from this thermistor will be connected later to the differential temperature flow controller. Use two

of the CPVC plastic couplings described later in this chapter as thermal insulation to keep the inlet and outlet panel tubing from being in direct contact with the collector bay frame. They will need to be reamed as there is a small shoulder inside in the middle of the coupling. Slip the coupling on the panel tubing as shown in Figure 10-30. The blocks that were removed earlier to form the notches in the collector bay frames are now put back into place and sealed with duct seal. The remaining flashing where the inlet and outlet tubing pass through the collector bay is installed and sealed with roofing cement. The panels in each bay are then connected together in series as shown in Figure 10-33 with high-temperature hose.

After all panels in the bay have been installed, the polyvinyl fluoride cover is installed

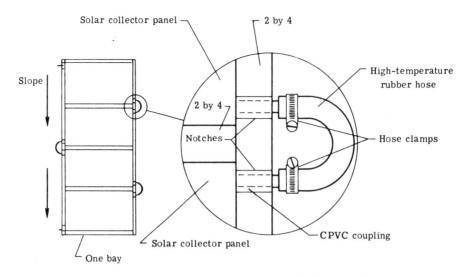

Typical connection between off-the-shelf
standard panels
Figure 10-33

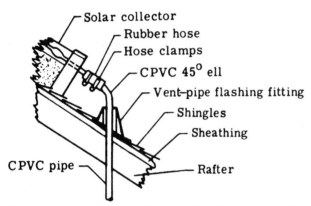

Typical connection at inlet and outlet of panels
Figure 10-34

in place. The plastic film should be stretched taut and stapled in place. Then the batten strips, ¼ inch by 2 inches, are nailed in place on top of the staples. This increases the holding surface

and prevents the plastic from tearing around the staples. This process is repeated until all the solar collector bays have been installed and sealed.

At each collector bay where inlet and outlet tubing exists from the bay and enters the roof, a vent-pipe flashing fitting will be required. A hole is cut in the roof with a hole saw and electric drill. To install vent-pipe flashing, lift the shingles on the upward side of the hole, slipping the flashing underneath as the vent-pipe flashing fitting is pushed through the hole. (See Figure 10-34 for details.) After the connections have been made, cover the connection with a water-tight boot. This boot should come down over the vent-pipe flashing. (See Figure 10-35.)

One or more of the uppermost exits from the collector bays must have vacuum breakers

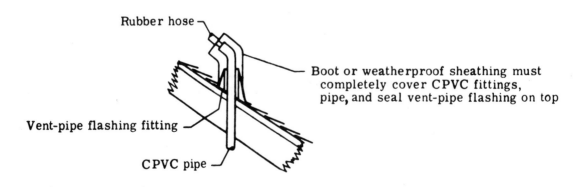

Weather covering installation
Figure 10-35

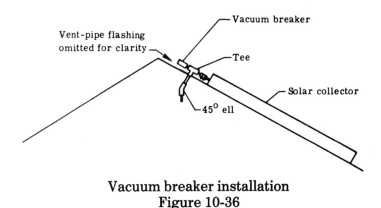

Vacuum breaker installation
Figure 10-36

installed in the highest point in the system for drainage. A vacuum breaker is shown installed in Figure 10-36. Remember the vacuum breakers must not be covered. Although the CPVC piping does not need insulation because it has a very low thermal conductivity coefficient, it must be shielded from long-term exposure to direct sunlight. A word of caution: Be sure that you are getting CPVC pipe and fittings, not PVC. Only CPVC will endure hot water at elevated pressures. CPVC piping has an ASTM (American Society for Testing Materials) rating of 100 pounds per square inch at 180°F. The plastic pipe and fittings should be marked with the ASTM designation D2846 to be genuine CPVC.

Storage Tank and Foundation

The storage tank may be installed either inside the garage or outside behind the house. You could use a foundation similar to the one shown in Figure 10-37 if you use a steel tank. The steel tank illustrated is approximately 4 feet in diameter and 10 feet 8 inches long.

A concrete storage tank (septic tank) above ground is recommended instead of a steel tank since it is less expensive and simpler to install. The concrete tank can be placed in the backyard similar to oil and gas tanks above ground. The size of a 1000-gallon tank is approximately 9 feet long, 5 feet wide, and 6 feet high. Contact your local septic tank subcontractor for information about what can be supplied for a water storage tank to be mounted on the ground. Some tanks are not recommended for use above ground because the sidewalls do not have sufficient strength to support the water in the tanks. Your local building inspector will know where the tank should be located in the yard and how the tank can be installed. Build the tank supports similar to that shown in Figure 10-38. Ask the tank supplier to place the tank on the supports when it is delivered. The storage tank must be installed so that the inlet to the pump is a minimum of 2 feet below the surface of the water level in the tank. A decorative fence may be placed around the tank.

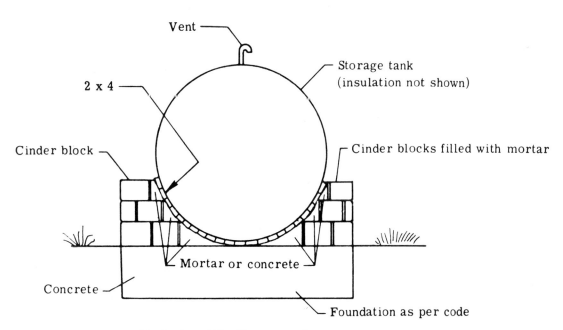

Typical saddle (2 required)
Outside foundation tank
Figure 10-37

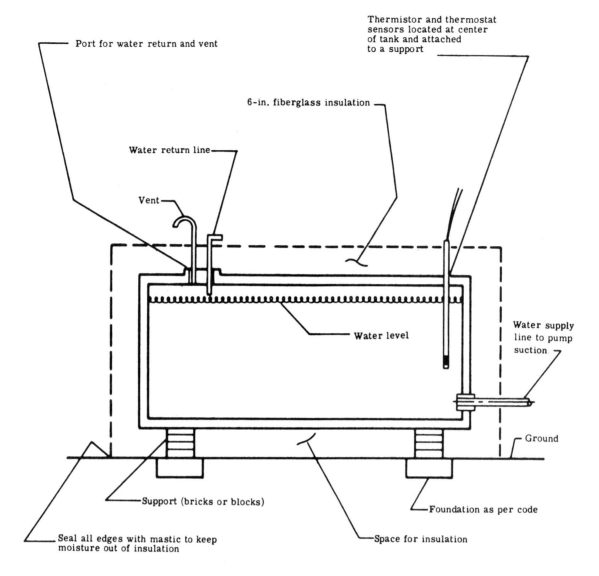

Port for water return and vent

Thermistor and thermostat
sensors located at center
of tank and attached
to a support

6-in. fiberglass insulation

Water return line

Vent

Water level

Water supply
line to pump
suction

Ground

Support (bricks or blocks)

Foundation as per code

Seal all edges with mastic to keep
moisture out of insulation

Space for insulation

Typical tank installation
Figure 10-38

Underground installation of concrete storage tanks may present the following difficulties:

(1) The thermal insulation will be more difficult to install and seal from moisture.

(2) The tank and pump installation will be more difficult. A hole must be dug for the tank, and the pump would have to be installed in a dry well.

(3) Maintenance or repairs would be more difficult.

(4) The cost of water storage may exceed the cost of the rest of the system.

Whether the storage tank is installed indoors or outside, it should be insulated with a low-thermal-conductivity type insulation, such as 6-inch-thick fiberglass. If the storage tank is installed outside, the insulation must be waterproofed with roofing cement or enclosed in a tool shed or other weatherproof shelter.

Air-Duct Modification

The water-to-air heat exchanger which is to be installed in the cold-air return of the homeowner's warm-air furnace should have a cross-sectional dimension similar to the cold-air return duct to minimize changes to the duct. The heat exchanger in the bill of materials (Table 10-15) is ideally suited for duct installation since the flow of air through the heat exchanger is only slightly obstructed. It is important that when purchasing the heat exchanger the pressure drop of the air through the heat exchanger be no more than 0.1 inch of water. The heat exchanger described provides good

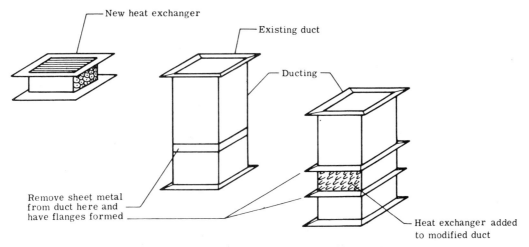

Details of duct modification and heat
exchanger installation
Figure 10-39

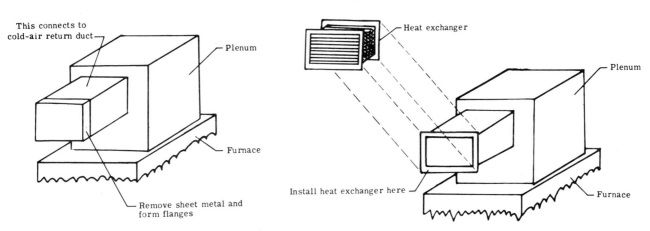

Modification of cold-air plenum for
installation of heat exchanger
Figure 10-40

performance at water temperatures available from solar collectors and air-duct flow velocities usually found in residential warm-air heating systems.

To install the heat exchanger, remove that part of the ducting where the heat exchanger is to be installed and take it to a sheet-metal shop or air-conditioning service company. They can cut the duct into two pieces and form the flanges so that the heat exchanger can be installed between the two pieces as shown in Figure 10-39. If the heat exchanger can be located next to an existing flange joint in the cold-air return duct, then only the end of a piece of ducting will need to be shortened and flanged as shown in Figure 10-40 to match the flanges of the heat exchanger. Drill the holes in the duct flanges before reinstalling the duct. Drill holes in duct

flanges to match the existing holes in the heat exchanger. Using sheet metal duct flange gasket material, a soft rubber stripping, make up the flange or flanges of the ducting and install the screws.

The Heat Exchanger

After the ducting has been reinstalled, the heat exchanger is ready to be installed. Place the heat exchanger into the opening in the cold-air return duct, matching up the screw holes in the flanges. Insert the rubber gasket materials and install the screws. Self-tapping screws are suitable for connecting duct flanges, but nuts and bolts may be required to connect the duct ends to the heat exchanger flange which is usually a thicker metal and predrilled.

If the heat exchanger cannot be installed

131

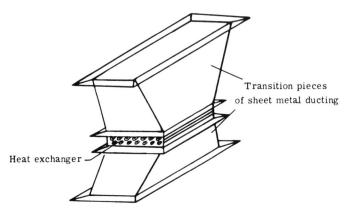

Heat exchanger

Transition pieces
of sheet metal ducting

Modification to duct where transition
section is required
Figure 10-41

adjacent to the cold-air plenum of the furnace, then that part of the duct adjacent to the plenum should be made as short as practicable, to prevent sagging of the duct. (See Figure 10-39.) This part of the ducting supports the weight of the heat exchanger.

If a heat exchanger cannot be obtained to fit the cross-sectional shape of the cold-air return duct, two transition pieces similar to those shown in Figure 10-41 will be needed. These transition pieces can also be made by a sheet metal shop. Installation of the heat exchanger by using transition pieces of ducting will be similar to the method just described. The cost will be somewhat higher because of the transition pieces needed.

The following procedure was used to select the heat exchanger for a 1500 square foot house with about 500 square feet of collector area. The water flow rate from the collectors and into the heat exchanger is about 0.8 gallon per minute for each 100 square foot of collector area or 4.0 gallons per minute for 500 square feet. A 1500 square foot house would typically have a furnace with an output of about 80,000 BTU per hour. The lowest reasonable water temperature for transferring usable quantities of heat to the air in the duct is about 105°F for any size collector system. It is desirable to be able to transfer at least 20,000 BTU per hour, one-fourth of the furnace output, of heat to the air which flows through the duct at about 900 cubic feet per minute. If the following information is given to an experienced heating and air-conditioning contractor, he can select a heat exchanger for you:

(1) Water flow rate of 4.0 gallons per minute
(2) Water inlet temperature of 105°F

(3) Air inlet temperature of 70°F
(4) Air outlet temperature of 90°F
(5) Heat to be transferred, 20,000 BTU per hour
(6) Air friction pressure drop across the heat exchanger to be no more than 0.1 inch of water

This information was used to size the heat exchanger for the system described. A similar procedure can be used for other size systems. For example, a 2,100 square foot home would require 700 square feet of collector area and would have a furnace output of about 110,000 BTU per hour. Again it is desirable to transfer at least one-fourth of the furnace output, 27,500 BTU per hour, to the air flowing through the duct at about 1,330 cubic feet per minute. In this case, the information to give to the heat exchanger supplier would be :

(1) Water flow rate of 5.6 gallons per minute (0.8 x 700/100 S.F.)
(2) Water inlet temperature of 105°F (same for any size system)
(3) Air inlet temperature of 70°F (same for any size system)
(4) Air outlet temperature of 90°F (same for any size system)
(5) Heat to be transferred, 27,500 BTU per hour (one-fourth) of 110,000 BTU per hour furnace output)
(6) Air friction pressure drop across the heat exchanger to be no more than 0.1 inch of water

The BTU output rating of the furnace is given on the metal nameplate attached to the furnace. The capability of the existing fan can also be found on the nameplate. This information should be given to the supplier of the heat exchanger since the heat exchanger will produce additional resistance to the airflow.

The Hot Water Distribution System

This system consists of check valves, electrically operated three-way valves (actuated by a differential temperature flow controller and a thermostatic electric switch), CPVC pipe, tees, ells, and couplings, vacuum breaker, hot-water storage tank, hot-water pump, and heat exchanger. Figure 10-42 shows a cap on the three-way valve. This valve serves as a drain valve. It is energized in the closed position when the other three-way valve is energized. The hot-water distribution system should be laid out as shown in Figure 10-42 with a slope of not less than 0.25 inch per foot. Horizontal piping must

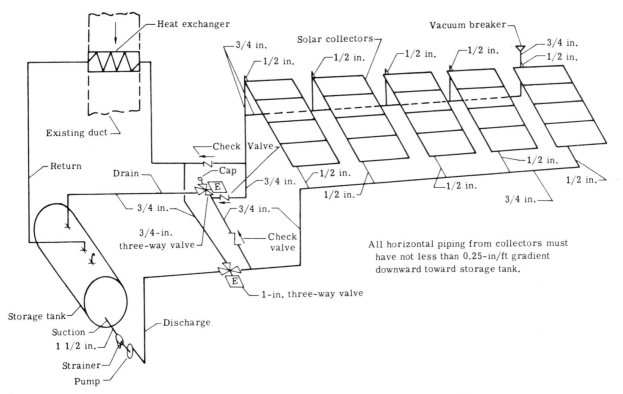

Schematic of hot-water distribution system. All
dimensions are nominal pipe sizes
Figure 10-42

slope so the solar panels can drain automatically
in case of a power failure.

Pipe Adapters

Plastic pipe to metal tube adapters are
soldered to the two three-way valves (Figure
10-43(a)). The pump is a high-temperature
positive displacement pump with an internal
relief valve which should be set at 50 pounds per
square inch. This pump should be installed in
the lowest elevation of the suction line as shown
in Figure 10-42. The heat exchanger will require
two threaded ferrule-type transition fittings, as
shown in Figure 10-43(b), to make the
connection from the copper tube of the heat
exchanger to the CPVC piping. The pump
suction strainer fitting shown in Figure 10-42
should be fitted with a 100-mesh-size stainless-
steel screen.

Assembly of the Pipe and Fitting

Storage and handling. - CPVC pipe, tubing,
and fittings should be stored indoors to avoid
unnecessary dirt accummulation and long-term
exposure to sunlight. Pipe and tubing should be
stored flat on continuous supports in straight
bundles. Avoid unnecessary abuse such as

crushing or abrasion on concrete.

Thermal expansion. - CPVC pipe has a linear
thermal expansion rate of approximately ½ inch
per 100°F. temperature change for each 10 feet
of pipe. The pipe should not be clamped rigidly
but rather supported by broad, smooth hangers
which will allow the pipe to move. The hangers
should be spaced not more than 3 feet apart.

Installation temperatures. - Solvent cement-
ing should not be attempted at temperatures
below 40°F., unless temporary heat can be
supplied, nor at temperatures above 110°F.

Cutting. - Pipe and tubing may be cut to
length with tubing cutters. Tubing cutters with
thin cutting wheels designed specifically for
plastic are recommended. When tubing cutters
are not available, a saw and miter box may be
used. Burrs and ridges caused by handling or
cutting must be filed off before assembling a
joint.

Solvent cleaning. - Cyclohexanone, 2-buta-
none, acetone, or a CPVC cleaner should be
used for cleaning the plastic pipe and fittings.
THF (tetrahydrofuran) should not be used for
cleaning CPVC piping and fittings.

Interference fit. - Components manufactured
according to ASTM D2846 will provide an

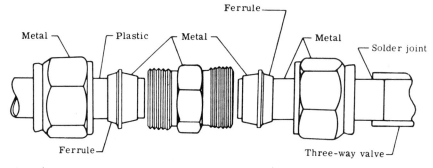

(a) Plastic pipe to metal tube.

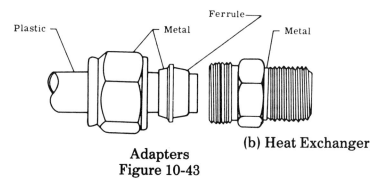

(b) Heat Exchanger

Adapters
Figure 10-43

"interference fit" between socket-type fittings and the plastic piping. Before making up a cemented joint, it is best to check for a dry interference fit. A good interference fit exists when the pipe or tubing makes contact with the fitting socket wall between one-third and two-thirds of the way into the socket.

Step-by-step assembly. - Correct assembly consists of the following steps:

(1) Cut the pipe square
(2) Remove burrs
(3) Check for interference fit
(4) Clean both pipe ends and fitting socket with a recommended CPVC cleaner or by light sanding, or both
(5) Apply a liberal coat of CPVC solvent cement to the pipe and apply a light coat of cement to the fitting socket
(6) Assemble immediately by bottoming the pipe in the socket and rotating a quarter of a turn as the joint is assembled
(7) Remove excess cement from the joint

If a joint has been properly made up, a small bead of cement will always appear at the juncture between the pipe or tubing and the fitting. Cement that becomes stringy or lumpy should not be used.

Plastic-to-metal transitions. - Union and compression type transition fittings are likely to include ferrules or O-rings which form an essential part of the assembly and should not be omitted. Plastic sockets to male threaded adapters should be installed with a recommended thread sealant, such as Teflon tape.

Pressure testing. - Refer to the cement manufacturer's recommendation on the can for joint curing time. The rate of cure depends on the cement formula, size of the joint, the air temperature, and the humidity. Generally, a solvent cemented CPVC system is ready for pressure testing with cold water after 16 hours at air temperatures above 60°F. Use the cold-water supply to check the system for leaks. Pressure should not exceed 100 pounds per square inch. The system should be kept pressurized for approximately 8 hours with several checks being made during the 8-hour period for joint leaks.

Repairs. - If a leak is discovered, that portion of the system should be drained and the joint and fittings should be cut out. The pipe should be dried and a new fitting installed using couplings and short lengths of pipe.

Soldering in the area. - No plastic-to-metal solder joints are required. However, if any soldering is performed on a metal joint, it should not be made any closer than 18 inches to an installed plastic-to-metal adapter in the same water line.

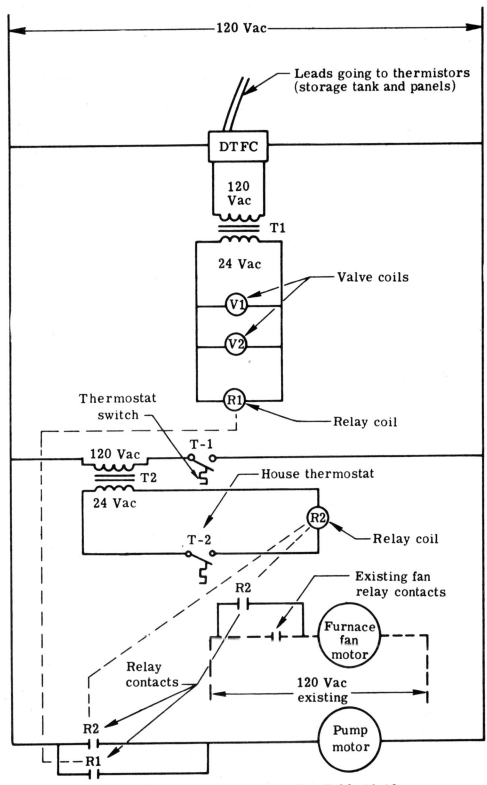

Electrical power schematic. (See Table 10-16
for description of components)
Figure 10-44

Electrical Work

Operation of the water pump and furnace fan motor are controlled by the components listed in Table 10-16. The differential temperature flow controller (DTFC) turns the water pump on when solar energy can be collected and off when solar energy cannot be collected. The component locations indicated by the component symbols are shown on the electrical power schematic (Figure 10-44). The name and type of each component are listed in Table 10-16 with the manufacturers of the components.

The electrical circuit shown in Figure 10-44 is designed to operate the water pump and furnace fan motor only when necessary and when certain temperature conditions are met. Electrical power will be supplied only to the water pump on sunny days when the home does not require heat. Electrical power will be supplied to both the water pump and the furnace fan motor on sunny days when the house requires heat. The fan motor will cut off when the house is heated to the desired temperature. The water pump will continue to run as long as heat is being collected. The control valves (V1 and V2 are the three-way valves listed in Table 10-15) are energized on sunny days so that water is directed through the collector and then through the heat exchanger as the water returns to the storage tank. However, on cloudy days or at night, electrical power is supplied to the pump and fan motor only when the house thermostat T-2 calls for heat. The valves which are de-energized for this operation allow the water to flow directly to the heat exchanger without going to the collector.

The differential temperature flow controller allows the entire system to be completely automatic. The controller compares the temperature of the storage tank to the temperature of the solar panels to determine if the system is collecting energy or losing energy to the atmosphere. The controller turns off the pump motor when the panel temperature drops to 5°F. above the storage tank temperature and automatically drains water out of the panels. The DTFC uses two thermistors as its primary sensing elements. One thermistor is attached to the underside of the panel at the water outlet of one of the bays and the other thermistor is located in the storage tank. The pump motor will start operating again when the panel temperature is 10°F. above the storage tank temperature.

The electrical power schematic shows the two circuitry conditions under which electrical power is supplied to the water pump motor to circulate water to the solar panel on sunny days or to the heat exchanger at night or on cloudy days. The first circuit shown at the top part of Figure 10-44 includes a transformer T1 which

provides 24 volts to the three-way valves V1 and V2 and to a relay R1. The contacts of this relay will close the circuit to supply power to the water pump motor for circulating water through the solar panel. The signal for this operation is controlled by the differential temperature flow controller which is available from several suppliers.

The other circuit shown in the center of Figure 10-44 includes a transformer T2, two thermostat switches and a relay. Two conditions must be satisfied before power can be supplied to the water pump and fan motor. First, the storage tank temperature must be 75°F. or higher to close the thermostat switch T-1. Second, the house solar thermostat T-2 must call for heat to be supplied to the house. If these two conditions are satisfied, relay R2 will close to supply electrical power to the water pump and fan motor. The water flows to the heat exchanger and then back to the storage tank as long as these two conditions are satisfied. The relay opens, when the conditions are not satisfied, to shut off electrical power to the water pump and fan motor. The solar thermostat should be set approximately 5°F. above the existing house thermostat so that the existing furnace does not cut on until the heat in the storage tank is used. When this heat is used, the house temperature will drop and be maintained by the existing furnace. Relay R-2 is connected parallel to the existing relay on the furnace fan.

The connecting wiring between each component should be sized as required by the component manufacturer and by the local electrical inspector. Sketches which show components, distance between components, size of connecting wire, and method of installation will help get the electrical inspector's approval.

Buying Parts or the Whole System

The solar heating industry is still in its infancy and is sure to develop rapidly during the 1980's. Solar collectors may one day be available through building supply dealers and hardware stores. Eventually the industry will be dominated by a few large producers with smaller producers handling specific applications and geographic areas. But today there are many small manufacturers selling through a limited number of dealers or direct to installers. If you can't locate the materials you need or get the technical assistance you would like to have, you should buy one of several catalogs which list manufacturers, products and applications. At least seven directories of solar energy manufacturers were available in the Fall of 1977. Most of the directories are revised periodically. Prices range from a few dollars to about $20.

Solar Industry Index
1001 Connecticut Avenue, NW
Washington, DC 20036

Directory of the Solar Industry
Solar Data
13 Evergreen Road
Hampton, NH 03842

Solar Energy Directory
Centerline Corporation
405 S. 36th Street
Phoenix, AZ 85034

Solar Directory
Home Free
4924 Greenville Avenue
Dallas, TX 75206

Sun Catalog
Solar Usage Now
450 E. Tiffin Street
Bascom, OH 44809

Information Directory of the Organizations and People Involved in the Solar Heating of Buildings
W. A. Shurcliff
19 Appleton Street
Cambridge, MA 02138

Solar Directory
Ann Arbor Science Publishers, Inc.
Ann Arbor, MI 48106

Many companies that sell collectors offer complete engineered domestic hot water, pool heating or space heating systems in a packaged unit that make buying and installation easier. Most manufacturers will provide technical assistance in designing a system to meet the requirements of a particular application. Often installation instructions are included with packaged heating systems.

Options in the Solar Energy Field for Builders
To enter the solar energy field as an active participant, one can choose from several options. At the current time, the most logical choice involves the growing market for solar space heating and hot water. To begin, one can select either products or services, or a combination of both. One can also select from several application areas, such as residential or agricultural processes; and from one of two modes--new construction or retrofit construction; or again, both.

Many types of businesses can follow one or several opportunities available. For example, using existing capital equipment, a vending machine company in Connecticut has become a major manufacturer of solar collector panels for an air-type system. On a smaller scale, home improvement contractors offer a solar energy package on jobs involving add-on rooms. In another case, a swimming pool installation company has added solar pool heating plus domestic heat and hot water systems to its existing business with little difficulty. Many such possibilities exist for involving already established businesses in the solar field. As the field advances further in the next few years, other opportunities will be created which can support entirely new companies.

The following sections will outline some of the basic steps involved with establishing a solar energy business. Our discussion of the various options for entering the solar field will begin with the dealer/installer, the backbone of the solar heating and cooling industry.

Discussion
Evaluating your local market potential will be one of the most valuable steps in the process of establishing a solar energy business. Few analysts doubt that a billion dollar solar energy industry will exist in the early 1980's. For a local entrepreneur, however, timing is the critical element. A proper analysis of market conditions will help indicate when a solar business in a particular area has a better chance of success.

One of the elements contributing most to timing will be cost of existing sources of energy used for heating and cooling. Adoption of solar energy in the residential field will be a function of its relative economic cost. As the market unfolds, such factors as acceptance, reliability, appearance, will have decreasing weight. Another factor determining timing is regional climatic conditions. The number of solar heating panels (and consequently the cost) necessary to economically heat a structure depends most on the weather. Thus, in certain regions, the larger sized system represents a greater first-cost investment, which can delay sales until fuel prices escalate even higher.

Initiates to solar energy use are surprised to find that solar heating systems are sometimes more economical in cold northern U.S. areas than in the south. A longer heating season in the northern U.S. lets the solar equipment be used for several more weeks or months, which means it saves more energy and pays for itself in a shorter period of time. Furthermore, the cost of conventional energy sources is frequently higher in the North than in the South. Thus, solar heating may actually be catching on more rapidly in states like Colorado than in some southern states.

To assess the competition in any particular locale, one should check the Yellow Pages to see how many companies are listed under "Solar..."-then find out what products and services they offer. One can also call the National Solar Heating and Cooling Information Center to locate solar companies and solar buildings in one's vicinity. What the local competition has or has not done will be vital information. How they are doing it is just as important.

One should also check for availability of local and state tax breaks or low-cost loans which serve as incentives. Some states will give consumers of solar energy equipment a tax rebate, or exempt solar energy systems from sales and property taxes. Tax incentives to cut initial costs of solar equipment can be a powerful selling tool since they dramatically improve the conditions determining payback on solar investment for home owners. Another determinant of potential solar sales is the degree of disposable (surplus) income available to individuals in the economic community. Consumers with discretionary income are responsible for most residential solar energy sales thus far. Another group buying solar energy for heating are individuals concerned about the environment, who have usually selected a simpler life style. The market hasn't reached a point yet where many consumers will buy because solar saves them money. Thus, in the near term, a dealer's sales will depend on how much discretionary income is available and how great an understanding of energy consid-

erations exist.

To augment this market research and determine when solar energy will become competitive on its own economic merits, one should also determine what energy sources are being used for heating, hot water and cooling, and how much the energy and equipment costs. One may even find some energy sources such as natural gas no longer available. This prepares the potential dealer to discuss life-cycle costs of existing energy alternatives. This discussion will become important when selling solar energy equipment. For example, solar hot water heaters are generally competitive against electric resistance hot water heaters. And in many metropolitan areas where the cost of electricity (including taxes and surcharges) exceeds 5 cents per kilowatt hour (KWH) the solar heater's competitive position increases dramatically.

In the commercial and industrial area some of the same formulae apply. Many states are facing serious natural gas curtailments. Commercial and industrial enterprises are the first to be cut off. When they begin searching for energy alternatives, in some instances solar energy applications will be feasible. Thus, for any local area, data on energy use and cost should be gathered and analyzed. It will be available in many forms, and such a data base will be a valuable indicator of where and when solar energy applications will fit.

We have just touched on the more important elements of local market evaluation. Other points will come up as the research progresses, and turns up additional questions and information.

In review, a solar market research plan involves finding out about presently used energy sources and their cost and availability over the long term; weather data; types of existing construction and future construction market forecasts; general public attitudes and awareness about energy problems; and existing solar energy companies and resources located or available locally. Such a survey must be conducted carefully, since an accurate assessment of local market potential can save a new company many lean months by recommending a waiting period of months or years, or may identify a market ready to be tapped. Waiting should not be too serious a drawback in many cases because the present condition of the existing solar energy market and the scale of its future growth could still give entrants some ample opportunities for successful businesses.

Locate Equipment

The next step is to locate manufacturers, distributors or wholesalers of solar energy equipment. Start with local firms (if any exist) so they may be visited. But do not neglect distant firms, because they may be seeking outlets across the U.S. as part of a national marketing plan.

Finding sources of solar equipment can be easy. Remember it is a buyer's market at the present time. Consequently, any issue of a solar magazine carries advertisements soliciting dealers. One need only circle a reader inquiry card, and a package of material will arrive. Such ads also appear in local newspapers and in many heating and plumbing periodicals.

There is a large number of manufacturers to choose from. One hundred and fifty manufacturers of solar collectors are listed in several surveys of collector manufacturing. Some are multimillion dollar companies like Grumman Aerospace, Inc. Others are small firms which may have grown from a garage experimenter's ideas to make a better system. You must be careful, however, as a number of small companies come into the field with such an idea and do not last very long.

Decide What to Do, What To Carry

Deciding what to do in order to actually start a dealership can be as simple as arbitrarily choosing one solar company's package, inventorying all the components and beginning to sell. Or, one can be more selective, choose components from many different manufacturers, and assemble a custom package.

Either choice is less frightening if one can add the solar equipment line to an existing business. Not many solar manufacturing companies generate enough income now to be able to rely solely on solar sales as their sole source of revenue. This situation is especially true for the lowest echelon in the solar field, which is selling to the public. Yet, in some parts of the U.S. where the market is somewhat more developed, the picture is already much brighter.

One way to begin as a dealer is to start with an established manufacturer's system. Offer the whole package. It will be comforting to some degree to select a manufacturer with several years experience, and a documented track record. An easy way to judge a firm's record is to look for a number of federally-funded residential or commercial solar energy systems a manufacturer has participated in. But, do not eliminate a firm just because it has not gotten a HUD or ERDA demonstration grant. Receiving federal money usally requires spending your own first. Newer solar companies cannot afford, in some cases, to make the expenditure, but will have a perfectly good system. Nor should one be swayed because a manufacturer carries a well-known name, such as Grumman or Lennox. One of the most successful solar companies to date is called Solaron.

Once a package has been selected, use it as the core for building a business, department, or division. One will have to add support, a sales effort, service, and maintenance capability.

At the same time, continue to canvass other manufacturers until satisfied that the company selected initially is on the right track; that is, making improvements in its system to make it cost less, be more durable, and operate more efficiently. At some point in this process, you may discover a new innovation, such as a better and cheaper glazing or coating, that might give one manufacturer a potential lead over his competitors. Or, since solar collectors are really rather basic, you may find an inventor with a new design concept which could lead you, the new dealer, to begin considering a custom system.

Realistically, however, only when well established can you afford, perhaps, to take on an experimental or new product and add it to an existing line. Some analysts do not recommend that new entrants in a field select totally new equipment for sale, since an "established" solar company is probably offering a system that is less than four years old. In addition, the manufacturer you start with is likely to emulate new developments since the field is so new. Finally, increased experience with consumer demand, which is not yet completely understood regarding solar energy, should indicate what physical and psychological considerations will govern the market, and thereby affect selection of additional types of solar equipment.

An alternative to selecting one manufacturer's solar package is to select components from various manufacturers in order to fashion a "custom" system. Such a selection process is not easy. There are many choices between types of systems, air or hydronic, and types of collectors or parts, aluminum, copper, iron, flat plate, concentrating, tracking, selective coated, single, double, or triple glazed, glass, plastic or fiberglass covered to name a few variables.

The solar collector should be regarded as the heart of the system. Be sure the collector is made of high quality components, is designed properly and is put together with expert workmanship. Too often, people forget that a flat plate collector is basically an assembly of insulation, absorber plate (and tubing), transparent covers, seals, and fasteners, all held together in a frame or box. Bearing this in mind makes inspection easier. For example, make sure dissimilar metals are isolated from each other in liquid systems to avoid electrical galvanic reaction. Also, room for thermal expansion must be provided, or piping, plates and covers can be damaged. The entire collector should be air or liquid leak-proof, except for vents in certain designs. Collectors with coated absorber surfaces should have easily removable covers, since the surface may have to be retreated after a number of years. It is also helpful to have collector frames with adequate provision for mounting supports, and for attaching flashing to provide leak protection when they are integrated into or mounted on a roof.

Many analysts in the solar field have noted that quality collectors which meet existing standards, no matter who manufactures them, generally perform similarly. Such similar data on performance tends to create a premium on continually seeking the right combination of price, design, and durability in order to offer a "superior" collector that could subsequently lead the market. This means that once a buyer is satisfied with workmanship and guarantees offered by a solar company, selection of a collector may come down to comparing prices.

It is still too early to determine who or what will in fact give rise to a lead in the class of solar collector manufacturers. Given the number of alternative designs, several dozen firms may be solid leaders, each specializing in a certain type of system, or offering a particularly competitive combination of components that make them able to be a leader in some region of the U.S.

This competition, to quote one solar analyst,

"involves, mainly, petty detail. No new principles of physics are expected, or sought." Thus, anyone with a really innovative idea might be able to rearrange the rank ordering of solar collector manufacturers. And, such improvement could come from any direction since Federal funding for solar research and development has quadrupled in recent years. In addition, many firms are investing their own R & D capital.

This situation does have its drawbacks. The possibility of important new developments could tend to make some firms conservative about launching a new design. The "game" is so young that some may be tempted to wait, afraid of being outclassed by a competitor who waited a little longer and was able to shave off an edge somewhere. As a result, many new developments are held close-to-the-vest. Then, a lack of information makes it harder to select those firms and ideas that have a good chance of being a potential "winner."

To evaluate and select system components, compare performance statistics with documented performance of well-established companies' products. Most manufacturers offer graphs which indicate relative performance of collectors under identical conditions. Similar tests can be used as a guide, and test results in manufacturers' literature (which should be performed by an independent testing facility) can be carefully compared to determine if the equipment being considered performs up to general standards. Sophisticated evaluation must give due consideration to price, long-term durability, reliability, etc., as well as performance. When such comparisons are made, a better understanding of what a component actually offers will result.

Alternative designs other than flat plate collectors do exist and should be considered. For example, a California company is marketing a cylindrical collector for water heating which is made out of glass. The manufacturer claims that, based on the amount of money spent for the collectors, one receives more heat from this type than the more familiar flat plate collector. Without passing judgment on this claim, we offer it as an example of one of the comparative concepts just mentioned. The California company is asking for a performance comparison based on price and output, that is, in terms of dollars and heat units.

Although very valuable, such a comparison does have limitations. Some collectors are more expensive because they are designed to meet more rigorous operating requirements. For example, a design to attain a higher collection efficiency at outlet temperatures near 190° F. may make the resultant collector a poor performer at lower temperature ranges, and therefore, not really an economic bargain if it is being purchased to operate in the lower temperature range. By the same token, a plastic, unglazed swimming pool collector can have excellent dollar-per-BTU-delivered figures, for its application, but should not be expected to provide adequate temperatures for domestic hot water. In short, when a manufacturer speaks of BTU's to dollars, or lower cost per-square-foot-of collector, the listener has to know what the collector panel will be asked to do, and in what environment.

If after all this, you determine that two or more collectors perform similarly, and are of equal quality, price again is of major importance. The high initial cost for a solar heating system weighs heavily on the consumer. Generally, collector costs represent about fifty percent of the installed cost of a heating system, so a prospective dealer should carefully consider price, all else equal or nearly equal, when selecting from several candidates.

Selecting the Solar Manufacturer

Don't get carried away selecting equipment based on its performance and cost alone. The quality, stability, and "personality" of the solar manufacturer also counts for a great deal. You may choose a slightly more expensive design and be justified if the supplier will provide more follow-up support. Such help can be crucial for those new to the solar energy field, since they will have to rely on a supportive source of information in their initial learning period.

For this reason, some analysts suggest turning to a medium sized firm. Smaller companies operating on a shoestring may have a good product, but be incapable of providing the support a new dealer needs. On the other hand, large firms with a solar energy division may just be keeping their hand in; and the division, whose personnel realize a shakeout period exists, may be coasting and not providing the kind of support they could. Of course, certain advantages come with a well-established com-

pany name on a solar energy system; but quality in the solar field will not necessarily be determined by the company size.

Another danger might be selection of a firm with too popular a system. Delivery then becomes a problem, and the dealer will have nothing to sell. This can be avoided by getting an estimate of a manufacturer's existing back orders (some are reported to be $1.5 million behind; most wish they were) and capability of expanding production to meet demand.

Thus far, we have rapidly covered a lot of ground regarding selection of equipment. The reader should realize the material presented has concentrated on collectors and really only talked about very basic considerations. More help is readily available from many sources when the prospective dealer is ready to begin his own selection process. He should now know, however, what questions to ask.

Getting Information and Support

The first information a prospective dealer is likely to need is the names and addresses of solar manufacturers. These can be obtained from several sources. Some solar research companies put out their own solar directories. Several directories were listed earlier in this chapter.

Solar magazines and newsletters are also a valuable source of company names and addresses. Moreover, these periodicals feature new products and developments, which keeps their readers abreast of progress in the solar field and what others are doing.

Finding solar installations in one's own area is useful and can be fairly easy. A helpful guide to solar heated buildings is published by Dr. William Shurcliff, Cambridge, Massachusetts. In his 13th edition of Solar Heated Buildings: *A Brief Survey*, he describes over 300 solar heated buildings located in the U.S. and abroad. This handy book tells where, who, how, and what for each of the buildings. Similar guides are published by the Housing and Urban Development Administration, and sold by the U.S. Government Printing Office, Washington, D.C. 20402. However, these are limited to the residences and buildings which have received a HUD grant as part of the solar demonstration program.

Any of these guides can provide valuable information about owners, projects, equipment, manufacturers and installers located in one's geographical area.

Another way to obtain similar information is to write or call the National Solar Heating and Cooling Information Center, P.O. Box 1807, Rockville, Maryland 20850, or call, 800-523-2929. (In Pennsylvania call 800-462-4983).

Also of help in your own area are the Yellow Pages listings in the telephone directory. In major metropolitan areas one should easily find a dozen solar firms listed. Contact with them can be the beginning of your own survey.

An additional valuable source of information may be a local chapter of the American Section of the International Solar Energy Society. This Society is a non-profit association of solar researchers, educators, advocates, or those just interested in the field. Primarily, the ISES serves the scientific community. Many states have their own chapters and some areas have local chapters. Contact the American Section ISES at 301 State Road 400, Cape Canaveral, Florida 32920, for the address of a local ISES chapter. Attending meetings will introduce you to those actively involved in solar energy in your area and will provide a well-spring of information on solar energy.

Of additional value to businesses will be the activities of local chapters of the American Society of Heating, Refrigerating and Air Conditioning Engineers. ASHRAE publishes material on solar energy, and sponsors several workshops each year on energy. Local chapters have guest speakers at their meetings, and solar energy is a frequent topic. To locate a chapter contact ASHRAE, 345 East 47th Street, New York, NY 10017.

Finally, the Solar Energy Industries Association (1001 Connecticut Avenue, N.W. Suite 632, Washington, D.C. 20036) provides to its members association sources to support their businesses. The SEIA publishes market forecasts and its legislative proposals and a newsletter, organizes business conferences and seminars, and sponsors a solar magazine. As the solar energy market grows, it will be a still more valuable association.

Once You Have A Project

Once a dealership is established, first priority should be demonstration of your equipment. Sell a system to yourself, a friend or co-worker. If at all possible, get coverage in the local newspaper. The demonstration adds credibility to your company's efforts immediately. It will be important to notify the National Solar Heating and Cooling Information Center. They have been receiving up to 500 calls a day asking about solar energy. One should also notify the usual local business and trade associations, in order to get referrals. A Yellow Pages advertisement should generate a few calls each week.

Be careful that your solar business isn't a drag on your contracting business. The drawing power is there, but one can spend a great deal of time answering questions for the curious. If a display is set up, make an effort to provide answers to general questions with visual aids or handouts. These questions are generally: How does it work? How much does it cost to heat a house or heat water? Will it work here? How long does it take to install? By providing this information, time-consuming general questions will be avoided.

Write and ask the National Solar Heating and Cooling Information Center for as many copies of their pamphlet, *Solar Energy and Your Home* as you need. It is a small eight-page booklet which answers many of the questions mentioned above.

Preparation of material to support sales efforts should have high priority once products have been selected. Recalling information gained in your market survey, and using cost figures on the solar equipment chosen for the business, prepare a concise worksheet for potential customers. This sheet can show where the user will stand financially five, ten, fifteen and twenty years in the future if he invests or does not invest in a solar energy system. Insurance salesmen successfully employ this technique. Such a worksheet has the added advantage of helping organize the sellers thoughts and presentation. One could engage, if necessary, a solar consulting firm for professional help in preparation of such a document.

From the above, and earlier discussion, you can already see that much of your sales activity is going to involve educating the consumer. He or she should be well prepared for this role, especially if entering the solar market now.

Wholesaling Solar Equipment

For a potential wholesaler, evaluation of

local market potential should be the same as for a dealer. Energy sources and costs, plus status of the housing industry, plus number of families or businesses with disposable income are key elements. A feeling for the state of the HVAC and plumbing business will also be helpful. Sales will come slowly, if at all, if a wholesaler has to rely on consumers to make the plumbing and heating companies come looking for solar equipment. A potential wholesaler should begin cultivating local construction business people to have them suggesting solar to the consumers. In the early learning period, some crucial back-up work should be made available to the contractors so they feel at ease selling something new.

A wholesaler could also establish relations with home improvement contractors. In areas where families are buying older homes and improving or repairing them, fertile ground exists for the contractors to suggest incorporation of solar energy into the projects. Again, this represents an area which will require initiative on the part of the wholesaler since his customers are likely to have little, if any, experience with solar energy installations.

Selecting Manufacturers and Equipment

The wholesaler can fill the needs of many solar manufacturers for a sales medium. The manufacturer wants to avoid really grass-roots sales work. They have been faced with such work because not enough outlets exist to interface with consumers. Consequently, the manufacturer carries on a sales effort at more expense than he cares to bear. Thus, opportunity for wholesale operations appear fairly good. The problem will be one of volume.

A prospective wholesaler of solar equipment should have a clear picture of the national sales efforts and plans of the solar manufacturers being considered. Because sales are still low volume for many manufacturers, they often attempt to market nationally right from the beginning. Such outreach may not be sound, since several solar analysts feel solar collector and system manufacturing may actually be a regional business. Care should be taken to make sure a manufacturer's outreach can be supported, at the same time, representing a sound competitive position.

On the other hand, a wholesaler that can represent a distant manufacturer should be able to achieve an ideal position; particularly if the equipment or system being offered is sound.

Your local survey may also determine that certain types of equipment, air systems for example, are not well supplied regionally. In such cases, a wholesale operation emphasizing, but not limited to, a particular type of system could represent an attractive option.

A wholesale operation might also do well to concentrate on commercial solar installations. These projects can run from twenty thousand to a half million dollars or more in cost. Because manufacturers are anxious to increase their volume quickly, they frequently focus on large projects. Many design and engineering firms feel the same. A wholesale operation should be able to work equally as hard at developing commerical projects, and should be better prepared to handle them than dealers. Furthermore, wholesalers with close ties to manufacturing suppliers can be supported effectively by the solar manufacturer in concluding such deals. Ideally, a wholesaler should have a more thorough knowledge of a manufacturer's position with regard to back orders, supplies, capacity and cost situations than a dealer.

In the start-up period, a wholesaler may have to deal with potential customers who feel the wholesaler is too inexperienced to provide necessary answers regarding equipment. Such concern is natural because the field is new, and solar projects are regarded as "custom" jobs. In addition, more searching and researching is frequently justified in the minds of customers. (To halt this tendency, one has to be well prepared to provide specifications and performance data). A wholesaler may lose sales if not able to satisfy such psychological needs.

Wholesale operations can also be planned to deal with new equipment, processes, and designs that are not yet widely known or accepted, but which represent future potential. A most likely possibility could be solar concentrating collectors. They do not presently represent major sales, in volume terms. However, for solar cooling, or for high temperature applications associated with industrial processes, they fill a present need.

Northrup Inc. of Hutchins, Texas has had its fresnel lens concentrator used for federally funded solar cooling projects. Owens-Illinois also has a collector concept which can achieve higher temperatures needed to power an air-conditioning unit. Banks of evacuated glass tubes are the heart of this system. Another type of concentrator is under development and should be marketed soon. Invented by a University of Chicago physicist and tested by the Argonne National Laboratory, this collector uses compound parabolic mirrored surfaces to focus solar radiation on a narrow area. Externally, this collector resembles a flat-plate collector, but it is actually a concentrator. A wholesaler might choose to carry such specialized equipment, and be prepared to wait for necessary volume to increase.

Thus far, discussion of wholesaling has implied marketing solar manufacturers' goods to consumers. What about potential for the reverse, wholesaling to manufacturers of solar equipment? The prospects don't appear good, because just about everything that goes into a solar system is "on-the-shelf" equipment and components and are already part of a distribution system. However, such thinking can be carried further. Although young, the solar industry represents rapid potential growth. Such growth will create additional business for existing suppliers of conventional equipment and services. Many companies should consider keeping up on the needs of the solar industry. By making contacts now with manufacturers, they may be able to create a solid relationship for future sales.

Conclusion

Deciding to become a solar energy equipment wholesaler will require careful thought and investigation. Much will depend on an accurate assessment of the market. Still, one could discover, in the course of investigation, a manufacturer, or a market which presents a one-time opportunity to establish a company, or division in a company, to service an area needing help. But, by the same token, an opportunity may never appear to be completely obvious but still exist. Thorough research is the key. A prospective wholesaler should also concern himself with much more than collectors. Controls, tanks, air handling units, tracking devices, etc. can all offer opportunity for wholesale marketing. Again, careful investigation of these components as well as the potential market, is necessary.

Manufacturing

Becoming a manufacturer of solar energy equipment can be an easy as it may be unprofitable. This section is not going to fully outline procedures such as those outlined for a potential dealer because the process of becoming a manufacturer is too complex and depends on many subjective and objective conditions. No one should invest time and capital to become a manufacturer without full consideration of the factors involved.

Because becoming a solar system or collector "manufacturer" can be as easy as setting aside assembly tables in a sheet metal shop, many companies have entered the field. In 1974 it was estimated that 45 firms produced 1,243,736 square feet of solar collectors. (Six of these firms producing low temperature collectors for swimming pool heating accounted for 1,137,196 square feet of this production). By July 1976, the number of firms had grown to 156, with production in six months of 1976 at 2,273,170 square feet of collectors. Of these 156 companies, 14 firms produced 1,568,777 square feet of low temperature (swimming pool) collector panels.

Of the 142 firms producing medium temperature (suitable for water or space heating) or special collectors (concentrators or evacuated tube type) in early 1976, 70 companies were selling for the first time. Twenty two companies that had been operating in 1975 reported decreased production, while the remaining companies increased or maintained the same (2 companies) level of production.

Given that 100 firms produced medium temperature or special collectors in 1975, these figures indicate that 28 companies were no longer reporting manufacturing. In fact, 21 stopped manufacture of collectors; four were absorbed, losing their identity; two disappeared entirely, and one will not report its production. These figures show that a great deal of turbulence exists, and the solar industry is undergoing a shake-out period.

Part of the reason such turbulence can exist is the simple design requirements for flat plate collectors. This situation allows many new entrants who really risk very little if they already possess a "metal bending" capacity.

A success story which best illustrates this situation involves Solaron Corporation of Colorado. A leading designer and supplier of solar air-type systems, Solaron is also a manufacturer. To overcome transportation costs to the

Eastern U.S., Solaron has given a manufacturing contract for its collectors to Choice Vend, Inc., of Windsor Locks, Connecticut. In the September 1976 issue of *Solar Engineering Magazine*, Choice Vend was reported to be producing 500 collectors a month. *Solar Engineering* says that, "The collector has been adapted to mass production with the same equipment and dies used in refrigerated vending machines that are produced by Choice Vend. Jerome Nathan (Choice Vend vice president) said the plant has the capacity to produce six times its current volume with existing equipment."

This example illustrates an ideal situation. A well-established solar company with a competent design takes advantage of existing capital equipment and capacity to develop and market its system. The potential for many such arrangements exists, especially since many new designs are being introduced. However, the owner of the manufacturing capability will have to be cautious and secure in his own independent evaluation of the solar design offered for technical and economic validity. In addition, he should seek marketing expertise in the solar field to determine if this product has a chance to "fly." Many sheet metal contractors can make collectors, but not every one can make money doing it.

The example just described involved a metal-fabricating firm. Other types of firms have good potential for entering the solar market place with their existing capital equipment. For example, a patent holder of a solar swimming pool heating design searching for a company to produce his system feels a present manufacturer of plastic children's swimming pools would be an ideal type of company. Electronics firms are making specialized solar controls, pump manufacturers are offering "solar pumps", hot water heater companies are modifying existing products and offering them as solar tanks. There are many such areas in which existing manufacturing concerns can adapt existing products, or develop a new one using existing capability in order to enter the solar industry as a manufacturer. A short product or component list might be helpful.

- Metal extrusions
- Piping and tubing
- Glass and plastics
- Electronic controls
- Coatings and paints
- Insulation materials
- Storage tanks and containers
- Fasteners
- Sealants
- Sheet metal
- Antifreezes and thermal transfer fluids
- Storage chemical compounds
- Pumps
- Heat exchangers
- Valves, dampers, and vents

It is beyond the scope of this book to discuss creation of the manufacturing capability from absolute ground zero. At the present time, and with present technology, such a choice does not appear to offer solid chances for success except for specialized systems or components which will require new capital equipment and production techniques. In such areas as concentrating collectors, or in solar photoelectric cell production, such an option might appear to be realistic. However, given present development in the state of the art, use of existing techniques and capability probably offers the greatest chance of success.

In the next few years, many analysts predict rapid growth of the solar hot water heating business, followed by space heating. A shift could gradually occur from the present buyer's market to a more balanced position, and eventually a seller's market if and when a rapid expansion take-off occurs. In that event, more room for expanded capacity will exist, and opportunity for creating new solar manufacturing companies. One suspects, however, that many "new" manufacturers may select existing products and secure manufacturing licenses for them.

Throughout the market growth process, new ideas for solar component designs will develop, and in some cases, a new manufacturing facility will result. Few people will have the understanding and insight about the solar energy market and solar technology to know when an idea can support a new company. Those who do carry such knowledge, or acquire it, will avoid disaster and achieve success.

Insulation and Weatherstripping 11

The point has been made rather emphatically by now that insulation is the single most important contribution to the energywise house. Every home that has a heating system to protect it against cold or that is exposed to warm weather in the summer needs insulating, which is surely every home in existence or to be built in the U.S. If all homes in the U.S. were fully insulated, energy for residential heating would be reduced by approximately 42%. By adding 1 inch of insulation to a typical wall with 2½ inches of glass fiber insulation, conductive heat loss would be reduced by 21%.

Understanding Heat Loss

Heat always tends to flow from wherever the temperature is higher to wherever the temperature is lower. For example, put a pan of cold water on a hot stove and heat flows from the stove through the bottom of the pan into the water, heating it up to a higher temperature. Pan bottoms are, therefore, made of materials which *conduct* heat easily. To keep the pan from losing heat after it comes off the stove, we can stand it on an asbestos pad—a material which resists passage of heat, or provides insulation.

Heat escapes from a building primarily in two ways: by *conduction* and *infiltration*. Conduction loss is through the exterior surface of the building. See Figure 11-1. The rate of heat loss from the warm side to the cold side through the exterior surface depends upon the size of the surface, the length of time the heat flow occurs, the temperature difference between the two sides of the exposed area, and the construction of the section, that is the type of material used in the construction. All materials used in building construction reduce the flow of heat. Some materials are much better than others at reducing heat flow. The more effective materials are used as insulation.

Infiltration heat loss is the replacement of interior air with exterior air. Any building will constantly exchange air with its environment—outside air leaks in—inside air leaks out. A certain amount of this exchange (not more than one complete air change per hour) is necessary for ventilation. Most buildings have much more than is needed. In winter, the air that leaks in is cold; the air that leaks out is warm; fuel is consumed to supply this temperature difference.

This leakage or infiltration is caused by wind, the building acting as a chimney, and the opening of outside doors. The effect of door openings and wind needs little explanation; but the chimney effect may not be obvious. See Figure 11-2. When air in a building is warmer than the outside air, the entire building acts like a chimney—hot air tends to rise and leak out of cracks at the upper levels and suck cold air in through cracks at the lower levels. Both the temperature difference and building height contribute to this effect. A two story house with a 68°F. inside temperature and a 30°F. outside temperature will produce a "chimney" leakage equivalent to a ten mile per hour wind blowing against the building.

Insulation Means Quality

Home owners and buyers are becoming more and more aware of how important insulation is. A well insulated home can save about 40% of the cost of heating and cooling an

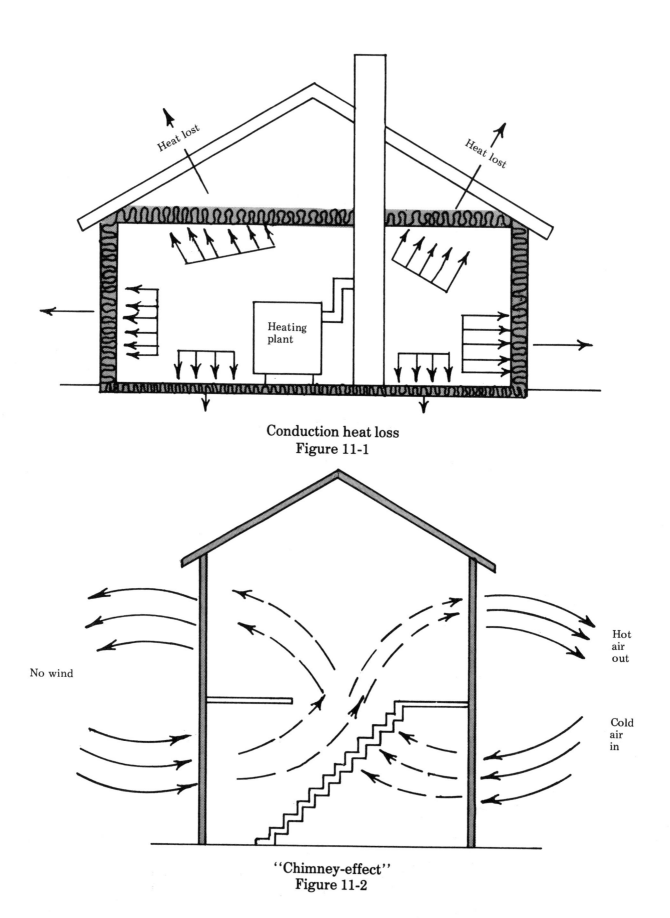

Conduction heat loss
Figure 11-1

''Chimney-effect''
Figure 11-2

uninsulated home. You know and most of your clients understand that no home is really first quality unless it is adequately insulated.

Insulation is, for the most part, invisible. It is placed in walls, ceilings, floors, and under roofing material. For your client to know that his builder has done a good job in providing this precious unseen asset is to be reassured that there has been incorporated one of the major bulwarks of quality building within the house. The thought cannot help occurring to your buyer that you have probably not skimped on other hidden but vital quality features if you have been fastidious in insulating the home.

The presence of insulation in outside walls can be detected by removing cover plates from telephone, TV, or electrical outlets in the walls and examining the surrounding wall cavities for signs of fiberglass, rockwool, or the other insulation products used. Another method of gaining this assurance in a room heated to sixty-eight degrees, with an outdoor temperature of fifty degrees, is to place a thermometer against the outside wall and see if the temperature is about sixty-five degrees. If it is much lower than that, the wall is probably not insulated.

Insulating New Construction

In the schedule of production, insulation is added after all rough plumbing and wiring of all kinds is complete. The roof should be finished, including the insulation that goes between the roof sheathing and the roofing material, which the roofer applies right along with the waterproofing membrane. The outside of the house should be wrapped with building paper so the insulation will not be damaged by wind or rain once it is in place.

The insulation contractor is often the same person who applies weatherstripping, which is scheduled very late in the construction program. This subcontractor will apply the specified insulating material at a firm figure of so much a square foot. It takes very little time to insulate a house, and labor costs do not go up with better quality material, so it pays to stick with the best. In small additions, or remodeling, the regular carpenter can install the insulation which is obtainable at the lumber yard or building materials store.

How Insulation is Rated

Many types and forms of materials are used in manufacturing building insulation. Also, there are many building materials which are mistakenly assumed by the uninformed to have much more insulation value than they really have.

Because of these variations and misunderstandings, it is unrealistic to compare insulating values of materials by thickness in inches. For example, many people are shocked when told that 1 inch of mineral wool insulation has more insulating value than an 18 inch masonry wall of common brick.

Fortunately, reliable standard rating methods have been developed to help you rate various insulations. Although the rating method is quite reliable, some of the terms used to explain it may be new and somewhat confusing.

Effectiveness of insulation is specified in two ways. One is stated as the resistance offered by a material or materials to the flow of heat under known conditions. This "Resistance" is generally designated by the letter "R". The second specification is stated as the amount of heat that will pass through a material or materials under known conditions. This is designated by the letters "C" or "U".

Most manufacturers of insulation have adopted the "R" rating and stamp it on their product for easy evaluation by the purchaser. For example, a 3 inch thick batt of one insulation might have an R10 rating, whereas a 3 inch batt of another type might have an R12 rating. On the other hand a 2 inch thick rigid foam material might have an R10 rating stamped on it. In all cases when you are given the "R" rating it is a simple matter to evaluate and make comparisons.

When you are building a wall containing several materials and have the "R" values for each, you can determine the total "R" value or insulating value by simply adding them directly. For example: R4 + R10 + R5 = R19 total. Table 11-3 gives the "R" value of many common building materials.

Another example of how the rating can be used is in determining values of various thicknesses of materials. If 2 inches of insulation "A" has a rating of R8 then 4 inches would have a rating of R16, for all practical purposes.

You cannot add the "C" or "U" values directly. When you can only find the "C" or the "U" rating you change them to "R" before adding. Simply stated the procedure is this: when you know the "C" or "U" value, you divide one (1) by this value to get "R". Example: a "C" or "U" value is .5, then "R" = 1 ÷ .5 = 2.

These simple rating designations also make

Material	Thickness	"R" Value
Air Film and Spaces		
Air space		
Bounded by ordinary mat.	¾" or more	0.91
Bounded by aluminum foil	¾" or more	2.17
Exterior surface resistance	---	0.17
Interior surface resistance	---	0.68
Masonry		
Sand and gravel conc. block	8"	1.11
Sand and gravel conc. block	12"	1.28
Lightweight concrete block	8"	2.00
Lightweight concrete block	12"	2.13
Face brick	4"	0.44
Concrete cast in place	8"	0.64
Building Materials		
Wood sheathing or subfloor	¾"	1.00
Fiber board insulating sheathing	¾"	2.10
Plywood	5/8"	0.79
Plywood	1/2"	0.63
Plywood	3/8"	0.47
Bevel lapped siding	½" x 8"	0.81
Bevel lapped siding	¾" x 10"	1.05
Vertical tongue & groove board	3/4"	1.00
Drop siding	3/4"	0.94
Asbestos board	1/4"	0.13
3/8" gypsum lath and 3/8" plaster	3/4"	0.42
Gypsum board	3/8"	0.32
Interior plywood panel	1/4"	0.31
Building paper	---	0.06
Vapor barrier	---	0.00
Wood shingles	---	0.87
Asphalt shingles	---	0.44
Linoleum	---	0.08
Carpet with fiber pad	---	2.08
Hardwood floor	---	0.71
Windows and Doors		
Single window	---	Approx 1.00
Double window	---	Approx 2.00
Exterior door	---	Approx 2.00

Insulation value of common materials
Table 11-3

it easy to compare costs of insulations. If one insulation rated R13 meets your job requirements and costs 10 cents per square foot, and another is identical in every way except cost, your choice is clear. Also, you can easily determine the amount of insulation required for a desired "R" value for any type of construction.

Some characteristics or features of insulation materials besides "R" values and cost could influence your choice of materials used for particular conditions. A few of these are:

1. Structural requirements, which must be considered when you want to use rigid insulation for such things as sheathing, plaster base, interior ceiling or wall finish, and roof decks.

2. Fire resistance of any insulating material should be considered regardless of where it is used in the house.

3. Effects of moisture on an insulation material sometimes determine whether or not it can be used for some jobs such as perimeter insulation under concrete slabs. When any insulation material becomes saturated, the insulating value decreases to practically nothing.

4. Vermin resistance is an important consideration, but you must make relative evaluations. No material is absolutely vermin proof.

Insulation Materials

Building insulation materials are developed specifically to reduce heat transfer. Insulation materials are generally very light in weight and are produced in five common forms. These are batts or blankets, loose fill, rigid boards, reflective, and foamed in place materials.

There are two types of blankets or batts: glass fiber and rock wool. The difference between the two materials is that rock wool is denser and has a slightly higher "R" value per unit of thickness than glass fiber (3.7 vs. 3.1 to 3.4). Normally the two materials can be used interchangeably, but there may be cases where the thickness of material that can fit in a space is limited, and a rock wool batt of a given "R" value will fit while a corresponding glass fiber batt will not.

Both types of batts and blankets are sold on the basis of their "R" value and both cost about the same for a given "R" value. Prices and availability of materials vary from locality to locality. Rock wool is relatively heavy and its shipping costs are high. Its prices vary with distance from the plants where it is manufactured. In some places it is not available at all. The prices of glass fiber batts conform to the prices of rock wool.

Insulation batts or blankets are usually encased in paper, one face of which is made to serve as a vapor barrier. This may be an asphalt paper or a paper with a reflective metal foil backing. Proper installation of this vapor barrier is very important. Chapter 12 covers the use of vapor barriers.

The "R" values, types, and thicknesses of batts and blankets that are available are given in Tables 11-4 and 11-5.

Blankets and batts are manufactured in widths to fit between joists, rafters, and studs spaced 12, 16 and 24 inches on center. Blanket insulation may come in lengths of 50 feet or

Rated R	Thickness	Kraft paper faced	Foil faced
7	2	X	X
11	3	X	X
13	3-5/8	X	
19	5-1/4	X	X
22	6	X	X

Rock wool
Table 11-4

Rated R	Thickness	Kraft paper faced	Foil faced	Unfaced
3.5	1			X
4	1-1/8			X
5	1-1/2			X
7	2¼-2¾	X	X	
11	3½-4	X	X	X
13	3-5/8			X
14	5			X
19	6-6½	X	X	X
21	7	X	X	
22	6-1/2	X		X

Glass fiber
Table 11-5

more. Batts generally are between 2 feet and 8 feet in length. The batt and blanket type insulation is normally used during initial construction when it can be easily placed between structural members of the sidewall, ceiling and floor.

Loose Fill

There are four types of loose-fill materials in common use: glass fiber, rock wool, cellulosic fiber, and vermiculite. There are two types of application methods: pouring and blowing. Pouring materials require no special equipment. Blowing materials are installed by means of special insulation blowing machines. Any of the four materials is suitable for pouring. Any of them except vermiculite is used for blowing. The "R" value per inch of the different blowing and pouring materials is given below. The material that accounts for most of the vermiculite market is produced under the trade name of Zonolite. It is actually a mixture of vermiculite and polystyrene beads and has a somewhat higher R-factor than pure vermiculite.

	R Per Inch	
	Pouring	Blowing
Glass fiber, rock wool	2.2	2.2
Rock wool	n.a.	2.8
Cellulose fiber	3.7	3.7
Zonolite	3.0	----

An R-value per inch for pouring rock wool is not given here because it is sold under a labeling system which relates the "R" value desired to the square foot coverage that can be attained per 24 pound bag. The formula is:

$$\text{Square foot coverage} = \frac{250}{\text{Desired R-Value}}$$

Pour-in loose fill is designed primarily for application to easily accessible horizontal spaces in floors or ceilings. Placing loose fill insulation into sidewalls and ceilings of existing houses by special blowers is about the only method of insulating when the spaces are inaccessible otherwise. The method used is to fill the cavities through holes of approximately 2'' diameter drilled at suitable intervals. Application methods for blown materials are explained later in this chapter. Note carefully that moisture problems may develop as a result of using blown insulation or any insulation.

Rigid Boards

There are four main types of rigid board insulations: expanded polystyrene, commonly known as "beadboard" because of its appearance (though smooth, it can be seen that it is basically a compressed collection of polystyrene beads); extruded polystyrene or "styrofoam"; urethane board; and rigid glass fiber board. The three types of plastic board are commonly used to insulate masonry walls.

The big advantage of rigid board insulations is their relatively high "R" value per inch. The R's per inch of the four types of boards are given below:

	R Per Inch
Polystyrene	4.17
Styrofoam	5.41
Urethane	7.14
Glass fiber	4.30

These boards have the additional advantage that they are to varying degrees resistant to transmission and absorption of moisture. This is especially true of styrofoam, and somewhat less true of polystyrene. Polystyrene, styrofoam, and urethane boards, however, have the important disadvantage that they are flammable and give off noxious smoke. Therefore, when used in the interior spaces of houses, they must be covered over completely and tightly with drywall or paneling immediately after installation. In some areas there may be code restrictions to their use.

Rigid insulation boards 1 to 2 feet wide and 1 to 4 inches thick are used as perimeter insulation around the outside edges of houses built with concrete slab floors. This insulation must be moisture resistant so it is generally made of foamed glass, or foamed plastic such as urethane or styrofoam. Plastic foam insulation board is also available in larger tongue and groove panels which are glued to the sheathing to cover all exterior wall surfaces from the front line to the roof line. One inch urethane insulation panels glued to the exterior of an insulated R11 2''x4'' stud wall raises the insulating value to a R19 rating and cuts down the air infiltration through the wall. As will be explained later in this chapter, R19 wall insulation is suggested for most parts of the country and the 3-5/8'' cavity in a standard 4'' stud wall can be insulated to a maximum of R13. Plastic foam board insulation is popular because it increases the insulating value of a wall to the modern standard without altering traditional construction practice. Urea-formaldehyde and urethane foams using isocyanates compounds should be used only when surrounded by fireproof materials. Urea tri-polymer and low flame spread styrofoam are considered fire-resistant.

Metallic Insulation

Reflective insulation is made from reflective foils such as aluminum, or polished metallic flake adhered to a reinforced paper. It retards the flow of infra-red heat rays passing across an air space. To be effective, the foil surface must face an air space of ¾ inch or more. Reflective insulation is available in single sheets, strips formed to create 3 or 4 separated air spaces of ¾ inch each and as a combination vapor barrier and reflective surface attached to batts or blankets.

The critical factor to insure efficiency of reflective insulation is installing it so the reflective surface always faces an air space of ¾ inch or more. Once the reflective surface touches surrounding materials it is ineffective as an insulator because it does not retard

conducted heat or heat of convection.

Foam-In-Place

Urea-formaldehyde is only one type of foam-in-place material that is widely used at present for residential retrofit. Urea-formaldehyde is a material of sponge-cake consistency with an R of 4.2 per inch. Its handling characteristics are like those of loose fill: it can be spread in an open horizontal space to any thickness or it can be injected into a closed cavity. In a horizontal or sloping cavity, it is, as with loose fill, generally necessary to fill that cavity completely; it is impossible to leave an air space above the foam. The principle use of urea-formaldehyde foam is in the side walls of a house, where thickness is limited.

The material has several advantages over loose fill materials. It does not settle; it is not affected by moisture; it is nonflammable; and its R per inch is relatively high. It has the problems that it shrinks away from framing members when it cures (shrinkage is from 1-3%), and it gives off a smelly gas while curing that can cause problems if it vents into a closed living space.

The cost of urea-formaldehyde is comparable to the cost of loose fill on an R-by-R basis. Its cost is higher, however, on a per-unit-thickness basis. In situations such as sidewalls where the thickness of insulation is fixed, the higher performance of foam must be traded off with its higher cost.

Urethane foam is not suitable for application to existing residence. It is technically feasible to spray it into open spaces, but it is not generally economical to do so. In cases where a very high R is needed in a limited space, it is cheaper to use rigid urethane board which has the same "R" value. As far as closed cavities are concerned, it is not technically feasible to try and fill them with urethane foam. Unlike urea-formaldehyde, which goes into the cavity already foamed to its ultimate dimensions, urethane foams *after* it has gone into the cavity. It is a very tricky process to ensure that it foams up just enough to fill the cavity, but not to burst it. Bursting of cavities is a real possibility with urethane foam, and it is not worth the risk to try and fill them with this material.

Selecting The Right Material

In some applications it is immaterial what the thickness of the insulating layer is. For example, you could use most any material in an unfloored, unfinished attic. On a strict cost basis, there is no reason for preferring one material over the other in these applications. In other applications, the thickness may be restricted: in frame walls the stud spaces are usually 3½'' or 3-5/8'' thick. Since whatever material is used must fill this space completely. your choice of R-factor and price determines your choice of material. Also, in closed horizontal ceiling spaces, the ''R'' value that can be reached with a given material is limited by the maximum height available in that cavity. To get a higher R-factor above a certain point, you must switch to a material with a higher ''R'' per inch. Don't choose materials on a strict cost basis. Materials have different desirable and undesirable characteristics that need to be taken into account.

Cellulosic fiber is made by a number of different manufacturers and is not a uniform product. When manufactured to federal and industry specifications, the material will have the following characteristics:

• It will be chemically treated to resist fire, with a flame spread rating of 35 and no smoke contribution.

• It will have a neutral pH and will not corrode metals such as electrical conduits.

• It should maintain these properties for the lifetime of the house.

Not all cellulose meets these standards. Some is little more than old newspapers turned into coarse powder. It will perform in a wall about the same as you would expect an equivalent volume of old newspapers to perform.

Rock wool and glass fiber are inherently fireproof and nearly vermin-proof. They do, however, have disadvantages when they are installed in closed cavities, particularly frame sidewalls. They have a lower R per inch than cellulosic fiber. They also consist of relatively long fibers bonded into relatively large tufts. A major problem with these large tufts is that they are liable to get hung up on nails and other obstructions in cavities and not fill the cavity as completely as they are supposed to. Cellulosic fibers are very small and are more likely to penetrate all areas of a cavity.

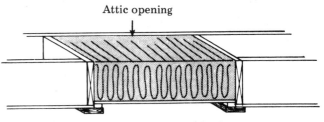

Insulating an access door
Figure 11-6

Insulating Roofs and Ceilings

Most houses have an accessible attic with exposed ceiling framing so that any type of insulation can easily be applied. If batt or blanket type is used, get the width that will conform to joist spacing—usually 16 or 24 inches. Loose-fill type would also be used by simply dumping the insulation between joists and screeding it off to the desired thickness. See Figure 11-6.

Preformed insulation blankets or batts may be more attractive from a labor standpoint than loose fill materials in an unobstructed attic area with no flooring. These blankets or batts can be rolled out quickly and minimize the raising of fibers into the air which create an uncomfortable working environment. Where studs are not spaced at 16'' or 24'' centers, loose fill may be a much better choice.

Give close attention to the places and spaces in an attic where air infiltration can add to the heating load of a home. Attic access doors should be weatherstripped. In addition, a piece of insulation board cut to the size of the attic door and tacked to the attic side of the door can materially improve the thermal characteristics of a panel or hollow core door. See Figure 11-6. If there is an attic scuttle hole, weatherstrip it and insulate the back of the scuttle closure panel. Stuff insulation around pipes, flues, or chimneys penetrating into the attic space, especially in cold climates.

When insulating a ceiling, extend the insulation over the top of the top plate as in Figure 11-7B. Mineral fiber blankets are installed in ceilings by stapling vapor barrier flanges from below, installing unfaced pressure-fit blankets, or laying blankets in from above after the ceiling is in place. Install insulation so the vapor barrier side faces the interior of the home—that is, the area heated in winter. Place insulation on the cold side (in winter) of pipes and ducts. Repair rips or tears in the vapor

153

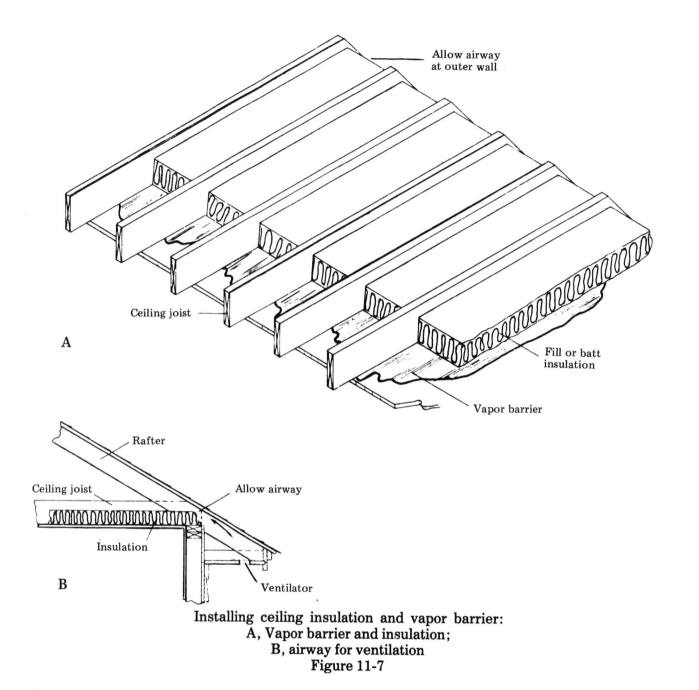

Installing ceiling insulation and vapor barrier:
A, Vapor barrier and insulation;
B, airway for ventilation
Figure 11-7

barrier by stapling vapor barrier material over the tear or by taping the torn barrier back into place.

When adding batts over existing insulation, it is preferable to install unfaced batts. These are generally cheaper, and prevent moisture from condensing in the existing insulation. If unfaced batts are not available or cannot be purchased for less than faced batts, faced batts can be used if the facing is stripped off or slashed at frequent intervals to allow free passage to moisture. Unfaced pressure-fit batts are held between joists without fastening. When installing blankets or batts above the joists it

may be useful to run the batts perpendicular to the joists in order to cover the attic more thoroughly.

Loose fill insulation may be preferred when the attic access is difficult or flooring is present. If flooring is present, some strips may be pulled up or holes can be drilled in the floor at intervals between the joists. This insulation is usually pneumatically pumped or blown into the attic through flexible tubing by a small machine which puffs up the insulation as it pushes it through. This may cause some settling after the insulation is in place so that some margin of safety should be allowed in measuring depth.

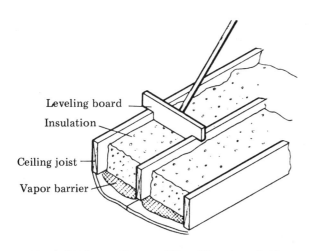

Leveling board
Insulation
Ceiling joist
Vapor barrier

Installation of loose-fill ceiling insulation
Figure 11-8

For this reason the densities recommended by the manufacturer for different desired R values should be carefully followed.

Pouring wool may be applied in unfinished attic areas by emptying the bags evenly between ceiling joists, paying particular attention to the manufacturer's recommendations as to proper thickness and coverage per bag. The wool may be leveled with a wood slat or garden rake. See Figure 11-8. Be sure that eave ventilation openings are not blocked. Small openings, such as those around a chimney, should be hand packed. Cavities, drops, or scuttles should be covered with insulation or the sides and bottom areas should be insulated. Be sure that recessed lighting fixtures and exhaust fan motors protruding into the ceiling are *not* covered with insulation. In floored attics, if you pull up alternate boards or drill holes to allow insertion of insulation, watch out for obstructions such as bridging and conduit between openings.

There is no reason to restrict the depth of attic insulation to the height of the ceiling joists in areas not needed for storage if more insulation is warranted. However, insulation should not come in contact with the roof above at any point.

Blown Insulation in Walls

Wood-frame walls in existing houses are usually covered both inside and out, so application of batt or blanket insulation is impractical in such renovating. It is possible, however, to blow fill-type insulation into each of the stud spaces. More information on blown insulation appears later in this chapter. On

houses having wood siding, the top strip just below the top plates and strips below each window are removed. Two inch diameter holes are cut through the sheathing into each stud space. The depth of each stud space is determined by using a plumb bob, and additional holes are made below obstructions in the spaces. Insulation is forced under slight pressure through a hose and nozzle into the stud space until it is completely filled. Special care should be taken to insulate spaces around doors and windows and at intersections of partition and outside walls.

One problem which may occur within the wall is settling or shrinkage of the insulation materials over time. This problem is both hard to remedy and difficult to detect. While many insulation installers will guarantee that there will be no settling, in general there will be some, and its effect may be significant. As the settling occurs no insulation is protecting the top of the wall, and heat transfer through this area resumes its pre-insulation rate. A 10 percent allowance for settling and unfilled cavities would probably be normal. Over a period of many years the settling of some types of insulating materials may amount to more than this, however. With urea-formaldehyde foam some shrinkage occurs rather than settling—this is claimed by the manufacturers to be about 2 percent. However, improper installation and curing can cause shrinkage to be considerably higher.

The only sure means of monitoring settling at the time of installation and at periodic intervals is through thermographic imagery. An infra-red "picture" of the wall taken from the outside on a cold day will show "hot spots" which are most likely uninsulated areas. Unfortunately, such systems are quite expensive and limited in use.

In addition to the conductive heat savings due to the addition of insulation, a blown wall may offer some savings in convective heat transfer i.e., infiltration through the wall may be slowed. While infiltration through walls may be small for well-constructed homes, it may be significant in older homes or in walls which were not well sealed. One suggested way to detect the relative amount of infiltration entering through a wall is to remove a switch plate cover from the inside of an exterior wall on a windy day and hold a buring match close to the opening. If it

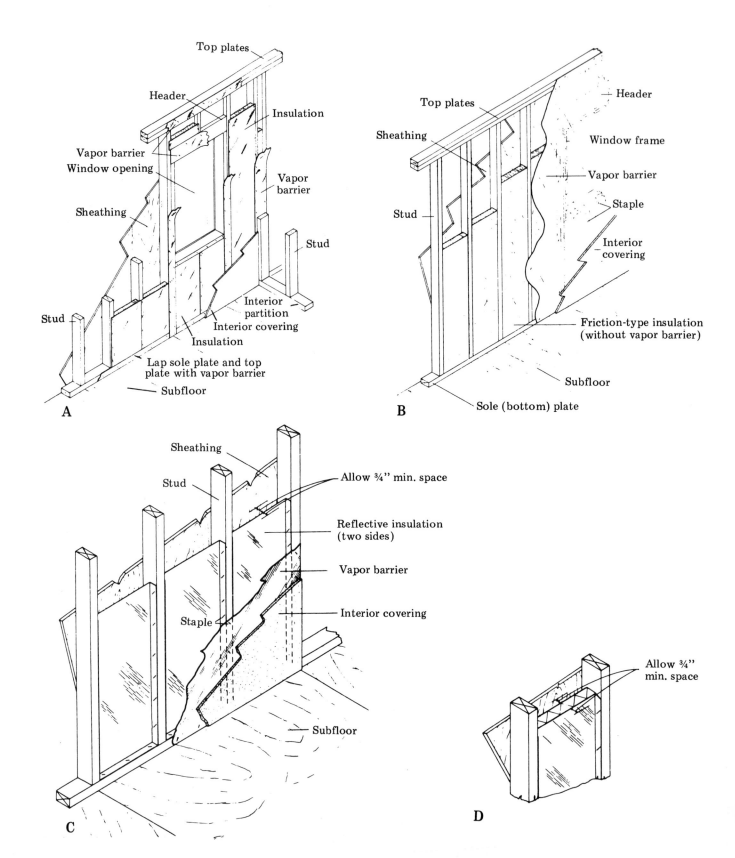

Installing Insulation:
A, Blanket insulation and vapor barriers in exterior wall. B, Vapor barrier over friction-type insulation (enveloping). C, Single sheet two side reflective insulation. D, Multiple sheet reflective insulation.

Figure 11-9

flickers wildly or blows out, there may be significant air infiltration leaking into the house. Filling the wall with insulation will stop much of this air leakage, but it is difficult to assess the savings available under the wide variety of conditions that may exist.

Insulating Walls In New Construction

By far the best and least expensive way to insulate is during the original building process. Flexible insulation in blanket or batt form is normally manufactured with a vapor barrier. These vapor barriers contain tabs at each side which are stapled to the frame members. To minimize vapor loss and possible condensation problems, the best method of attaching consists of stapling the tabs over the edge of the studs as shown in Figure 11-9A. However, many contractors do not follow this procedure because it is more difficult and may cause some problems in nailing of the rock lath or drywall to the studs. Consequently, in many cases, the tabs are fastened to the inner faces of the studs. This usually results in some openings along the edge of the vapor barrier and, of course, a chance for vapor to escape and cause problems. When insulation is placed in this manner, it is well to use a vapor barrier over the entire wall. This method is described in the next section.

Insulate non-standard width spaces by cutting the insulation and the vapor barrier an inch or so wider than the space to be filled. Staple the uncut flange as usual. Pull the vapor barrier on the cut side to the other stud, compressing the insulation behind it, and staple through the vapor barrier to the stud. Unfaced blankets are cut slightly oversize and wedged into place.

Another factor in the use of flexible insulation having an integral vapor barrier is the protection required around window and door openings. Where the vapor barrier on the insulation does not cover doubled studs and header areas, additional vapor barrier materials should be used for protection (Figure 11-9A). Most well informed contractors include such details in the application of their insulation.

At junctions of interior partitions with exterior walls, care should be taken to cover this intersection with some type of vapor barrier. For best protection, insulating the space between the doubled exterior wall studs and the application of a vapor barrier should be done before the corner post is assembled (Figure 11-9A). However, the vapor barrier should at least cover the stud intersections at each side of the partition wall.

Some of the newer insulation forms, such as the friction-type without covers, have resulted in the development of a new process of installing insulation and vapor barriers so as to practically eliminate condensation problems in the walls. An unfaced friction-type insulation batt is used. It fits tightly between frame members spaced 16 or 24 inches on center. "Enveloping" is the process of installing a vapor barrier over the entire wall (Figure 11-9B). This type vapor barrier often consists of 4-mil or thicker polyethylene or similar material used in 8 foot wide rolls. After insulation has been placed, rough wiring or duct work finished, and window frames installed, the vapor barrier is placed over the entire wall, stapling when necessary to hold it in place. Window and door headers, top and bottom plates, and other framing are completely covered. After plaster base or drywall finish is installed, the vapor barrier can be trimmed around window openings.

Reflective insulations used in walls ordinarily consist of either a kraft sheet faced on two sides with aluminum foil, Figure 11-C, or the multiple-reflective "accordion" type, Figure 11-9D. Both are made to use between studs or joists. To be effective, it is important in using such insulation that there is at least a ¾ inch space between the reflective surface and the wall, floor, or ceiling surface. When a reflective insulation is used, it is good practice to use a vapor barrier over the studs or joists. The barrier should be placed over the frame members just under the drywall or plaster base (Figure 11-9C). Gypsum board commonly used as a drywall finish can be obtained with aluminum foil on the inside face which serves as a vapor barrier. When such material is used, the need for a separate vapor barrier is eliminated.

Push insulation behind pipes, ducts, and electrical boxes. Note Figure 11-10. The space may be packed with loose insulation or a piece of insulation of the proper size can be cut and fitted into place. Pack small spaces between rough framing and door and window headers, jambs, and sills with pieces of insulation. Note Figure 11-11. Staple insulation vapor barrier paper or polyethylene over these small spaces.

Regardless of type and location of insulation,

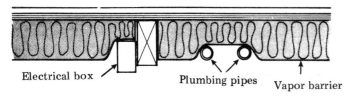

Insulate behind pipes and electrical boxes
Figure 11-10

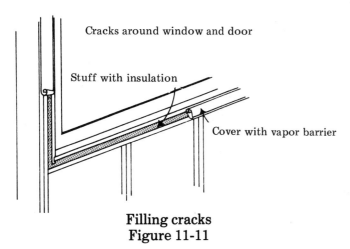

Filling cracks
Figure 11-11

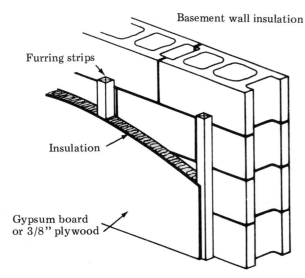

Masonry wall insulation
Figure 11-12

vapor barriers are required on the warm side of the insulation. Vapor barriers will be discussed in Chapter 12.

Masonry Walls

Solid masonry walls, such as brick stone, and concrete, can be insulated only by applying insulation to the interior surface. Remember that in doing this some space is being lost. One method of installing such insulation is to adhesively bond insulating board directly to the interior surface.

The insulating board can be plastered, left exposed, or covered with any desired finish material. Thicker insulating board can be used for added effectiveness. Another method of installing insulation on the inside surface of masonry walls is through attachment of 2 by 2, 1 by 2, or 2 by 4 inch furring strips 16 or 24 inches on center. Note Figure 11-12. Staple vapor barrier flanges to the faces of the furring strips. With 1 by 2 furring, wedge unfaced masonry wall blankets (normally 1 inch thick) between the furring strips; apply a separate polyethylene vapor barrier over the insulation or use foil-backed gypsum board as the interior finish. With the 2 by 4 furring frequently used in colder climates, insulation blankets are stapled to the sides of the furring strips.

Insulating Floors

Insulating batts, with an attached vapor barrier, are easily located between the floor joists. They can be fastened by placing the tabs over the edge of the joists before the subfloor is installed when the cover (vapor barrier) is strong enough to support the insulation batt. However, there is often a hazard of the insulation becoming wet before the subfloor is installed and the house enclosed. Thus, it is advisable to use one of the following alternate methods:

Friction type batt insulation is made to fit tightly between joists and may be installed from the crawl space as shown in Figure 11-13. It is good practice to use small "dabs" of mastic adhesive to insure that it remains in place against the subfloor. When the vapor barrier is not a part of the insulation, a separate film should be placed between the subfloor and the finish floor.

Plenum Chamber Heating

One method of heating which is sometimes used for crawl space houses utilizes the crawl space as a plenum chamber. Warm air is forced into the crawl space, which is somewhat shallower than those normally used without heat, and through wall-floor registers, around the outer walls, into the rooms above. When such a system is used, insulation is placed along the perimeter walls as shown in Figure 11-14. Flexible insulation, with the vapor barrier facing

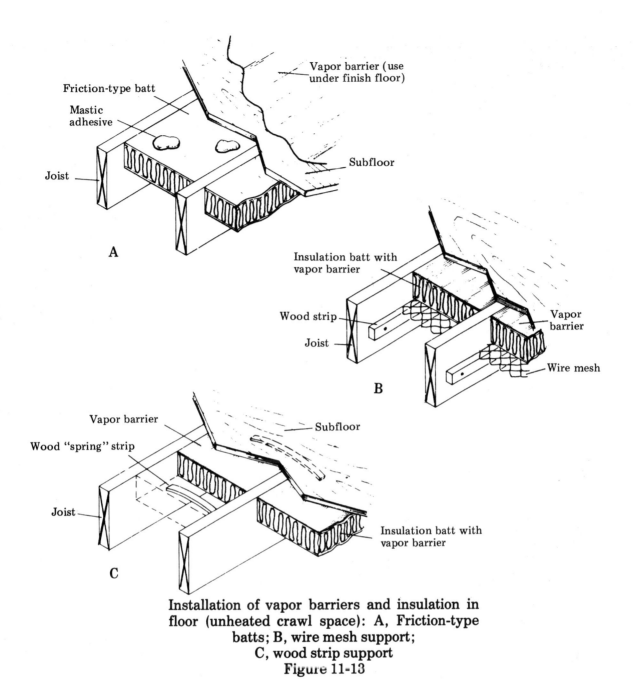

Installation of vapor barriers and insulation in floor (unheated crawl space): A, Friction-type batts; B, wire mesh support; C, wood strip support

Figure 11-13

the interior, is used between joists, at the top of the foundation wall. A rigid insulation such as expanded polystyrene is placed along the inside of the wall extending below the groundline to reduce heat loss. Insulation may be held in place with an approved mastic adhesive. To protect the insulation from moisture and to prevent moisture entry into the crawl space from the soil, a vapor barrier is used over the insulation below the groundline (Figure 11-14). Seams of the ground cover should be lapped and held in place with bricks or other bits of masonry. Some builders pour a thin concrete slab over the vapor

barrier. The crawl space of such construction is not ventilated.

Protecting Supply and Drain Lines

Once the floor is adequately insulated, the crawl space below the house may be below freezing during cold weather. An unheated crawl space in cold climates offers insufficient protection to supply and disposal pipes during winter months. It is common practice to use a large vitrified or similar tile to enclose the water and sewer lines in the crawl space. Insulation is then placed within the tile to the floor level.

159

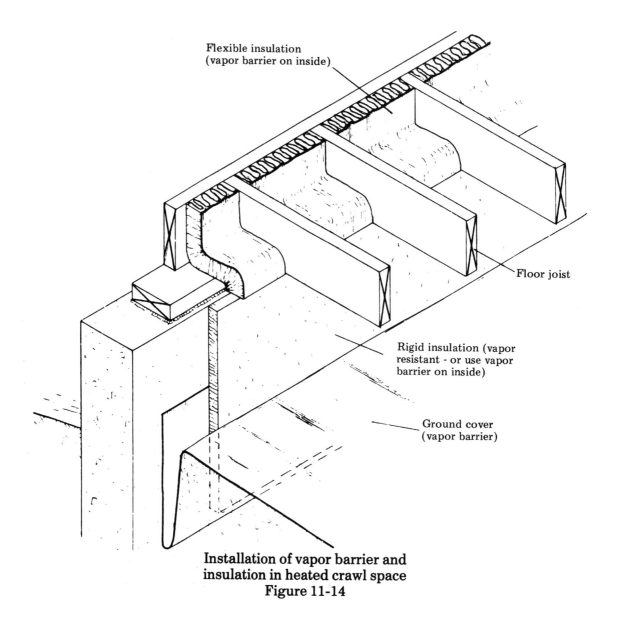

Flexible insulation
(vapor barrier on inside)

Floor joist

Rigid insulation (vapor
resistant - or use vapor
barrier on inside)

Ground cover
(vapor barrier)

Installation of vapor barrier and
insulation in heated crawl space
Figure 11-14

Where heat escaping from the furnace or hot water heater raises the temperature of an otherwise unheated basement or crawl space, the level of insulation may be somewhat less for both the floor and supply or waste lines.

Insulation of Exposed Ducting

Heating and cooling ducts which run through unconditioned spaces (especially attics, garages and crawlspaces) can be a major source of heat loss (or gain) if not properly taped and insulated. Even where an adequate amount of insulation exists, it may be worthwhile removing this temporarily to check on the condition of the ducts. Escaping air indicates the need for retaping the joints. This is especially important if the warm air in the duct is humid, as condensation inside the moisture barrier surrounding the insulation will result.

Most homes have no more than one or two inches of insulation wrapped around the exposed ducting. Considerably more than this may be economically desirable in colder climates, especially for electrically heated homes.

Duct wrap insulation is available in a wide variety of widths up to about two inches. Where more than two inches are needed, several layers of duct wrap should be used. Unfaced wrap should be installed beneath the outer layer. A heavy foil face is usually used on the outer layer as a vapor barrier. Alternatively, regular unfaced batts can be wrapped around the ducts and covered with a vinyl wrapping sealed to form an adequate vapor barrier. In either case it is important to avoid crushing the insulation or binding it too tightly in order to maximize its resistance to heat flow.

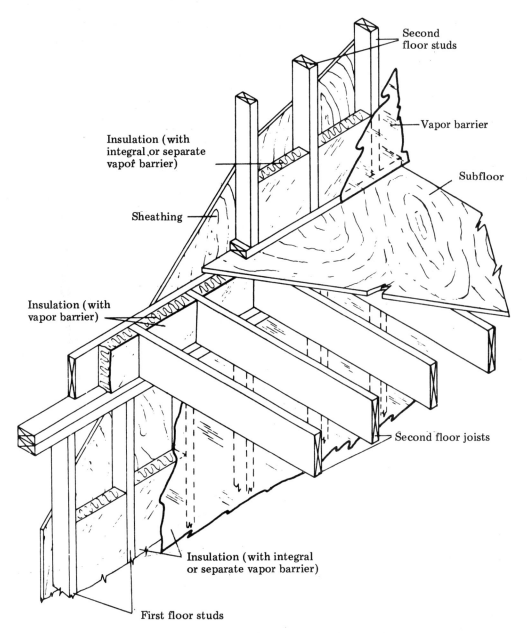

Second floor studs

Vapor barrier

Subfloor

Insulation (with integral or separate vapor barrier)

Sheathing

Insulation (with vapor barrier)

Second floor joists

Insulation (with integral or separate vapor barrier)

First floor studs

**Insulation in walls and joist space of
two-story house
Figure 11-15**

Ducting insulation requirements are not directly proportional to the climate. Rather they are a function of the climate, the general insulation level of the building and heat or cooling system efficiency. In a well-insulated home, other things held equal, the heating/cooling system will be used less and the heat loss and gain through the duct work will be lower. For this reason, insulation requirements for exposed ducting depend on other insulation levels. In general, the poorer the insulation, the higher the heating bill, the more important duct insulation will be.

Insulating Second Stories

One of the areas of a two-story house where the requirement of a vapor barrier and insulation is often overlooked is at the perimeter area of the second floor joists. The space between the joists at the header and along the stringer joists should be protected by sections of batt insulation which contain a vapor barrier (Figure 11-15). The sections should fit tightly so that both the vapor barriers and the insulation fill the joist spaces. Insulation and vapor barriers in exposed second floor walls (Figure 11-15) should be installed in the same manner as

161

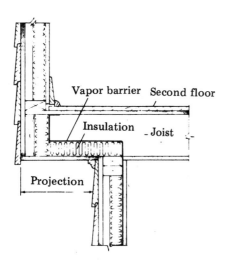

Insulation and vapor barrier at
second floor projection
Figure 11-16

for walls of single-story houses.

A two-story house is sometimes designed so that part of the second floor projects beyond the first. This projection varies but is often about 12 inches. In such designs, the projections should be insulated and vapor barriers installed as shown in Figure 11-16.

In 1½-story houses containing bedrooms and other occupied rooms on the second floor, it is common practice to include knee walls. These are partial walls which extend from the floor to the rafters (Figure 11-17). Their height usually varies between 4 and 6 feet. Such areas must normally contain vapor barriers and insulation in the following areas: (a) In the first floor ceiling area, (b) at the knee wall, and (c) between the rafters. Insulation batts with the vapor barrier facing down should be placed between joists from the outside wall plate to the knee wall. The insulation should also fill the entire joist space directly under the knee wall (Figure 11-17). Care should be taken when placing the insulating batt to allow an airway for attic ventilation at the junction of the rafter and exterior wall.

Insulation in the knee wall can consist of blanket or batt type insulation with integral vapor barrier or with separately applied vapor barriers, as described for first and second floor walls.

Batt or blanket insulation is commonly used between the rafters at the sloping portion of the heated room. As in the application of all insulations, the vapor barrier should face the inner or warm side of the roof or wall. An airway should always be allowed between the top of the insulation and the roof sheathing at each rafter space. This should be at least a one inch clear space without obstructions such as might occur with solid blocking. This will allow movement of air in the area behind the knee wall to the attic area above the second floor rooms.

Finished Basement Rooms

Finished rooms in basement areas with fully or partly exposed walls should be treated much the same as a framed wall with respect to the use of vapor barriers and insulation (Figure 11-18). When a full masonry wall is involved, several factors should be considered: (a) When drainage in the area is poor and soil is wet or when the basement has a history of dampness, drain tile should be installed on the outside of the footing for removing excess water; (b) in addition to an exterior wall coating, a waterproof coating should also be applied to the interior surface of the masonry to insure a dry wall.

Furring strips (2 by 2 or 2 by 3 inch members) used on the wall provide (a) space for the blanket insulation with the attached vapor barrier and (b) nailing surfaces for interior finish, (Figure 11-18). One or 1½ inch thicknesses of friction-type insulation with a vapor barrier of plastic film such as 4-mil polyethylene or other materials might also be used for the walls.

Other materials which are used over masonry walls consist of rigid insulation such as expanded polystyrene. These are installed with a thin slurry of cement mortar and the wall completed with a plaster finish. The expanded plastic insulations normally have moderate resistance to vapor movement and require no other vapor barrier.

When a vapor barrier has not been used under the concrete slab, it is good practice to place some type over the slab itself before applying the sleepers. One such system for unprotected in-place slabs involves the use of treated 1 by 4 inch sleepers fastened to the slab with a mastic. This is followed by the vapor barrier and further by second sets of 1 by 4 inch sleepers placed over and nailed to the first set. Subfloor and finish floor are then applied over the sleepers.

To prevent heat loss and minimize escape of

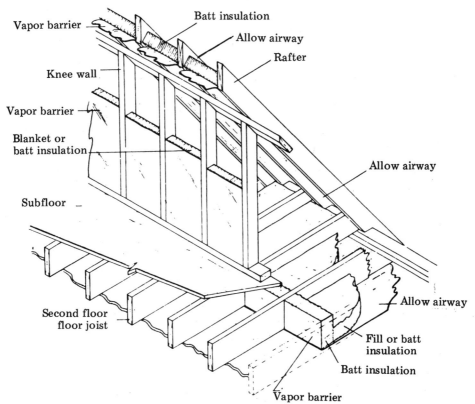

Installing vapor barrier and insulation in
knee-wall areas of 1½ story house
Figure 11-17

water vapor, blanket or batt insulation with
attached vapor barriers should be used around
the perimeter of the floor framing above the
foundation walls (Figure 11-18). Place the
insulation between the joists or along stringer
joists with the vapor barrier facing the basement
side. The vapor barrier should fit tightly against
the joists and subfloor.

How Much Insulation Is Needed?

Figure 11-19 summarizes the optimum
insulation values for residential heating and
cooling as calculated for each climate zone. The
figures are the recommendation of Owens-Corn-
ing Fiberglas and take into account national
weather data, energy costs and projected
increases, and insulation costs. Table 11-20
shows how much insulation is required to reach
the recommended "R" values.

The Modern Standard: 2"x6" @24" o.c.

Figure 11-19 shows that most areas in the
United States required R-19 walls insulation.
Filling the cavity in a 2 by 4 inch frame wall will
produce no more than a R-13 rating. A nominal 6

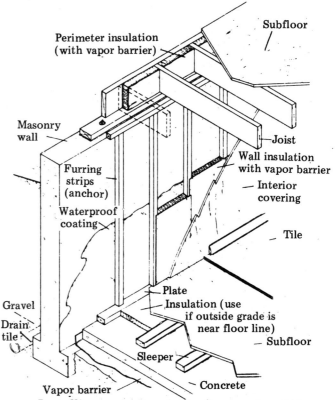

Installing vapor barrier in floor and wall
of finished basement
Figure 11-18

163

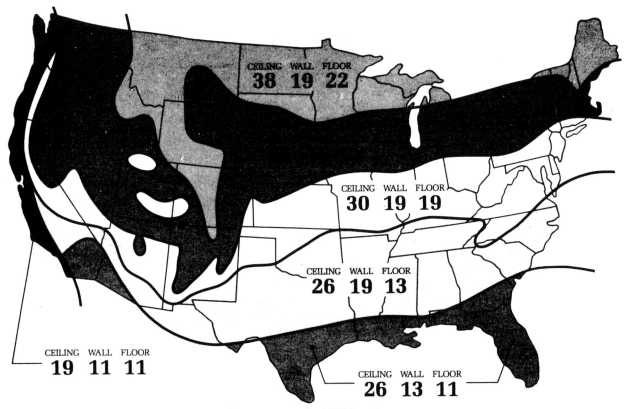

CEILING WALL FLOOR
38 19 22

CEILING WALL FLOOR
30 19 19

CEILING WALL FLOOR
26 19 13

CEILING WALL FLOOR
19 11 11

CEILING WALL FLOOR
26 13 11

Recommended "R" values
Figure 11-19

Ceilings, double layers of batts
    R-38, Two layers of R-19 (6'') mineral fiber
    R-33, One layer of R-22 (6½'') and one layer
        of R-11 (3½'') mineral fiber
    R-30, One layer of R-19 (6'') and one layer of
        R-11 (3½'') mineral fiber
    R-26, Two layers of R-13 (3-5/8'') mineral
        fiber

Ceilings, loose fill mineral wool and batts
    R-38, R-19 (6'') mineral fiber and 20 bags of
        wool per 1,000 S.F. (8¾'')
    R-33, R-22 (6½'') mineral fiber and 11 bags
        of wool per 1,000 S.F. (5'')
    R-30, R-19 (6'') mineral fiber and 11 bags of
        wool per 1,000 S.F. (5'')

    R-26, R-19 (6'') mineral fiber and 8 bags of
        wool per 1,000 S.F. (3¼'')

Walls, using 2''x6'' framing
    R-19, R-19 (6'') mineral fiber batts

Walls, using 2''x4'' framing
    R-19, R-13 (3-5/8'') mineral fiber batts and
        1'' plastic foam sheathing
    R-11, R-11 (3½'') mineral fiber batts

Floors
    R-22, R-22 (6½'') mineral fiber
    R-19, R-19 (6'') mineral fiber
    R-13, R-13 (3-5/8'') mineral fiber
    R-11, R-11 (3½'') mineral fiber

Insulation recommendations
Table 11-20

inch cavity wall carry R-19 insulation. Six inch studs spaced 24 inches on center (Figure 11-21) will give the same strength as 4 inch studs 16 inches on center but use fewer studs, less lumber, and provide better insulation because the studs transmit heat better than the fully insulated spaces between the studs.

In most parts of the country, 2'' x 6'' lumber in short lengths used for studs is considerably less expensive per board foot than 2'' x 4''

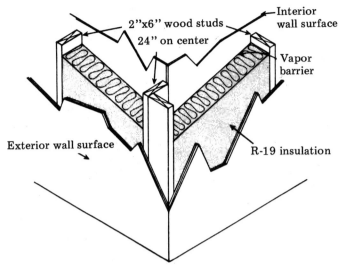

Modern 2''x6'' framing
Figure 11-21

studs. Also, it is usually possible to use 2'' x 6'' lumber in the No. 3 or utility grade of most species rather than the higher "Stud" grade of 2'' x 4''. Consequently, the energy conserving home requires less lumber when compared with conventional 16'' member spacing, and uses lumber at lower cost per board foot. The American Plywood Association estimates that using 2'' x 6'' lumber 24'' o.c. saves about $200 per house in material and labor when compared to 2'' x 4'' lumber 16'' o.c. The A.P.A. at 1119 A Street, Tacoma, Washington 98401 explains the use of 24'' o.c. framing in a free booklet titled "MOD 24 Building Guide."

The 2'' x 6'' studs in the house corners are set so one is flush to the outside sheathing and the other starting the connecting wall is at right angles 6'' from and parallel to the sheathing. See Figure 11-21. This permits the corner to be insulated. Similarly, where a partition meets an outside wall, a single stud is used. At the center bottom of each stud through which wiring is going to be passed a hole is augered or vee cut. This avoids having wiring interfere with insulation installation.

Many contractors retain their standard 2'' x 4'', 16'' o.c. wall and add foam insulation to the exterior. The old 16'' o.c. wall contains a greater area of semi-conductive studs. The problem with this is that unless the inside vapor barrier is better than the exterior insulating foam, water will condense in the wall, nullifying the thermal resistance of the insulation. Based on thermal resistance, the 6'' insulated stud design 24'' on

centers is 30% more efficient and much less likely to develop moisture problems that destroy the insulation.

Blown Insulation

Loose-fill blown insulation for reinsulation of ceilings and outside walls can be very effective in reducing heating and cooling energy requirements. Three or 4 inches of insulation properly placed in wall air space can reduce the heat transfer through the walls by as much as two thirds. Blown wall insulation in a 3½ inch cavity wall is usually given a R14 rating. Typically, blown wall and ceiling insulation alone will reduce heating costs by about 35 percent in houses with little or no insulation. Savings and improved comfort begin immediately when a good insulation job is done and continues throughout all seasons.

The advantage of blown insulation is that you are able to reinsulate exterior walls without tearing up the interior surface. The lightweight material is fed by a machine, located outside the building, through a flexible hose to the point of installation. Holes are bored through sidings and later covered with an inconspicuous plug, or a section of the exterior facing material can be removed and replaced. The fibers can be blown over existing insulation, filling voids which might have occurred with older insulation. It can be put into a ceiling, for example, where extra weight might be a problem and where long spans might otherwise require reduced insulation depth or special trussing.

Loose-fill materials, usually mineral fiber or cellulose, are the insulation forms best suited for this job. Cellulose is remarkably well suited for reinsulation jobs. The pneumatic blowing of short fibers results in a completely filled cavity without "hang-up" on wiring, nails, rough plaster or splinters. The monolith of millions of wood pulp particles retains its density over years of service. Moisture dissipation properties also are significant. When moisture vapor enters the wall it is held in suspension within the natural cellular fibers preventing it from collecting at the base of the wall. The moisture dissipates naturally, during temperature changes, similar to the evaporation of perspiration from the skin. It is essential that proper insulation be installed in all building areas exposed to the outside. Blown insulation generally can be applied to all ceiling and sidewall areas as well as to other exposed areas such as overhanging floors. For those areas where it is not practical to install loose fill insulation, such as under floors, batts or blankets should be installed.

In some older houses, access can be gained to the wall space from the attic. In this case, loose fill insulation material can be dropped into the space from above at very low cost, making this economical in all but the mildest climates with low fuel prices. (Make sure the insulation doesn't fall all the way into the basement!)

A potential problem with insulation in closed cavities in some climates is the possibility of moisture accumulation. This may be difficult to detect until moisture begins to show through the wall. If moisture problems occur, they can be minimized, however. The interior surface of the wall can be made vapor resistant with a paint or covering that has low moisture permeability. Cracks around windows and door frames, electrical outlets, and baseboards should be sealed at the surface facing the room. Outside surfaces should not be tightly sealed but allowed to "breathe."

The Job Crew

A well trained crew is absolutely essential, both to insure that the insulation work is installed correctly and to see that a profit is made on the job. The size of the crew will vary, depending upon the type of blowing equipment and the particular job. A minimum of two men is recommended even on ceiling jobs with automatic machines. Where both ceilings and sidewalls are to be installed, it may be advisable to use as many as four men, one of whom should be a competent carpenter.

Before starting any work, the foreman should make a thorough survey of the job to note any pre-existing damage to the property. Any damage which could be blamed upon the insulation crew should be shown to the homeowner. The foreman should request permission to enter the house to check the condition of interior walls and to suggest removal of dishes on shelves, mirrors, and pictures which might be dislodged during the application process. At job completion, the foreman should supervise the careful cleaning of buildings and grounds. It is generally an excellent idea for the foreman to offer the homeowner the opportunity of seeing those parts of the completed insulation job which are accessible.

Frequently the foreman can pick up leads to other prospective insulation purchasers. Although it is not his specific responsibility, a good foreman never misses the opportunity to get his company's name to an interested prospect or to turn the prospect's name over to his boss. Make sure your foreman has a supply of your business cards and receives a commission on jobs he sells.

Attics

Since the attic area is generally the most accessible part of the house to be insulated, most crews will start in this area. For practical scheduling, the attic area should always be saved for inclement weather.

Be sure there is sufficient light by which to work. Every crew should carry a long extension cord with extra bulbs for use whenever the attic is not well lighted. The hoseman should also have a flashlight available.

Before starting to blow insulation in the attic, anything which might interfere with the movement of the hoseman or proper application should be placed in an area where it will give the least amount of trouble. Items stored in the attic should be protected as much as possible. Clothes and other items which could be damaged by the insulation should be removed from the attic.

Before beginning the blowing, a batt or other baffle should be placed around the perimeter of houses having eave ventilation. This batt or baffle prevents the loss of insulation into the eave vents and, more important, prevents air moving through the eave vents from moving the insulation back away from the plate. Apply batts over the tops of wells and drop ceilings to assure that there is a continuous insulating blanket over the top floor ceiling.

In an unfloored attic, keep the hose parallel to the floor with insulation falling 6 to 8 feet in front. Where possible, back away from the work to prevent packing. Where work space is tight, prevent insulation from packing by allowing it to blow off your hand.

Blow three or four joists from one position by aiming the hose to the right or left. Always blow in the direction of the joists, not across them. Keep the hose close to the floor where the insulation must go underneath obstructions such as cross-bracing and wiring. Insulation must be blown on both sides of this kind of obstruction. Where an obstruction may cause a low spot to occur, move around, check this spot and, if necessary, fill in the low area. Be sure that the insulation is installed on both sides of obstructions such as solid cross bracing. (If an area is not properly blown, dust marks will appear on the ceiling below after a short time due to the difference in temperature of the surface.)

If a batt or blanket is not used to block off the ends of joists, be sure that the full depth of insulation is applied all the way to the end of the plate. When roof construction does not allow the application to go to the ends of the joists to assure full depth, it is possible to bounce the insulation off the underside of the roof in order to build up the required depth at the plate. Care should be taken, however, not to get the eave vents blocked.

There are two areas in the attic over which insulation must not be placed. One is on top of exhaust fans and the other on top of recessed light fixtures commonly used in kitchens and bathrooms. A recessed fixture must dissipate the heat upward and it is absolutely essential that no insulation be on top of its box.

Water pipes run in the attic area must be given protection, since the attic temperature during cold weather will now be very close to that of the outdoors. The severity of the winters and the location of the pipes will determine what additional protection must be given to prevent freezing. As a minimum, however, apply the same depth of insulation on top of pipes as there is between pipes and the warm surface.

After the attic is blown, smooth down the job as much as possible to make it look neater and to even out any of the high and low spots. Do not remove the hose from the attic until the foreman has inspected and determined that no areas have been accidently missed. Install a batt or blanket on top of areas where loose fill has not been applied, such as access panels, stair wells, and fan covers. The completed job should provide a continuous blanket of insulation over the ceiling area.

Many attic areas contain some floored areas which present no real problem. It is not advisable to attempt to blow more than six feet under flooring, so a floor board should be removed approximately every twelve feet. If some flooring is difficult to remove because of its nailing pattern, take care during removal to

prevent any possible damage to the ceiling surface below. Since it is difficult to see bracing underneath the flooring, take particular care to assume that the flow of insulation under the floor is not being blocked. When there is a large amount of bracing under the floor, it may be necessary to take off several boards in a small area. Insert the hose approximately six feet under the floor and gradually pull it out as the joist area fills. Twist and turn the hose as it is removed to assure complete coverage of the area under the floor.

Knee Walls

Although it is possible to put up a retainer and blow knee walls, the easiest method is to use a batt or blanket for the height of the knee wall. Slopes, if not too long, can be insulated with batts, or the bottom of the slopes may be blocked off and the area blown full of insulation. When blowing slopes, be sure that trapped air does not leave void spots. When insulating story and a half houses or houses with attic rooms, be sure not to miss any flat areas beyond the knee walls. Many times these flat areas are accessible by cutting a hole through a closet wall or by making a roof opening which should be patched immediately. These flat areas are very easy to miss if the job is not thoroughly checked.

Attic Stairways

Many older homes have an attic stairway. A ceiling insulation job is not complete until the stairway is insulated, including the soffit area, the walls, and the door. Many times the soffit area can be insulated by either removing the treads or drilling holes and filling with insulation. Close holes by means of plugs. Plugs can be finished and restained if necessary. Stairway walls can be insulated in the same manner as any other wall. Finish the openings as required to match the existing stairway finish. An alternate to insulating the entire stairway assembly is to install a trap door, operated by a counter-balance, over the top of the stairway, and insulate it by means of batts or blankets.

Sidewalls

Insulation of sidewalls is not a difficult job, providing you understand how sidewalls are framed out. A crew that has not previously blown a sidewall of an existing house should spend some time studying the general framing principles in a house which is under construction. By studying a wall section before the interior finish is put up, a man has a much better idea of how such things as fire stops, junction boxes, romex cables, and bracing will affect his job.

Regardless of the outside finish, all sidewalls are insulated in a similar manner. Some of the outside finish is removed and openings are made in the sheathing so that insulation can be blown into the empty stud area.

Some blown insulation principles apply to all types of wall construction:

1. The "double blow" method (Figure 11-22), with two openings, for sidewalls is recommended, although some reliable applicators can fill the spaces with one opening. Some stud sections may even require three or more openings because of construction features. Openings should be made into the stud area for each eight to ten feet of height. This is essential to assure that the stud area is completely full. Never try to blow more than 4 feet down or 18 inches up unless you have made two openings. Blowing through a single opening in an 8 foot wall could leave the bottom of the stud space with no insulation.

2. Remove the trim whenever possible. Generally this will expose studding.

3. Many homes have eaves which are actually below the level of the plate. Frequently access to the stud area can be gained by removing the eave panels. As with trim, the removal of eave sections will generally open a large amount of stud area with very little work.

4. Plumb bob all openings to determine the amount of area that can be filled through that opening. A plumb bob should be of sufficient size to readily reveal objects which would stop the flow of insulation. Areas under windows and below fire stops and bracing must be opened to completely fill the area.

Siding, shingles and brick veneer can be opened and replaced in many cases. Plywood panel siding and stucco are usually bored and slugged to match the previous condition as much as possible.

After the sidewall has been properly opened, insulation is blown into all areas. It is strongly recommended that a sidewall nozzle be used in blowing sidewalls so that the applicator can best control the direction in which his insulation is

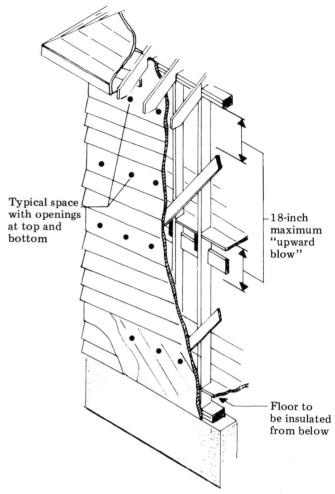

Typical space with openings at top and bottom

18-inch maximum "upward blow"

Floor to be insulated from below

Blown sidewall insulation
Figure 11-22

being blown. Your material manufacturer or equipment supplier can recommend the best nozzle for your needs.

Different applicators have different methods for filling up sidewall panels. It is generally recommended that the lower holes be filled first, particularly if the wall is partially insulated. If not, some lower holes will appear to be filled from the opening above. The hose should always be inserted in such holes to make sure that the insulation in the lower stud space is at the correct density.

Machine Pressure

The amount of pressure at which a machine should operate will vary with the job. The blowing machine should be equipped with a properly operating pop-off valve so that when the wall section is filled, pressure will bleed off at the machine rather than into the sidewall section, eliminating the danger of blowing out the inside surface. Considerably less pressure should be used on a sidewall in which the inner surface is drywall construction than on one in which the inner surface is metal lath and plaster. As the insulation is being blown into the sidewall, continually move the blowing nozzle from one side to the other so that the entire stud area will be filled.

The hoseman should be able to judge the approximate length of time it will take to fill any opening. If an opening is filled too quickly, it probably indicates that the insulation is hung up on some type of obstruction. When this occurs, it may be possible, by adjusting the nozzle, to break the insulation away from whatever it is hung on. However, it may also be necessary to make another opening below the stoppage. The applicator should remember that any sidewall section which is not properly insulated will be very evident to the homeowner as it will appear as a cold surface on his inside wall.

Houses Without Sheathing

On some houses, siding is nailed directly to the face of the studs without any sheathing. With this type of construction, removal of the outside facing will result in an opening into the stud area which is too large for proper use of the sidewall nozzle. In such cases, use a length of lumber approximately 24 inches long and the appropriate width as a substitute for sheathing, drilling a hole in it for inserting the sidewall nozzle.

Opening Procedures For Sidewalls

The information contained in the following paragraphs covers the procedure for the removal and replacement of different types of sidewall materials. There can be many variations of the procedures shown, and any method which gives efficient access to the sidewall area can be used.

Since the removal of the outside finishes on any existing home largely involves the principles of good carpentry, it is strongly recommended that one of the crew be a proficient carpenter. If one of the crew is not a carpenter, it is suggested that a carpenter be hired to work and train your men on the first few sidewall jobs. For brick or stone sidewalls it is recommended that an experienced mason be used until your crew is familiar with the procedure for entering these walls.

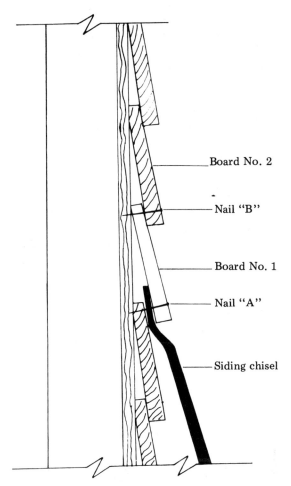

Opening in bevel siding
Figure 11-23

Bevel Siding

Tools usually required are a wide-faced chisel, curved siding chisel, claw hammer, nail set, nail saw, and back saws. The siding to be removed is shown as board Number 1 in Figure 11.23. Removal and preparatory steps are as follows:

1. Using the back saw, free the vertical end joints of the board on either side, or cut new vertical joints if only a portion of the board has to be removed.

2. Using the chisel, pry up the bottom of the board leaving a space at least the width of the chisel between the edge of board Number 1 and the one below. With the board in this position, cut with the nail saw nail "A" holding the bottom of the board.

3. Pry board Number 2 with the chisel in the same manner as board Number 1 and, at the same time, kink the nail holding the Number 2 board to the sheathing.

4. Tap the Number 2 board back gently,

169

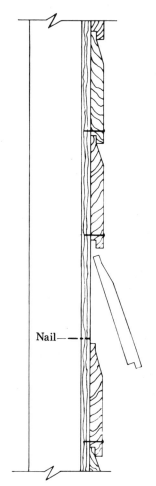

Nail—

Opening shiplap siding
Figure 11-24

thus forcing out nail "B" previously kinked.

5. Carefully remove the Number 1 board, using the chisel if the board is not free enough to fall out by itself.

6. After the board is removed, the building paper, usually found between siding and sheathing, should not be removed or damaged any more than necessary. Start by cutting the paper along the horizontal edge about 1 inch above the board still in place.

7. Cut the paper vertically on either side of the board and at least 6 inches on either side of the last hole at the end of the row.

8. Bend up the paper and tack to the board above, allowing free access to the sheathing.

9. Drill the hole and blow the insulation.

After the wall section is blown, replace the siding in a workmanlike manner, filling any nail holes or splits with putty, and touch up. If possible, leave a very slight opening between the replaced board and the ones already on the house in order to permit breathing in the wall.

A chisel may be used instead of a nail saw for cutting nails. In isolated cases it may be necessary to set the nails with nail sets through both boards and into the sheathing. This method is not recommended unless absolutely necessary. The bottom of the board may be split and the nail set creates large holes requiring a large amount of puttying.

Jointed Siding

Novelty siding (regardless of its exterior appearance) usually has one common characteristic—the boards are joined together by some form of shiplap or tongue and groove joint. In this type of work there is no opportunity to pry the boards loose. Therefore, the following steps are practically the only methods by which the work should be handled. Tools required are a claw hammer, wood chisel, nail set, and a broad curved blade knife with a striking plate on the back side of the blade. The procedure for shiplap siding (Figure 11.24) is as follows:

1. Set the nails directly through the board.

2. After setting the nails, the procedure is practically the same as that for bevel siding. The chisel is inserted under the lower edge of the board to be removed and it is pried outward (Figure 11-24). As the illustration of the shiplap joint shows in Figure 11-24, there is nothing to prevent the removal of the board.

3. Preparations for blowing (treatment of sheathing, etc., and drilling) are the same as for bevel siding.

4. Replacement of the siding is the same as for bevel siding.

Tongue and Groove Siding

With tongue and groove work a slightly different procedure is necessary as the boards cannot be pried out without breaking either the tongue or one of the edges. Two methods are in use at present. Both can be recommended, although where the boards are very tightly fitted, Method Number 1 is likely to split off the top outer edge of the board.

Method 1

1. Set all nails directly through to the sheathing.

2. At the lower edge of the board to be removed, insert an electrician's chisel and pry out and down at the point "A" as shown in Figure 11.25. This will usually cause the board

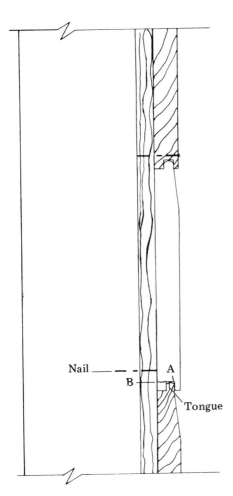

Opening tongue-and-groove siding
Figure 11-25

to split off at the rear along the line "B", leaving the tongue of the board below intact.

3. By proper manipulation, board Number 1 will come away from the top groove in the board above and can be removed.

4. Preparations for blowing (treatment of sheathing, etc., and drilling) are the same as for bevel siding.

To replace the siding, set the edge of the tongue into the groove of the upper board and tap the board along the edges until the tongue is started in the groove along the entire length. When the tongue has entered the groove far enough so that bottom edges are level, the bottom edge can be knocked straight in and the board is now ready for face nailing. Finishing nails are used in the same manner as for bevel siding.

Method 2

Where the boards are set in tightly and there is danger that the board cannot be freed at the top tongue, the following alternate method is suggested:

1. Set the nails through the board.

2. Use a broad bladed knife about 12 inches long, with a slight curvature to the blade face and a welded striking plate on the blade. The knife blade is inserted in the groove at both top and bottom of the board to be removed and driven in, in order to cut off the tongue.

3. After the tongues are completely cut away from the board, top and bottom, the board can be removed easily. If the board is toenailed at the top edge through the groove instead of straight-nailed, the procedure is the same except that slightly more prying is required.

4. Preparations for blowing (treatment of sheathing, etc., and drilling) are the same as for bevel siding.

After blowing, cover the sheathing behind the top and bottom edges of the board with mastic the full length of the cut and at least 1 inch either side of the tongue and groove. The mastic should be sufficiently thick so that when the board is pushed back into place, the mastic will work into place between the upper and lower joints, serving in place of the tongue and groove as a protection against the weather. Since the board is absolutely free, it can be easily put in place. Finishing nails are used in the same manner as for bevel siding.

Vertical Siding

Vertical novelty siding is sometimes applied to the face of the house without sheathing. In such cases, there are usually several horizontal stops or nailers in the wall. When this construction is encountered, the only suitable method is removal of all vertical siding or removal of sufficient siding in each panel to provide for blowing or hand packing as the case may be.

The method of removing and replacing vertical siding is exactly the same as for horizontal siding. However, since there is no sheathing behind the siding, the edges must be butted with either white lead or mastic compound to provide a water seal at the joint. If there is an appreciable opening on either side of the board after replacement, the joints should be further sealed by caulking with a fine-pointed caulking gun.

Siding Shingles

Where Method 1 is to be used, the owner

should be informed of the procedure. Otherwise, the shingles should be pulled as shown under Method 2. Method 1 requires the cutting of the outer course of shingles and involves the use of a claw hammer and a 2½ inch wide blade steel chisel no greater than 8 inches in overall length, the taper of the blade to range from 0 to 3/16 of an inch. The various steps are as follows:

Method 1

1. Beginning at a distance of about 3/8 inch up under the butt edge of the shingle course above, start to cut the shingle to be removed on a 45 degree angle upward being careful that each chisel width of cut overlaps the previous cut and that the cutting line is kept straight. (See Figure 11-26.). The first cut across should only go half way through the shingle thickness to prevent unnecessary splitting of the shingle.

2. Repeat the cutting across the shingle in the same manner, finishing the cut.

3. Carefully break the paint seal at the bottom and sides of the shingle with a jackknife and remove the shingle.

4. Drill through the lower course of shingles and through the sheathing. Pieces of shingles usually cannot be saved.

After blowing, replace the shingles:

1. If the lower course of shingles is in poor condition, place a piece of asphalt paper over the hole to entirely cover the under surface of the shingle removed and press the paper down into mastic.

2. Lightly daub the cut edge of the removed shingle with the mastic and drive it up solidly against the section of the shingle still in place.

3. Face-nail the shingle with 4d or 6d galvanized finishing nails top and bottom, driving the top nails through the butt of the course above to catch the upper edge of the cut shingle.

4. Touch edges and other necessary spots with paint.

Method 2

If the owner should object to cutting the shingles as in Method 1, a procedure consisting of pulling shingles can be used. Essential tools are a shingle or slate ripper and a nail saw.

1. With a jackknife, free the edges of the shingle by cutting the paint seal.

2. Pry up the course above the shingle to be removed. Then, pry up the shingle to be

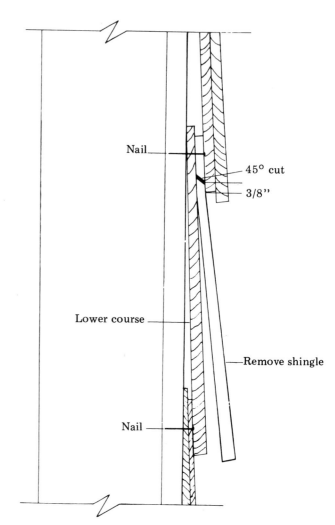

Opening sidewall shingles
Figure 11-26

removed.

3. Running the ripper or saw above the shingles to be removed, cut the nails holding the course to this shingle.

4. Inserting the ripper or saw under the shingle to be removed, cut or pull the nails holding this shingle.

5. Holding the shingle by the butt, work the shingle loose and pull out.

6. Drill through the lower course shingle and through the sheathing.

Replace the shingles as in Method 1:

1. Insert the shingle into the space it is to occupy and drive upwards until the edge of the butt lines up with the rest of the course. Use a block of wood against the butt end in driving in order to save the shingle edge.

2. Face-nail the course above with 6d or 8d galvanized finishing nails through the butt and shingle below.

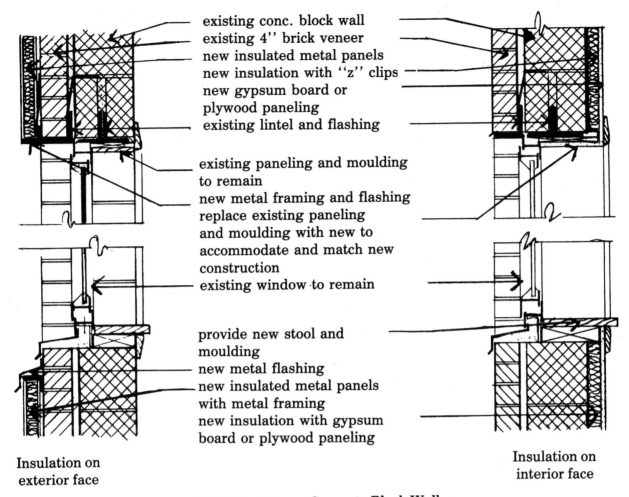

existing conc. block wall
existing 4'' brick veneer
new insulated metal panels
new insulation with ''z'' clips
new gypsum board or
plywood paneling
existing lintel and flashing

existing paneling and moulding
to remain
new metal framing and flashing
replace existing paneling
and moulding with new to
accommodate and match new
construction
existing window to remain

provide new stool and
moulding
new metal flashing
new insulated metal panels
with metal framing
new insulation with gypsum
board or plywood paneling

Insulation on
exterior face

Insulation on
interior face

Insulating Over a Concrete Block Wall
Figure 11-27

3. Face-nail the shingle just replaced at the butt, setting the nails and puttying.

4. Touch edges and other necessary spots with paint.

Brick Veneer

Brick veneer construction consists of a 4 inch brick wall attached to sheathing which is nailed to studs. Where entrance by removal of the trim or eaves is not possible, it will be necessary to remove the brick. It is of utmost importance that the number of openings be minimized. Thus, it is desirable to make openings straddling the studding, as this permits two panels to be serviced through one opening. The removal of one brick will usually give access to two stud spaces. Where it is necessary to remove two or three bricks, the combination may be two bricks beside each other or two beside each other and one above or below. When servicing only one panel, the removal of a single brick will usually

suffice.

When blowing brick veneer walls, a 2 inch nozzle rather than a 2½ inch nozzle will make the job easier. When doing brick walls, consider the use of an experienced mason if your crews are not experienced in this type of construction.

There are two methods of removing brick: (1) Removal of the brick itself by removing the mortar around it; or (2) by actually breaking the brick out in pieces. Whenever possible the former method should be used.

To remove the brick in its entirety, it is necessary to remove the mortar around it. This can be done by drilling four holes at the corners of the brick and chiseling out the mortar between them. Power chisels make this a relatively easy operation on some jobs. Another method of removing the mortar joint is by the use of a skill saw and a special cement cutting blade.

After the panels are filled, the bricks should

173

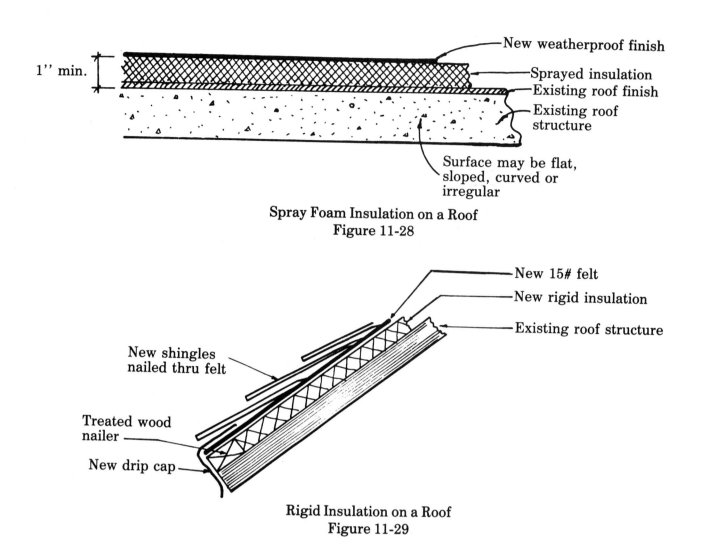

1'' min.

New weatherproof finish
Sprayed insulation
Existing roof finish
Existing roof structure

Surface may be flat, sloped, curved or irregular

Spray Foam Insulation on a Roof
Figure 11-28

New 15# felt
New rigid insulation
Existing roof structure

New shingles nailed thru felt

Treated wood nailer

New drip cap

Rigid Insulation on a Roof
Figure 11-29

be carefully replaced, matching the old mortar as closely as possible. Mortar may be given an aged appearance with the aid of a blow torch.

Adding Insulation to Wall Surfaces

In an existing building it may be possible to add insulation to the wall surface, either interior or exterior. Figure 11-27 shows examples of insulating materials added over a concrete block wall. This is the only practical way to insulate solid masonry or concrete and may cost less than filling wall cavities if the wall has few openings and new exterior or interior wall cover was needed. Be sure that the insulating material you select meets local code requirements for fastening security, fire resistance and smoke or fume production.

Internal insulation must be protected from moisture by a vapor barrier and from degradation by wear and tear either by having an integral finished surface or by being covered by a protective finish such as wood paneling or gypsum wallboard. Design problems likely to occur when adding insulation to the internal surfaces of walls are treatment of window and door openings, the junction between the insulation and the floor and ceiling, and repositioning equipment such as heaters and electric receptacles that are in the existing wall.

Adding Insulation to the Roof Surface

Where an existing roof has deteriorated and is scheduled for extensive repair or replacement, you could spray on polyurethane foam or install rigid insulation. The roof surface must be cleaned of all loose debris and, if necessary, cut back to provide a good bonding surface. It is not necessary, however, to provide a completely smooth surface as the foam will conform to any irregularities. The existing roof structure must be vented as necessary and protection provided against overspray. Even though the insulation will not absorb water, it must be protected by a weatherproof finish such as butyl. Whatever finish is selected must be applied cold as heat

174

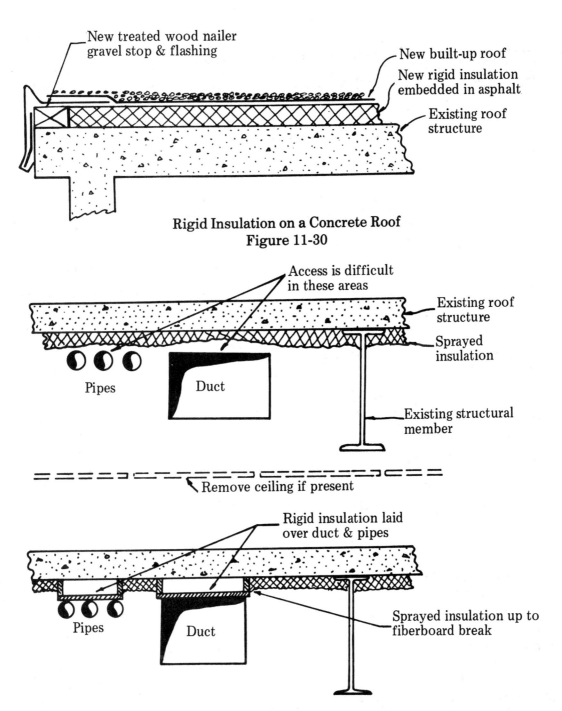

New treated wood nailer
gravel stop & flashing

New built-up roof

New rigid insulation
embedded in asphalt

Existing roof
structure

Rigid Insulation on a Concrete Roof
Figure 11-30

Access is difficult
in these areas

Existing roof
structure

Sprayed
insulation

Pipes

Duct

Existing structural
member

Remove ceiling if present

Rigid insulation laid
over duct & pipes

Pipes

Duct

Sprayed insulation up to
fiberboard break

Insulation on the Inside Surface of a Roof
Figure 11-31

can damage the insulation. A minimum thickness of 1'' spray foam is required to provide acceptable bond strength and integrity. See Figure 11-28.

For rigid insulation, the roof surface must be cleaned of all loose debris and a smooth surface provided. Treated wood nailers should be used at all joints, roof penetrations, gravel stops, and as required to fit new flashing. For sloping roofs of angles greater than 5°, treated wood nailers

should be provided between insulation boards. See Figure 11-29. Rigid insulation made of fiberglass fiberboard, cellular glass, or perlite boards should be embedded in a solid mopping of hot asphalt and then protected with a built up roof. See Figure 11-30.

Adding Insulation to the Inside Surface

Where the existing roof is sound and the underside is directly accessible, polyurethane

175

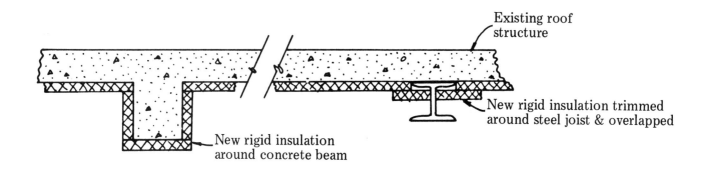

New rigid insulation trimmed around steel joist & overlapped

Existing roof structure

New rigid insulation around concrete beam

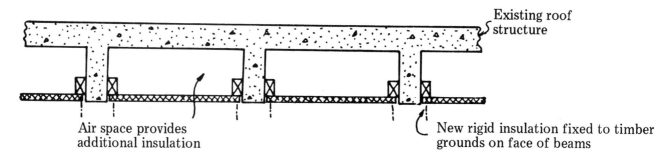

Existing roof structure

Air space provides additional insulation

New rigid insulation fixed to timber grounds on face of beams

Rigid Insulation on the Underside of a Roof
Figure 11-32

spray foam, mineral fiber spray, or rigid insulation may be added to the inside surface.

For sprayed foam insulation, access must be provided over the whole area. The underside must be brushed clean of all loose debris and any ducts or pipes masked from the spray. A minimum thickness of 1'' sprayed insulation is required. Difficulty may be experienced in reaching all the roof area where ducts and pipes are installed close to the roof and where structural members protrude. See Figure 11-31 for possible solutions.

Spray insulation is quick and easy to apply, but will require either removal of furnishings or protection to prevent spoiling by overspray and droppings. Polyurethane spray and mineral fiber spray both involve health hazards and the immediate building area must be evacuated while the work is done. As a side benefit, mineral fiber sprays will generally improve the fire rating of the structure and provide good noise control if exposed to the occupied space below.

To apply rigid insulation to the underside of the roof, direct access is required over the whole area. The surface should be brushed free of all loose debris and be relatively smooth. The

insulation may be glued, nailed or fixed with special clips and must be trimmed to fit around obstructions. See Figure 11-32. Installation is less rapid than spray but can be restricted to small areas at any one time, causing minimum inconvenience. It is impractical, however, in nearly all wood-frame dwellings.

Although most insulating materials are light and unlikely to exceed the permissible loading of the existing structure, you should be sure that the work you do complies with the local building code.

Check with the local fire department on the acceptability of insulating materials. In some areas plastic insulation is considered a fire and smoke hazard. Check with the local office of the Food and Drug Administration (Health, Education and Welfare Dept.) to determine whether the insulation considered is listed as hazardous if work is being done in a retail store that sells food.

Soffits of roof overhangs and roof facias are frequently left uninsulated and can result in high heat loss. If the building you are working on has these features, they should be insulated at the same time as the main roof. If the soffit is accessible, sprayed or rigid insulation may be

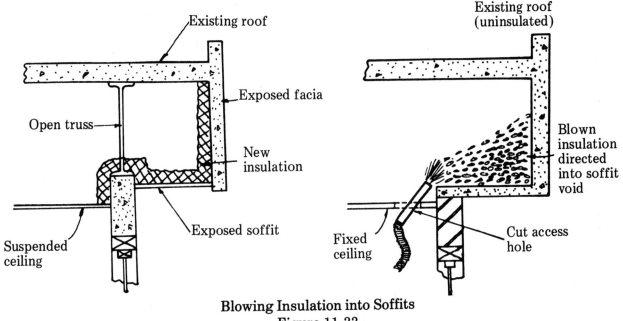

Blowing Insulation into Soffits
Figure 11-33

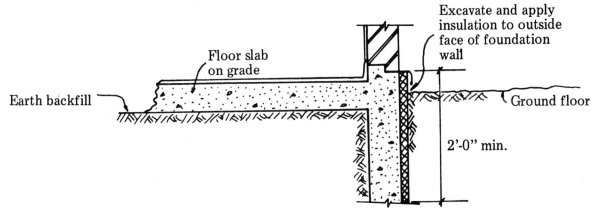

Slab-on-Grade Floor Insulation
Figure 11-34

used. If the soffit is not accessible, a hole can be cut in the structure for blowing mineral fiber. See Figure 11-33.

Improving Floor Insulation

Heat loss from slab-on-grade floors occurs mainly around the perimeter. Very little heat is lost from the center of the floor. This is because the insulating effect of the earth is greatest in the center and least in the perimeter. Heat loss from suspended floors over an unheated space, however, occurs evenly over the whole floor area and is proportional to the difference between inside and outside temperatures. In existing buildings it is impracticable to add insulation to the top of existing floors.

Uninsulated slab-on-grade floors should be insulated around the perimeter. This insulation should be placed vertically on the outside edge of the floor and should extend at least 2'-0" below the floor surface. See Figures 11-34 to 11-36.

Insulation materials may be rigid board or foam as described for walls. Insulation below ground should be applied in a bedding of hot asphalt. Existing flashing at ground floor level may have to be extended to cover the insulation top edge.

The savings due to edge insulation cannot be predicted with any accuracy. If, however, condensation occurs on the floor perimeter in cold weather or if the floor surface temperature close to the outside wall is more than 10°F. lower than the indoor temperature, then

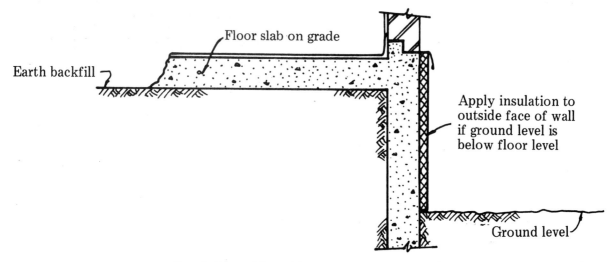

Insulating a Floor above Ground Level
Figure 11-35

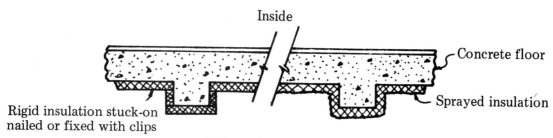

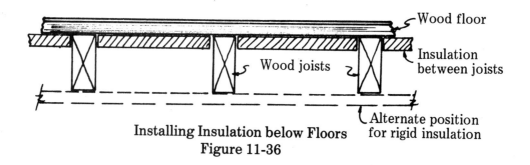

Installing Insulation below Floors
Figure 11-36

insulation will be beneficial and should be added.

Suspended floors over an unheated space (garage, crawlway, etc.) may be insulated on the underside by applying spray foam or rigid insulation as described for roofs.

Improve Air Duct Insulation

Warm air ducts are commonly installed without insulation. Typically they are routed from the equipment through unoccupied spaces, shafts, and ceiling voids where their heat loss is unproductive in meeting the occupied space heating load. Even when the temperature difference between ducts and the air temperature is relatively small, heat loss in long duct runs can be significant. Ducts run above a well insulated ceiling will waste much more fuel.

Of equal importance is the temperature drop of air moving in the duct. In long duct runs serving many rooms, this will result in the last room having a lower supply air temperature

City	Type of work	Add storm sash	Add 6" to uninsulated attic	Increase 3½" in attic to 6"	Blow 3½" in sidewalls
Atlanta, GA	Heat pump	8	2	6	8
	Electric resistance	4	1	4	5
	Gas	14	3	7	12
	Oil	6	2	5	7
Boston, MA	Heat pump	4	1	4	5
	Electric resistance	2	1	2	3
	Gas	4	2	4	6
	Oil	4	1	3	5
Cheyenne, WY	Heat pump	4	2	7	6
	Electric resistance	3	1	3	4
	Gas	12	4	11	16
	Oil	3	1	3	4
Chicago, IL	Heat pump	5	2	6	7
	Electric resistance	3	1	3	5
	Gas	6	2	5	8
	Oil	3	1	3	4
Dallas, TX	Heat pump	12	3	7	12
	Electric resistance	7	2	5	8
	Gas	16	3	8	14
	Oil	6	2	5	8
Kansas City, KS	Heat pump	8	2	7	10
	Electric resistance	5	2	4	7
	Gas	13	3	8	13
	Oil	4	1	4	6
Knoxville, TN	Heat pump	10	3	7	12
	Electric resistance	5	2	5	7
	Gas	9	3	8	12
	Oil	5	2	5	7
Minneapolis, MN	Heat pump	3	2	4	5
	Electric resistance	3	1	2	3
	Gas	6	2	5	8
	Oil	3	1	3	4
Philadelphia, PA	Heat pump	4	2	4	6
	Electric resistance	3	1	2	4
	Gas	6	2	5	7
	Oil	4	1	4	5
Phoenix, AZ	Heat pump	9	2	5	8
	Electric resistance	6	2	4	7
	Gas	10	2	5	9
	Oil	7	2	4	7
San Diego, CA	Heat pump	35	3	11	25
	Electric resistance	11	2	7	13
	Gas	54	4	13	31
	Oil	18	3	9	19
Seattle, WA	Heat pump	14	4	12	16
	Electric resistance	6	2	6	8
	Gas	7	3	8	12
	Oil	4	2	4	6
Washington, DC	Heat pump	5	2	5	6
	Electric resistance	3	1	3	4
	Gas	7	2	5	9
	Oil	4	2	4	6

Payback periods for existing homes
Table 11-37

than the first. The tendency in this case is to heat the last room to comfort conditions, resulting in overheating in each preceding room. This wastes energy over and above the duct heat loss.

Warm air ducts may be insulated with rigid fibrous material stuck on or fixed with special clips or bands. They may also be insulated with flexible mats clipped or wired on (this is particularly applicable for round or oval ducts). Ducts may also be insulated with spray-on foam or fibrous material as described for insulating undersides of roofs. Consider insulating roofs and ducts at the same time.

Insulation applied to ducts supplying only warm air need not be vapor sealed. Insulation applied to ducts supplying warm air in winter and cold air in summer must be vapor sealed to prevent condensation forming within the insulation.

Check with the local fire department to determine whether the selected insulation is acceptable or whether it is considered a fire and smoke hazard.

Savings In An Existing Home

How much can be saved by adding insulation to an existing home depends on the cost of fuel, the cost of the improvement and the type of heating system in use. In general, it almost always pays to bring attic insulation up to R19 or 6 inches of insulation. Table 11-37 shows how long it will take to recover the initial investment under most conditions in 13 U.S. cities. In the table all periods are rounded off to the next higher whole year. Note that any payback period less than 5 years is a sure money maker. Periods of from 6 to 10 years depend on the home owner's personal finances and preferences. If he has the money available and plans to stay in the house for some time, the improvement will save him money over the longer period. Payback periods over 10 years are advisable if fuel prices rise faster than most experts expect them to or if utility company or government incentive are available to encourage the investment. The payback periods here were calculated by the Oak Ridge National Laboratory for the U.S. Energy Research and Development Administration.

You can calculate the savings for adding or improving insulation fairly easily by determining the BTU's of energy that are saved. Once the BTU's per year saving is known, convert the total to dollars by using certain constants that relate to the type of fuel used. Chapter 15 shows how to use the calculated fuel savings as a selling tool and has the forms you need to develop a complete retrofit proposal and savings estimate.

The charts and explanations that follow show a convenient way of figuring the dollar savings for several key projects outlined earlier. They give the total in thousands of BTU's saved per year. To convert 1000 BTU's to units of fuel, divide by the constants below. Multiply the result by the cost per unit of fuel to find the actual dollars saved.

Units of Fuel Saved	Thousands of BTU's saved
No.2 Heating oil, gallon	138
No.6 Heating Oil, gallon	146
Natural Gas, cubic foot	1
Manufactured gas, cubic foot	.8
Coal, short ton	26,000
Steam, 1000 pounds	900
Propane gas, pound	21.5
Electricity, 1000 watt hours	3.413

You will also have to know the "U" value or heat transfer coefficients of both the existing and proposed wall, ceiling, floor or window. Tables 11-38 and 11-39 list "U" values for various constructions.

Component	Insulation	"U" Value
Ceiling	None	0.29[a]
	3½" glass fiber	0.07
	6" glass fiber	0.045
	7½" glass fiber	0.037
Wall	None	0.19
	1-7/8" glass fiber	0.090
	2½" glass fiber	0.077
	3½" glass fiber	0.062
Floor	None	0.28
	Foil with air gap	0.093
	3½" glass fiber	0.069
Windows	Single pane	1.02 + 0.44[b] = 1.46
	Double glazed	0.58 + 0.44[b] = 1.02
	Storm sash	0.48 + 0.22[b] = 0.70

[a] Includes effect of attic on heat transmission.
[b] First value is conduction U; second value is infiltration equivalent U. Effective U is sum of two.

Typical wood frame structure "U" values
Table 11-38

Wall Savings

To determine the heating energy saved by insulating walls, refer to Figures 11-40 and 11-41, then carry out the following procedure:

1. Determine your latitude from Figure 11-48 and select the appropriate graph.

2. Determine from the table at the end of Chapter 15 the heating degree days for your location. See pages 261 to 266.

3. Determine from Figure 10-12 the mean daily solar radiation in Langleys for your location.

4. Determine the orientation and area of the wall or walls to be insulated.

Material	"U" Value per inch of thickness
Acoustical ceiling tile	.42
Asbestos cement board	4.00
Brick, common	5.00
Brick, face	9.01
Carpet	.45
Ceramic tile	.45
Celotex	.25
Clay tile, 6 inch	3.95
Concrete block, 4", light	2.68
Concrete block, 6", light	3.36
Concrete block, 8", light	4.00
Concrete block, 4", regular	5.59
Concrete block, 6", regular	6.90
Concrete block, 8", regular	7.19
Concrete	12.05
Door, hollow core	.42
Drywall	3.30
Earth	6.49
Felt (asphalt saturated)	1.33
Glass block	.40
Gypsum deck	1.60
Gypsum plaster board(lath)	1.15
Hardboard	1.40
Insulation, fiber	.17

Material	"U" Value per inch of thickness
Insulation, rigid	.36
Insulation, mineral wool batt	.32
Insulation, roof deck	.38
Linoleum	1.57
Perlite	1.50
Plaster, sand aggregate	5.59
Plaster, light aggregate	1.60
Plywood	.80
Rockwool batt	.27
Roofing, built-up	1.13
Roofing, asphalt shingles	.30
Roofing, wood shingles	.40
Stones, 4" diameter	12.50
Stucco	4.00
Styrofoam	.60
Terrazzo	12.50
Tile, asphalt	2.50
Tile, vinyl	2.00
Urethane foam	.17
Vermiculite, loose	.30
Wood, hard	1.10
Wood, soft	1.38
Zonolite, loose	.39

"U" values per inch thickness of materials
Table 11-39

5. Determine the initial "U" value of the wall and the improved "U" value after insulation. Use table 11-38 or 11-39.

6. Determine the absorption coefficient of the outside surface of the wall. Use 0.3 for white walls and higher values to 0.8 for black walls. Most walls will be about 0.5.

7. Begin with the initial "U" value of the wall. Enter the graph at the appropriate degree days and follow the direction of the example line. Intersect the appropriate points for Langleys, orientation and "U" value. Read out the yearly heat loss in thousand BTU's per square foot of wall on the appropriate absorption coefficient line. Interpolate the results for absorption coefficients other than the 0.3 and 0.8 shown. Repeat this procedure using the improved "U" value and subtract the energy used before insulation to find the energy saving per square foot of wall. Multiply this saving by the area of the wall insulated. Convert the BTU's saved to units of fuel with the energy constants.

8. Repeat the complete procedure outlined in (7) above for each different orientation of wall to be insulated. The graph shows orientation for the four cardinal points (north, east, south, and west.) Interpolate for other orientations. Note that the heat losses derived from the graph assume that the wall is not shaded from direct sunshine. If shading occurs, then regardless of the actual orientation of the wall, treat it as a north wall, as this does not include a direct sunshine component.

Total the yearly fuel savings of all walls insulated to obtain total saving of fuel. Multiply the units of fuel saved by the cost per unit to find the dollars saved per year. In addition, wall insulation will also reduce summer heat gains. This extra saving is small but nevertheless should be recognized.

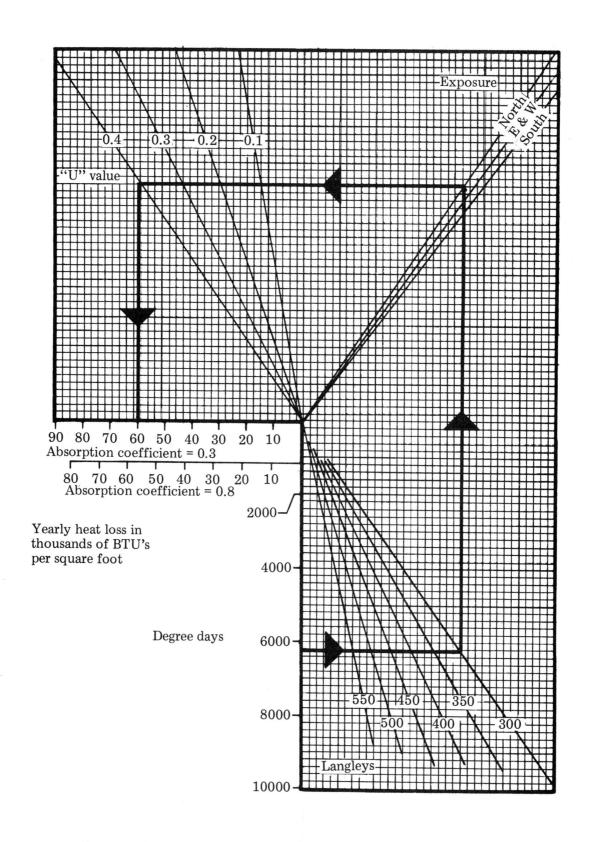

Yearly heat loss through walls,
latitude 25°N to 35°N
Figure 11-40

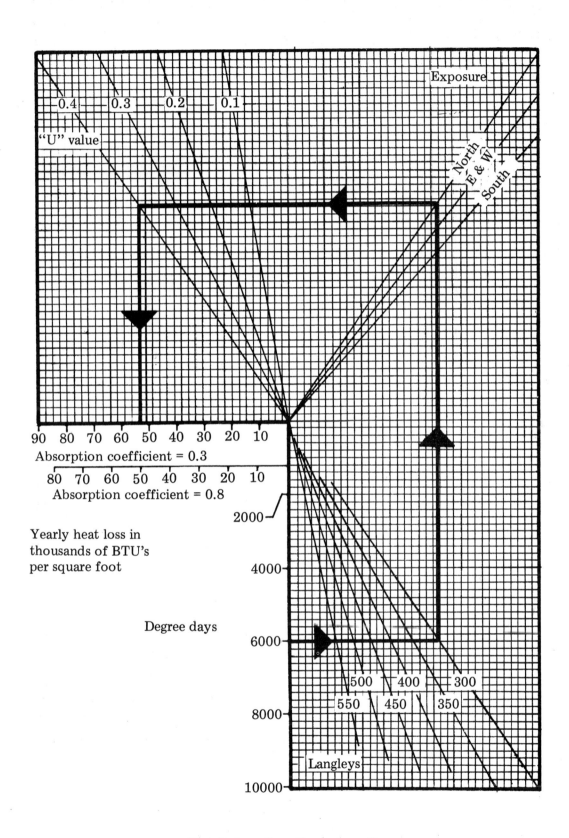

Yearly heat loss through walls,
latitude 35°N to 45°N
Figure 11-41

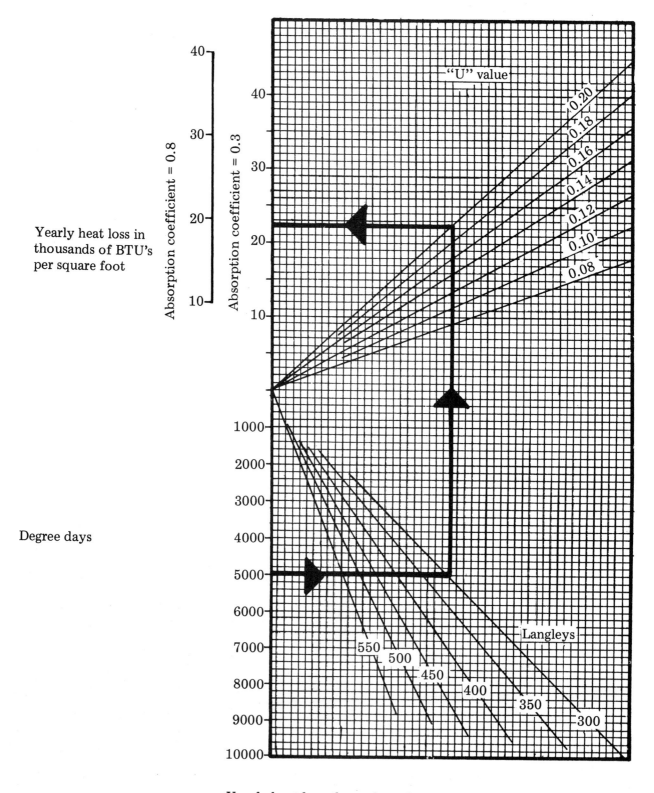

Yearly heat loss through roofs
Figure 11-42

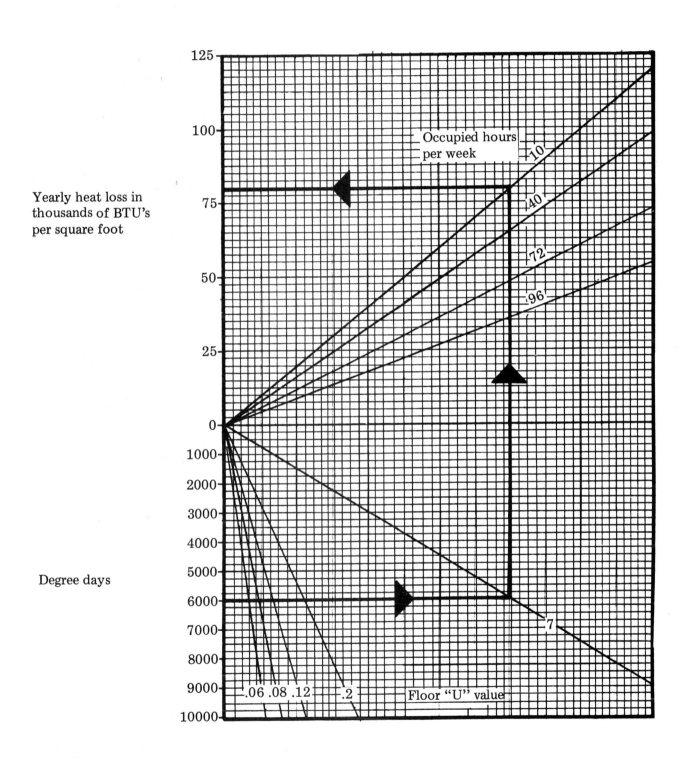

Yearly heat loss through floors
Figure 11-43

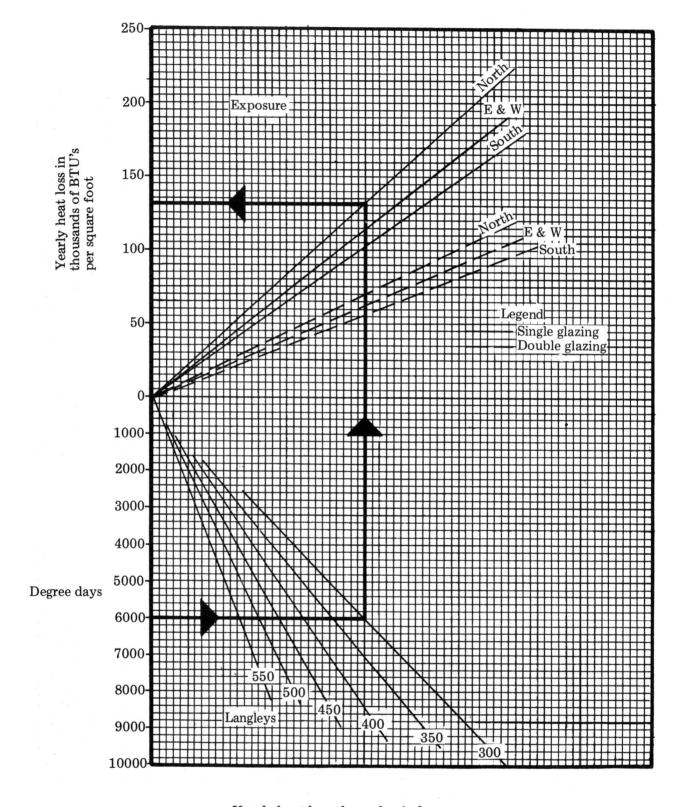

Yearly heat loss through windows,
latitude 25°N to 35°N
Figure 11-44

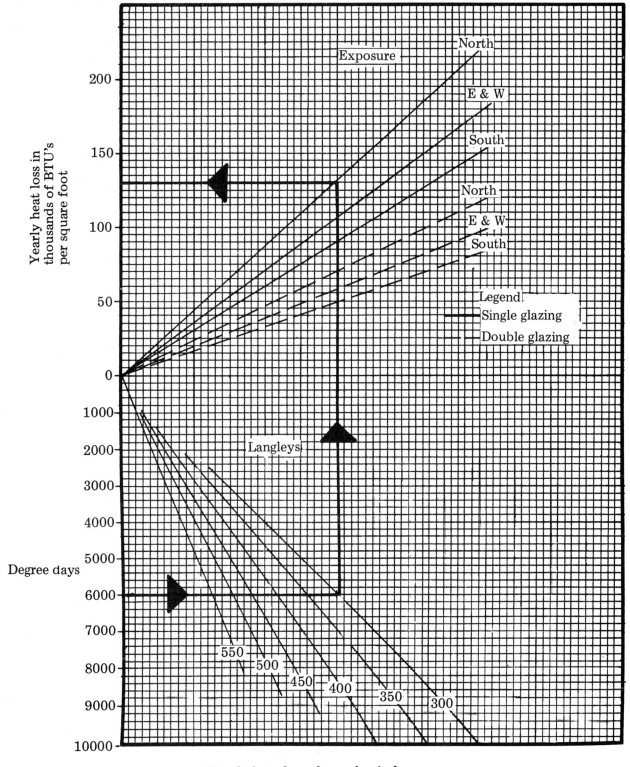

Yearly heat loss through windows,
latitude 35°N to 45°N
Figure 11-45

Roof Savings

To determine the heating energy saved by insulating roofs, refer to Figure 11-42 and carry out the following procedure:

1. Determine your latitude from Figure 11-48 and select the appropriate graph.

2. Determine from the table at the end of Chapter 15 the heating degree days for your location.

3. Determine from Figure 10-12 the mean daily solar radiation in Langleys for your location.

4. Determine the initial "U" value and the improved "U" value after insulation. Use Table 11-38 or 11-39.

5. Determine the absorption coefficient of the roof outside surface. Use 0.3 for white roofs and 0.8 for black roofs.

6. Begin with the initial "U" value of the roof. Enter the graph at the appropriate degree days and follow the direction of the example line. Intersect the appropriate points for Langleys and "U" value. Read out the yearly heat loss per square foot of roof on the appropriate absorption coefficient line. Interpolate to obtain answers for absorption coefficients other than the 0.3 and 0.8 shown. Convert the BTU's saved to units of fuel with the energy constants.

7. Repeat this complete procedure using the improved "U" value. Subtract the answer from the energy used before insulating to find the energy saving per square foot of insulated roof. Multiply this saving by the area of the insulated roof to determine the total yearly reduction. Multiply the units of fuel saved by the cost per unit to find the dollars saved per year.

In addition to savings achieved by reducing winter heat losses, roof insulation will also reduce summer heat gains. When adding roof insulation to the outside surface of a roof, it is possible to change the absorption coefficient (roof surface color) at the same time. A judgment must be made whether it is better to have a dark surface to improve the heating effect of the sun in winter or whether it is better to have a light surface and sacrifice the winter benefits in favor of reflecting unwanted solar gains in summer.

Floor Savings

To determine the heating energy saved by insulating floors, refer to Figure 11-43 and carry out the following procedure:

1. Determine from the table at the end of Chapter 15 the heating degree days for your location.

2. Determine the initial "U" value and the improved "U" value after insulation. See Table 11-38 or 11-39.

3. Using the initial "U" value of the floor, enter the graph at the appropriate degree days. Follow the direction of the example line. Intersect at the appropriate point for "U" value. Read out the yearly heat loss per square foot of floor area after crossing the line indicating the hours the building is heated.

4. Repeat this complete procedure using the improved "U" value. Subtract the answer from the energy used before insulating to find the energy saving per square foot of insulated floor. Multiply this saving by the area of the insulated floor to find total yearly heat load reduction. Convert BTU's saved to units of fuel saved with the energy constants. Convert units of fuel to dollars saved per year.

Window Savings

To determine the energy saved by double glazing, refer to Figures 11-44 and 11-45 and then carry out the following procedure:

1. Determine your latitude from Figure 11-48 and select the appropriate graph.

2. Determine from the table at the end of Chapter 15 the heating degree days for your location.

3. Determine from Figure 10-12 the mean daily solar radiation in Langleys for your location.

4. Select the orientation and determine the area of the windows to be double glazed.

5. Enter the graph at the appropriate degree days. Following the direction of the example line, intersect with the appropriate Langleys and orientation. Read out the yearly energy requirements for one square foot of single glazed window. Repeat the procedure for double glazing and subtract this value from the energy required for single glazing to find the load reduction in BTU's per year per square foot of double-glazed window. Multiply by the area of window to determine the total yearly heating load reduction for the orientation considered. Divide the BTU's saved by the energy constant to find the amount of fuel saved.

6. Repeat the procedure for other orientations. Note that the heat losses derived from the graph assume that the windows are subjected to direct sunshine and are not shaded by adjacent

buildings, structures, trees, etc. If shading occurs, then regardless of the actual orientation, use the figures for north facing windows as these do not include a direct-sunshine component. Multiply the total units of fuel saved by the appropriate fuel cost to get the dollars saved per year.

Interpolate for orientations other than the four cardinal points shown. In addition to the energy savings made by reducing heat losses, double glazing also reduces heat gain in summer, resulting in a slight reduction of cooling loads.

Existing single glazed windows may be converted permanently to double glazed windows by the addition of a new glazing frame to accept the additional pane of glass. The space between the glazing should be vented and drained to the outside and provisions made for cleaning both sides of each sheet of glass.

Where the existing window frame is in good condition and the glazing system permits, a single sheet of glass may be replaced by a sealed double glazing unit. In all cases whether storm windows are added or single windows are replaced by double, the frame of the selected unit should not form a heat bridge. Each frame should incorporate a thermal break between inside and outside surfaces. Such frames are commercially available. This is particularly important in frames made of metal, which readily conducts heat. Wood frames are better because wood is a poor heat conductor.

Before installing double glazing check the applicable local and national codes. Some building codes specify tempered glass. Glazing fitted outside existing windows must be fastened in an acceptable manner. Local fire codes often specify a certain percentage or number of windows per floor that must be operable. In this case, and also where operable windows are required for ventilation, the additional glazing should also be operable.

Savings for Cooling

Dark walls have a high absorption coefficient (0.7 or greater) and may be resurfaced or coated to reduce the heat absorbed. Use light colored paint or finish. Silver is best but white may be more acceptable if reflections on the surrounding properties are objectionable. Theoretically, it is possible to reduce the external absorption coefficient to 0.1, but in practice

dirt accumulates on building surfaces and an absorption coefficient of 0.3 for white and 0.5 for light colors (pastel shades of yellow, green, etc.) is more realistic.

To determine the reduction of heat gain through walls due to a reduction in absorption coefficient, use Figure 11-46 or 11-47 and interpolate as necessary for changes in the coefficient. Figure 11-48 gives the annual dry bulb degree hours figure you need for determining the heat gain in your area. Langley radiation values are listed in Figure 10-12.

Savings from Reduced Cooling Loads

Buildings with mechanical cooling will use less energy if the ceiling, walls and floor are well insulated and the roof surface is a light color. The reduced absorption coefficient of a light colored roof may be more important from an energy conservation standpoint than good thermal insulation. White paint or light colored roofing will usually save more than its cost over a short period in most air conditioned single story buildings.

Any paint or reflective finish must be compatible with the existing roof and capable of withstanding abrasion. The absorption coefficient of roofs may also be reduced by adding a surface layer of white pebbles or gravel. Check that the weight of the additional layer does not exceed the structural bearing capacity, and that gravel stops are fitted around rain water drains and the perimeter of the roof. If insulation is added to the surface of the roof for the purpose of reducing heat loss or heat gain, select the most desirable absorption coefficient. Change in roofing materials to effect changes of absorption coefficient are subject to building or fire code compliance. In some cases color and texture change may require architectural review and approval.

To determine the cooling energy saved by insulating roofs or changing the absorption coefficient, refer to Figures 11-49 and 11-50 and carry out the following procedure:

1. Determine from Figure 11-48 the cooling degree hours above a dry bulb reading of 78° for your location.
2. Determine from Figure 10-12 the mean daily solar radiation in Langleys for your location.
3. Determine the initial "U" value and improved "U" value after insulation. See Tables 11-38 and 11-39.

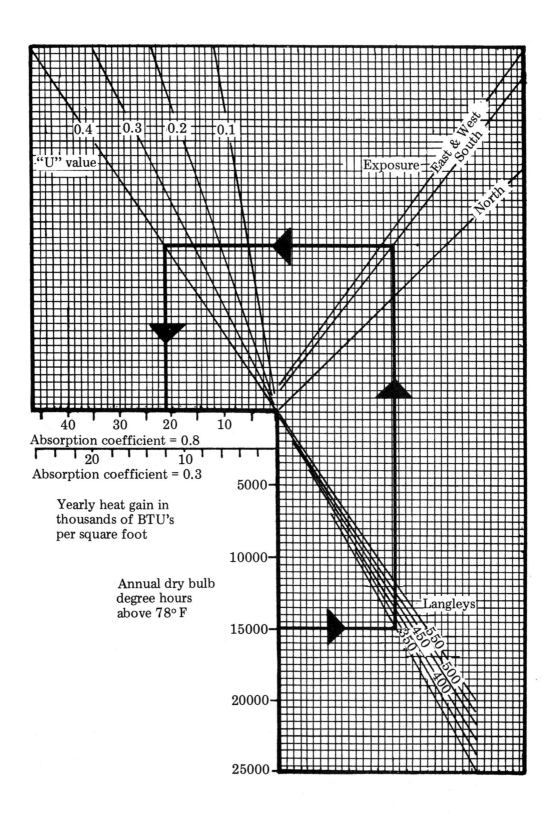

Yearly solar heat gain through walls,
latitude 25°N to 35°N
Figure 11-46

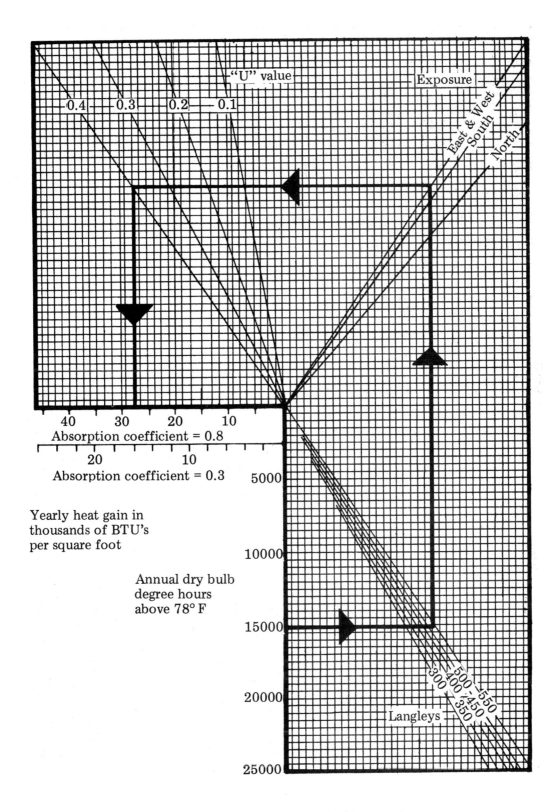

Yearly solar heat gain through walls,
latitude 35°N to 45°N
Figure 11-47

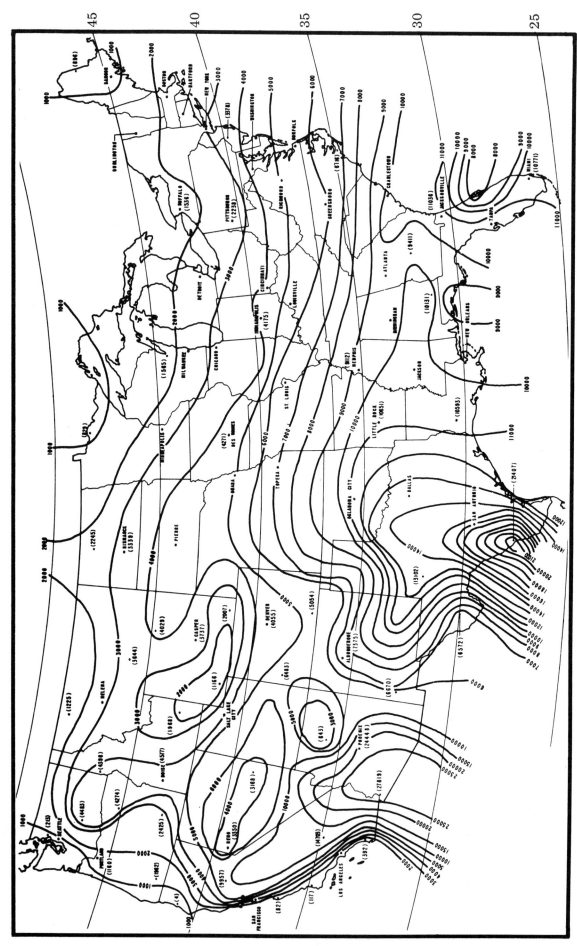

**Annual degree hours for dry bulb temperatures
greater than 78°**

Figure 11-48

Yearly heat gain in
thousands of BTU's
per square foot

Annual dry bulb
degree hours
above 78° F

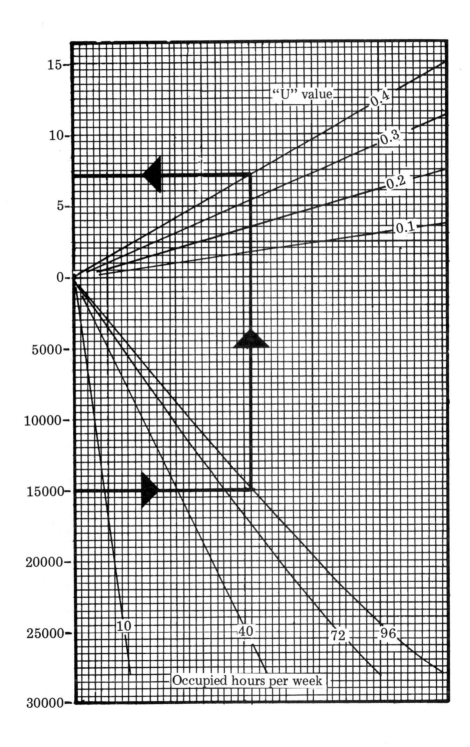

Yearly conduction heat gain through walls,
roofs and floors
Figure 11-49

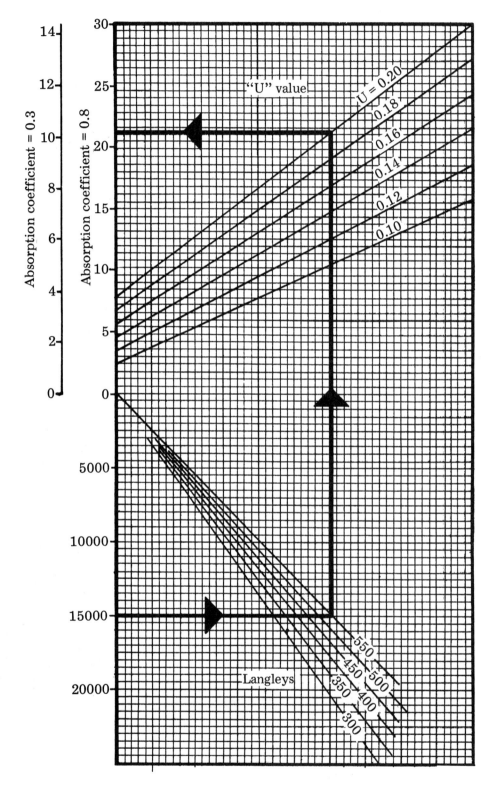

Yearly solar heat gain through roofs
Figure 11-50

194

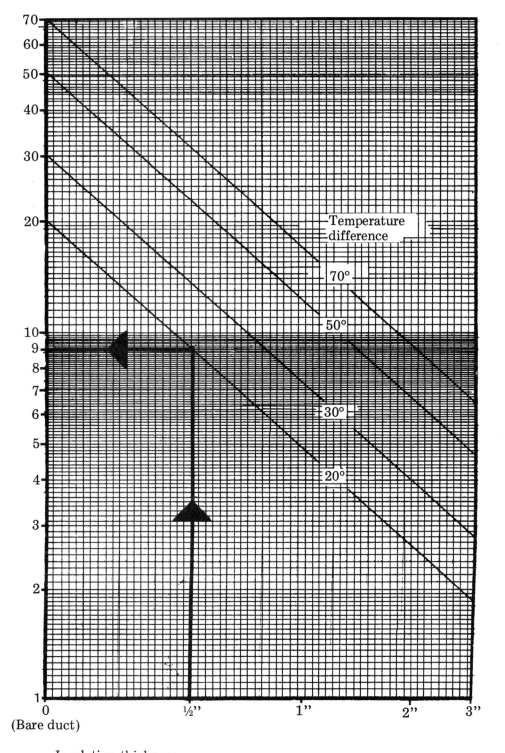

Heat loss or gain
in BTU's per hour
per square foot of
duct

Insulation thickness
in inches

Heat loss or gain for various duct
insulation thicknesses
Figure 11-51

4. Determine the initial absorption coefficient and the improved absorption coefficient.

5. Refer to Figure 11-49. Use the initial "U" value of the roof. Enter the graph at the selected degree hours and follow direction of the example line, intersecting at the appropriate points for hours of use per week and "U" value. Read out the yearly heat gain due only to conduction per square foot of roof.

6. Now, refer to Figure 11-50. Use the existing "U" value and absorption coefficient of the roof. Enter the graph at the selected degree hours and, following the direction of the example line, intersect at the appropriate points for Langleys and "U" value. Read out the yearly heat gain per square foot of roof on the appropriate absorption coefficient line. Interpolate to obtain answers for absorption coefficients other than the 0.3 and 0.8 shown.

7. Repeat steps 1 to 6 using the improved "U" value or the improved absorption coefficient. By subtraction, obtain the cooling load reduction due to insulation or modified absorption coefficient per square foot of roof.

Duct Insulation Savings

To determine the heating energy saved by insulating ducts, refer to Figure 11-51 and then carry out the following procedure:

1. Calculate the exposed surface area of uninsulated ductwork.

2. Estimate the average temperature differential between the duct and the surrounding air.

3. Enter the graph at the insulation thickness and, following the direction of the example line, intersect with the appropriate temperature differential line. Read out the heat loss in BTU per square foot per hour.

4. Read out the bare duct heat loss from the graph.

5. Subtract the insulated duct loss from the bare duct heat loss and multiply by the surface area of insulated duct to derive the saving in BTU per hour.

6. Estimate the hours of system operation per year and multiply by the hourly saving to derive the total yearly saving in BTU's.

If the air temperature varies by more than 5° F. over the year, determine and use the average temperature for the time considered in the calculation.

Weatherstripping and Caulking

In a well insulated house, the largest source of heat loss is from air leaks, especially around windows and doors. Good weatherstripping and caulking of exterior window and door frames will not only reduce the heat loss in winter and heat gain in summer, but they will reduce uncomfortable drafts as well.

Weatherstripping and caulking are generally economical in all climates. This is especially true for drafty windows and doors. Weatherstripping is available in a wide selection of shapes and materials. Caulking materials vary greatly in quality as well. More durable varieties will not have to be replaced as often, which is an important consideration.

A home needs some ventilation even in cold weather to release built-up moisture, cooking fumes and odors. Generally, one quarter to one half of the air volume in a home should be changed each hour, to keep the house from seeming "stuffy." Unfortunately, most houses have far more ventilation than they need, even if the doors and windows are never opened. All this extra air change means the heating and cooling systems have to run overtime to maintain comfortable room temperatures.

As a maximum, a house should have one complete air change per hour. Use Table 11-52 to estimate the excessive air change rate for a home:

Building Foundation. To determine leakage around sills and cellar windows, examine the structure from the inside. Look for "daylight" between the sill and the foundation. Feel for drafts at cellar windows. Push on windows to see if they are loose or rattle. Check for missing putty on sash.

If the building is on posts, infiltration must be evaluated by an examination of the floor. Open kitchen floor cabinets and look at pipe holes for the sink drain, etc. If these are tight, the building is category 1. . .if very open, category 3. Check the construction of the floor: if made of plywood or subfloor, paper, and finished floor, it is category 1. If board floor with visible cracks and discernible drafts, category 3.

Doors. Open the door quickly. A good fit will create a vacuum and resist the effort to open. A loose door will offer very little resistance. An on-hands-and-knees examination of the crack between the door and sill will also help. If a twenty-five cent piece can be pushed under the door, it is category 2, if two twenty-five cent pieces can be used, it is category 3.

Windows. The same evaluation can be used

Building Component	"Standard" One Air Change Per Hour	"Below Standard" Two Air Changes Per Hour	"Poor" Three Air Changes Per Hour
Building with cellar OR	Tight, no cracks, caulked sills, sealed cellar windows, no grade entrance leaks.	Some foundation cracks, no weatherstripping on cellar windows, grade entrance not tight.	Stone foundation, considerable leakage area, poor seal around grade entrance.
Building with crawl space or on posts	Plywood floor, no trap door leaks, no leaks around water, sewer and electrical openings.	Tongue-and-groove board floor, reasonable fit on trap doors, around pipes, etc.	Board floor, loose fit around pipes, etc.
Windows	Storm windows with good fit.	No storm windows, good fit on regular windows.	No storm windows, loose fit on regular windows.
Doors	Good fit on storm doors.	Loose storm doors, poor fit on inside door.	No storm doors, loose fit on inside door.
Walls	Caulked windows and doors building paper used under siding.	Caulking in poor repair, building needs paint.	No indication of building paper, evident cracks around door and window frame.

Usually building components are not all in the same infiltration category. You can estimate the approximate rate by considering how many of the components are in each category. For example, if two components are in the three air change category and two are in the two air change category, the overall infiltration would be 2 ½ air changes per hour.

Air infiltration categories
Figure 11-52

on windows. . .push hard on the window. . .if a twenty-five cent piece can be pushed between the window and the casing, it is category 2, if two can be used, it is category 3.

Walls. To determine infiltration through the walls, feel for drafts around outside wall electrical outlets. Check for caulking around doors and windows, condition of paint, check for building paper.

Cutting Down Infiltration

All wood doors and wood sashes must be weatherstripped. The cheapest type is a sort of plastic or rubber gasket that comes in a roll and creates a seal when the windows and doors are closed. This is an inferior and temporary method. The gasket material eventually hardens or manifests an uneven pressure and, needless to say, a number of air leaks are the result.

A spring bronze material is next in line, but it too operates under pressure and does not necessarily produce the best seal. Even better weatherstripping is interlocking bronze flanges that do not operate by pressure at all but actually form a tiny interlocking seal all around the windows and doors. This product will permit a certain play in the windows and doors and still not destroy the effect of the seal—an important feature in wood houses. By all means, favor the interlocking method of weatherstripping. The best seal against air infiltration is provided by magnetic strips that attach themselves to a metal skin door as the door is closed. Be sure,

however, that the door itself is adequately insulated. A number of good quality foam core metal doors are available.

When a garage is attached to the house, a plastic blade should be installed on the bottom edge of the garage door so that wind, leaves, and cold do not enter so easily through the large gap. The door from the garage into the house should also be weatherstripped to protect the house when the garage door is open.

For remodeling work, there are several good weatherstripping systems and each has its own level of effectiveness, durability and installation problems. Figures 11-53 and 11-54 show several practical methods for both doors and windows. No matter what system you use, attention to detail is the key. Even the best weatherstripping is useless when it isn't positioned to cover the opening it is intended to seal.

The Importance of Caulking

A few cracks around a few windows or the foundation can turn an otherwise energy efficient home into a real energy "disaster." Air enters the sidewalls through cracks in the building shell, moves vertically or horizontally in the walls and then into rooms through cracks in the internal wall cover. Even a well designed and carefully built home should be caulked carefully and then recaulked every 5 or ten years to close cracks that result from settlement, shrinkage of materials and deterioration of the caulking material. In an older home a few tubes

197

Thin spring metal

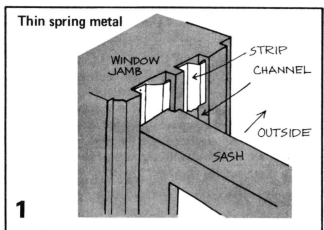

1

Install by moving sash to the open position and sliding strip in between the sash and the channel. Tack in place into the casing. Do not cover the pulleys in the upper channels.

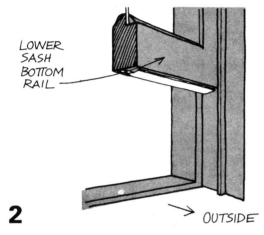

2

Install strips the full width of the sash on the bottom of the lower sash bottom rail and the top of the upper sash top rail.

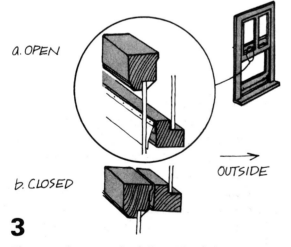

3

Then attach a strip the full width of the window to the upper sash bottom rail. Countersink the nails slightly so they won't catch on the lower sash top rail.

Rolled vinyl

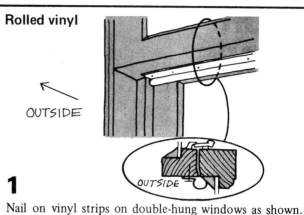

1

Nail on vinyl strips on double-hung windows as shown. A sliding window is much the same and can be treated as a double-hung window turned on its side. Casement and

2

tilting windows should be weatherstripped with the vinyl nailed to the window casing so that, as the window shuts, it compresses the roll.

Adhesive-backed foam strip

Install adhesive backed foam, on all types of windows, only where there is no friction. On double-hung windows, this is only on the bottom (as shown) and top rails. Other types of windows can use foam strips in many more places.

Weatherstripping windows
Figure 11-53

1. Adhesive backed foam:

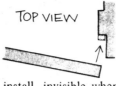

Evaluation — extremely easy to install, invisible when installed, not very durable, more effective on doors than windows.

Installation — stick foam to inside face of jamb.

2. Rolled vinyl with aluminum channel backing:

Evaluation — easy to install, visible when installed, durable.

Installation — nail strip snugly against door on the casing

3. Foam rubber with wood backing:

Evaluation — easy to install, visible when installed, not very durable.

Installation — nail strip snugly against the closed door. Space nails 8 to 12 inches apart.

4. Spring metal:

Evaluation — easy to install, invisible when installed, extremely durable.

Installation — cut to length and tack in place. Lift outer edge of strip with screwdriver after tacking, for better seal.

Weatherstripping doors
Figure 11-54

of caulking compound and an hour of labor will probably yield a larger dividend in energy saved per dollar invested than anything else that can be done. Every home insulation program should begin with caulking at the points where different materials or parts of the house come together.

Caulking compound is available in these basic types:

1. Oil or resin base caulk; readily available and will bond to most surfaces — wood, masonry and metal; not very durable but lowest in first cost for this type of application.

2. Latex, butyl or polyvinyl based caulk; all readily available and will bond to most surfaces, more durable, but more expensive than oil or resin based caulk.

3. Elastomeric caulks; most durable and most expensive; includes silicones, polysulfides and polyurethanes; the instructions provided on the labels should be followed.

4. Filler; includes oakum, caulking cotton, sponge rubber, and glass fiber types; used to fill extra wide cracks or as a backup for elastomeric caulks.

Of the types of caulks and sealants available, the preferred types are either polysulfide, polyurethane or silicone material. These types may more than pay for their high initial cost by eliminating the need for recaulking.

Be careful to caulk at these locations:

Note: These methods are harder than 1 through 4.

5. Interlocking metal channels:

Tools

Hack saw,
Hammer, nails,
Tape measure

Evaluation — difficult to install (alignment is critical), visible when installed, durable but subject to damage, because they're exposed, excellent seal.

Installation — cut and fit strips to head of door first: male strip on door, female on head; then hinge side of door: male strip on jamb, female on door; finally lock side on door, female on jamb.

6. Fitted interlocking metal channels: (J-Strips)

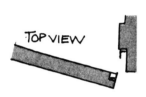

Evaluation — very difficult to install, exceptionally good weather seal, invisible when installed, not exposed to possible damage.

Installation — should be installed by a carpenter. Not appropriate for do-it-yourself installation unless done by an accomplished handyman.

7. Sweeps:

Tools

Screwdriver,
Hack saw,
Tape measure

Evaluation — useful for flat threshholds, may drag on carpet or rug.

Installation — cut sweep to fit 1/16 inch in from the edges of the door. Some sweeps are installed on the inside and some outside. Check instructions for your particular type.

8. Door Shoes:

Tools

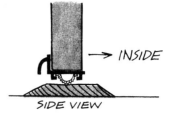

Screwdriver,
Hack saw,
Plane,
Tape measure

Evaluation — useful with wooden threshhold that is not worn, very durable, difficult to install (must remove door).

Installation — remove door and trim required amount off bottom. Cut to door width. Install by sliding vinyl out and fasten with screws.

9. Vinyl bulb threshold:

Tools

Screwdriver,
Hack saw,
Plane,
Tape measure

Evaluation — useful where there is no threshhold or wooden one is worn out, difficult to install, vinyl will wear but replacements are available.

Installation — remove door and trim required amount off bottom. Bottom should have about 1/8" bevel to seal against vinyl. Be sure bevel is cut in right direction for opening.

10. Interlocking threshold:

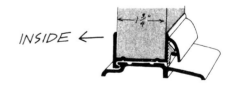

Evaluation — very difficult to install, exceptionally good weather seal.

Installation — should be installed by a skilled carpenter.

Weatherstripping doors
Figure 11-54, continued

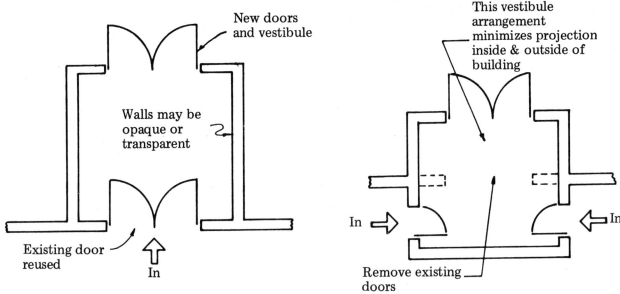

**Forming an "air lock" through
vestibule arrangement
Figure 11-55**

- Between drip caps and siding (windows and doors).
- At joints between window and door frames and siding.
- Between window sills and siding.
- At corners formed by siding.
- At sills where wood structure meets the foundation.
- Around outside water faucets, electrical outlets or other breaks in the outside house surfaces.
- Where pipes and wires penetrate the ceiling below an unheated attic.
- Between porches and the main body of the house.
- Where the chimney or masonry meets siding.
- Where the wall meets the eave at the gable ends of a heated attic.

Estimating the number of cartridges of caulking compound required is difficult since the number needed will vary greatly with the size of cracks to be filled. Rough estimates for recaulking an older home would be about as follows:

½ cartridge per window or door
4 cartridges for the foundation sill
2 cartridges for a two story chimney

Be sure to clean out any paint build-up, dirt or deteriorated caulking material before applying the new caulk. Paint thinner may be used to dissolve oil based paint or caulking material. Force the caulk into gaps to make sure that the material adheres to both sides and fills the crack completely. Extra wide cracks such as those at the sill should be stuffed with oakum, glass fiber or fiber weatherstripping before the caulk is applied. Any unsupported bead of caulk over about ¼ inch wide can be counted on to shrink away from one or both sides of the gap eventually and is vulnerable to accidental damage. Some wider cracks can be filled with rope form caulking, especially where the crack is several feet long and about uniform in width. Rope type caulking tends to shrink less than similar materials in cartridge form.

Other Considerations

If you provide a range hood, use the recirculation type in cold climates and the exhaust-to-outside air type in warm climates where the air conditioning load is more significant than the heating load.

Exhaust fans are essential in high moisture areas like bathrooms. Research has shown, however, that a home can lose large amounts of heated air through them, so use a model with a positive shutter closure.

If a fireplace is used, be sure to install a damper and instruct the homeowner to close it whenever the fireplace is not in use. A properly constructed fireplace draws air up through the chimney to expel smoke from the fire, but without a damper, it will continually draw out heated room air in the winter when the fireplace is not in use.

In buildings that experience fairly continuous traffic through external doors, infiltration

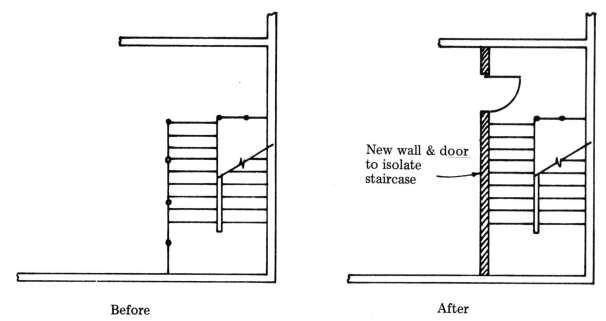

Before   After

New wall & door
to isolate
staircase

Reducing stack action in stairwells
Figure 11-56

may be reduced by building vestibules to form an "air lock". See Figure 11-55. The vestibule should be sufficiently long so that the external door closes before the internal door is opened. Depending on the particular characteristic of the building, the vestibule may be constructed inside or outside the building.

Vestibule doors may be either manually operated and self-closing or, if traffic is particularly dense, can be automatically opened and closed by a pressure pad or photo-electric cell. Revolving doors may be fitted in place of the existing doors. Although maximum reduction in infiltration will be achieved if they are used in conjunction with vestibules, they may also be used alone. When fitting revolving doors, it is always necessary to provide a hinged door in addition for use by handicapped people and to allow bulky objects to be taken in and out of the building. Check applicable fire codes and the local fire department to insure that

installation of a vestibule or revolving door does not infringe fire exit requirements.

To reduce the effect of potential stack action present in vertical shafts and stairs, these areas should be sealed from the rest of the building. Open stairwells in high rise buildings that connect with circulation spaces at each floor level should be provided with walls and self-closing doors to isolate them. See Figure 11-56. Check the local fire codes before isolating stairs from the remainder of the building to insure that fire exit requirements are met.

Consider installing a wind screen in front of an exposed front door to protect the interior from direct blasts of prevailing winds. Screens can be constructed cheaply from concrete block or can be constructed of metal framing with armored glass or Lexan fill. Careful positioning can reduce infiltration through external doors by about 50% of that obtained by fitting a vestibule.

Avoiding Condensation 12

Every house must cope with moisture that is produced in the interior. Cooking, bathing, laundry and all the actions associated with human habitation release water vapor into the air. Most families introduce 20 gallons or more of water into the home each week. This presents no problem when the windows are open. The humidity level on the interior will be no higher than on the exterior. But when a home is closed for winter heating or summer cooling the natural means of escape is eliminated. The water vapor still escapes, of course, but now through cracks around windows and doors, open chimney flues, and even directly through walls and the roof. But now assume that the energy saving measures described in the last chapter are used. Cracks and loose windows are sealed to cut down air infiltration and insulation is installed in walls, ceiling and floor. The result: many of those 20 gallons of water per week will go through the walls and ceiling to equalize the interior and exterior moisture level. In cold weather the water vapor condenses or freezes on the insulation, leaving the house encased in a cold cocoon of frozen, useless insulation. Eventually the insulation turns into a sodden mass, studs and joists are transformed into the consistency of balsa wood, and the whole structure deteriorates into an unholy shambles.

Fortunately, reduced air infiltration and improved insulation doesn't have to lead to condensation problems. Proper use of vapor barriers and adequate ventilation will minimize or eliminate most condensation, even when you insulate, caulk and weatherstrip a home that had condensation problems previously. It's relatively easy and inexpensive to reduce moisture problems in most homes. It takes some planning and care, but should be well worth the additional trouble to you and undoubtedly will be worth the added expense to your client. Ignoring potential condensation problems when building or insulating a home could be both very expensive for your client and expose you to legal liability for your negligence. This chapter is intended to help you understand the cause of moisture problems and suggest what you should do to prevent problems in new and newly insulated homes and remedy excessive moisture conditions in existing structures.

Most remodeling and repair jobs deal in some way with moisture problems. Any time you remove and replace siding, flooring, roofing or wall covering you have a chance to evaluate the work from a moisture control standpoint. You will have the opportunity to observe condensation problems and will have the chance to recommend an appropriate solution. Any time you add floor space to a house or convert an attic, basement or garage, you will have to deal with moisture. Everyone in the construction industry should be aware that professional workmanship demands attention to preventing moisture problems.

Moisture Sources

Moisture, which is produced in or which enters a home, changes the relative humidity of the interior atmosphere. Ordinary household functions which generate a good share of the total amount of water vapor include dishwashing, cooking, bathing, and laundry work, to say nothing of human respiration and evaporation from plants. Houses may also be equipped with central air conditioners or room humidifiers. Still another source of moisture may be from unvented or poorly vented clothes dryers. Several sources and their effect in adding water vapor to the interior of the house are as listed below in pints of water given off:

Plants = 1.7 for each plant per week.

Showers = 0.5 for each shower and 0.1 for each bath.

Floor mopping = 2.9 per 100 square feet, each washing.

Kettles and cooking = 5.5 per day.

Clothes (washing, steam ironing, drying) = 29.4 per week.

Water vapor from the soil of crawl-space houses does not normally affect the occupied areas. However, without good construction practices or proper precautions it can be a factor in causing problems in exterior walls over the area as well as in the crawl space itself. It is another source of moisture that must be considered in providing protection.

People moving into a newly constructed house or room addition in the fall or early winter sometimes experience temporary moisture problems. Surface condensation on windows, damp areas on cold closet walls where air movement is restricted, and even stained siding all indicate an excessive amount of moisture. Such conditions can often be traced to water used in the construction of a house.

There are other sources of moisture, often unsuspected, which could be the cause of condensation problems. One such source can be a gas fired furnace. It is desirable to maintain flue gas temperatures within the recommended limits throughout the appliance, in the flue, the connecting vent, and other areas. Otherwise, excessive condensation problems can result. If all sources of excessive moisture have been exhausted in determining the reasons for a condensation problem, it is best to have the heating unit examined by a competent heating engineer.

There is a distinct relationship in all homes between indoor relative humidity and outdoor temperature. The humidity is generally high indoors when outdoor temperatures are high and decreases as outdoor temperatures drop. In an exceptionally tight modern house where moisture buildup may be a problem, outside air should be introduced into the cold air return ducts to reduce relative humidity.

Condensation Damage

Condensation can be described as the change in moisture from a vapor to a liquid. In homes not properly protected, condensation caused by high humidities often results in unnecessarily rapid deterioration. Water vapor within the house, when unrestricted, moves through the wall or ceiling during the heating season to some cold surface where it condenses, collecting generally in the form of ice or frost. During warm periods the frost melts. When conditions are severe, the water from melting ice in unvented attics may drip to the ceiling below and cause damage to the interior finish. Moisture can also soak into the roof sheathing or rafters and set up conditions which could lead to decay. In walls, water from melting frost may run out between the siding laps and cause staining or soak into the siding and cause paint blistering and peeling.

Wood and wood-base materials used for sheathing and panel siding may swell from this added moisture and result in bowing, cupping, or buckling. Thermal insulation becomes wet and provides less resistance to heat loss. Efflorescence may occur on brick or stone of an exterior wall because of such condensation.

The cost of heat losses, painting and redecorating, and excessive maintenance and repair caused by cold weather condensation can be easily reduced or eliminated when proper construction details are used.

Changes in design, materials and construction methods have resulted in houses that are easier to heat and more comfortable, but these changes have accentuated the potential for condensation problems. New types of weatherstripping, storm sash, and sheet material for sheathing in new houses provide tight air-resistant construction which restricts the escape of moisture generated in the house. Newer houses are also generally smaller and may have lower ceilings, resulting in less atmosphere to hold moisture.

Unless excess water vapor is properly removed in some way (ventilation usually), it will either increase the humidity or condense on cold surfaces such as window glass. More serious, however, it can move in or through the construction, often condensing within the wall,

Darkened areas on roof boards and rafters in attic indicate stain that stemmed from condensation. This usually could be prevented by vapor barrier below the insulation and good attic ventilation

Figure 12-1

roof, or floor cavities. Heating systems equipped with winter air-conditioning (humidifier) systems also increase the humidity.

Most new houses have 3½ inches of insulation in the walls and 6 or more inches in the ceilings. Unfortunately, the more efficient the insulation is in retarding heat transfer, the colder the outer surfaces become and unless moisture is restricted from entering the wall or ceiling, the greater the potential for moisture condensation. Moisture migrates toward cold surfaces and will condense or form as frost or ice on these surfaces.

Inexpensive methods of preventing condensation problems are available. They mainly involve the proper use of vapor barriers and good ventilating practices. Naturally it is simpler, less expensive, and more effective to employ these during the construction of a house than to add them to existing homes. But most condensation problems can be solved at a reasonable cost and with little extra effort when insulating, remodeling or repairing the home.

Condensation will take place anytime the temperature drops below dewpoint (100 percent saturation of the air with water vapor at a given temperature). Commonly, under such conditions some surface accessible to the moisture in the air is cooler than the dewpoint and the moisture condenses on that surface.

Visible Condensation

During cold weather, visible condensation is usually first noticed on window glass but may also be discovered on cold surfaces of closets and unheated bedroom walls and ceilings. Visible surface condensation on the interior glass surfaces of windows can be minimized by the use of storm windows or by replacing single glass with insulated glass. However, when this does not prevent condensation on the surface, the relative humidity in the room must be reduced. Drapes or curtains across the windows hinder rather than help. Not only do they increase surface condensation because of colder glass surfaces, but they also prevent the air movement that would warm the glass surface and aid in dispersing some of the moisture.

Reducing high relative humidities within the house to permissible levels is often necessary to minimize condensation problems. Discontinuing the use of room-size humidifiers or reducing the output of automatic humidifiers until conditions are improved is helpful. The use of exhaust fans

Surface condensation on floor joists in crawl space. A vapor barrier ground cover can prevent this because it restricts water vapor movement from the soil and thus avoids high humidity of crawl space and subsequent surface condensation

Figure 12-2

and dehumidifiers can also be of value in eliminating high relative humidities within the house. When possible, decreasing the activities which produce excessive moisture, as discussed later in this chapter, is sometimes necessary. This is especially important for homes with electric heat.

Concrete slabs without radiant heat are sometimes subjected to surface condensation in late spring when warm humid air enters the house. Because the temperature of some areas of the concrete slab or its covering is below the dewpoint, surface condensation can occur. Keeping the windows closed during the day, using a dehumidifier, and raising the inside temperature aid in minimizing this problem. When the concrete slab reaches normal room temperatures, this inconvenience is eliminated.

Condensation might also be visible in attic spaces on rafters or roof boards near the cold cornice area (Figure 12-1) or form as frost. Such condensation or melting frost can result in excessive maintenance, such as the need for refinishing of window sash and trim, or even decay. Water from melting frost in the attic can

also damage ceilings below. Condensation or frost on protruding nails, on the surfaces of roof boards, or other members in attic areas normally indicates the escape of excessive amounts of water vapor from the heated rooms below. If a vapor barrier is not already present, place one between joists under the insulation. Make sure the vapor barrier fits tightly around ceiling lights and exhaust fans, caulking if necessary. In addition, increase both inlet and outlet ventilators to levels recommended later in this chapter. Decreasing the amount of water vapor produced in the living areas is also helpful.

Another area where visible condensation can occur is in crawl spaces under occupied rooms. This area usually differs from those on the interior of the house and in the attic because the source of the moisture is usually from the soil or from warm moisture-laden air which enters through foundation ventilators. Moisture vapor then condenses on the cooler surfaces in the crawl space (Figure 12-2). Such conditions often occur during warm periods in late spring. To eliminate this problem, place a vapor barrier

206

over the soil and use the proper amount of ventilation as recommended later in this chapter.

An increase in relative humidity of the inside atmosphere increases the potential for condensation on inside surfaces. For example, when inside temperature is 70°F., surface condensation will occur on a single glass window when outside temperature falls to -10°F. and inside relative humidity is 10 percent. When inside relative humidity is 20 percent, condensation can occur on the single glass when outside temperature only falls to about +7°F. When a storm window is added or insulated glass is used, surface condensation will not occur until the relative humidity has reached 38 percent when the outdoor temperature is -10°F. The above conditions apply only where storm windows are tight and there is good circulation of air on the inside surface of the window. Where drapes or shades restrict circulation of air, storm windows are not tight, or lower temperatures are maintained in such areas as bedrooms, condensation will occur at a higher outside temperature.

Concealed Condensation

Condensation in concealed areas, such as wall spaces, often is first noticed by stains on the siding or by paint peeling. Water vapor moving through permeable walls and ceilings is normally responsible for such damage. Water vapor also escapes from houses by constant outleakage through cracks and crevices, around doors and windows, and by ventilation, but this moisture-vapor loss is usually insufficient to eliminate condensation problems.

Concealed condensation takes place when a condensing surface is below the dewpoint. In cold weather, condensation often forms as frost. The resulting problems are usually not detected until spring after the heating season has ended. The remedies and solutions to the problems should be taken care of before repainting, residing or reinsulating is attempted. Several methods can be used to correct this problem.

1. Reduce or control the relative humidity within the house.

2. Improve the vapor resistance by adding a vapor barrier.

3. Add a vapor-resistant paint coating such as aluminum paint to the interior of walls and ceilings.

4. Improve crawl space and attic ventilation to the minimums recommended in this chapter.

5. Seal off areas where air or water enters walls and attics.

It has already been suggested that the family living in the home can reduce condensation by controlling the relative humidity. Steps 2 thru 5 above are effective ways to eliminate or reduce condensation regardless of the moisture present and are explained in the remainder of this chapter.

Vapor Barriers

Many materials used as interior coverings for exposed walls and ceilings, such as plaster, drywall, wood paneling, and plywood, permit water vapor to pass slowly through them during cold weather. Temperatures of the sheathing or siding on the outside of the wall are often low enough to cause condensation of water vapor within the cavities of a framed wall. When the relative humidity within the house at the surface of an unprotected wall is greater than that within the wall, water vapor will migrate through the plaster or other finish into the stud space; there it will condense if it comes in contact with surfaces colder than its dewpoint temperature. Vapor barriers are used to resist this movement of water vapor or moisture in various areas of the house.

The most effective vapor barrier is a continuous membrane which is applied to the inside face of studs and joists in new construction. In rehabilitation, such a membrane can be used only where new interior covering materials are to be applied.

The amount of condensation that can develop within a wall depends upon (a) the resistance of the intervening materials to vapor transfusion, (b) differences in vapor pressure, and (c) time. Plastering walls or ordinary drywalls have little resistance to vapor movement. However, when the surfaces are painted with oil base paint, the resistance is increased. High indoor temperature and relative humidities result in high indoor vapor pressures. Low outdoor vapor pressures always exist at low temperatures. Thus, a combination of high inside temperatures and humidities and low outside temperatures will normally result in vapor movement into the wall if no vapor barrier is present. Long periods of severe weather will result in condensation problems. Though fewer homes are affected by condensation in mild winter weather, many problems have been reported. Where information is available, it appears that the minimum relative humidities in the affected homes are 35 percent or higher.

Vapor barrier requirements are sometimes satisfied by one of the materials used in construction. In addition to integral vapor barriers which are a part of many types of insulation, such materials as plastic-faced hardboard and similar interior coverings may have sufficient resistance when the permeability of the exterior construction is not too low. The permeability of the surface to such vapor movement is usually expressed in "perms," which are grams (438 grams per ounce) of water vapor passing through a square foot of material per hour per inch of mercury difference in vapor pressure. A material with a low perm value (1.0 or less) is a barrier, while one with a high perm value (greater than 1.0) is a "breather."

The perm value of the cold side materials should be several times greater than those on the warm side. A ratio of 1 to 5 or greater from inside to outside is sometimes used as a rule of thumb in selecting materials and finish. When this is not possible because of virtually impermeable outside construction (such as a built-up roof or resistant exterior wall membranes), research has indicated the need to ventilate the space between the insulation and the outer covering.

Vapor barriers are used in three general areas of the house to minimize condensation or moisture problems:

Walls, ceilings, floors. — Vapor barriers used on the warm side of all exposed walls, ceilings, and floors greatly reduce movement of water vapor to colder surfaces where harmful condensation can occur. For such uses it is good practice to select materials with perm values of 0.25 or less. Such vapor barriers can be a part of the insulation or a separate film. Commonly used materials are (a) asphalt coated or laminated papers, (b) kraft backed aluminum foil, and (c) plastic films such as polyethylene, and others. Foil backed gypsum board and various coatings also serve as vapor barriers. Oil base or aluminum paints, or similar coatings are often used in houses which did not have other vapor barriers installed during their construction.

Concrete slabs. — Vapor barriers under concrete slabs resist the movement of moisture through the concrete and into living areas. Such vapor barriers should normally have a maximum perm value of 0.50. But the material must also have adequate resistance to the hazards of pouring concrete. Thus, a satisfactory material must be heavy enough to withstand such damage and at the same time have an adequate perm value. Heavy asphalt laminated papers, papers with laminated films, roll roofing, heavy films such as polyethylene, and other materials are commonly used as vapor barriers under slabs.

Crawl space covers. — Vapor barriers in crawl spaces prevent ground moisture from moving up and condensing on wood members, (Figure 12-2). A perm value of 1.0 or less is considered satisfactory for such use. Asphalt laminated paper, polyethylene, and similar materials are commonly used. Strength and resistance of crawl space covering to mechanical damage can be lower than that for vapor barriers used under concrete slabs.

Vapor Barriers and Location

The control of condensation through the use of vapor barriers and ventilation should be practiced regardless of the amount of insulation used. Normally, winter condensation problems occur in those parts of the United States where the average January temperature is 35°F. or lower. Figure 12-3 illustrates this condensation zone. The northern half of the condensation zone has a lower average winter temperature and, of course, more severe conditions than the southern portion. Areas outside this zone, such as the southeast and west coastal areas and the southern states, seldom have condensation problems. Vapor barriers should be installed in all houses built within the condensation zone outlined in Figure 12-3 and proper ventilation procedures should be followed. These will insure control over normal condensation problems.

Installing Vapor Barriers

A good general rule to keep in mind when installing vapor barriers in a house is as follows: Place the vapor barrier as close as possible to the interior or warm surface of all exposed walls, ceilings, and floors. This normally means placing the vapor barrier (separately or as a part

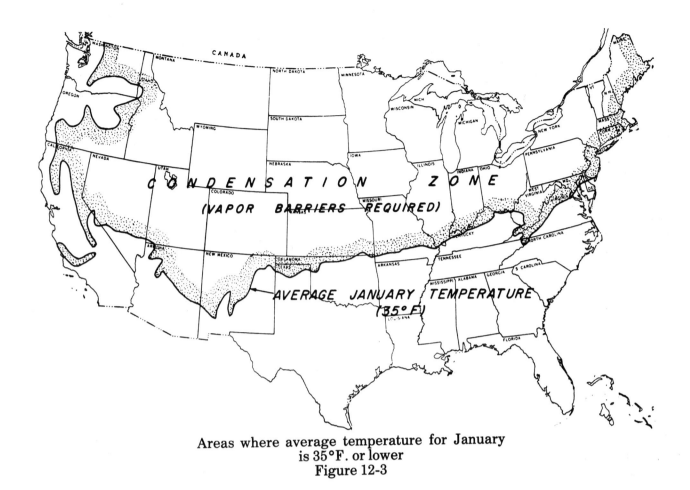

Areas where average temperature for January
is 35°F. or lower
Figure 12-3

of the insulation) on (a) the inside edge of the studs just under the rock lath or drywall finish, (b) on the under side of the ceiling joists of a one-story house or the second floor ceiling joists of a two-story house, and (c) between the subfloor and finish floor (or just under the subfloor of a house with an unheated crawl space in addition to the one placed on the ground). The insulation, of course, is normally placed between studs or other frame members on the outside of the vapor barrier. The exception is the insulation used in concrete floor slabs where a barrier is used under the insulation to protect it from ground moisture.

Placement of vapor barriers and insulation in one-story houses is shown in Figure 12-4 (flat roof and concrete floor slab) and Figure 12-5 (pitched roof and crawl space). Figure 12-6 shows barriers and insulation in a 1½ story house with a full basement. Figure 12-7 depicts a two-story house with a full basement. Other combinations of slabs, crawl spaces, and basements in houses with 1, 1½, or 2 stories, should follow the same general recommendations. Detailed descriptions in the use of vapor

barriers will be covered in the following sections.

Slabs and Crawl Spaces

Every house or room addition constructed over a concrete slab must be protected from soil moisture which may enter the slab. Protection is normally provided by a vapor barrier, which completely isolates the concrete and perimeter

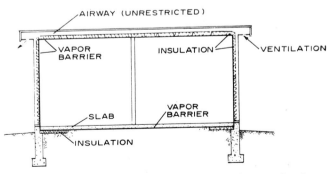

Location of vapor barriers and insulation
in concrete slab and flatdeck roof
Figure 12-4

209

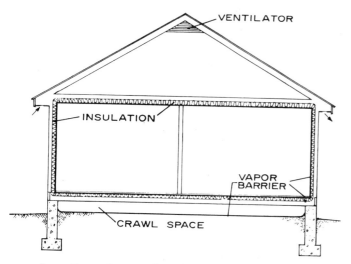

Location of vapor barriers and insulation in crawl space of another one-story house
Figure 12-5

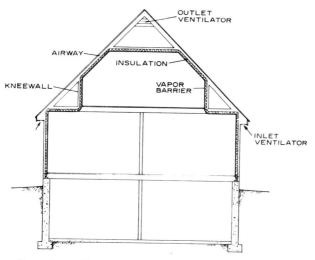

Location of vapor barriers and insulation in 1½ story house with basement
Figure 12-6

insulation is placed vertically, it should extend a minimum of 12 inches below the outside finish grade. In the colder climates a minimum 24 inch width or depth should be used.

In late spring or early summer, periods of high humidity may cause surface condensation on exposed concrete slabs or on coverings such as resilient tile before the concrete has reached normal temperatures. A fully insulated slab or a wood floor installed over wood furring strips minimizes if not eliminates such problems.

Because the vapor barriers slow the curing process of the concrete, final steel troweling of the surface is somewhat delayed. Do not punch holes through the barrier to hasten the curing process as this will destroy its effectiveness!

In placing the vapor barrier over the crawl space soil, adjoining edges should be lapped slightly and ends turned up on the foundation wall (Figure 12-9). To prevent movement of the barrier, it is good practice to weight down laps and edges with bricks or other small masonry sections.

Vapor Resistant Coatings

Where loose fill insulation has been used in walls and ceilings and no new interior covering is planned, a vapor resistant coating should be applied to the inside surface. One method for applying such a coating is to paint the interior surface of all outside walls with two coats of aluminum primer, which are subsequently covered with decorative paint. This does not

insulation from the soil. Thermal insulation of some type is required around the house perimeter in the colder climates, not only to reduce heat loss but also to minimize condensation on the colder concrete surfaces. Some types of rigid insulation impervious to moisture absorption should be used. Expanded plastic insulation such as polystyrene is commonly used.

One method of installing this insulation is shown in Figure 12-8. Another method consists of placing it vertically along the inside of the foundation wall. Both methods require insulation at the slab notch of the wall. If the

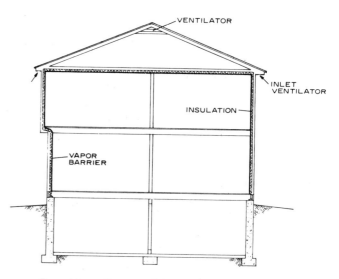

Location of vapor barriers and insulation in full two-story house with basement
Figure 12-7

210

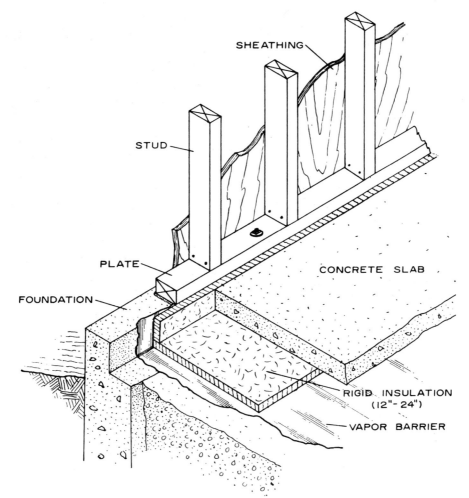

Installation of vapor barrier under concrete slab
Figure 12-8

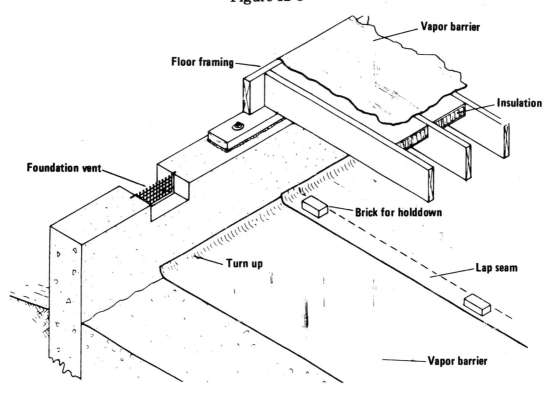

Vapor barrier for crawl space [ground cover]
Figure 12-9

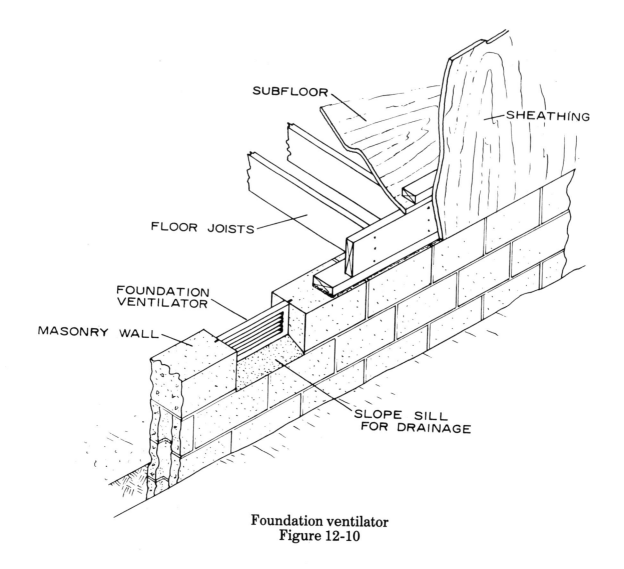

SUBFLOOR

SHEATHING

FLOOR JOISTS

FOUNDATION
VENTILATOR

MASONRY WALL

SLOPE SILL
FOR DRAINAGE

Foundation ventilator
Figure 12-10

offer as much resistance to vapor movement as a membrane, so it should be used only where other types cannot be used. If the exterior wall covering is permeable enough to allow moisture to escape from the wall, a vapor resistant coating on the inside should be adequate. This will not, however, prevent moisture from collecting in the insulation.

You can minimize condensation in the insulation by removing any low permeance coating on the exterior and replacing it with a high permeance coating. A low permeance material or coating on the outside can retard the escape of moisture which has been forced into the wall from the inside. An alternative finish for such situations is a penetrating stain, which does not form a coating on the wood surface and so does not retard the movement of moisture. Penetrating stains are very durable and easily refinished because they do not fail by blistering or peeling. Where the older home has a paint peeling problem due to condensation, the siding should be painted with white latex paint, which is very porous, and then spot painted annually wherever peeling occurs. White paint is recommended because it does not fade and retains a good exterior appearance between yearly touchups.

Ventilation

Ventilation of attics and crawl spaces is essential in all houses located where the average January temperature is 35°F. or lower. Vapor barriers help to control moisture problems, but there are always places, such as around utility pipes, where some moisture escapes. In the older house that does not have proper vapor barriers, ventilation is especially important.

Enclosed crawl spaces require some protection to prevent problems caused by excessive soil moisture. To provide complete protection from condensation problems, the conventional unheated crawl space usually contains (a) foundation ventilators, (b) a ground cover (vapor

212

Crawl space	Ratio of total net ventilating area to floor area[1]	Minimum number of ventilators[2]
Without vapor barrier	1/150	4
With vapor barrier	1/1500	2

[1] The actual area of the ventilators depends on the type of louvers and size of screen used - see Table 12-12.

[2] Foundation ventilators should be distributed around foundation to provide best air movement. When two are used, place one toward the side of prevailing wind and the other on opposite side.

Crawl-space ventilation
Table 12-11

barrier), and (c) thermal insulation between the floor joists. Foundation ventilators are normally located near the top of the masonry wall. In concrete block foundations, the ventilator is often made in a size to replace a full block (Figure 12-10). In heated crawl spaces, a vapor barrier and perimeter insulation is used but foundation ventilators are eliminated.

The amount of ventilation required for a crawl space is based on the total area of the house in square feet and the presence of a vapor barrier soil cover. Table 12-11 lists the recommended minimum net ventilating areas for crawl spaces with or without vapor barriers.

The flow of air through a ventilator is restricted by the presence of screening and by the louvers. This reduction varies with the size of the screening or mesh and by the type of louvers used. Louvers are sloped about 45 degrees to shed rain when used in a vertical position. Table 12-12 outlines the amount by which the total calculated net area of the ventilators must be increased to compensate for screens and the thickness of the louvers.

Several types of foundation vents can be purchased commercially for easy installation in the appropriate size opening. Screen sizes vary, depending on whether they are insect-proof or rodent-proof. Manufactured vents usually have a statement of free area. Often it may be sufficient to attach a screen over an opening rather than to purchase a manufactured vent.

Attic and Roof

Moisture escaping from the house into the attic tends to collect in the coldest part of the attic. Relatively impermeable roofing, such as asphalt shingles or a built-up roof, complicates

the problem by preventing the moisture from escaping to the outside. The only way to get the moisture out is to ventilate the attic. Attic ventilation also helps keep a house cool during hot weather.

Where possible, inlet vents should be provided in the soffit area and outlet vents should be provided near the ridge. This results in natural circulation regardless of wind direction. The warm air in the attic rises to the peak, goes out the vents, and fresh air enters through the inlet vents to replace the exhausted air. In some attics only gable vents can be used. Air movement is then somewhat dependent upon wind. The open area of the vent must be larger than where both inlet and outlet vents are provided.

Obstructions in ventilators- louvers and screens[1]	To determine total area of ventilators, multiply required net area in square feet by[2]
1/4 inch mesh hardware cloth	1
1/8 inch mesh screen	1¼
No. 16 mesh insect screen (with or without plain metal louvers)	2
Wood louvers and 1/4 inch mesh hardware cloth[3]	2
Wood louvers and 1/8 inch mesh screen[3]	2¼
Wood louvers and No. 16 mesh insect screen[3]	3

[1] In crawl-space ventilators, screen openings should not be larger than ¼ inch; in attic spaces no larger than 1/8 inch.

[2] Net area for attics determined by ratios in Figures 12-13, 12-14, and 12-15.

[3] If metal louvers have drip edges that reduce the opening, use same ratio as shown for wood louvers.

Ventilating area increase required if louvers and screening are used in crawl spaces and attics
Figure 12-12

Ventilation of attic spaces and roof areas is important in minimizing water vapor buildup. However, while good ventilation is important, there is still a need for vapor barriers in ceiling areas. This is especially true of the flat or low-slope roof where only a 1 to 3 inch space above the insulation might be available for ventilation.

The minimum amount of attic or roof space ventilation required is determined by the total ceiling area. These ratios are shown in Figures

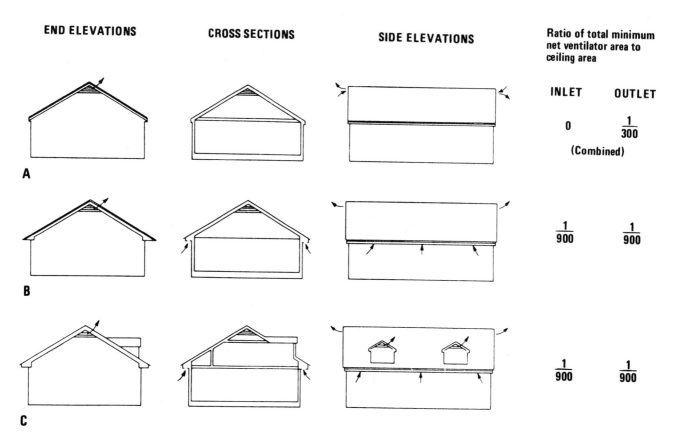

Ventilating area of gable roofs: A, louvers in end walls; B, louvers in end walls with additional openings at eaves; C, louvers at end walls with additional openings at eaves and dormers. Cross section of C shows free opening for air movement between roof boards and ceiling insulation of attic room

Figure 12-13

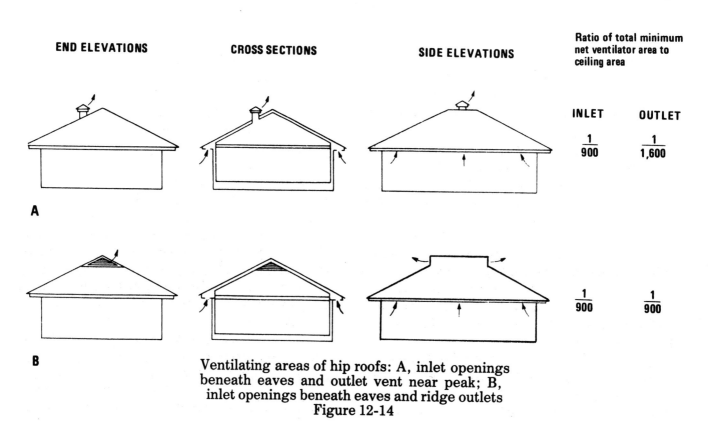

Ventilating areas of hip roofs: A, inlet openings beneath eaves and outlet vent near peak; B, inlet openings beneath eaves and ridge outlets

Figure 12-14

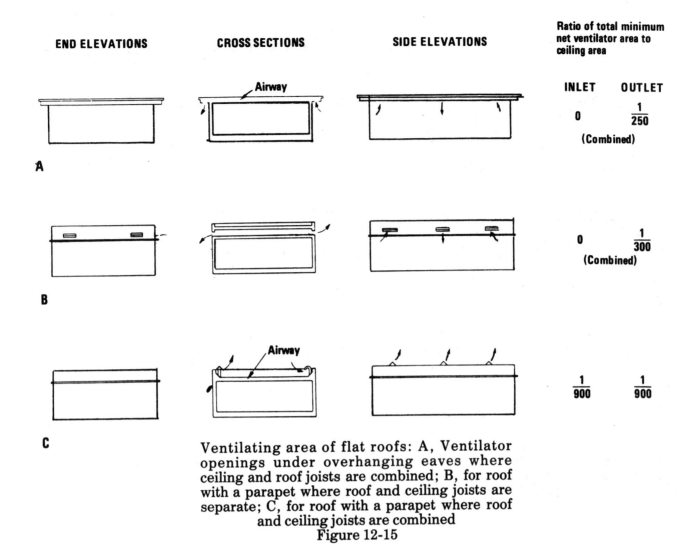

END ELEVATIONS	CROSS SECTIONS	SIDE ELEVATIONS	Ratio of total minimum net ventilator area to ceiling area	
			INLET	OUTLET
A	Airway		0	$\frac{1}{250}$
			(Combined)	
B			0	$\frac{1}{300}$
			(Combined)	
C	Airway		$\frac{1}{900}$	$\frac{1}{900}$

Ventilating area of flat roofs: A, Ventilator openings under overhanging eaves where ceiling and roof joists are combined; B, for roof with a parapet where roof and ceiling joists are separate; C, for roof with a parapet where roof and ceiling joists are combined
Figure 12-15

12-13, 12-14 and 12-15, for various types of roofs. The use of both inlet and outlet ventilators is recommended whenever possible. The total net area of ventilators is found by application of the ratios shown in Figures 12-13, 12-14 and 12-15. The total area of the ventilators can be found by using the data in Table 12-12. Divide this total area by the number of ventilators used to find the recommended square foot area of each.

For example, a gable roof similar to Figure 12-13, B with inlet and outlet ventilators has a minimum required total inlet and outlet ratio of 1/900 of the ceiling area. If the ceiling area of the house is 1,350 square feet, each net inlet and outlet ventilating area should be 1,350 divided by 900 or 1½ square feet.

If ventilators are protected with Number 16 mesh insect screen and plain metal louvers (Table 12-12) the minimum gross area must be 2 x 1½ or 3 square feet. When one outlet ventilator is used at each gable end, each should have a gross area of 1½ square feet (3 divided by 2). When distributing the soffit inlet ventilators to three on each side, for a small house (total of 6), each ventilator should have a gross area of 0.5 square feet. For long houses, use 6 or more on each side.

Hip roofs cannot have gable vents near the peak, so some other type of outlet ventilator must be provided (Figure 12-14). This can be either a ventilator near the ridge, or a special flue provided in the chimney with openings into the attic space. Both types require inlet vents in the soffit area. The hip roof can also be modified to provide a small gable for a conventional louvered vent.

Flat roofs with no attic require some type of ventilation above the ceiling insulation. If this space is divided by joists, each joist space must be ventilated. This is often accomplished by a continuous vent strip in the soffit. Drill through

215

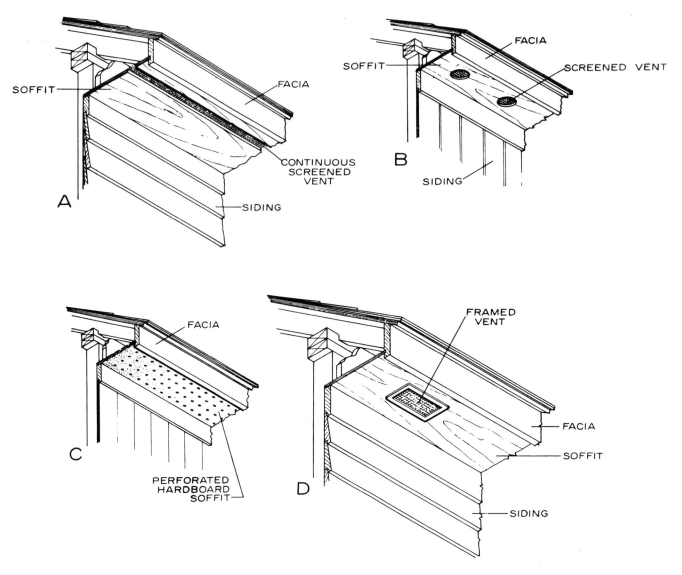

Inlet ventilators in soffits: A, Continuous vent;
B, round vents; C, perforated;
D, single ventilator
Figure 12-16

all headers that impede passage of air to the opposite eave. Other methods are illustrated in Figure 12-15.

Cathedral ceilings require the same type of ventilation as flat roofs. A continuous ridge vent is also desirable because even with holes in the ridge rafter, air movement through rafter space is very sluggish without a ridge vent.

Inlet ventilators in the soffit may consist of several designs. It is good practice to distribute them as much as possible to prevent "dead" air pockets in the attic where moisture might collect. A continuous screened slot (Figure 12-16, A) satisfies this requirement. Small screened openings might also be used (Figure 12-16, B). Continuous slots or individual ventilators between roof members should be used for flat roof houses where roof members serve as both rafters and ceiling joists. Locate the openings away from the wall line to minimize the possible entry of wind driven snow. A soffit consisting of perforated hardboard (Figure 12-16, C) can also be used to advantage but holes should be no larger than 1/8 inch in diameter. Small metal frames with screened openings are also available and may be used in soffit areas (Figure 12-16, D). For open cornice design, the use of a frieze board with

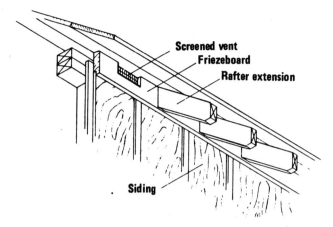

Frieze ventilator (for open cornice)
Figure 12-17

screen ventilating slots would be satisfactory (Figure 12-17). Perforated hardboard might also be used for this purpose. The recommended minimum inlet ventilating ratios shown in Figures 12-13, 12-14 and 12-15 should be followed in determining total net ventilating areas for both inlet and outlet ventilators.

Outlet ventilators to be most effective should be located as close to the highest portion of the ridge as possible. They may be placed in the upper wall section of a gable roofed house in various forms as shown in Figure 12-18, A and

B. In wide gable-end overhangs with ladder framing, a number of screened openings can be located in the soffit area of the lookouts. (Figure 12-18,C). Ventilating openings to the attic space should not be restricted by blocking. Outlet ventilators on gable or hip roofs might also consist of some type of roof ventilator (Figure 12-19, A and B). Hip roofs can utilize a ventilating gable (modified hip) (Figure 12-19, C). Protection from blowing snow must be considered, which often restricts the use of a continuous ridge vent. Locate the single roof ventilators (Figure 12-19, A and B) along the ridge toward the rear of the house so they are not visible from the front. Outlet ventilators might also be located in a chimney as a false flue which has a screened opening to the attic area.

Other Protective Measures

Water leakage into walls and interiors of houses in the snow belt areas of the country is sometimes caused by ice dams and is often mistaken for condensation. Such problems occur after heavy snowfalls when there is sufficient heat loss from the living quarters to melt the snow along the roof surface. The water moves down the roof surface to the colder overhang of the roof where it freezes. This causes a ledge of ice and backs up water, which can enter the wall

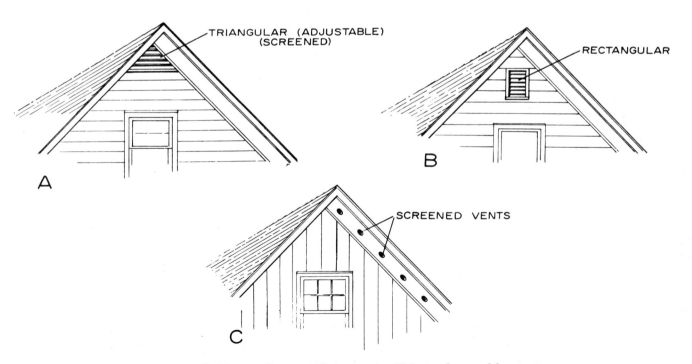

Gable outlet ventilators: A, Triangular gable end ventilator; B, rectangular gable end ventilator; C, soffit ventilators
Figure 12-18

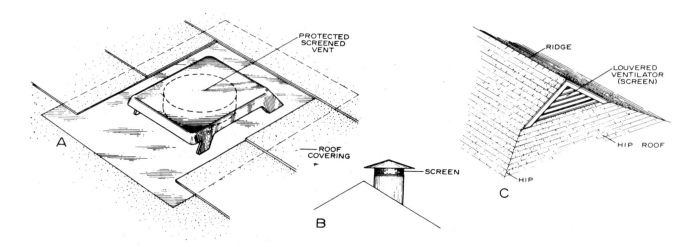

Ridge outlet ventilators: A, Low silhouette type;
B, pipe ventilator; C, modified hip ventilator
Figure 12-19

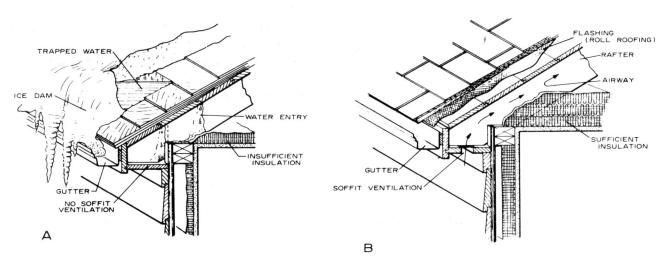

Ice dams: A, insufficient insulation and ventilation can cause ice dams and water damage; B,
good ventilation, insulation, and roof flashing
Figure 12-20

or drip down onto the ceiling finish (Figure
12-20,A).

Several methods can be used to minimize
this problem caused by melting snow. By
reducing the attic temperatures in the winter so
that they are only slightly above outdoor
temperatures, most ice dams can be eliminated.
This can be accomplished in the following
manner:

1. Add insulation to the ceiling area in the
attic to reduce heat loss from living areas below.
This added insulation and ventilation will also
be helpful by reducing summer temperatures in
the living areas below.

2. Provide additional inlet ventilation in the
soffit area of the cornice as well as better outlet
ventilation near the ridge.

3. When reroofing, use a flashing strip of 36
inch wide roll roofing paper of 45 pound weight
along the eave line before reshingling. See
Figure12-20. While this does not prevent ice
dams, it is a worthwhile precaution.

4. Under severe conditions, or when only
some portions of a roof produce ice dams (such
as at valleys), the use of electric-thermal wire
laid in a zig-zag pattern and in gutters may
prove effective. The wire is connected and
heated during periods of snowfall and at other
times as needed to maintain channels for
drainage.

218

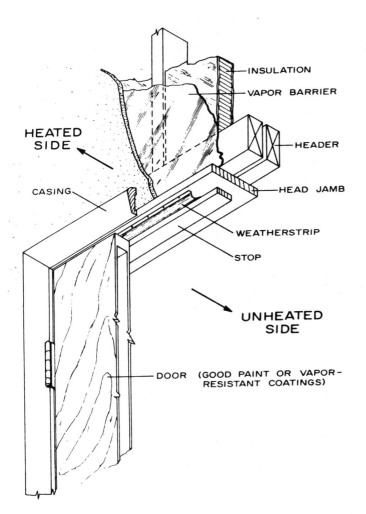

HEATED SIDE

UNHEATED SIDE

INSULATION
VAPOR BARRIER
HEADER
HEAD JAMB
WEATHERSTRIP
STOP
CASING
DOOR (GOOD PAINT OR VAPOR-RESISTANT COATINGS)

Insulating door to unheated attic space
Figure 12-21

Walls and doors to unheated areas such as attic spaces should be treated to resist water vapor movement as well as to minimize heat loss. This includes the use of insulation and vapor barriers on all wall areas adjacent to the cold attic (Figure 12-21). Vapor barriers should face the warm side of the room. In addition, some means should be used to prevent heat and vapor loss around the perimeter of the door. One method is through some type of weatherstrip (Figure 12-21). The door itself should be given several finish coats of paint or varnish which will resist the movement of water vapor.

If further resistance to heat loss is desired, a covering of ½ inch or thicker rigid insulation such as insulation board or foamed plastic can be attached to the back of the door.

Outlet or switch boxes or other openings in exposed (cold) walls often are difficult to treat to prevent water vapor escape. Initially, whether the vapor barrier is a separate sheet or part of the insulation, as tight a fit as possible should be made when trimming the barrier around the box (Figure 12-22). This is less difficult when the barrier is separate. As an additional precaution, a bead of caulking compound should be applied around the box after the drywall or the plaster base has been installed (Figure 12-22). The same caulking can be used around the cold air return ducts or other openings in exterior walls. This type of sealing may appear unnecessary, but laboratory tests have shown that there is enough moisture loss through the perimeter of an outlet box to form a large ball of frost on the back face during extended cold periods. Melting of this frost can adversely affect the exterior paint films. In the colder areas of the country and in rooms where there is excess water vapor, such as the bath and kitchen, this added protection is good insurance from future problems. Some switch and junction boxes are more difficult to seal than others because of their makeup. A simple polyethylene bag or other enclosure around such boxes will provide some protection.

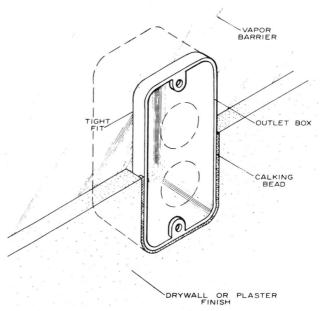

VAPOR BARRIER
TIGHT FIT
OUTLET BOX
CALKING BEAD
DRYWALL OR PLASTER FINISH

Protection around outlet boxes in exposed walls
Figure 12-22

Condensation problems caused by water vapor movement through unprotected outlet box areas in exposed walls are often due to poor workmanship during application of the insulation. Figure 12-23 shows a section of exterior

219

wall with the vapor barrier loosely stapled to the face of the studs. Because of poor application, a small space is sometimes left at the top and bottom of the insulation in the stud space. Water vapor escaping through the unprotected outlet box travels by convection, on the warm side, to the top of the wall, where it moves to the cold side and condenses on the inner face of the colder siding or sheathing. Continued movement of vapor can saturate these materials and in severe conditions cause decay. Buckling of single panel siding, such as hardboard or similar materials, can result as the moisture content of the material increases. Such problems can be minimized by "enveloping" of the inner face of exposed walls with a continuous membrane. Sealing the outlet box in some manner will also aid in restricting water vapor movement into the wall cavity.

The same principles used in sealing outlet boxes should be applied to all openings in an outside wall or ceiling. Openings may include exhaust fans in the kitchen or the bathroom, hot air registers, cold air return registers, and plumbing. Openings are also required in ceilings for light fixtures, ventilation fans, and plumbing vents. Regardless of the type of opening, the vapor barrier should be trimmed to fit as tightly as possible.

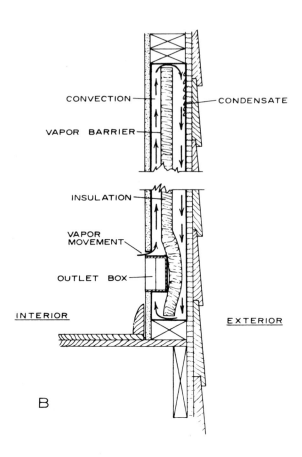

Results of water vapor loss around outlet box
Figure 12-23

Decorating and Painting for Energy Savings 13

Insist on *exterior paints* that reduce maintenance and do not cause a build-up of pigmentation. Light and heavy-bodied stains are best for this and best for preserving wood. The use of regular paints on the outside of a house causes ever-thickening layers of paint to build up. This "skin" must eventually be stripped off or it will make the house look "paint sick"- samples of which you can see in old wharves and derelict wooden boats.

We have harangued copiously in previous books about the desirability of using rough, rough-sawn, resawn, or sandblasted wood surfaces on a house's exterior. These rough textured surfaces allow light stains to be applied in initial construction, and then the wood surfaces need not be recoated for years and, even then, only with a thin, easily applied film of more stain. Furthermore, the drudgery of preparatory work is eliminated, since the surface to be stained needs only be whisked clean with a stiff brush before staining.

The delicate soft wood rails, stiles, muntins, and panels of wood windows and doors need the solid protection (in most climates) of at least three coats of regular paint. However, even on the largest house this relatively small amount of "trim" is not burdensome to maintain. What is emphasized here is avoidance of committing vast amounts of siding, eaves, beam and beam ends, trim, railings, balconies, soffits, and posts to an annual expensive paint job. There is no reason why all of these elements cannot be treated with protective stains and left to weather pleasantly if a little extra is spent to obtain the slightly roughed up surfaces to begin with.

Where regular paint is applied, the lighter colors are less heat absorbent and will maintain the home at cooler temperatures. Paint can also be used to lighten rooms as in the case of basement light wells or sides of fences, trellises, or walls facing dark rooms.

Keep paint off masonry materials like brick, concrete block, slump stone, adobe, stone, etc., as much as possible, because it will require constant maintenance. Apply paint to masonry only where it is absolutely demanded for important decorative and illuminative effect.

Interior paints can help you take a long initial step toward lightening a dark room. This assist is customarily needed on the north side of the house or in any room or hallway with undersized windows.

Actually there are hundreds of shades of white one can use without resorting to hospital-operating-room white. These white tones are able to lighten a room and they tend to blend more satisfactorily with other colors than does pure white, since pure white is not a color.

In rooms that have colored painted walls or wallpapered walls or paneled walls, a very light ceiling not only makes the room appear larger and makes a pleasant contrast, but it also maximizes the light sources of the room, both natural and artificial.

Areas around skylight soffits or in light soffits should be painted white to aid in light transmission.

Window Coverings as Insulation

Draperies over sliding glass doors, large panels of glass, and all windows help to keep

221

heat in and keep cold out. In summer they can serve to partially block the sun.

A tendency has grown to allow some sliding patio doors and large sections of glass to remain undraped. You should visualize how this appears in the black of night when you are trying to enjoy the coziness of a room and are faced with a gigantic gaping maw of blackness. Draperies or shutters would visually close off this black cavern and further aid in preserving heat.

Basically for safety, and for interior aesthetic enjoyment and energy conservation, all openings should be covered in some fashion. Additionally, where heat can become severe, as in southern or western exposures, draperies covering these windows should be lined. In fact all draperies hang better, function better, and last longer if they are lined.

Bear in mind the effectiveness of blinds or shades as a protective shelter for windows on the southern and western side of the house in summer. They can greatly reduce the need for excessive air conditioning.

Shutters

As window coverings, shutters are decorative, stylish, and long-lasting. They are available in infinite varieties of design, colors, textures. As energy conservers they are formidable tools, with their adjustability and retractability. Careful study of the exterior of houses will reveal to you that certain house styles really benefit on the outside as well as the inside by the installation of shutters. They can help complete the textural statement desired on the exterior in a way that draperies and curtains fail to do.

One word of caution. Consult the shutter supplier before installing decorative moldings around windows and doors. Sometimes the shutters will occupy the place of the casing, and you will be doing the same job twice or having to remove the casing before the shutters can be installed.

Wall Coverings

Wallpapers and wall fabrics offer a multitude of ways to aid in energy conservation. How? Light papers, of course, aid rooms that are deficient in natural light, and the same is true of fabrics. Warm colors can aid in bathroom and dressing room papers whereby the rooms actually feel warmer through visual suggestion.

Papers suggesting trellis work or treillage open up smallish rooms and impart feelings of light and air.

Another room-enlarging trick, like the use of mirrors, is to use scenic wallpapers. These can be environmentally suggestive as well, admitting an expression of light or of ascension in a stairwell, and of garden tranquillity in a breakfast room or dining room—many things. They are most effective in dining rooms, halls, foyers, bars, stairwells, and telephone niches. They are very hard to choose with taste, and they are especially difficult to work in with the necessary architectural interruptions of doors and windows. Scenics, to be successful, almost have to be a part of the integral planning of the house.

Mirrors-Like Adding onto a Room

These fantastically versatile and functional elements are a relatively low-cost means of enlarging, or seeming to enlarge, a smallish entry, bath, dressing room, powder room, hall, niche, or dining room. They push out walls without a carpenter lifting a finger. From an energy standpoint they can multiply light and partially reflect heat. They are the unsung tool of the imaginative decorator.

Kitchen and Bathroom

Ceramic Tile for Showers-This material should generally be kept very light, preferably white, since showers are usually recessed in a cranny of the bathroom. Without the help of very light tile, this area can be dark and demand special lighting, which should be unnecessary if care is exercised in tile selection.

Kitchen Cabinet Interiors-There is sometimes a tendency on the part of the painter to talk the general contractor or decorator into applying the same stain he uses on the exterior of the cabinets to the interiors. You should disabuse him of this thought and insist that these cavities be kept very light, preferably some shade of white. There is no illumination inside cabinets, and the home owner will be totally dependent on light spilling over from the kitchen ceiling sources, which may not be adequate to begin with. Therefore, you need as much reflected light as possible in order to be able to see the contents easily.

Flowers and Plants

Flowers are such a smashing contribution to

Cast iron fireback

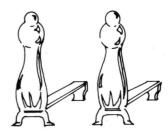
Antique andirons

the decor of your rooms that effort should be made for their inclusion in the landscaping plan in order to have them available for continuing interior enhancement. They use nothing of our precious energy except a little water, yet they impart a warm feeling in cold weather and an airy feeling in summer. However, there is a current fad rampant in the "house" magazines for placing vast bunches of flowers in clusters everywhere, even on the floor. We shall dub this "the Florist Look." Moderation in this as in most things is essential. Michael Greer, the nationally reknowned interior designer pronounced the final word on excessive floral exuberance when he wrote, "Too many flowers in a room imply the presence of a corpse." Avoid the florist look.

Plants are a great asset in building an attractive room environment. Tall ones can give the feeling of heightened ceilings. One in front of an unappealing window can help to make the vista more palatable. They can last forever and are quite hardy. As in regulating thermostats for people, do not keep temperatures too high for plants-another plus.

Furniture and Antiques, as Energy Savers

The actor, Robert Redford, in speaking about his rustic home in Sundance, Utah, said: "The answer to our future may lie in our past...There's a great deal we can absorb from history that would improve the quality of life today."

As far as furnishing the home is concerned, you can take a comtemplative look at the contents of any good quality antique store, and you will see what Mr. Redford means. By "good quality antique store" is meant an establishment featuring seventeenth and eighteenth-century furniture and accessories, as opposed to a "daisies and buttons" shop full of nineteenth-century cranberry glass, or one of those monstrosities of American merchandising rejoicing in the name Antique Shop that is simply a warehouse full of used furniture.

Semi-Architectural Items

A typical accoutrement of seventeenth-century houses was the iron fireback mentioned previously. These heavy metal plaques were decorative and, when mounted at the back of the firebox against the firebrick, multiplied the radiating effect of the warm bricks. If you cannot find these in an antique store, reproductions can be obtained from Kingsworthy Foundry Co., Ltd., Kingsworthy, Winchester, Hants, Great Britain, who also have an illustrated catalogue with related items.

Other kitchen-fireplace features are the andirons that have movable hooks for swinging

223

pots out over the fire and receptacles for bowls at their tops.

Although associated more with the nineteenth than the eighteenth century, the free-standing cast-iron stove fueled by wood or coal served an important heat-producing function. Requiring nowhere near the space and expense of a masonry fireplace, the cast-iron stove, when properly vented, was a safe, inexpensive, and effective method of sending radiated heat out into a room. Who does not remember drawings and paintings of the country store or farm workroom of early America with its worthies sitting around the cast-iron stove, the cracker barrel not far distant?

Actually, Benjamin Franklin's iron stove for heating rooms first appeared in 1874, and though initially unpopular, it grew into an institution in the nineteenth century. It was the grandparent of the cook stove, which was not actually popularized until the middle of the nineteenth century, up until which time cooking was still being done by the old open-hearth method. These cast-iron stoves are still available from the Portland Stove Foundry Co., as mentioned in the chapter on heating.

Additionally, around the kitchen-oriented fireplace there were also more swinging pothooks and trays that could be rotated out into the room or back into the recesses of the fireplace, depending on the heat desired. Built-in seats in inglenooks were the ultimate in creating a snug region in the immediate influence of the fire.

Attractive old shutters verify the reliance in the past on these sensible protectors from storms and oppressive sun. The attractive S-shaped shutter hooks are frequently found in the hardware trays of such stores.

Furniture with an Energy Function

Related to the inglenook and the fireplace was the wing chair, whose high, protruding sides both kept the sitter's face from being scorched and saved him from the errant drafts that were common in less snug houses of the period.

Francis I of France, like many monarchs of his time, slept in a "great curtained and canopied bed," which was almost a necessity in a cold and drafty palace that lacked both heat and privacy. A double bed with four posts, a top, and side curtains of heavy fabric was a vital ingredient for comfort in early Gothic times.

What About the Pool? 14

Does high cost energy make the backyard swimming pool obsolete? Once you have sold your client on an energy efficient home, can you recommend the pool he wants without blowing the whole energy conservation program? What should you advise your client about pools and the energy shortage?

Fortunately, there is plenty that can be done to make a pool or "spa" as energy efficient as a well planned and carefully built home. Heating and filtering water use nearly all the energy required for most pools and there are now better ways to heat and filter water than conventional pools of the 1960's used. A pool can be an asset to most any home and doesn't have to squander energy to be useful.

Basic Orientation

Because of competitive market conditions in most areas of the country where pools are desirable, they represent an excellent value for the money. For after all, in most types of soils the pool can be regarded fundamentally as a large hole lined with steel and concrete and filled with water. When you consider that a more or less standard pool with heater and filter can cost less than a medium-priced automobile, the value is astonishing. Moreover, the pool becomes a permanent minimally depreciating asset enhancing the home, and it truly heightens the overall investment value of your property. The only problem comes in attempting to organize pool installation and use so it does not conflict with our objectives here and become an excessive energy consumer and money waster.

An unbelievable amount of heat is lost from a pool due to the wind blowing over its surface. Much like a fresh-baked pie placed on a window sill for the express purpose of cooling, it loses much heat from wind blowing over it. Therefore, in planning for a swimming pool, try to locate it in such a way that the contours of the lot or the house or other structures shield it from the prevailing wind.

If the pool is already installed, work with the landscaper in positioning a hedge to create this vital shelter. Or, if it is possible, suggest a cabana or masonry decorative wall that can also serve as a windbreak. Remember that half of the heat loss from a pool is due to evaporation, and this is greatly accelerated by the wind.

What About the Water Itself?

Chemical balance of the water is extremely important in controlling heat loss; this balance is necessary in order to keep the heater working at top efficiency. Incorrect balance of the "pH" factor and alkalinity cause scales to build up inside the heat exchange tubes leading to and from the pool. This condition is made manifest by a banging sound inside the heater and a jetting of some of the scaly particles into the pool itself.

The proper pH reading is somewhere between 7.2 and 7.4, and the total alkalinity from 80 to 150 parts per million. If you can make a suggestion about pool maintenance, never miss these two vital counts.

If the heater gets noisy and scaling is evident, have the heater checked right away. It may need to be descaled. Thus, in making an

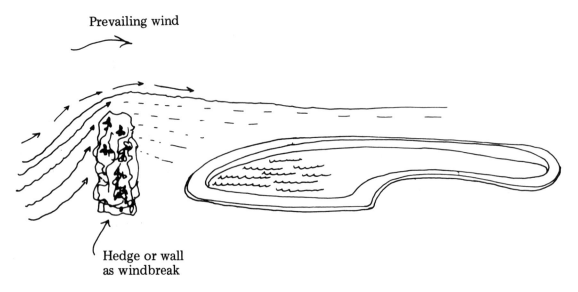

Prevailing wind

Hedge or wall
as windbreak

Controlling Pool Temperature with a Windbreak

energy survey of a home with a pool, a check for scale buildup should be made at the outset. A whirlpool "spa" with its higher temperature is even more vulnerable than the big pool to this scaling, so watch it particularly.

The Temperature of the Pool

Obviously just as filtering time should be reduced to the bare minimum, so should pool temperature be reduced. A setting of 78 degrees Fahrenheit is advocated by the American Red Cross.

As far as the cost of fuel is concerned, observe this chart:

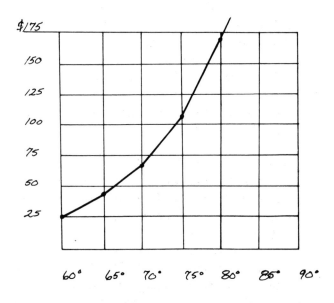

Cost of Pool Temperature

This shows that with each added degree of heat, the heating cost goes up 10 percent. Thus, with five degrees added, the cost goes up more than 50 percent.

Where pool use is confined to weekends, the thermostat should be at a standby temperature of 70 degrees during the week. Raise it to the temperature the family agrees upon on the weekend.

Do not shut down the pool heater for short periods. Any saving will be offset by having it struggle for hours getting the water temperature back up again, especially under a reduced filtration program. A good mental note to make in this regard is that pool heaters are sized to allow for heating that specific quantity of water in the pool a little over *a degree an hour*. Thus, a rise of ten degrees takes something over ten hours.

However, if the owners leave on a vacation or for any extended period of time, they should turn the heater down completely and turn off the pilot light. Otherwise, it can continue to burn about one thousand B.T.U.'s an hour.

Pool Heater Size

In recommending a pool you should know that the heater size is one of the pool salesman's tools in making his price competitive. You should also know his minimum formula, for this sizing technique is not governed by any local building codes; the building departments are generally only concerned with the safety of the heater and the method of installation. To determine heater size, the pool area is multiplied by the temperature rise, which is multiplied by a factor of fifteen. Here is the way it works out in a specific example.

Pool area (in square feet) x temperature rise x 15 = heater size.

If, for example, we have a 16-by-32 foot pool, we multiply that by a rise of 23 degrees-figuring that the low point for the coldest unheated water we are likely to have during a swimming season, is 55 degrees and our optimum swimming temperature is 78 degrees, the rise would be 23 degrees.

$$(16 \times 32) \times (78-55) \times 15 = \text{Htr.Size}$$
$$512 \times 23 \times 15 = \text{Htr.Size}$$
$$\text{or } 176,640 \text{ B.T.U.}$$

A larger heater tends to conserve fuel, because of its quicker heating ability; and considering that you want to reduce filtration time, this precious circulation time through the heater provides a double incentive to have a larger rather than minimal pool heater. The cost difference between a 250,000-B.T.U. heater, for example, and a heater 25 percent larger, 325,000 B.T.U.'s is only about $100.

Using the Sun

Solar energy and swimming pools make an excellent match. Unlike home space heating, the season when you need pool heat is the season when the sun shines most: summer and early fall. All solar heating systems use a ''heat sink'' of some sort to store collected energy and most any pool by itself makes an excellent heat storage reservoir. Solar space heating and domestic water heating systems require high temperatures (about 140 degrees) that make the collectors operate inefficiently. Pool heating needs collector temperatures of only 80 to 90 degrees. At temperatures in this range, plastic collectors are effective, thus nearly eliminating corrosion, breakage and freezing problems and cutting the cost significantly. No special heat transfer liquid is required. Pool water can flow directly through the collector. The conventional pool filter pump is all that is needed to maintain a water flow through the collector if the pressure drop in the collector is not too large. Orientation of the collector is still important, however. The collector should face due south and be inclined at an angle equal to 15 degrees less than the latitude. The collector area should be equivalent to at least 50% of the pool surface. A collector area equal to 100% of the pool surface will just about double the number of months the pool is a comfortable temperature for swimming.

Conventional glazed and double glazed collectors are used for spas and soaking tubs where temperatures above 80 degrees are desirable and for installations where there are wind problems, low solar radiation or low design temperatures. Even more expensive glazed collectors will usually repay the additional installation cost in ten years through lower fuel bills.

Controlling Water Evaporation

The loss of heat by evaporation is staggering, for when water evaporates it must absorb heat to do so. In our temperate climates, a standard pool would lose about an inch and a half a week. If the pool were 20 x 40 feet, that would be five hundred gallons a week, of which each gallon absorbs about six thousand B.T.U.'s of heat. This means that 3 million B.T.U.'s-3 million-are lost each week, and it takes the average heater sixteen hours merely to replace those lost B.T.U.'s.

An indoor pool is the most obvious solution of all, and, of course, it requires less heat even without the evaporation control it provides. Second best is a pool cover, either the air-supported vinyl bubble or the accordian-fold type that retracts into a storage compartment. The cheapest and most popular cover is simply the lightweight plastic kind that the owner lays down with weights at the edge. It may not win any *House and Garden* awards for beauty but it truly gets the job done. All the cover methods have the extra dividends of holding down maintenance costs and increasing safety. Heat costs can be expected to plummet by 30 percent if a cover is employed.

The Greatest Saver of Heat?

Research in oil coagulants to gather oil spill material from coastal waters has likely created some fallout of other chemicals that can perform wonders in related areas.

A chemical has been developed that covers the water's surface with a film that is one molecule thick. Originating in the petroleum industry, where it was used to cover reservoirs in the Southwest, this acts as a heat sealant that can be effective as a swimming pool cover without ever giving away its presence.

It is a relatively cheap product made of alcohol and oils of high molecular weight. Its microscopically thin layer is broken when you swim or dive in it, or otherwise disturb the water, but it is able to reconstitute itself afterward. Initial results indicate that it cuts heating costs by 50 percent. Unfortunately, the product is not yet available nationwide, but should be in the very near future.

For Gaylord Hauser Types

There is no reason why swimming in fifty-five-degree water could not be as enjoyable as surfing in a fifty-five-degree ocean. It is all a matter of dress-surfers wear rubber ''wet suits.'' These rubber shirts and trousers entirely contain the body with the exception of hands, feet, and face, and therefore keep 90 percent of the body in a reasonably comfortable state.

The Final Decision

As to the overall idea of whether you should include a pool or not in the face of energy shortages and energy expense, there is a special way to look at this problem. The time when the family will spend more time together, use the home more, enjoy recreation and leisure together more is near at hand. A swimming pool is one of the few major recreational items available that does not require transportation by camper, boat, or automobile. In fact, using a filter pump for an eight-hour period consumes the same energy as one evening's viewing of color television. So, why not build a pool? But follow the suggestions on managing the heating of it.

Opportunities for Building Contractors 15

The potential for energy conservation in existing homes is enormous. There are about 47.5 million single-family detached dwellings in this country. Much of that existing housing inventory was built when energy was readily available and cheap. In the late 1950's, the surge of interest in central residential air conditioning and electric heating combined to provide a new viewpoint with respect to thermal protection for new homes. It was not until then that the manufacture of insulation became a major industry and double glazing or storm windows were considered for new housing. Even so, energy was relatively cheap and extensive thermal protection was not widely justifiable on an economic basis.

Perhaps 75 percent or about 35 million existing single-family detached homes were built prior to 1960. There is little doubt that it would be economically justifiable to add additional thermal protection to nearly all of these homes and to most of those built since 1960. It is estimated that retrofitting just half of these homes with economically justifiable energy saving features will save the equivalent of 650,000 to 1,000,000 barrels of oil per day and create thousands of construction industry jobs during the 1980's with encouragement from the Federal and State governments in the form of tax incentives and mass media campaigns, scare headlines about shortages and high energy costs. Thus, it is easy to see that builders ready to meet the challenge of high cost energy have a bright future. This chapter is intended to help you understand the nature of the retrofit contracting business and equip you with some of the advertising, sales, production and contracting information you will need to succeed in business as a retrofit contractor during the 1980's.

There is broad support for energy conservation in the home. Owners of residences and businesses are reminded almost daily of the need to retrofit their homes:

- The President has proposed and Congress has enacted a number of incentives for owners who retrofit their homes.
- The major electric and gas utility associations and many gas and electric utility companies are actively encouraging conserving energy in homes.
- Manufacturers are advertising on television, radio and in the newspapers to encourage people to retrofit their homes energy conserving features.
- All of the states and many cities have energy conservation offices and engage in a number of different energy conservation programs.
- The mounting pressure of high monthly bills for heating and cooling can be expected to stimulate increasing home owner interest in the program.
- While no one can predict future fuel and energy prices accurately, most experts believe that rates will continue to rise indefinitely at 10 or perhaps 15 percent per year.

All of these factors are helping to create an increasingly favorable climate for getting into the retrofit business.

The "Retrofit" Business

Retrofitting existing homes for energy conservation on a large scale is a new business opportunity. It is very likely to be a different type of business situation for many builders, remodelers or contractors wishing to enter the field. Thousands of builders and contractors presently in home building may become successful retrofit prime contractors.

Energy retrofit may be viewed as an extension or diversification of a present business, or it may be considered as an entirely new business. Some examples of existing businessmen who are probably best suited to enter the retrofit field are builders, home remodelers, and contractors now in the HVAC, insulation or rehabilitation businesses. Regardless of your background, a prerequisite for success is basic business experience. Recognize the unique nature of the housing retrofit business and make your plans accordingly. New technical skills may need to be developed. Subcontracting portions of the work may be a new experience. Coordination of promotion and selling techniques with national advertising and working with local utilities, building officials and others will be necessary.

There are other unique features about retrofit work. Few people are now qualified to identify the appropriate energy saving features, estimate the price and supervise all of the work. Some training will be necessary.

Retrofit will be accomplished mostly while the home is occupied, and that will be a new experience for workmen accustomed to new housing construction. Not all workmen can be expected to adjust to working in occupied homes. For those accustomed to new home construction, business insurance policies may need to be examined to make certain that they cover the home owner's personal property and valuables as well as damage to their furniture and furnishings.

What makes energy retrofitting different from other types of home building and related remodeling work?

- The contractor, his salesmen and craftsmen are dealing directly with the public. They sell customers something for their home and work in the home to install the retrofit package.

- Some people may resent the implication that their home has some deficiencies, energy related or not.

- Retrofit packages will be tailored to the needs of each customer. Making estimates of energy benefits and savings in utilities costs requires new skills. Some subcontractors may be required to provide the necessary items to complete the package.

- Retrofit items are installed in homes where people are living. Thus, a different kind of scheduling is required. The needs of the home owner and the businessman must be meshed. Working in the home requires considerate, trustworthy workmen, good workmanship and good manners.

- The retrofit business consists of a large number of "small" dollar volume jobs sold to one-time customers. The recommendation of each customer to friends and neighbors is invaluable.

- It is likely that issuing a certificate that work meets the specifications will be good business. Eventually, it may be required in some areas.

- The relatively small dollar volume of the basic package means that your advertising can only be geared to identifying your availability to do the work once the home owner has been convinced by the public awareness advertising that he should install some energy conserving items.

- You will need to arrange some financing. Verifying owners' credit is part of your responsibility.

What types of labor skills and operations are required for energy conservation retrofitting?

- The installation of the retrofit items includes installation of insulation of all types (ceiling, wall, floor, basement wall and crawl space), storm windows and doors, clock thermostat, caulking and weatherstripping, attic or crawl space ventilation, HVAC inspection and tune-up and carpentry.

- In addition to these specific technical skills, you must be able to supervise, schedule and control the quality of the installation.

What types of equipment are required to

successfully engage in retrofitting?

- The usual light vehicles such as pickup trucks, vans and passenger cars are required for transportation of men and materials to the job site. Specialized equipment is available for blowing insulation. Otherwise, the usual carpentry items and tools involved in HVAC work are all that are necessary.

What basic decisions must be made in establishing a business organization for retrofitting?

- An entirely new company may be established, or a new department or profit center may be added to an existing business.
- In many cases, the retrofit business will be of a sufficiently different character to warrant lines of authority and responsibility clearly separating retrofit from the rest of your business.
- Obviously, the number of employees depends on the volume of business and the proportion of work that is subcontracted.

Advertising

The right advertising program for retrofit contractors is very much like that of home remodeling contractors. The best advertising is a sustained good reputation. Word-of-mouth advertising and referrals are a very effective method of obtaining customers. It is estimated that the average well established remodeling contractor with a good reputation and in a good location spends approximately 2 percent of gross sales on advertising. Perhaps twice this much or more may be necessary as your retrofit business is being started to create an initial awareness of your availability for doing this work. Advertising possibilities include the following:

- For creating mass market demand, insulation manufacturers have found TV to be most effective. This is too costly for most retrofit contractors. Of course, it is possible for a group of retrofit contractors, manufacturers, subcontractors and local suppliers to join in such a program.
- Advertising in local area weekly papers has been found to be inexpensive and effective for remodeling contractors. This is particularly appropriate for large communities where the contractor may want to concen-

trate in one geographic area.

- Yellow pages advertising is considered to be very important.
- Utility bill "stuffers" can be very effective. The credibility of a utility company trying to show people how to reduce their monthly bill is naturally very high.
- General newspaper ads and radio spots are another means of identifying yourself as a retrofit contractor.
- Your advertising will be more effective when its timing and content are related to the basic awareness promotion and advertising referred to before.
- The most effective advertising effort is *not* geared to the "hard sell" approach used by unscrupulous operators. Experience indicates that potential retrofit customers mistrust such "high power" operators.

Selling

The builder who is likely to be successful as a retrofit contractor already has much more selling knowledge and ability than can be put in this chapter. While there are many similiarities between retrofit selling and successful sales efforts in related businesses, there also are some differences. The retrofit sales persons not only need to have selling competency but also need to be technically competent. Their job requires that they analyze the home's energy characteristics, recommend a package of retrofit items, calculate energy savings and relate that to the cost of the retrofit package.

As a retrofit contractor you can develop your own unique selling plan and methods. However, there are some points that are particularly important to all successful retrofit sales efforts:

- After initial contact with the potential customer, the appointment to inspect the home and offer retrofit services should be made promptly.
- Both husband and wife should be present during inspection, job description and contract arrangements. Otherwise, it is quite likely that additional follow-up calls will be necessary.
- The job should be "qualified" as soon as possible in discussions with the customers. Their concept of the scope of work needed and an evaluation of their willingness and ability to pay for the work should be determined as early as possible.

231

- Sell both the *estimated* savings and the comfort that will result due to reduction in drafts and a more pleasant temperature. The surrounding wall, floor and ceiling surfaces, when retrofitted, will be warmer in winter and cooler in summer. An appeal to patriotism to help solve our nation's energy problem may help in some areas, but comfort and savings should be emphasized.

- Financing is often a necessary sales tool. Total job costs can then be discussed in terms of monthly payments for a specific package of items and a specific financing plan. Many retrofit contractors ask and receive an initial payment when they get agreement to do the work. They get one-third or more on completion and the balance in 30, 60 or 90 days. Stretching out the payments without charging interest or entering into a time payment plan will simplify your sales job. If you agree to accept payment over a two or three month period, your prospect should fill out a credit application similar to that shown. If your prospect wants to pay for the work over a period of more than 2 or 3 months, your bank will probably be able to arrange the financing you need. Use their forms.

- A certificate of completion is a desirable selling tool. To be most effective, when signed by the retrofit contractor, it should certify that the work has been completed properly. Note that the certificate should make no promise about the fuel that will be saved and should not guarantee the performance of any products. Naturally, you should pass on to your customer any warranty the manufacturer makes on the products you install. Know how the manufacturer makes good on his warranty and explain that to your client. Most successful retrofit contractors also make good any part of the work they do which fails for the first one or two years after completion. If anything goes wrong with the job in the first year or two, your foreman should fix it, no questions asked. It's good business, costs very little and will pay a big dividend in customer satisfaction. If you feel it is necessary, include $25 or $50 in your bid to cover the cost of service calls. If you make any warranty of your own you must comply with Federal Trade Commission Rules enacted under the Magnuson - Moss Warranty Act. You must make clear in writing what is covered by your warranty and for how long, what you will do when something fails, and what your customer should do to have the warranty honored. You must also disclose any limitations you place on your warranty and warn that some states do not recognize certain limits on warranties. Finally, you must advise your customer that he has legal rights under the warranty.

Sales Tips

PTA's or Home Owners Associations in specific areas of a community might be helpful in initial contact work.

Trained sales women may have increased receptivity during the day for "surveying" energy conservation needs and making initial sales contact.

Utility companies have the expertise to survey individual dwellings to determine the need for the energy conserving items in the retrofit package.

Utility companies might provide a list of "qualified" retrofit contractors as a type of referral service for their customers.

Local experts such as people in universities, utilities and engineering firms might help in the preparation of scientifically sound "technical news releases" explaining energy conservation fundamentals for appropriate distribution in newspapers and other media.

After appropriate survey work, the local utility company might be induced to stamp on their bills, "You may be able to save 30% on this bill", or whatever is the appropriate percentage.

All states have energy conservation offices that may be able to supply helpful information, pamphlets, energy conservation awareness promotion or advertising material.

Many larger cities have either full-time or part-time personnel designated by the mayor or city manager to handle energy conservation matters. That person may be able to provide assistance of varying kinds.

A host of volunteer organizations such as the Junior Chamber of Commerce, Boy Scouts, Girl Scouts, environmental and conservation organizations, might assist in "surveying" energy conservation needs in homes.

Experimental programs are underway in a few grade schools using children to assess energy conservation needs in their homes.

When the job is finished, make a call-back to determine customer satisfaction, and then ask for leads for other possible customers. This provides an opportunity to remind satisfied customers that you also do remodeling and other building work (if you do) and to request that he be kept in mind when other work is contemplated.

You Sell Savings

Cold logic is really all you need to sell energy conserving home improvements. Unlike most home improvements projects that must be sold on the basis of eye appeal and convenience, energy conservation can be sold on dollars saved alone. Every month homeowners are reminded by their utility company that they are wasting money and energy. Your only task is to translate the service you sell into dollars saved.

Most everyone knows how important energy saving is. But when you meet your prospect it wouldn't hurt to emphasize points to your prospect like the following: "Mr. Prospect, you may not have thought about energy conservation as a good investment, but investing in insulation and reduced air infiltration is better than most long term investments you can make. When you invest in energy conservation improvements, you immediately begin to earn dividends in the form of reduced utility bills. These dividends not only pay off your investment, but they pay ''interest'' as well. And unlike dividends from many other investments, these are not subject to income taxes.

"At current fuel prices, improved insulation and reduced air infiltration will pay for itself many times over during the life of the house. The more poorly insulated the house is to begin with, the shorter the payback period.

"Even if you don't plan to live in your house long enough to reap the full return on your investment in the form of lowered utility bills, Mr. Prospect, it will probably still pay to invest in energy conservation improvements now. Because of higher energy prices, a well insulated house is likely to sell more quickly and at a higher price than a poorly insulated house that costs a lot to heat and cool. Show your fuel bills to prospective buyers. They will find the small increase in monthly mortgage payments will be more than offset by monthly fuel bill savings, possibly bringing the cost of living in the house within their reach. The increased value of the house alone might cover the cost to you of making the investment in energy conservation improvements.''

Explain that accepting your proposal should yield savings in fuel bills that will more than equal the cost of improvements in a relatively few years. Have some examples of savings on jobs you have done and offer references to satisfied past customers. If cost is the prime consideration, offer to do the more difficult work (walls, crawl spaces and attics) and give the homeowner assistance in completing the easier work (caulking and weatherstripping). Your approach will make sense and result in a sale to nearly anyone who has a high energy consumption home and is tired of wasting money on heating and cooling.

Why Use a Contract?

No retrofit contractor ever starts a job he doesn't expect to get paid for. Yet, every year thousands of builders and remodelers are stuck with uncollectable accounts or are forced to go to court to collect. The fewer legal problems and controversies you have, the more profitable your organization can become. When a dispute ends up in the offices of two attorneys, there is not going to be any real winner, only a losing side and a side that loses a little less. Any legal dispute over less than one or two thousand dollars is a waste of time. The attorney fees will probably be more than that if one side files suit and will certainly be more than that if the matter goes to trial. Even if you win and your contract provides that you are entitled to collect your attorney fees, you may not be awarded all of your cost, you certainly will not be reimbursed for your time, and you may find that your opponent has no assets or has been able to transfer his assets to someone else so that there is no practical way of collecting without months of delay. It is far better to try to settle smaller disputes by compromise and sue in small claims court if that fails.

You can do a lot to stay out of court when you prepare the contract. Use contract documents that you know and understand and make sure that the people who buy your services understand the contract to mean what you know it actually does mean. Put your agreements in writing, even when they are to be performed in a day or two. Don't rely on ''side agreements'' or oral understandings that modify a written agreement. Don't agree to do something you may not be able to do or pay a sum you may not have available.

Don't contract with anyone until you are sure that they have the ability and desire to pay their bills on time. If you have any doubt about prompt payment, put your credit application to use. It is a fact of life that many people do not pay their bills on time. They realize that even if you have a 100 percent valid claim against a solvent debtor, if you have to use an attorney to collect, you give up at least half the amount owed. The attorney's fee will be between one-third and one-half of the debt and you will probably waste between 1 and 3 years getting a judgment against your debtor. Somewhere during that time you will become anxious to settle for something less than the full amount of the debt. The result: you settle for 75 cents on the dollar and your attorney takes about half of that. Your "sharp" operator gets a 25 percent discount and delays payment several months at least. Meanwhile you have to pay your craftsmen and material suppliers.

To avoid disputes you should avoid surprises. No one is surprised if everyone does what is expected. The retrofit contract, whether written or oral, outlines what is expected of the parties contracting. These obligations should be as clear and precise as practical and should anticipate as many problems as can reasonably be foreseen. Don't experiment with drafting your own contract. Some contracts favor contractors and some don't. There are many local and national associations of builders and contractors who offer "standard" contracts that favor and protect the contractor. The contract included in this chapter is weighted in favor of contractors. Use one of these documents if possible.

The Statute of Frauds in most states won't let you collect on some oral contracts. At best you will have to convince a court that there was really a contract; at worst you will only be allowed to collect the reasonable value of your services rather than the full contract price. In either event you may have to go to court to collect what you are owed.

One excellent way to avoid surprises is to make clear what is *not* included. Naturally, you won't be able to list everything that is not included, but a list of items specifically excluded can save a dispute later and may even provide a little extra work for you if the owner wants that item included.

Your Contract

There are about as many building and retrofit contracts as there are construction contractors. Most of them are good...for those who use them. If you have a good basic contract and it works for you, stick to it. The contract in this chapter covers some things you may not have thought of or that may help settle disputes in the future. Use it or work part of it into your agreement if you prefer. The important thing is to develop and use a contract that covers as many possible points of conflict as possible. You are way ahead of the game if you can point to specific language in the agreement covering some minor point that your customer says is holding up payment.

Some retrofit contractors don't use a contract at all. At least they don't use a form they call a "contract." Instead, they draft a letter or use a description sheet spelling out in plain language what they plan to do, what they don't plan to do and how much and when they expect to be paid for it. Actually, this becomes the contract, whether it is signed and returned by the customer or not, once work begins. The customer agrees to the terms of the contract by letting the work go forward. Your contract could also be verbal, that is, just an oral agreement on what you and your customer are going to do. However, sometimes it is hard to remember exactly what was agreed on and some states won't enforce certain types of oral agreements. Put it in writing unless it is a very small, very simple, very quick job you are doing for a good friend.

Understand Your Contract

You should understand and be able to explain the contract you offer your client. No matter what contract you use, it will have many of the elements of the sample contract in this chapter. Many of these contract terms are in nearly every building contract you see. Know what they mean and where they apply and you should have no trouble staying out of disputes with your customers.

You should make up at least two copies of all contract documents and materials referred to in the contract documents: one copy for your file, one copy for your customer. A lender should get a third copy if there is a lending institution involved.

Proposal and Contract

Date _____ 19 _____

To _____

Dear Sir:

We propose to furnish all materials and perform all labor necessary to complete the following:

_____

_____

_____

_____

_____

_____

_____

Job Location: _____

All of the above work to be completed in a substantial and workmanlike manner according to the terms and conditions on the back of this form for the sum of:

_____ Dollars ($ _____)

Payments to be made as follows: _____

_____

_____

_____

the entire amount of the contract to be paid within _____ days after completion. The price quoted is for immediate acceptance only. Any delay in acceptance will require a verification of prevailing labor and material costs.

By _____

Company Name _____

Address _____

State Licence No. _____

"YOU, THE BUYER, MAY CANCEL THIS TRANSACTION AT ANY TIME PRIOR TO MIDNIGHT OF THE THIRD BUSINESS DAY AFTER THE DATE OF THIS TRANSACTION. SEE THE ATTACHED NOTICE OF CANCELLATION FORM FOR AN EXPLANATION OF THIS RIGHT."

You are hereby authorized to furnish all materials and labor required to complete the work according to the terms and conditions on the back of this proposal, for which we agree to pay the amounts itemized above

Owner _____

Owner _____ Date _____

Terms and Conditions

1. Contractor shall commence work under this agreement and prosecute the work hereunder to completion within a reasonable time, subject to such delays as are permissible under this contract. Contractor shall obtain a valid building permit from the appropriate Public Authority if such building permit is required. Any fee or charge which must be paid to the Public Authority in connection with the work will be paid by Owner unless provided otherwise under this contract.

2. Contractor shall pay all valid bills and charge for material and labor arising out of the construction of the structure and will hold Owner of the property free and harmless against all liens and claims of lien for labor and material filed against the property.

3. No payment under this contract shall be construed as an acceptance of any work done up to the time of such payment, except as to such items as are plainly evident to anyone not experienced in construction work, but the entire work is to be subject to the inspection and approval of the inspector for the Public Authority at the time when it shall be claimed by the Contractor that the work has been completed. At the completion of the work, acceptance by the Public Authority shall entitle Contractor to receive all payments set forth.

4. Unless otherwise specified, the contract price is based upon Owner's representation that there are no conditions preventing Contractor from proceeding with usual installation procedures for the materials required under this contract. Further, Owner represents that he will relocate furniture, clothing, draperies, personal effects and all personal property prior to the beginning of work so that Contractor has free access to portions of the building where installation of materials is required. In the event that Owner fails to relocate any personal property as provided hereunder, Contractor may relocate any of Owner's property as may be required and is not responsible for damage thereto which may result during prosecution of the work.

5. Owner agrees to pay Contractor its normal selling price for all additions, alterations or deviations. No additional work shall be done without the prior written authorization of Owner. Any such authorization shall be on a change-order form, approved by both parties, which shall become a part of this Contract. Where such additional work is added to this Contract, it is agreed that all terms and conditions of this Contract shall apply equally to such additional work.

6. The Contractor shall not be responsible for any damage occasioned by the Owner or Owner's agent, Acts of God, earthquake, or other causes beyond the control of Contractor, unless otherwise herein provided or unless he is obligated by the terms hereof to provide insurance against such harzards. Contractor shall not be liable for damages or defects resulting from work done by Subcontractors. In the event Owner authorizes access through adjacent properties for Contractor's use during construction, Owner is required to obtain permission from the owner(s) of the adjacent properties for such. Owner agrees to be responsible and to hold Contractor harmless and accept any risks resulting from access through adjacent properties.

7. The time during which the Contractor is delayed in his work by (a) the acts of Owner or his agents or employees or those claiming under agreement with or grant from Owner, including any notice to the Lien Holder to withhold progress payments, or by (b) any acts or delays occasioned by the Lien Holder, or by (c) the Acts of God which Contractor could not have reasonably foreseen and provided against, or by (d) stormy or inclement weather which necessarily delays the work, or by (e) any strikes, boycotts or like obstructive actions by employees or labor organizations and which are beyond the control of Contractor and which he cannot reasonably overcome, or by (f) extra work requested by the Owner, or by (g) failure of Owner to promptly pay for any extra work as authorized, shall be added to the time for completion by a fair and reasonable allowance.

8. Contractor shall at his own expense carry all workers' compensation insurance and public liability insurance necessary for the full protection of Contractor and Owner during the progress of the work. Certificates of such insurance shall be filed with Owner and said Lien Holder if Owner and Lien Holder so require. Owner agrees to procure at his own expense, prior to the commencement of any work, fire insurance with Course of Construction, All Physical Loss and Vandalism and Malicious Mischief clauses attached in a sum equal to the total cost of the improvements.

9. Where materials are to be matched, Contractor shall make every reasonable effort to do so using standard materials, but does not guarantee a perfect match.

10. Owner agrees to sign and file for record within five days after the completion and acceptance of work a notice of completion. Contractor agrees upon receipt of final payment to release the property from any and all claims that may have accrued by reason of the construction. If the Contractor faithfully performs the obligations of this part to be performed, he shall have the right to refuse to permit occupancy of the structure by the Owner or anyone claiming through the Owner until Contractor has received the payment due at completion of construction.

11. Any controversy or claim arising out of or relating to this contract, shall be settled by arbitration in accordance with the Rules of the American Arbitration Association, and judgment upon the award rendered by the Arbitrator(s) may be entered in any Court having jurisdiction.

12. Should either party hereto bring suit in court to enforce the terms of this agreement, any judgment awarded shall include court costs and reasonable attorney's fees to the successful party plus interest at the legal rate.

13. Owner grants to Contractor and Contractor's employees and subcontractors the right to enter the premises during daylight hours from Monday through Friday while work is in progress.

14. The Owner is solely responsible for providing Contractor prior to the commencing of construction with such water, electricity and refuse removal service at the job site as may be required by Contractor to effect the construction of the improvement covered by this Contract. Owner shall provide a toilet during the course of construction when required by law. Contractor shall leave living areas "broom clean" at the completion of work.

15. The Contractor shall not be responsible for damage to existing walks, curbs, driveways, cesspools, septic tanks, sewer lines, water or gas lines, arches, shrubs, lawn, trees, clotheslines, personal property, telephone and electric lines, by the Contractor, sub-contractor, or supplier incurred in the performance of work

16. Contractor shall issue a "Certificate of Completion" upon completion of the work. Owner acknowledges that he has reviewed the form of the Certificate and is satisfied therewith.

17. Contractor has the right to sub-contract any part, or all, of the work herein agreed to be performed.

18. Owner agrees to install and connect at owner's cost, such utilities and make such improvements in addition to work covered by this contract as may be required by Lien Holder or Public Authority prior to completion of work of Contractor.

19. Contractor makes no guarantee or promise concerning reduction in fuel bills as a result of any work performed. Heating and cooling costs are a function of utility rates, life style, activities of the occupants, temperature at which thermostats are set, hot water usage, ventilation and many other factors over which Contractor has no control.

20. Contractor shall have no liability for correcting any existing defect which is recognized during the coarse of work.

21. Owner hereby grants to Contractor the right to display signs and advertise at the building site.

22. Contractor shall have the right to stop work and keept the job idle if payments are not made to him when due. If any payments are not made to Contractor when due, Owner shall pay to Contractor an additional charge of 10% of the amount of such payment.

23. Within ten days after execution of this Contract, Contractor shall have the right to cancel this Contract should he determine that there is any uncertainty that all payments due under this Contract will be made when due or that an error has been made in computing the cost of completing the work.

24. This agreement constitutes the entire contract and the parties are not bound by oral expression or representation by any party or agent or either party.

25. The price quoted for completion of the structure is subject to change to the extent of any difference in the cost of labor and materials as of this date and the actual cost to contractor at the time materials are purchased and work is done.

26. The Contractor is not responsible for labor or materials furnished by Owner or anyone working under the direction of the Ower and any loss or additional work that results therefrom shall be the responsibility of the Owner.

27. No action arising from or related to the contract, or the performance thereof, shall be commenced by either party against the other more than two years after the completion or cessation of work under this Contract. This limitation applies to all actions of any character, whether at law or in equity, and whether sounding in contract, tort, or otherwise.

28. All taxes and special assessments levied against the property shall be paid by the Owner.

29. Contractor agrees to complete the work in a substantial and workmanlike manner but is not responsible for failures or defects that result from work done by others prior, at the time of or subsequent to work done under this agreement, failure to keep gutters, downspouts and valleys reasonably clear of leaves or obstructions, failure of the Owner to authorize Contractor to undertake needed repairs or replacement of fascia, vents, defective or deteriorated roofing or roofing felt, trim, sheathing, rafters, structural members, siding, masonry, caulking, metal edging, or flashing of any type, or any act of negligence or misuse by the Owner or any other party.

30. Contractor makes no warranty, express or implied (including warranty of fitness for purpose and merchantability). Any warranty or limited warranty shall be as provided by the manufacturer of the products and materials used in construction.

236

Notice To Customer Required By Federal Law

You have entered into a transaction on_____which may result in a lien, mortgage, or other security interest on your home. You have a legal right under federal law to cancel this transaction, if you desire to do so, without any penalty or obligation within three business days from the above date or any later date on which all material disclosures required under the Truth in Lending Act have been given to you. If you so cancel the transaction, any lien, mortgage, or other security interest on your home arising from this transaction is automatically void. You are also entitled to receive a refund of any down payment or other consideration if you cancel. If you decide to cancel this transaction, you may do so by notifying

_____
(Name of Creditor)

at_____
(Address of Creditor's Place of Business)

by mail or telegram sent not later than midnight of_____. You may also use any other form of written
(Date)

notice identifying the transaction if it is delivered to the above address not later than that time.

This notice may be used for the purpose by dating and signing below.

I hereby cancel this transaction.

_____   _____
(Date)   (Customer's Signature)

Effect of rescission. When a customer exercises his right to rescind under paragraph (a) of this section, he is not liable for any finance or other charge, and any security interest becomes void upon such a rescission. Within 10 days after receipt of a notice of rescission, the creditor shall return to the customer any money or property given as earnest money, downpayment, or otherwise, and shall take any action necessary or appropriate to reflect the termination of any security interest created under the transaction. If the creditor has delivered any property to the customer, the customer may retain possession of it. Upon the performance of the creditor's obligations under this section, the customer shall tender the property to the creditor, except that if return of the property in kind would be impracticable or inequitable, the customer shall tender its reasonable value. Tender shall be made at the location of the property or at the residence of the customer, at the option of the customer. If the creditor does not take possession of the property within 10 days after tender by the customer, ownership of the property vests in the customer without obligation on his part to pay for it.

Certificate of Completion
Retrofit Contracting Company

This certifies that Retrofit Construction Company on _____ 19,____ completed installation of the following in the structure located at _____ :
_____

Attic insulation consisting of_____ to an "R" value of_____
Wall insulation consisting of_____ to an "R" value of_____
Floor insulation consisting of_____ to an "R" value of_____
Insulation was installed in the following locations:
Attic_____Square feet _____
Walls_____Square feet _____
Floors_____Square feet _____

Other work done and materials installed:
_____
_____
_____
_____
_____
_____

All work was performed in a substantial and workman - like manner in accord with the manufacturers' instructions and generally accepted installation practices.

_____   _____
Date   Authorized Officer
                                          Retrofit Contracting Company

Credit Application

Name _____ Date of Birth _____
       First   Middle   Last

First Name of Spouse _____ Social Security Number. __ __ — __ __ — __ __

Home Address _____ City _____ State _____ Zip _____

Home Phone (_____) _____ Years at Present Address _____ Own Home ☐ Rent ☐ _____

Married ☐ Single ☐ Divorced ☐ Widow(er) ☐ Number of Dependents _____

Previous Home Address _____ How Long? _____

Firm Name or Employer's Name _____ Years There _____

Address _____ City _____ State _____ Zip _____

Business Phone _____ Position _____ Nature of Business _____

Previous Employer _____ Years There _____

Address _____ City _____ State _____ Zip _____

College/University (if recent graduate) _____ Year Graduated _____

Your Present Annual Salary _____ List Source & Amount of income other than salary _____

_____

Personal References: Name _____

Address _____ City _____ State _____ Zip _____

Name _____

Address _____ City _____ State _____ Zip _____

Credit References: 1. Name _____ No _____ Open ☐ Closed ☐

                    Address _____

                    2. Name _____ No _____ Open ☐ Closed ☐

                    Address _____

Bank   1. Name _____ Branch _____

                  _____ Type of Account _____ No _____

Bank   2. Name _____ Branch _____

                  _____ Type of Account _____ No _____

Finance Company Name _____ Address _____

Street _____ City _____ State _____ Zip _____

Nearest Relative or Friend Not Living with you _____

Address _____ Relationship _____

I hereby certify that the information in this credit application is correct. I hereby authorize you to investigate the data furnished by me.

X _____
          Signature Of Applicant   (Ink)   Date

The Sample Contract

The front of the contract is the basic contract though the small print on the back is as much a part of the agreement as the terms on the front. Identify your prospect by first and last name (use Mr. and Mrs. if that is appropriate) and date the agreement. Use the blank lines under the first printed line to identify the work you are going to do. Be specific. Name the maker, identify the products you are going to install and spell out how many square feet or linear feet or units you include in your proposal. Include in your description all the necessary associated work such as flashing, molding, trim, etc. Specifically exclude anything that your prospect might think is included but you have not included in your bid. If you need more than five or six lines to describe completely what you are going to do, refer to a sketch or plan that shows what the job includes. Identify the sketch or plan clearly by reference so there can be no mistakes about what the job is.

Next, fill in the job location. A street address is sufficient unless a lender is involved. A bank or saving association will need a legal description.

The next blank space has the payment amount and terms. On most small jobs it is reasonable for you to request payment upon completion or within 30 days after completion. Get an agreement to pay something before or at the time work begins. If you are going to have payment problems you should find that out as soon as possible. If the job is over $5,000, you should get 10 percent on signing the contract and the balance in three or four equal installments as the work goes on. The idea is to make payments roughly match your expenditures. If a lender is releasing funds to you, they will probably have their own schedule.

Under Regulation Z of the Truth in Lending Act you must notify the buyer of his right to cancel the transaction any time up to midnight of the third business day following the date the contract was signed. The law requires that a warning appear on the contract near the place for the signature of your customer. You must leave two copies of the separate right to cancel notice and the "Effect of Rescission" paragraph with your customer. You cannot start work until the three days are up (three days excluding Sundays and legal holidays) unless your customer gives up his cancellation right because there is a real emergency that requires repairs necessary to avoid danger to the buyer's family or property. Fill out the separate notice with the date the agreement is signed, the name and address of your company and the date three full days (excluding Sundays and holidays) later when the right to cancel expires.

If there is any finance charge or interest charged on an unpaid balance, you are required to make certain disclosures under Regulation Z of the Truth in Lending Act. If you are planning to charge interest or some finance fee, ask your bank for assistance in complying with Regulation Z. You can get a copy of "What You Ought to Know About Truth in Lending" from most banks and from the Board of Governors, Federal Reserve System, Washington, D.C. 20551. Any complaint your customer has against you for failing to live up to the contract can be used against whoever holds the right to collect the amount due. An appropriate notice must be included in the loan agreement. Again, your bank or whoever helps you set up credit transactions can provide the necessary forms.

Many states now license construction contractors and require that a notice concerning licensing requirements appear on the contract. Note also that many states require that a notice of the mechanics lien law appear on the contract. Be aware of any such requirements in the states where you do business.

The paragraphs on the reverse of the proposal and contract are numbered. Note especially the following points:

Paragraph 3 sets a standard by which completion can be judged if the owner refuses to agree that you have finished the work. The building inspector's standard will probably be far less exacting than an owner who stubbornly wants you to do some extra work.

Paragraph 5 requires change orders in writing and specifies that the owner pay your "normal selling price" which is more than the cost of the change. If you have to change the job to comply with building codes, you can collect for the additional work.

Paragraph 6 eliminates any responsibility you might have for acts over which you have no control.

Paragraph 7 extends the time you have to complete the contract under a number of conditions and gives you a way out of the contract if the delay goes beyond 30 days.

Paragraph 8 requires that you have workers' compensation and liability insurance and places the burden for other insurance on the owner.

Paragraph 11 means that the American Arbitration Association arbitration system will be used to settle disputes under the contract. The paragraph could have required settlement under the Better Business Bureau's National Program of Consumer Arbitration. Courts usually do not accept cases under contracts requiring arbitration until arbitration has been completed. This means you and your customer will have to arbitrate if you can't agree. Arbitration is much faster and cheaper than a court suit and should solve any problems you have.

Paragraph 12 will help you collect your attorney fees if you have to sue to enforce the contract.

Paragraph 15 absolves you of responsibility for a large number of conditions over which you have no control.

Paragraph 22 gives you the important right to stop work if a payment isn't made on time.

Paragraph 23 lets you cancel the contract if the credit check you make on your customer reveals a poor payment record or if there was a mistake in your estimate.

Paragraph 24 makes this contract the only agreement you have. In other words, the only promise you make to your customer is what the contract says, not what your salesman may have implied.

Paragraph 25 gives you the right to collect for higher labor and material costs if your labor and material costs go up after the contract is signed.

Paragraph 26 is important where the owner is furnishing materials or working on the job himself.

The contract does not make any warranty or guarantee concerning the work to be done. You should pass on the warranty made by manufacturers of the products you install, however.

Financing

Financing alternatives are essential to reduce the total price of the retrofit work to a monthly payment manageable by most prospective customers. The possible alternatives include personal bank loans, consumer credit organization loans and loans from banks for specific improvements to the home. Second mortgages are a possibility for jobs over $3,000. However, if available locally, HUD-insured Title 1 home improvement loans may offer the best alternative. Currently, the maximums for Title 1 loans are $10,000 and 12 years. Personal bank loans and consumer credit loans are generally available only on a short term basis, about one or two years. Bank loans involving specific home improvements are available for five years and second mortgages for longer terms. Re-financing of a first mortgage is not usually practical for the typical retrofit job.

In communities where energy rates have risen rapidly, institutions holding the first mortgages might be a special source for loans for retrofit. Otherwise, the cost of utilities may have risen to the point where the owner's ability to keep mortgage payments current may be jeopardized.

Your Survey and Estimate

One of your primary sales advantages as a retrofit contractor is your ability to offer a total energy conservation evaluation of the home and to tailor a balanced package of retrofit items to meet the home owner's needs. Your sales people should be responsible for making the evaluation and recommending the proper combination of items for the package. This involves a five-step process.

First, the existing characteristics of the home that affect energy use should be recorded. This includes certain dimensional measurements such as thickness of existing attic insulation, square feet of attic space, area of windows, etc.

Second, a recommended package of retrofit items should be selected based on the existing characteristics of the home, the climatic region and the desire and ability of the customer to pay for the work. A strong effort should be made to sell all of the appropriate items in at least the basic package and, where it seems appropriate, the better package including necessary supplemental items and custom options.

Third, the estimated energy savings are calculated.

Fourth, cost estimates for the individual items and the entire package are determined.

Fifth, the cost and savings benefits are related in terms of pay-back period at appropriate annual energy cost increase rates. These

Zone 1 Below 4500 degree days
Zone 2 4500 to 8000 degree days
Zone 3 Above 8000 degree days

United States climatic zones by degree days

and financing alternatives in terms of monthly costs are used with the customer as the basis for contract discussion.

The Packages

On the following page basic and better packages of energy saving items have been developed for each of three national climate zones. The map of the U.S. shows the three climate zones. Each package contains a balanced group of items what are considered to be "basic" and "better" levels of energy conservation protection. They were selected to reflect relatively similar benefit to cost relationships for each of the items in the packages. Each package is intended to represent a reasonable priority

basis for an appropriate value combination of energy conserving items, assuming that the home does not now have those items.

Of course, there is nothing hard and fast about each of the items in each of the packages. If the home owner already has storm windows and wants to have better than the basic level of thermal protection in the attic or other items in the better package, he should be encouraged to select items out of the better package, custom options or supplemental items, as appropriate.

In addition to the basic and better packages, another group of energy conservation items is listed under the heading of custom options. Most of these are applicable to homes in all

RETROFIT PACKAGES

Zone 1	Zone 2	Zone 3
Basic Package: Includes any or all items below, where applicable	**Basic Package:** Includes any or all items below, where applicable	**Basic Package:** Includes any or all items below, where applicable
Install day/night clock thermostat	Install day/night clock thermostat	Install day/night clock thermostat
Add ceiling insulation to achieve total of approximtely R-19	Add ceiling insulation to achieve total of approximately R-22	Add ceiling insulation to achieve total of approximately R-30
Tune-up furnace and air conditioning system	Install storm windows in all living areas	Install storm windows in all living areas
Weatherstrip exterior doors	Tune-up furnace and air conditioning system	Tune-up furnace and air conditioning system
Seal all openings and cracks in exterior walls	Install storm doors and weatherstrip exterior prime doors	Install storm doors and weatherstrip exterior prime doors
Calibrate water heater temperature	Seal all openings and cracks in exterior walls	Seal all openings and cracks in exterior walls
Weatherstrip and insulate attic access door	Calibrate water heater temperature	Calibrate water heater temperature
Inspection of entire house for additional recommendations	Weatherstrip and insulate attic access door	Weatherstrip and insulate attic access door
	Inspection of entire house for additional recommendations	Inspection of entire house for additional recommendations
Better Package: Includes items under basic package plus the following items, where applicable	**Better Package:** Includes items under basic package plus the following items, where applicable	**Better Package:** Includes items under basic package plus the following items, where applicable
Add ceiling insulation to achieve total of approximately R-22	Add ceiling insulation to achieve total of approximately R-30	Add ceiling insulation to achieve total of approximately R-38
Install R-11 floor insulation above unconditioned spaces	Install R-11 floor insulation over unconditioned spaces	Install R-11 floor insulation over unconditioned spaces
Tape duct joints and insulate ducts in unconditioned spaces	Tape duct joints and insulate ducts in unconditioned spaces	Tape duct joints and insulate ducts in unconditioned spaces
Install storm windows in all living areas	Blow insulation in uninsulated exterior wall cavities	Blow insulation in uninsulated exterior wall cavities
Blow insulation in uninsulated exterior wall cavities	Install 2x2 furring and R-7 insulation on basement walls	Install 2x3 framing (1" from wall) and R-11 insulation on basement walls
Add or increase natural attic ventilation, if necessary	Install basement storm windows and doors	Install basement storm windows and doors
Install ceiling fan for summer cooling	Add or increase natural attic ventilation	Add or increase natural attic ventilation

Custom options for all zones. The following items are in addition to the **basic** or **better packages.** They depend on the owner's preference. Replace shower heads with hot water saving type and replace defective washers in all faucets. Build in vestibule at entrances. Replace electric resistance heating with heat pump. Replace furnace heating system with properly sized efficient unit. Replace air conditioning with properly sized, high energy efficiency equipment. Install shades on east/west windows. Install attic exhaust fan. Install exhaust fan in window, wall or ceiling beneath attic for summer cooling. Install fan(s) hung from the ceiling for summer cooling. Replace incandescent lighting with fluorescent. Modify roof overhang for summer shading.

zones. Further, on the worksheets there are included a number of supplemental items that may be either a necessary adjunct to the installation of certain energy conserving items or they may be energy conserving items for which the exact savings are not readily measured. Examples of the first type of items are additional attic natural ventilation and a ground cover vapor barrier in the crawl space. Examples of the second type of items include insulating and weatherstripping an existing attic door and caulking and sealing the crack between the top of the foundation wall and the house framing. All of the supplemental items are either essential for the satisfactory performance of certain other retrofit items or have high benefit to cost ratios that are not individually identifiable.

The items in the basic package were selected to represent a first priority level of energy conservation for most climates and for most energy rates in view of the increasing cost and scarcity of energy. Home owners with limited ability to finance retrofit should consider the items in the basic package first. The better package contains additional energy conserving items that provide for a higher level of thermal protection although at a higher first cost.

The packages are modified for each of three climate zones because energy uses for heating and air conditioning vary significantly. The three climate zones are shown approximately on the map of the continental United States. Alaska is in Zone 3 and Hawaii is in Zone 1. The appendix at the end of this chapter lists the exact degree days and summer cooling hours over 80°F. for a selected group of cities. Sixty-five minus the average of the high and low temperature for the day equals the number of degree days in that day.

The pay back period will vary with each item, the current characteristics of the home and the cost of energy. Generally speaking, most of the items in both packages will have a pay back period (adjusted for probable increases in energy rates) under 10 years and many will be under 5 years. While all possible combinations of conditions are not considered, the pay back period of almost all of the items will be less than 15 years. Of course, each item adds to the resale value of the home. Further, that added value

will probably appreciate by the end of the pay back period. Except for mechanical and electrical equipment, caulking, weatherstripping and possibly storm doors (which may need replacing every decade or so), almost all of the items are appreciating assets that may be expected to continue to function and to produce cost savings for the life of the home.

As a rule, the pay back period will be a little longer for the items in the better package than those in the basic package. The items in the better package will also yield savings each year and better comfort conditions than those in the basic package.

All of the items in the basic and better packages, the custom options and the supplemental items reflect well established and technically sound methods for energy conservation in homes. None of these are experimental or of dubious value. Properly installed with adequate quality materials, they will all produce operating cost savings.

Doing the Work

Most of the retrofit work has been explained in previous chapters. Some items need special emphasis here. A few additional energy saving techniques are covered here because they are uniquely part of the package you should offer as a contractor specializing in retrofit work.

Installation of additional insulation to achieve the specified R-value for the ceiling can be accomplished in a number of ways. Cellulose fiber, mineral wool and glass fiber are the most commonly used materials. These materials can be installed in the form of batts, blankets or as poured or blown loose fill as explained in Chapter 11. It is usually installed between the ceiling joists or between the bottom chords of roof trusses. If these spaces are not readily accessible, batts or blankets may be installed between the rafters, collar beams and gable ends and between the framing members of the dormers and knee walls.

When installing additional insulation, the adequacy of the ventilation should be checked. See Chapter 12. Gable-end, ridge, soffit or through-the-roof vents can be used to obtain the required net free ventilation area. Care should be taken not to block existing or newly installed vents in soffits when insulation is added.

When there is no existing insulation, the preferred method is to install batts or blankets having either a kraft paper or foil-faced vapor barrier with the vapor barrier side placed face down. If there is any existing insulation, do not use a batt or blanket having a vapor barrier. Adding additional insulation does not require addition of another vapor barrier.

For unusual roof configurations, such as flat roofs, consider using rigid insulation applied over the entire roof surface. New roofing must then be applied over the rigid insulation. In that case, the total R-value of the entire roof section should be calculated before selecting a savings factor from the savings worksheets.

Walls

Wall insulation should be blown to the rejection point into the cavities of stud framed walls. If *any* insulation exists in the walls, it is probably not feasible to attempt to add additional blown material.

Two inch by two inch furring strips with R-7 batt insulation and a vapor barrier facing inside should be used to insulate basement walls. R-11 batt insulation, installed between a supplementary 2x4 or 2x3 wall frame, is referred to in the better package for the cold climates of Zone 3. Rigid wall insulation with appropriate resistance values can also be used. If not already present, pieces of R-11 batts placed between the floor joists and against the band joists are needed to complete the basement wall or floor insulation task.

Floors

Install R-11 batts between the floor joists if the basement is going to be used only occasionally in winter time, creating a relatively cold basement in winter. The batts may be installed with the vapor barrier side down for ease of installation. Temperature and vapor pressure differences between first floor rooms and the basement are probably not great enough to cause condensation problems unless some unusual condition exists.

For unvented crawl spaces, the preferred method is to add insulation to the perimeter wall and, in some climates, to the outer two feet of the crawl-space ground. For vented crawl spaces, install the insulation batts between floor joists with vapor barrier side *up*. When floor insulation is used, heating and cooling ducts and water lines below the floor insulation should be insulated. If a ground cover vapor barrier is not present, it should be installed.

Storm Windows and Doors

Storm windows serve the dual purpose of reducing infiltration around operable window sash and decreasing the heat loss through the window section. In very cold climates or in areas of high energy costs, storm windows can be considered for installation over double-glazed prime windows. In this case, the storm window cuts heat loss through the window section about 40 percent and also reduces wind infiltration.

Storm doors reduce infiltration and increase the thermal resistance value of the prime door. In cases where storm doors are not to be installed, all four sides around exterior doors should be weatherstripped.

Heating and Air Conditioning Tune-up

As part of a complete energy retrofit package, heating and air conditioning equipment should be inspected and tuned. For gas and oil furnaces, burners should be cleaned and adjusted and heat exchangers cleaned. The home owner should be instructed on the proper frequency for changing filters and a 1-year supply of filters could be a part of the package.

More extensive changes may be sometimes warranted. Many furnaces are either oversized or will be after the retrofit package is installed. It may be possible to "derate" the furnace by modifying the gas or oil burners. An older, oversized furnace may warrant replacement because overall efficiency will be increased when the size of the furnace is equal to the design load. Also, conversion from electric resistance heating to heat pumps is a retrofit alternative, since the heat pump is much more efficient, although its winter time coefficient of performance (COP) declines as the average outdoor temperature decreases. Air conditioner filters should be inspected and changed if required. Coolant should be recharged and line leaks repaired if indicated. Compressor and fan motors may also be serviced as part of the total heating and air conditioning tune-up.

Clock Thermostat

Clock thermostats are used to automatically "set back" the temperature to predetermined levels for fixed time periods, usually during the night. This, for example, removes the human element from setting back the thermostat during winter nights and allows the heat to be automatically turned up prior to awakening in the morning if desired. This can result in very substantial energy savings. An 8-hour night time set-back of 10°F, from 75°F to 65°F, should produce savings of 10 to 15 percent. Setting back the temperature from 70°F to 60°F would result in even greater savings. Even a 5° set back should yield savings of 6 to 12 percent.

Ducts

Heating and air conditioning supply ducts that run through unconditioned spaces should be insulated and the joints taped to reduce air leakage. Existing duct insulation may need to be repaired, replaced, taped or rewrapped to supplement tightly wrapped thin duct insulation. Adding additional duct insulation frequently may be justified in high energy cost areas or where the original insulation is only one inch thick.

Exhaust Fans

Window and ceiling exhaust fans, used in lieu of adding air conditioning, are options for retrofitting. They remove hot air from the house by exhausting it through windows or into the attic. They also create air movement which has a cooling effect.

Power attic exhaust fans, to lower air conditioning loads by reducing attic temperature, may be cost effective in some very hot climates. If a substantial amount of ceiling insulation is used, as indicated in the packages, power exhaust fans will not usually be cost effective in most climates.

Water Heater

Reducing the temperature setting of the hot water heater to about 125°F will save some energy and prolong the life of the heater. Most water heaters have the temperature set at 150°F or higher at the time of installation. This is substantially higher than necessary. After calibrating the hot water heater temperature setting, the home owner should be shown how to adjust the temperature, if necessary, and the benefits of the lower setting explained. The energy savings is hard to value but depends on original water temperature setting, volume and frequency of use and other factors.

Water Savings

Leaky faucets and high-rate-of-discharge shower heads waste energy by using excessive amounts of hot water. Replacing washers in leaky faucets and installing water-saver shower heads are two retrofit items that will help to save energy. The leakage from a tightly closed hot water faucet, with a worn washer, was measured and found to be a little over one gallon per hour. At that rate, the leakage was a series of nearly continuous drops, but not a continuous stream. This translates to about 6,000,000 BTU per year at usual water heater temperature settings. At $0.06 per kwh for electricity, that would cost $105 per year. At a gas cost of $0.30 per therm and a 50 percent efficiency, the cost would be $36 per year.

Managing Your Retrofit Operation

Good business management is essential to the success of retrofitting just as in any other business. Maintaining low overhead costs per job will be necessary because the average job size is relatively small.

All the usual principles of good business management are applicable to the retrofit business. But working in owner occupied homes will require a combination of management skills to evaluate the home owner's needs and to install the retrofit items with due consideration to their privacy requirements. Most of these management skills are similar to those required in all businesses, but there are a few that are especially worth noting for the retrofit business.

Scheduling

In addition to all the usual scheduling problems of building related to labor, materials and subcontractors, the retrofit contractor must coordinate with the home owner's scheduling needs. There are many possibilities for delays, nonproductive time, call-backs, dissatisfied customers, excessive cost for doing the job and missed opportunities for referrals for other work. Developing and maintaining a tight production schedule is quite important.

Efficient Operation Requires:
- A sales peson estimating the job, writing the sales contract, meshing home owner's time preference with the company's production capabilities and schedule and transmitting the work requirements to the production manager.
- A production manager coordinating materials, labor, subcontractors and the overall job scheduling and production in accord with the home owner's desires as identified by the sales person.
- A supervisor, on-site at least occasionally, responsible for production, quality control and customer satisfaction.

Each of the functions above is necessary. However it isn't necessary that three different people all be involved in performing these functions for the average size retrofit business. The best combination is a division of work between a sales person and a production manager who also performs the on-site supervision and quality control functions. However, there can be substantial differences in operating methods. The important thing is to adjust work assignments to the capabilities of the people working for you.

Good scheduling starts with the sales person's call on the prospective customer. The sales person needs to be knowledgeable and competent with respect to a number of subjects. However, there are a few scheduling related items that are particularly important for the salesman to understand:
- He must know the schedule and capabilities of the production crews. Work must be performed at the time that it is promised.
- The salesman must accurately estimate the total number of work days and number of times access to the property will be required to complete the job. Make sure that the customer is aware of these access requirements.
- He must establish a firm date for additional installations that might be required, such as for storm windows. The materials should arrive at mutually satisfactory approximate dates for installation. He should give the customer a card with the estimated dates and the name of a person and a number to call if there are any necessary changes in the schedule by the customer.
- He should call several days in advance of installation to confirm the schedule date.
- He must have an orderly and accurate written system for transmitting sales commitments to the production manager.

Production

The production manager is responsible for production scheduling within the limits previously established by the customer and the sales person, coordinating materials needs, supervising production crews, scheduling subcontractors and overall job production. For many retrofit contractors, the production manager is also responsible for the on-site supervision responsibilities for production, quality control and customer satisfaction. Some tips for successful production scheduling and supervision are as follows:

- Each job should have a back-up file that includes a copy of the contract, copies of the measurements, recommendations, cost estimate, savings and summary worksheets, required subcontractors, scheduled work time alternatives and any special occupant information that is appropriate (illness, deafness, etc.).
- A simplified form or wall chart showing each job, major tasks, location and start and finish time may be helpful in keeping track of the status of the various jobs.
- To minimize nonproductive travel time, keep a large scale map of the city marked with job locations. Clear, specific directions on how to reach the home scheduled for work that day will help the crews locate the home without delay.
- Use a specific worksheet for each home. This should be carried by the crew foreman to help avoid mistakes and costly re-work.
- There is not a great deal of variation in seasonal work patterns for remodeling items that can be accomplished indoors. However, the production manager should develop alternative work schedules for very bad weather days to help to minimize nonproductive time.

• Emphasize the importance of material costs to the workmen and accurate estimating of material needs for each job. Have a check - out - and - return - accountability - system for materials to reduce materials scrap and waste.

• Emphasize to subcontractors the importance of performing the jobs on time. If the subcontractors do not perform on schedule, your retrofit business costs will surely increase.

The amount of on-site supervision required depends on the experience and capabilities of work crews and the subcontractors. In some cases, the crew foreman may be able to perform all of the necessary functions of quality control and customer relations. However, in most construction work, self-inspection of work identifies only a small percentage of all defects. The crew foreman should report work progress to the production manager. The production manager should visit the site to be sure that work has been completed, and performed in accord with the contract. He should inspect the job quality, maintain good customer relations, deliver a signed certificate, and obtain any suggestions or leads for follow-up work, either with that customer at a later date or with other potential customers.

Volume Production

Substantial volume and low overhead are necessary to remain competitive. There are some economies of scale, but they are modest due to three unique features of the retrofit business:

First, the relatively small value of each job.

Second, the variation in each job related to the individual home owner's interests, ability to pay and the variable home characteristics.

Third, the requirement for a unique combination of technical skills.

A nationally coordinated promotion program to create basic demand for retrofit along with other financial incentives to home owners can create enough basic demand for retrofit to provide a steady flow of work for the competitive contractor. A 50 percent penetration of the existing single-family detached home market by 1985 will require about 6,000 contractors, each retrofitting 500 homes per year.

Maintaining a relatively level year-round volume of work is an important factor in keeping overhead reasonably constant, productivity high and in helping to achieve economics of scale. While there are variations in seasonal demand, these are modest based on the fact that most of the work can be accomplished indoors, except for hanging storm windows and doors, outside caulking and a small amount of other work on some homes. Data on the volume of remodeling work by seasons indicate that the second and third quarter are the best sales periods and the fourth quarter is nearly as good. The January to March quarter has the lowest volume of work. However, when these data are examined for seasonal variations of inside work only, it is noted that volume is relatively stable from quarter to quarter. If seasonal variations develop in your business, they may be partially overcome by emphasizing the year-round benefits of energy conservation. This is especially appropriate where a significant cooling season exists. Also, retrofit sales efforts can be stepped up during the first and fourth quarters when other building activity may be slack.

Developing an adequate volume in any given area is important. Travel time between small jobs and time wasted late in the day trying to "stretch-out-the-work" instead of moving to the next job can be minimized. Scheduling groups of jobs within the same neighborhood is more economical for the retrofit contractor and his subcontractors. Use direct mail advertising or neighborhood sales techniques, such as working through a home owners' neighborhood association, PTA or similar group to concentrate sales in one area of the city at a time.

It is possible to develop some economies of scale when retrofitting homes in a tract or subdivision. Many large tracts with repetitions of nearly identical models were built between 1947 and 1964. Unfortunately, home owners living in essentially identical homes have different desires and abilities to pay. Many may have already made some retrofit improvements. Nonetheless, you may be able to achieve some economies by estimating the costs only for each model of home in the subdivision so that it is not necessary to repeat this procedure for every sale. Also, you may be able to buy a larger volume of storm windows and doors that have identical dimensions.

A larger volume of work will certainly help you maintain a higher skill level for your crews and allow you to buy highly productive equipment. You might consider hiring tradesmen to do work you had been sending to subcontractors if volume permits. To be economical, this would require a substantial business volume, and warehousing facilities would be required. On the other hand, the economies inherent in absolute control of production and the economies of volume purchasing of materials could be significant. In part, of course, they are offset by higher overhead costs for equipment operation and depreciation, warehousing costs and inventory financing.

Overall, you should be able to develop some economies of scale as your experience and knowledge of the business increases.

The Energy Savings Analysis

Simplified worksheets are included here to assist you in estimating savings for each item in the packages. The worksheets cover all of the essential work elements, set forth a method of organizing the work to simplify the estimating and selling tasks, and present a logical, complete, easy to understand plan to the customer. Reproduce these sheets for use in your business or use them as a basis for developing your own worksheets. The worksheets establish a format for obtaining the required *measurements*, setting forth *recommendations*, *estimating installed costs*, *calculating energy savings* and *summarizing* the information.

The Measurements Worksheet is used for recording the required physical measurements. These are needed both for estimating costs and for calculating energy savings. These measurements do not need to be precise. For example, window measurements can be to the nearest inch and attic measurements to the nearest foot or two, since precise measurements are not necessary to establish costs or estimate savings. Reasonably accurate but not necessarily precise measurements will help to speed up the estimating processes. Some precise measurements will be needed, however. For example, measure exactly for storm windows and storm doors.

These measurements (excluding the precise measurements) should be recorded by the sales person when conducting the home energy inspection. Since the home owner will almost surely be present during that inspection and evaluation, the sales person has an excellent opportunity then to explain the potential retrofit options and their costs and benefits. The sales person, therefore, must be very familiar with the various retrofit items and must be able to calculate costs and benefits. Some remodelers prefer to develop a total price and sign a contract at the time of the first call. Others always insist on returning to the office to make the detailed cost calculations and prepare the contract. The advocates of the latter method prefer it because they say it provides them an opportunity to double check all of the figures and specifications and carefully prepare the contract. Also, they say it provides the home owner with an opportunity to make up his mind in a "non-pressure atmosphere".

The Recommendations and Estimate Worksheets

This is used to present a balanced package of retrofit items to the home owner. The package should generally follow the guidelines set forth for one of the two types of packages and one of the three climate zones. Of course, these can and should be tailored to the individual interest of the home owners and their ability to pay.

The Cost Estimate Worksheet, used together with the Measurement Worksheet provides the information needed for determining the installed cost of each item. You may want to do this right out of your established cost book in the presence of the home owner. You may prefer to do this at the office. Neither alternative is better than the other in all situations. Your method of doing business and the attitude of your customers will dictate the alternative to be used.

Estimating

Your cost book will be based on your experience with labor, material and overhead costs and subcontractor prices. Establishing unit prices will be relatively simple in some cases and more complex in others. In the case of work with which you have no previous experience, there is no substitute for accurate recording of direct labor, material and related overhead costs attributable to each retrofit item. Analysis of that data from a few representative jobs will provide a reasonable basis for developing unit prices.

Unit prices will vary because on-site conditions vary. Therefore, unit prices may need to reflect a price range or contain add-on and subtraction factors from an average price. For example, if there is easy access to an attic which has no sub-flooring and nothing stored, the unit price will be less than if the attic contains a large amount of storage or is covered with sub-flooring. Further, the unit price depends on the size of the job. The unit square-foot-cost of insulating 150 square feet over a previously missed room addition, for example, would certainly be more than insulating a 1,500 square foot attic. However, one of the advantages of the retrofit concept is that installing a package of items on a volume basis will help to average out the varying unit costs. This wouldn't be true if you were installing only one type of item on a one-at-a-time, small volume basis.

Developing a cost book, good pricing methods and effective policies will require your personal attention in the early stages of starting your retrofit business, especially if you have had little experience with the type of items involved.

The annual energy cost savings for each item can be determined by selecting the appropriate savings factor from the worksheet for that item and the existing house condition, selecting the proper number of units, area and climate factors as appropriate, and multiplying the product of these by the product of the number of degree days (or cooling hours) and the unit energy costs. This product divided by the cost factor is equal to the annual savings in dollars (refer to the formulas on the Savings Worksheets). The savings factors, number of units, area and climate factors and cost factor are selected from either the Measurement Worksheet or the Savings Worksheet.

The fuel cost is determined locally from the utility, oil or propane company, taking into account the appropriate step rate. The sales person only needs to select the correct factors and numbers, enter them into the formula and perform the simple multiplications. The fuel or

energy cost should be adjusted each time there is a rate change. The savings factor, though a single number, builds in all conditions that need to be considered. Use the Energy Savings Worksheets to make calculations for your home and some other home so you are familiar with the calculations required and can explain them to your sales people.

The Summary Worksheet is a method of presenting to your client in a clear form the cost, savings, and pay back period (based on energy costs continuing to increase) for each quantifiable item. The data on costs and savings are merely transferred onto the Summary Worksheet for each item for the Cost Estimate and Savings Worksheets. Some calculations are then performed on the Summary Worksheet. These are important in presenting the data in a form that will help the home owner to understand the benefit from each item. Also, it should be helpful in closing the sale.

First, the simple pay back period is calculated. This is equal to the total installed cost in dollars, divided by the annual benefit in dollars. This shows your customers the number of years necessary to pay off or get back their investment in that particular retrofit item. The second calculation shows the pay back period assuming that energy costs increase at a certain percent per year. Virtually everyone believes that the cost of energy will go up at least as fast as the rate of inflation and probably faster. Page 251 shows pay-back multipliers for various combinations of simple pay back periods and annual energy cost increase percentage rates. Interpolations for pay back periods and energy cost increase rates not shown in the table can be made easily because the increments in the table are small. For example, if the simple pay back period is 4 years and the annual energy cost increase rate is assumed to be 13 percent, the pay back multiplier would be 0.81 (that is one-third of the difference between the multiplier for 12 percent and 15 percent subtracted from the multiplier for 12 percent).

When you can show that the cost of your service will be paid back in five or six years, it shouldn't take very much creative salesmanship to close the deal. Still, remember to emphasize that the savings are like getting tax free income because it will be extra money available to the home owner and no taxes have to be paid, unlike most other income. Further, the home will be permanently more comfortable and be worth more when it is offered for sale. What you are offering is an unbeatable deal. You only have to explain it carefully and make sure your crews do what you promise.

Be careful to explain that these are *estimated* savings and depend on many factors which your customer alone can control. For example, the time the doors and windows are left open and the setting of the thermostat will affect heating cost. You can assure your prospect that no matter what their fuel consumption habits are, what you do will save them money.

As can be seen from the worksheets, the exact savings of some of the items cannot be predicted. This is so for one or more of the four following reasons:

First, the amount of savings is dependent on action by the home owner. For example, the savings attributable to setting back the temperature on the hot water heater will depend on the initial temperature setting and the amount and frequency of use of hot water.

Second, house characteristics vary. For example, the size of an existing crack between the top of the foundation and the house framing determines the amount of energy savings available from a reduction in wind infiltration.

Third, the savings depend on the interrelationship between the modified and the other items. For example, the amount of savings due installing a clock thermostat set-back, even for a fixed number of degrees of decrease and a fixed number of hours of set-back, vary with the extent other retrofit items are installed.

Fourth, the original conditions or characteristics of the equipment, as they relate to energy conservation, cannot be determined. For example, a furnace tune-up may contribute as much as a 10 percent savings if it is a gas or oil furnace that has been operated for some time without a tune-up or other adjustments. However, if that has been done recently or if the furnace is in a relatively efficient operating condition, the savings could be much less.

There are some items that are known to have a high benefit to cost ratio but for which the dollar saving cannot be predicted. For example, savings due to insulating and weatherstripping an existing attic door would be small if the door fits tight but large if the fit was very loose. You should be able to spot these major energy waste items very easily. Your counsel here will be worth far more than it costs.

PAYBACK MULTIPLIERS AT VARIOUS ENERGY COST INCREASE RATES

Simple pay back period (years)	Annual energy cost increase (percent)						
	3	5	6	8	10	12	15
3	0.96	0.93	0.92	0.90	0.88	0.86	0.83
4	0.95	0.91	0.90	0.87	0.84	0.82	0.79
5	0.93	0.89	0.88	0.84	0.81	0.79	0.75
6	0.92	0.88	0.86	0.82	0.79	0.76	0.72
7	0.91	0.86	0.84	0.80	0.76	0.73	0.69
8	0.90	0.84	0.82	0.78	0.74	0.70	0.66
9	0.89	0.83	0.80	0.76	0.72	0.66	0.64
10	0.88	0.81	0.79	0.74	0.70	0.66	0.61
12	0.86	0.78	0.76	0.70	0.66	0.62	0.58
15	0.83	0.75	0.71	0.66	0.61	0.57	0.53
20	0.78	0.69	0.66	0.60	0.55	0.51	0.46

Simple payback period X Multiplier from above = Payback period at assumed energy cost rate increase

Example:
8 x 0.70 (12% per year increase rate assumed) = 5.6 years

MEASUREMENTS WORKSHEET

Owner_____ Address_____

Company_____ Address_____

Rep_____

Storm Windows and Doors
Add storm sash:_____Windows; average size_____SF

Add storm doors:_____ Doors; _____ Average fit, _____Loose fit

Existing Windows
Type:_____; Material_____; Total area_____SF

Glazing:_____ SF single; _____SF insulating glass

Fit:_____ SF loose; _____SF average

Picture window:_____Window(s); Total of approximately_____SF

Weatherstripping of Windows and Doors
Windows: _____Windows; Average size;_____; Weatherstrip type_____

Doors:_____doors; Average fit_____; Loose fit_____; Weatherstrip type_____

Caulking and Sealing of Openings in: Frame ☐ Masonry ☐
Windows:_____SF with_____Doors with_____

Other or special conditions:

_____

Ceilings and Attics
Existing insulation_____Inches average thickness; gross area_____SF

Attic floor coverage_____percent, adequate ventilation ☐Yes ☐No

Access to attic: type and location _____; Size_____

Special conditions:_____

_____

Exterior Walls
Cladding type:_____; Sheathing type_____SF

Gross wall area (including window and door areas):_____SF

Special conditions:_____

_____

_____

Basements and Crawl Spaces
Basement wall area:_____SF; Above grade:_____SF

Add storm sash:_____Windows; average size_____SF

Crawl space perimeter wall area:_____SF or floor area_____SF

Crawl space vents: Number_____, Area_____SF, Type_____; None

Ground cover vapor barriers: ☐Yes; ☐No; Type_____

Special condition _____

_____

Uninsulated Ducts
Attic   ☐; Length of trunk_____LF; Length of branches_____LF

Basement   ☐; Length of trunk_____LF; Length of branches_____LF

Crawl space ☐; Length of trunk_____LF; Length of branches_____LF

Average trunk size_____Average branch size_____

Special conditions:_____

_____

Thermostat setting: Winter day_____°; Night_____°; Summer day_____°

Description of heating and cooling equipment:_____

_____

_____

Additional information and measurements:_____

_____

_____

RECOMMENDATIONS WORKSHEET

Owner_____ Address _____

Company_____ Address _____

Rep. _____

Your home is in climate zone_____. The following balance package is recommended.

Item		Circle Item Recommended
Storm windows	Install_____Storm windows, model_____	Yes No
Picture window	Install storm sash _____	Yes No
Windows	Weatherstrip_____windows _____	Yes No
Storm doors	Install_____Storm doors, model_____	Yes No
Exterior doors	Weatherstrip_____doors _____	Yes No
Window frames	Caulk and seal_____frames_____	Yes No
Exterior door frames	Caulk and seal_____frames_____	Yes No
Ceilings	Insulate to achieve a total R-_____value _____	Yes No
Exterior walls	Add R-_____value insulation_____	Yes No
Crawl spaces	Add R-_____value insulation between joists_____	Yes No
	Add R-_____value insulation around perimeter_____	Yes No
Basement walls	Add R-_____value insulation on exterior walls_____	Yes No
	Add R-_____value insulation at band joists_____	Yes No
Duct insulation	Add__inches insulation in: ☐attic ☐crawl space ☐basement	Yes No
Clock thermostat ⎫ See	Install thermostat and wiring_____	Yes No
Furnace/AC tune-up ⎬ note	Service heating and/or AC unit_____	Yes No
Water heater ⎭ below	Calibrate temperature_____	Yes No

NOTE: Savings due to these three items will vary, depending upon how many degrees the water heater is set-back, how much and for what duration the thermostat reduction is in effect, the present condition of the heating or cooling unit, the existing temperature setting of the hot water heater and the pattern and volume of use of hot water. Combined savings of about 10 to 15 percent or more of present heating and cooling bills may be generally anticipated. Higher savings are possible, depending primarily on occupants' patterns of use of the clock thermostat and hot water, climate and original furnace/AC condition.

Supplement Items

The following items are not common to a majority of existing homes. One or more may be desired to complete the retrofit package. All have high benefit/cost ratios.

Attic area	Install insulated access opening to attic_____SF	Yes No.
	Weatherstrip and insulate existing attic door_____	Yes No
	Insulate attic stair sidewalls above ceiling line _____	Yes No
	Install adequate natural ventilation by adding _____ SF of_____ type vents_____	Yes No
	Insulate rafters, collar beams, knee walls, dormers and gable end walls_____SF	Yes No
	(Where attic floor insulation is impractical)	
Crawl spaces	Install ground cover vapor barrier_____	Yes No
Other	Insulate second floor overhangs, floors over unheated porches, breezeways, garages, etc. _____	Yes No
Foundation	Insulate, caulk or seal cracks, if any, between top of foundation wall and framing_____	Yes No
Heating systems	Replace furnace heating system with properly sized, efficient unit	Yes No
Air conditioning	Replace air conditioning with properly sized, high EER equipment	Yes No
Other items _____		Yes No
_____		Yes No
Custom options_____		Yes No
_____		Yes No

COST ESTIMATE WORKSHEET

Owner_____ Address_____

Company_____ Address_____

Rep. _____

Windows and doors
Storm windows: Install____, model(s)_____ @ $_____ Ea.   = $_____
Picture window(s):   Install_____ storm sash _____ @ $_____ Ea.   =   _____
Storm doors: Install____, model(s)_____ @ $_____ Ea.   =   _____
Weatherstrip: _____windows w/_____ @ $_____ Ea.   =   _____
                      _____doors w/_____ @ $_____ Ea.   =   _____
                      Install _____threshold   =   _____
Caulk and seal: _____windows and_____door frames   =   _____
Other door, window and frame work: _____
_____   =   _____

Ceilings, attics and walls
Ceiling/attic insulation: Add____insulation for total insulation R-___value using_____   = $_____
Access: Install opening and insulated panel; location_____   =   _____
Ventilation: Install_____vents; location and size _____   =   _____
Exterior wall insulation: Fill all cavities with_____insulation   =   _____
Other ceiling, attic and wall work: _____
_____
_____   =   _____

Basements
Walls: Add R-___value wall insulation; type_____   = $_____
Furring and other basement work: _____
_____   =   _____
Storm windows: Install_____sash @ $_____ Ea   =   _____

Crawl spaces
Floors over crawl spaces: Install R-_____value; Type_____   = $_____
Crawl space walls: Install R-_____value; Type_____   =   _____
                             Method of attachment_____
Ground cover: Install_____Type vapor barrier_____   =   _____

Ducts
Location: □ attics; □ basement; □ crawl space
Insulation: Install___inches; Type_____
                    _____LF trunk duct and_____LF branch ducts   =   _____
Subtotal of construction items _____   = $_____

Mechanical equipment
Thermostat(s):   Install Model(s) _____; Location(s)_____   = $_____
Heating equipment: Furnace tune-up to include_____
_____   =   _____
Water heater: Set outlet temperature_____º; setting marked
                    as follows _____   =   _____
Air conditioning: Tune-up include_____
_____   =   _____

Equipment replacement, supplemental items and custom options
_____
_____
_____
_____

Subtotal of equipment replacement, etc. _____   = $_____
Total cost of all work (sum of subtotals)_____   = $_____

SAVINGS WORKSHEET

This worksheet is divided into two parts. Part 1 is used to determine heating savings. Using the information from the Measurements Worksheet, select the appropriate savings factor for each recommended item and calculate the annual savings for each. These savings are entered on Lines 1 through 14 of the Summary Worksheet. Part 2 is used if air conditioning exists. Annual savings are entered on lines 15 through 18 of the Summary Worksheet.

Use the Degree Days Table that follows to determine heating degree days and air conditioning cooling hours for your area. Energy costs for your area are available from the energy supplier. They are divided by the cost factors shown below for the appropriate energy type.

Degree Days: _____ Cooling Hours: _____

Heating Energy Type	Energy Cost	Cost Factor
Natural gas	$ _____ /Therm	100,000
No. 2 fuel oil	$ _____ /Gallon	138,000
Propane	$ _____ /Gallon	82,000
Resistance electric*	$ _____ /Kwh	8,000
Cooling - electricity	$ _____ /Kwh	7,000

*Heat Pump Cost Factor = 8,000 x C.O.P. (Contact your local equipment supplier)

Part 1 = Heating Savings

A. Storm Windows:

Type of Window	Savings Factor	
	Storm Windows Over Metal Prime Windows	Storm Windows Over Wood Prime Windows
Operable: loose fit; no weather-stripping	38.5	35.1
Operable; average fit; no weather-stripping	29.7	26.2
Operable; loose fit; weatherstripped	31.4	28.0
Operable; average fit; weather-stripped	28.6	25.2
Fixed sash (picture windows)	29.3	25.9

Operable windows: _____ X _____ X _____ X _____ X _____ = $ _____ (Line 1)
Savings Factor — No. of Windows — Average Size (SF) — Degree Days — Energy Cost / Cost Factor — Annual Savings

Picture windows: _____ X _____ X _____ X _____ X _____ = $ _____ (Line 2)
Savings Factor — No. of Windows — Average Size (SF) — Degree Days — Energy Cost / Cost Factor — Annual Savings

B. Storm Doors:

Existing Door Fit	Savings Factor	
	Existing Door	
	Weatherstripped	Not Weatherstripped
Loose fit	250	360
Average fit	220	300

Storm Doors: _____ X _____ X _____ X _____ = $ _____ (Line 3)
Savings Factor — No. of Doors — Degree Days — Energy Cost / Cost Factor — Annual Savings

C. Weatherstripping only (no storm windows or doors added):

Existing Fit	Savings Factor	
	Windows	Doors
Loose fit	15	240
Average fit	5	180

Windows: ____ X ____ X ____ X ____ X ____ = $ _____ (Line 4)
Savings Factor / No. of Windows / Average Size (SF) / Degree Days / Energy Cost Cost Factor / Annual Savings

Doors: ____ X ____ X ____ X ____ = $ _____ (Line 5)
Savings Factor / No. of Doors / Degree Days / Energy Cost Cost Factor / Annual Savings

D. Caulking and sealing window and door frames:

Wall Construction	Savings Factor	
	Window Frames	Door Frames
Frame or 4" masonry veneer	3	40
8" masonry	5	55

Windows: ____ X ____ X ____ X ____ X ____ = $ _____ (Line 6)
Savings Factor / No. of Windows / Average Size (SF) / Degree Days / Energy Cost Cost Factor / Annual Savings

Doors: ____ X ____ X ____ X ____ = $ _____ (Line 7)
Savings Factor / No. of Doors / Degree Days / Energy Cost Cost Factor / Annual Savings

E. Ceiling Insulation:*

Recommended Total R-Value of Insulation	Savings Factor — Existing insulation thickness and R-value					
	0" (R-0)	1" (R-3)	2" (R-6)	3" (R-9)	4" (R-12)	6" (R-18)
R-19	22.5	6.7	3.3	1.8	--	--
R-22	22.7	6.9	3.5	2.0	1.2	--
R-30	23.1	7.3	3.9	2.4	1.6	0.7
R-38	23.3	7.5	4.1	2.6	1.7	0.9

Ceiling insulation: ____ X ____ X ____ X ____ X ____ = $ _____ (Line 8)
Savings Factor / Savings (SF) / Gross Area Days / Degree Days / Energy Cost Cost Factor / Annual Savings

*Note - Attic area assumed to be adequately ventilated

F. Exterior wall insulation: (Blow into stud cavities)

Type of Exterior Finish	Savings Factor — Type of Exterior Sheathing					
	None	1/2" Fiberboard	25/32" Fiberboard	Plywood	Gypsum Board	1" Boards
Wood siding or shingles	6.4	4.1	3.3	5.1	5.4	4.5
Metal or vinyl insulated siding	4.5	3.1	2.6	3.7	3.9	3.4
Plywood	7.5	4.5	3.6	5.8	6.2	5.1
Hardboard	6.9	4.3	3.4	5.4	5.7	4.8
Asphalt siding or shingles	8.8	5.1	4.0	6.6	7.1	5.7
Asbestos cement siding or shingles	9.3	5.3	4.1	6.9	7.5	6.0
Stucco	8.6	5.0	3.9	6.9	6.9	5.5
Face brick veneer on wood frame	7.6	4.6	3.7	5.9	6.3	4.2
Common brick veneer on wood frame	6.5	4.1	3.3	5.2	5.5	4.6
Regular concrete block on wood frame	5.8	3.7	3.0	4.6	4.9	4.1
Lightweight aggregate block on wood frame	4.3	3.0	2.5	3.6	3.7	3.2
Metal or vinyl uninsulated siding	9.5	5.3	4.2	7.0	7.6	6.1

F. Exterior Walls: (Continued)

	Normal Proportion of Glass (10% to 20%)	High Proportion of Glass (Greater than 20%)
Glass Factor	1.00	0.85

Exterior Walls: ____ X ____ X ____ X ____ X _____ = $ _____ (Line 9)

Savings Factor — Glass Factor — Gross Wall Area (SF) — Degree Days — Energy Cost Cost Factor — Annual Savings

G. Crawl Spaces Without Ducts:

Type of Crawl Space	Savings Factor
Vented crawl space; add R-11 floor insulation	8.3/Sq. Ft. of floor
Unvented crawl space; add R-4 (Min.) perimeter wall insulation	5.0/Sq. Ft. of perimeter wall
Unvented crawl space; add R-11 floor insulation	3.0/Sq. Ft. of floor

Crawl Spaces w/o ducts: ____ X _____ X ____ X _____ = $ _____ (Line 10)

Savings Factor — Floor or perimeter wall area (SF) — Degree Days — Energy Cost Cost Factor — Annual Savings

H. Crawl Space With Ducts:

Type of Crawl Space	Savings Factor
Unvented crawl space; no duct insulation; add R-4 (minimum) perimeter wall insulation	6.8 Sq. Ft. of perimeter wall
Unvented crawl space; with duct insulation; Add R-4 (mininum) perimeter wall insulation	5.3/Sq. Ft. of perimeter wall
Unvented crawl space; with duct insulation; Add R-11 floor insulation	2.7/Sq. Ft. of floor

Crawl Spaces with ducts: ____ X _____ X ____ X _____ = $ _____ (Line 11)

Savings Factor — Floor or perimeter wall area (SF) — Degree Days — Energy Cost Cost Factor — Annual Savings

I. Basement Walls:

	Basement With Uninsulated Ducts	Savings Factor Basement With Insulated Ducts or Uninsulated Pipes	Basement Without Ducts or Pipes
Add 2" x 2" wall furring and R-7 wall insulation	3.7	2.9	2.4

Basement Walls: ____ X ____ X ____ X _____ = $ _____ (Line 12)

Savings Factor — Gross Wall Area (SF) — Degree Days — Energy Cost Cost Factor — Annual Savings

J. Duct Insulation:

Location of Ducts	Savings Factor Trunk Ducts (or greater than 8" diameter)	Branch Ducts (or less than 8" diameter)
In attic; with attic insulation	80	30
In vented crawl spaces; with floor insulation	80	30
In unvented crawl spaces; with perimeter wall insulation	15	5
In unvented crawl spaces; with floor insulation	50	20
In unvented crawl spaces; with no insulation	25	10
In basements; with perimeter wall insulation	20	5
In basements; with floor insulation	55	20
In basements; with no insulation	35	15

J. Duct Insulation: Continued

Trunk Duct Installation: _____X_____X_____X_____ = $_____(Line 13)
  Savings   Linear Feet   Degree   Energy Cost   Annual
  Factor   of Trunk   Days   Cost Factor   Savings

Branch Duct Insulation: _____X_____X_____X_____ = $_____(Line 14)
  Savings   Linear Feet   Degree   Energy Cost   Annual
  Factor   of Branches   Days   Cost Factor   Savings

Part II - Air Conditioning Savings

K. Ceiling Insulation:*

Summer Temperature (See page 261)	Climate Factor
Mild summer (92° F or less)	0.90
Hot summer (93° F to 97° F)	1.00
Very hot summer (98° F to 102° F)	1.10
Extremely hot summer (103° F or more)	1.25

Recommended Total R-Value of Insulation	Savings Factor Existing Insulation Thickness and R-Value					
	0" (R-0)	1" (R-3)	2" (R-6)	3" (R-9)	4" (R-12)	6" (R-18)
R-19	20.0	9.0	5.0	2.9	--	--
R-22	20.4	9.4	5.4	3.3	2.0	--
R-30	21.1	10.1	6.1	4.0	2.7	1.3
R-38	21.6	10.6	6.5	4.4	3.1	1.7

Ceilings: _____X_____X_____X_____X_____ = $_____(Line 15)
  Climate   Savings   Gross   Cooling   Energy Cost   Annual
  Factor   Factor   Area (SF)   Hours   Cost Factor   Savings

*Note - Attic area assumed to be adequately ventilated

L. Exterior Wall Insulation (Blow into stud cavities)

Summer Temperature (See page 261)	Glass and Climate Factor	
	Normal Proportion of Glass (10% to 20%)	High Proportion of Glass (Greater than 20%)
Mild summer (92° F or less)	0.80	0.65
Hot summer (93° F to 97° F)	1.00	0.85
Very hot summer (98° F to 102° F)	1.20	1.05
Extremely hot summer (103° F or more)	1.40	1.20

Type of Exterior Finish	Savings Factor Type of Exterior Sheathing					
	None	1/2" Fiberboard	25/32" Fiberboard	Plywood	Gypsum Board	1" Boards
Wood siding or shingles	7.5	4.7	3.8	5.9	6.3	5.2
Metal or vinyl insulated siding	5.2	3.6	3.0	4.3	4.6	3.9
Plywood	8.8	5.3	4.2	6.8	7.2	5.9
Hardboard	8.0	5.0	4.0	6.3	6.7	5.5
Asphalt siding or shingles	10.2	5.9	4.6	7.7	8.3	6.7
Asbestos cement siding or shingles	10.9	6.1	4.8	8.1	8.7	7.0
Stucco	10.0	5.8	4.6	7.5	8.1	6.5
Face brick veneer on wood frame	8.9	5.3	4.3	6.8	7.3	6.0
Common brick veneer on wood frame	7.6	4.8	3.9	6.0	6.4	5.3
Regular concrete block on wood frame	4.6	3.0	2.5	3.7	3.9	3.3
Lightweight aggregate block on wood frame	3.4	2.4	2.0	2.9	3.0	2.6
Metal or vinyl uninsulated siding	11.1	6.2	4.8	8.2	8.8	7.1

L. Exterior Walls: (Continued)

Exterior Walls: _____ X _____ X _____ X _____ X _____ = $ _____ (Line 16)
$\quad\quad\quad\quad\quad$ Glass and $\quad\quad$ Savings $\quad$ Gross Wall $\quad$ Cooling $\quad\quad$ Energy Cost $\quad\quad$ Annual
$\quad\quad\quad\quad\quad$ Climate Factor $\quad$ Factor $\quad$ Area (SF) $\quad$ Hours $\quad\quad$ Cost Factor $\quad\quad$ Savings

M. Duct Insulation:

Location of Ducts	Savings Factor	
	Trunk Ducts (Or greater than 8" diameter)	Branch Ducts (Or less than 8" diameter)
In basements; with perimeter wall insulation	55	20
In basements; with floor insulation	50	20
In basements; with no insulation	60	20

Trunk Duct
Insulation: $\quad$ _____ X _____ X _____ X _____ = $ _____ (Line 17)
$\quad\quad\quad\quad\quad$ Savings $\quad$ Linear Feet $\quad$ Cooling $\quad$ Energy Cost $\quad\quad$ Annual
$\quad\quad\quad\quad\quad$ Factor $\quad$ of Branches $\quad$ Hours $\quad$ Cost Factor $\quad\quad$ Savings

Branch Duct
Insulation $\quad\quad$ _____ X _____ X _____ X _____ = $ _____ (Line 18)
$\quad\quad\quad\quad\quad$ Savings $\quad$ Linear Feet $\quad$ Cooling $\quad$ Energy Cost $\quad\quad$ Annual
$\quad\quad\quad\quad\quad$ Factor $\quad$ of Branches $\quad$ Hours $\quad$ Cost Factor $\quad\quad$ Savings

SUMMARY WORKSHEET

Owner_____ Address_____

Company_____ Address_____

Rep. _____

Basic and Better Package Items

Heating Items:	$ Cost	Annual $ Savings	Simple Pay Back Period (Years)	Pay Back Period With Energy Cost Increasing At ___ % Per Year (Years)
1. Storm Windows				
2. Picture Windows				
3. Storm Doors				
4. Weatherstrip Windows				
5. Weatherstrip Doors				
6. Caulk and Seal Window Frames				
7. Caulk and Seal Door Frames				
8. Ceiling Insulation				
9. Insulate Walls				
10. Insulate Crawl Spaces Without Ducts				
11. Insulate Crawl Spaces With Ducts				
12. Insulate Basement Walls				
13. Insulate Trunk Duct				
14. Insulate Branch Ducts				
Air Conditioning Items:	///	/////	/////	//////
15. Ceiling Insulation*				
16. Insulate Walls*				
17. Insulate Trunk Duct*				
18. Insulate Branch Ducts*				
Subtotal (Items Numbers 1-18)				

Other, Supplemental and Custom Items

Other Items

	$ Cost	Annual $ Savings	Simple Pay Back Period (Years)	Pay Back Period With Energy Cost Increasing (Years)
19. Clock Thermostat	} /////	/////	/////	/////
20. Furnace A/C Tune-Up	}			
21. Calibrate Water Heater	} /////	/////	/////	/////
Subtotal (Items Number 19-21)				

Supplemental Items

_____

_____

_____

_____

_____

Custom Options

_____

_____

_____

_____

_____

Total of All Items

*Costs noted under heating items; savings cumulative in determining pay back period.

DEGREE DAYS TABLE

Location	Winter Degree Days	Summer Cooling Hours Over 80°F	Summer Design Temp. (°F)	Location	Winter Degree Days	Summer Cooling Hours Over 80°F	Summer Design Temp. (°F)
ALABAMA				**CALIFORNIA**			
Andalusia	1800	1500	95	Alameda	2800	100	84
Anniston	2600	1350	96	Anaheim	2000	750	93
Bessemer	2600	1350	97	Bakersfield	2200	1650	103
Birmingham	2600	1350	98	Berkeley	3000	(b)	79
Decatur	3000	1450	97	Eureka	4600	(b)	67
Dothan	1800	1450	97	Fresno	2600	1350	101
Florence	3000	1450	97	Lafayette	3000	1050	103
Huntsville	3000	1250	97	Long Beach	1800	250	87
Mobile	1600	1850	95	Los Angeles	2000	550	94
Montgomery	2200	1600	98	Los Gatos	3000	100	87
Muscle Shoals	3000	1450	98	Merced	2400	1300	102
Phenix City	2400	1500	98	Modesto	2400	1200	101
Selma	2200	1700	98	Oakland	2800	100	85
Sheffield	3000	1450	98	Pasadena	2000	900	96
Talladega	2600	1350	97	Redding	4600	1550	103
Tuscaloosa	2600	1550	98	Sacramento	2600	1000	100
				San Bernardino	2000	1200	101
ALASKA				San Diego	1400	150	86
Anchorage	10800	(a)	73	San Francisco	3000	(b)	83
				San Jose	3000	150	90
ARIZONA				San Leandro	2800	100	85
Bisbee	2600	1250	95	San Mateo	2800	100	83
Chandler	1800	2800	108	San Rafael	3000	250	89
Douglas	2600	1250	100	Santa Ana	2000	750	92
Flagstaff	7200	200	84	Santa Barbara	2000	(b)	87
Gila Bend	1400	3100	111	Santa Clara	3000	150	87
Mesa	1800	2800	108	Santa Cruz	2800	(b)	87
Phoenix	1800	2750	108	Santa Maria	3000	(b)	85
Prescott	4600	1650	96	Santa Monica	2200	150	80
Scottsdale	1800	2750	109	Santa Rosa	3000	200	95
Tombstone	2400	1250	95	Stockton	2600	1000	101
Tucson	1800	2450	105	Yreka	5400	(a)	96
Winslow	4800	950	97				
Yuma	1000	3150	111	**COLORADO**			
				Boulder	5600	(a)	92
ARKANSAS				Colo. Springs	6400	500	90
Benton	3000	1800	100	Denver	6200	650	90
Blytheville	3400	1250	98	Fort Collins	7000	(a)	91
Dumas	2400	1600	98	Grand Junction	5600	1000	96
El Dorado	2200	1750	99	Leadville	10600	(a)	76
Fayetteville	3400	1200	97	Pueblo	5400	900	96
Fort Smith	3200	1500	101	Sheridan	6200	650	93
Hot Springs	3000	1550	99	Trinidad	5400	750	93
Jonesboro	3600	1350	98				
Little Rock	3200	2000	99	**CONNECTICUT**			
Mountain Home	3600	1150	100	Bridgeport	5600	300	90
Pine Bluff	2800	1650	99	Danbury	6000	350	90
Searcy	3400	1450	97	Greenwich	5400	300	88
Stuttgart	3000	1300	96	Hartford	6200	500	90
Texarkana	2600	1750	99	Meriden	6000	500	91
Walnut Ridge	3400	1400	99	New Britain	6000	500	91

Location	Winter Degree Days	Summer Cooling Hours Over 80° F	Summer Design Temp. (° F)	Location	Winter Degree Days	Summer Cooling Hours Over 80° F	Summer Design Temp. (° F)
CONN. (cont'd.)				**GA. (cont'd.)**			
New Haven	5800	200	88	Dalton	3400	1200	97
Norwalk	5400	300	91	Gainesville	3200	1400	94
Stamford	5400	300	88	La Grange	2600	1350	96
				Macon	2200	1550	98
DELAWARE				Marietta	3200	1150	95
Dover	4600	700	93	Moultrie	1600	1750	97
Newark	5000	600	93	Rome	3400	1100	97
Wilmington	5000	600	93	Savannah	1800	1450	96
				Valdosta	1600	1550	96
DIST. OF COLUMBIA							
Washington	4200	1000	94	**HAWAII**			
				Honolulu	(d)	1350	87
FLORIDA							
Cocoa Beach	600	2100	90	**IDAHO**			
Daytona Beach	800	1600	94	Aberdeen	7000	600	94
Deland	800	1600	93	Boise	5800	700	96
Fort Lauderdale	200	2050	91	Burley	5800	850	95
Fort Meade	600	1750	95	Coeur D'Alene	6600	350	94
Fort Myers	400	1850	94	Idaho Falls	7200	350	91
Fort Pierce	400	2000	93	Lewiston	5600	900	98
Ft. Walton Beach	1200	2000	92	Moscow	5800	900	91
Gainesville	1000	1700	96	Mountain Home	6400	900	99
Jacksonville	1200	1800	96	Nampa	5800	700	97
Lakeland	600	1750	95	Pocatello	7000	600	94
Lake Wales	600	1750	95	Twin Falls	5400	850	96
Lake Worth	200	2400	92				
Melbourne	600	2100	90	**ILLINOIS**			
Miami	200	2400	91	Alton	5000	1150	97
Ocala	800	1650	96	Aurora	6600	700	93
Orlando	800	1600	96	Belleville	4800	800	97
Panama City	1400	2100	92	Bloomington	5600	800	94
Pensacola	1400	1900	92	Cairo	3800	1150	98
Punta Gorda	400	1850	94	Carbondale	4200	1150	98
St. Augustine	1000	1800	94	Champaign	5800	800	96
St. Petersburg	600	2150	93	Chicago	6600	750	95
Sarasota	600	1800	93	Danville	5400	800	96
Tallahassee	1400	1550	96	Decatur	5400	950	96
Tampa	600	1800	92	De Kalb	6600	700	94
Titusville	600	2100	90	Elgin	6600	700	92
Venice	600	1600	92	Evanston	6600	400	92
West Palm Beach	200	2400	92	Galesburg	6200	700	95
Winter Haven	600	1750	95	Joliet	6600	700	94
Winter Park	800	1600	93	Kankakee	6000	650	94
				Moline	6400	700	94
GEORGIA				Ottawa	6400	600	94
Albany	1800	1750	98	Peoria	6000	600	94
Athens	3000	1400	96	Quincy	5400	800	97
Atlanta	3000	1000	95	Rantoul	5800	800	94
Augusta	2400	1400	96	Rockford	6800	700	92
Brunswick	1200	1600	97	Rock Island	6400	600	94
Columbus	2400	1500	98	Springfield	5400	950	95

Location	Winter Degree Days	Summer Cooling Hours Over 80° F	Summer Design Temp. (°F)	Location	Winter Degree Days	Summer Cooling Hours Over 80° F	Summer Design Temp. (°F)
ILL. (cont'd.)				**KANSAS (cont'd.)**			
Urbana	5800	800	96	Leavenworth	5000	1000	98
				Salina	5000	1400	101
INDIANA				Topeka	5200	1150	99
Anderson	5400	750	93	Wichita	4600	1300	102
Bloomington	4800	850	95				
Columbus	5400	850	95	**KENTUCKY**			
Connersville	5400	750	94	Covington	5200	750	93
Elkhart	6400	550	92	Hopkinsville	4000	1150	97
Evansville	4400	1100	96	Lexington	4600	950	94
Fort Wayne	6200	600	93	Louisville	4600	1050	96
Gary	6200	550	92	Murray	4000	1150	97
Greensburg	5200	850	95	Owensboro	4400	1200	96
Hammond	6200	550	92	Paducah	4200	1100	97
Indianapolis	5600	750	93				
Kokomo	5600	700	94	**LOUISIANA**			
Lafayette	5800	800	94	Alexandria	2000	1700	97
Marion	5800	700	93	Baton Rouge	1600	1650	96
Muncie	5600	650	93	Bossier City	2200	1850	99
New Albany	4600	1050	95	Lafayette	1400	1800	95
Richmond	5400	750	93	Lake Charles	1400	1800	95
Seymour	4800	850	95	Monroe	2200	1850	98
South Bend	6400	550	92	New Orleans	1400	1750	93
Terre Haute	5400	850	95	Shreveport	2200	1850	99
IOWA				**MAINE**			
Algona	7400	450	91	Bangor	8000	200	88
Ames	6800	600	94	Lewiston	7800	300	88
Burlington	6200	600	95	Portland	7600	250	88
Cedar Falls	7400	450	92				
Cedar Rapids	6600	550	92	**MARYLAND**			
Clinton	6800	550	92	Annapolis	4400	650	91
Council Bluffs	6600	900	97	Baltimore	4600	850	94
Davenport	6400	600	94	Cambridge	4200	800	93
Des Moines	6600	600	95	College Park	4400	900	95
Dubuque	7400	400	92	Cumberland	5200	650	94
Fort Dodge	7400	600	94	Frederick	5000	750	94
Iowa City	6400	600	94	Hagerstown	5200	550	94
Keokuk	5600	600	95	Rockville	4400	900	95
Marshalltown	6800	600	93	Silver Spring	4400	900	95
Mason City	7600	450	91	Wheaton	4400	900	95
Muscatine	6400	600	94				
Ottumwa	6400	900	95	**MASSACHUSETTS**			
Sioux City	7000	800	96	Attleboro	5800	300	90
Waterloo	7400	450	95	Boston	5600	400	90
				Cape Cod	6000	150	85
KANSAS				Fall River	5800	150	88
Coffeyville	4000	1350	99	Lawrence	6800	500	90
Dodge City	5000	1150	99	Lowell	6800	500	91
Garden City	5200	1150	100	Pittsfield	7600	200	86
Hutchinson	4600	1300	101	Springfield	6600	400	91
Kansas City	4800	1100	100	Worcester	7000	300	89

Location	Winter Degree Days	Summer Cooling Hours Over 80° F	Summer Design Temp. (°F)	Location	Winter Degree Days	Summer Cooling Hours Over 80° F	Summer Design Temp. (°F)
MICHIGAN				**MO. (cont'd.)**			
Adrian	6400	500	93	Hannibal	5400	850	96
Alpena	8600	300	87	Jefferson City	4800	1100	97
Ann Arbor	6800	400	90	Joplin	4000	1050	97
Battle Creek	6600	500	92	Kansas City	4800	1100	100
Benton Harbor	6200	350	90	St. Joseph	5400	1150	97
Coldwater	6400	500	92	St. Louis	5000	1150	98
Detroit	6200	500	92	Sedalia	5000	1100	97
Escanaba	8600	250	82	Springfield	5000	950	97
Flint	7400	500	89				
Grand Rapids	6800	400	91	**MONTANA**			
Holland	6400	300	90	Billings	7000	500	94
Jackson	6400	500	92	Butte	9800	200	86
Kalamazoo	6600	500	92	Great Falls	7800	300	91
Lansing	7000	300	89	Helena	8200	250	90
Ludington	7400	400	91	Missoula	8200	300	92
Marquette	8400	100	88				
Midland	7200	400	91	**NEBRASKA**			
Monroe	6200	550	93	Columbus	6600	850	98
Mt. Pleasant	7200	400	89	Grand Island	6600	850	98
Muskegon	6600	250	87	Hastings	6200	850	98
Port Huron	7200	400	90	Lincoln	5800	1000	100
Saginaw	7000	400	88	Norfolk	7000	800	97
Sault Ste. Marie	9400	100	83	North Platte	6600	700	97
				Omaha	6600	900	97
MINNESOTA				Scottsbluff	6600	850	96
Austin	8000	350	90				
Bloomington	8400	500	92	**NEVADA**			
Duluth	10000	(b)	83	Elko	7400	650	94
Minneapolis	8400	500	92	Las Vegas	2800	2350	100
Moorhead	9400	400	92	Reno	6400	650	95
Rochester	8200	350	90				
St. Cloud	8800	450	90	**NEW HAMPSHIRE**			
St. Paul	8400	500	92	Concord	7400	400	91
				Dover	7200	300	88
MISSISSIPPI				Keene	7400	500	90
Biloxi	1600	2050	93	Laconia	7800	400	89
Columbus	2600	1400	97	Manchester	7200	500	92
Greenville	2400	1700	98	Nashua	7000	500	92
Gulfport	1600	2050	93	Portsmouth	7200	300	88
Hattiesburg	1800	1600	97				
Jackson	2200	1600	98	**NEW JERSEY**			
Laurel	2000	1650	97	Atlantic City	4800	450	91
Meridian	2200	1550	97	Bernardsville	5400	600	94
Natchez	1800	1650	96	Camden	4600	700	94
Pascagoula	1600	2050	93	Cape May	4800	450	91
Picayune	1600	2050	93	Clinton	5200	550	91
Vicksburg	2000	1600	97	Edison	5000	600	93
				Flemington	5200	550	91
MISSOURI				Lakewood	5400	600	93
Cape Girardeau	4200	1300	98	Morristown	5600	650	91
Columbia	5000	1050	97	Newark	5000	600	94

Location	Winter Degree Days	Summer Cooling Hours Over 80° F	Summer Design Temp. (°F)	Location	Winter Degree Days	Summer Cooling Hours Over 80° F	Summer Design Temp. (°F)
				NORTH DAKOTA			
				Bismarck	8800	450	95
N.J. (cont'd.)				Fargo	9200	400	92
New Brunswick	5000	600	91	Grand Forks	9800	350	91
New Milford	5400	600	94	Minot	9600	300	91
Paterson	5400	600	93				
Trenton	5000	450	92	**OHIO**			
				Akron	6000	400	89
NEW MEXICO				Ashland	5800	450	90
Alamagordo	3000	1500	100	Ashtabula	6400	400	89
Albuquerque	4400	1150	96	Canton	6000	400	89
Carlsbad	2600	1800	101	Chillicothe	5000	900	93
Clovis	4200	1200	99	Cincinnati	4400	800	94
Hobbs	2600	1800	101	Cleveland	6400	500	91
Las Cruces	2800	1850	102	Columbus	5600	600	92
Roswell	3800	1600	101	Dayton	5600	700	92
Santa Fe	6200	700	90	Defiance	6200	600	93
				Dover	6000	450	90
NEW YORK				Elyria	6400	500	92
Albany	6800	400	91	Findlay	6200	650	92
Binghamton	7200	250	91	Greenville	5800	650	93
Buffalo	7000	350	88	Lancaster	5200	600	93
Elmira	6400	400	92	Lima	6000	650	93
Glens Falls	7200	400	88	Mansfield	6400	450	91
Hempstead	5200	450	91	Marietta	4800	800	96
New City-Nyack	5800	500	92	Newark	5600	700	92
New York	5000	650	94	Norwalk	6200	750	92
Niagara Falls	7000	350	88	Sandusky	5800	400	92
Poughkeepsie	6200	600	93	Sidney	5800	650	93
Rochester	6800	400	91	Springfield	5600	800	93
Rome	7400	350	90	Toledo	5800	600	92
Schenectady	6800	350	90	Troy	5600	700	93
Syracuse	6800	450	90	Wintersville	5800	450	90
Watertown	7200	200	86	Youngstown	6400	400	89
White Plains	5600	400	90				
				OKLAHOMA			
NORTH CAROLINA				Altus	3000	1850	103
Asheville	4000	600	91	Bartlesville	4000	1350	101
Burlington	3800	900	94	Enid	3800	1550	103
Charlotte	3200	1150	96	Lawton	3000	1750	103
Durham	3400	1050	94	Moore	3200	1550	101
Elizabeth City	3400	1000	93	Norman	3200	1600	101
Fayetteville	3000	1250	97	Oklahoma City	3200	1450	100
Gastonia	3200	1150	95	Ponca City	4000	1450	102
Greensboro	3800	900	94	Shawnee	3200	1500	100
Jacksonville	2600	1250	94	Stillwater	3800	1450	101
Kinston	2800	1150	97	Tulsa	3800	1600	102
Raleigh	3400	1050	95				
Rocky Mount	3600	1150	95	**OREGON**			
Salisbury	3200	1350	98	Baker	7000	200	94
Wilmington	2400	1250	93	Corvallis	4800	400	91
Winston-Salem	3600	800	94	Eugene	4800	450	91

Location	Winter Degree Days	Summer Cooling Hours Over 80° F	Summer Design Temp. (°F)	Location	Winter Degree Days	Summer Cooling Hours Over 80° F	Summer Design Temp. (°F)
ORE. (cont'd.)				**TENNESSEE**			
Grants Pass	5000	850	94	Chattanooga	3200	1250	97
Klamath Falls	6400	350	89	Jackson	3400	1500	97
Medford	5000	650	98	Johnson City	4000	850	92
Pendleton	5200	650	97	Knoxville	3400	1000	95
Portland	4600	200	89	Memphis	3200	1500	98
Salem	4800	300	92	Nashville	3600	1300	97
				Oak Ridge	3800	1050	94
PENNSYLVANIA							
Allentown	5800	500	92	**TEXAS**			
Altoona	6200	350	89	Abilene	2600	2000	101
Chambersburg	5400	650	94	Amarillo	4000	1200	98
Erie	6400	250	88	Austin	1800	2250	101
Gettysburg	5200	700	94	Beaumont	1000	1800	96
Harrisburg	5200	750	92	Brownsville	600	2300	94
Johnstown	5600	450	91	Brownwood	2200	1800	102
Kingston	6200	400	89	Corpus Christi	1000	2550	95
Lancaster	5400	650	92	Dallas	2400	2300	101
Philadelphia	4400	700	93	El Paso	2800	1850	100
Phila. Suburban	5200	550	91	Fort Worth	2400	2200	102
Pittsburgh	6000	450	90	Galveston	1200	2650	91
Reading	5000	800	93	Houston	1400	1900	96
Scranton	6200	450	89	Killeen	2000	2000	100
State College	6200	250	89	Longview	2400	1850	100
Sunbury	5600	650	91	Lubbock	3600	1350	99
Uniontown	5200	600	90	Lufkin	1800	2050	98
Washington	5400	450	90	Midland	2600	1900	100
Wilkes-Barre	6200	400	89	Paris	2600	1850	100
Williamsport	5800	550	91	San Angelo	2200	2100	101
York	5400	750	93	San Antonio	1600	2000	99
				Sherman	2600	1850	101
RHODE ISLAND				Texarkana	2600	1750	99
Newport	5800	250	86	Victoria	1200	2300	98
Providence	6000	300	89	Waco	2000	2200	101
Westerly	5800	250	87	Wichita Falls	2800	2050	103
SOUTH CAROLINA				**UTAH**			
Charleston	2000	1250	95	Ogden	5600	800	94
Columbia	2400	1350	98	Salt Lake City	6000	900	97
Florence	2600	1400	96				
Greenville	3000	1100	95	**VERMONT**			
Myrtle Beach	(c)	1200	92	Burlington	8200	300	88
Spartanburg	3000	1100	95	Montpelier	8800	300	90
Walhalla	3200	1100	95	Rutland	8000	300	87
SOUTH DAKOTA				**VIRGINIA**			
Aberdeen	8600	550	95	Alexandria	4200	1000	95
Huron	8200	650	97	Charlottesville	4200	850	93
Rapid City	7400	550	96	Danville	3600	700	95
Sioux Falls	7800	500	95	Lynchburg	4200	650	94
Watertown	8400	500	93	Martinsville	3800	700	95
				Newport News	3400	950	95

Location	Winter Degree Days	Summer Cooling Hours Over 80° F	Summer Design Temp. (°F)	Location	Winter Degree Days	Summer Cooling Hours Over 80° F	Summer Design Temp. (°F)
VA. (cont'd)				**WV (cont'd)**			
Norfolk	3400	1000	94	Parkersburg	4800	650	93
Petersburg	3600	1000	96	Wheeling	5200	450	91
Richmond	3800	1000	96				
Roanoke	4200	800	94	**WISCONSIN**			
				Appleton	7800	350	89
WASHINGTON				Beloit	6800	600	92
Bellingham	5400	150	76	Eau Claire	8000	400	90
Kennewick	5200	700	98	Fond du Lac	7600	350	89
Longview	5200	250	88	Green Bay	8000	250	88
Olympia	5200	100	85	La Crosse	7600	500	90
Poulsbo	5200	100	85	Madison	7800	500	92
Seattle	5200	100	85	Milwaukee	7600	350	90
Spokane	6600	350	93	Racine	7400	350	90
Tacoma	5200	100	85	Superior	9800	200	87
Walla Walla	4800	600	98	Watertown	7800	500	92
Yakima	6000	550	94	Wausau	8400	300	89
WEST VIRGINIA				**WYOMING**			
Charleston	4400	800	92	Casper	7400	550	92
Clarksburg	5000	750	92	Cheyenne	7400	350	89
Fairmont	5000	800	94	Lander	7800	200	92
Huntington	4400	1000	95	Sheridan	7600	600	95

Winter Degree Days are taken from the ASHRAE Handbook of Fundamental and other reference sources. Values have been rounded to the nearest 200 degree days.

Summer Cooling Hours are from the Engineering Weather Data Manual and are shown to the nearest 50 hours per cooling season.

Summer Design Temperatures are taken principally from the ASHRAE Handbook of Fundamentals and the Engineering Weather Data Manual (U.S. Government Printing Office).
   (a) Cooling data unavailable or cooling not normally considered.
   (b) Cooling hours less than 50 per year.
   (c) Heating data unavailable.
   (d) No heating required.

Appendix 1
Master Checklist For Energy Savings

Use the list on the following pages to recall the key energy saving concepts used in building or remodeling homes or light commercial structures. The list both summarizes concepts presented in the first 14 chapters of this book and includes many points which were not explained fully but should be remembered when planning any job.

Naturally not every building can use all or even most of the suggestions presented here. At best, you will be able to use only many of the most important points. Go over the list when you are in the planning stages to find key areas where energy savings are possible. Usually a little planning on your part will save a considerable amount of energy and add little or nothing to the cost of the home. Every professional builder has this obligation to his clients.

Use good judgment when going over this checklist. It is intended as a reminder system of *possible* ways to save energy, not as a set of specifications for every job. Some of the points apply only in extreme climates. Some principles work against other principles. For example, large windows are desirable because they admit energy saving light and heat. But large windows also increase the heating and cooling load. It is as important to know how and where to use large glass areas as it is to know that glass can cut energy requirements.

Site Selection

☐ When you have a choice of sites, take advantage of the site which offers opportunities for conservation of energy.

☐ Select a site which has year-round temperatures close to or somewhat lower than those desired within the occupied spaces.

☐ Select a site with high air quality (free of pollution) to enhance natural ventilation.

☐ Select a site that allows the best building orientation and configuration to minimize yearly energy consumption.

☐ Select a site that has topographical features and adjacent structures that provide desirable shading.

☐ Select a site that has topographical features and adjacent structures that provide wind and noise buffers.

☐ Select a site to reduce unwanted heat reflections from water.

☐ Minimize transportation costs; attempt to reduce dependence on the automobile.

☐ Locate the building in close proximity to as many services and and conveniences as possible.

☐ Consider convenience of recreation.

☐ Include the dual role of the home: its expanded use in the future for work and recreation.

☐ Be wary of second homes that are inaccessible to public transportation.

☐ Research utility costs in the area.

☐ Favor a direct sewer connection over septic tank or cesspool.

☐ Water service should have sufficient pressure, large enough meter, and large service line.

☐ Favor planning of a house with balanced utility use (gas and electricity) rather than one that is all electric.

☐ Avoid gerrymandered telephone districts that penalize the caller for "local" calls.

☐ Investigate alternative utility and fuel sources.

Site Development

☐ Utilize a sloping site to partially bury the building or use earth berms to reduce solar radiation.

☐ Use ponds and water fountains to reduce outdoor air temperature around the building.

☐ Collect rain water for use in the building and for care of the landscape.

☐ Locate the building on the site to induce air flow for natural ventilation and cooling.

☐ Locate the building to minimize adverse wind effects on exterior surfaces.

☐ Utilize photographic shots of the site.

☐ Introduce natural gas to the project.

☐ Reckon with any drainage problems.

☐ Be conscious of the importance of sewer depth.

☐ Research the nature of the soil.

☐ Use consistent and homogeneous building materials.

☐ Plan the lot as a single entity.

☐ Have a total grading plan related to final landscaping.

☐ Maximize privacy.

☐ Invite the morning sun into breakfast and bedrooms.

☐ Shield rooms from the setting western sun.

Landscaping

The types of trees, shrubs, and ground cover that can be grown in an area is dependent upon the climate. However, sufficient number and types of plants can be grown in any climate to provide either shade or windbreaks. The types of plants that can be planted adjacent to a building depends primarily upon the actual site selected and particularly upon the sub-surface soil and water conditions. Plants emit water vapor into the environment and may locally modify the outdoor humidity.

The relative advantages and disadvantages of plants in terms of energy conservation must be weighed in relation to the building envelope and orientation. However, no design should rely entirely on the presence of trees, since they may be destroyed through disease or accident, and it takes many years for new growth.

☐ Shade walls and paved areas adjacent to the building to reduce solar radiation striking the building. Shading reduces heat build-up and is therefore desirable where cooling is a problem. (Note that heat build-up will, however, reduce the use of energy during the heating season).

☐ Plant deciduous trees for their summer sun shading and windbreak effect.

☐ Plant coniferous trees for summer and winter shading and windbreak effects.

☐ Cover exterior walls with plantings to reduce heat transmission and solar gain. Select materials carefully so that the planting will not damage the building.

☐ Plant shrubs or lawn between the building perimeter and sidewalk to reduce heat build-up.

☐ Plant lawn between the building and the street to reduce heat build-up, if maintenance is possible.

☐ Plan paved areas to reduce energy consumption. The combination of paved areas, solar angle, and type of surface will control the majority of heat reflected onto most buildings. For example, a concrete (light) surface to the south of a building will reflect *light* on the south facade of the building, while a dark asphalt surface will absorb the sunlight but re-radiate the energy as heat which has very different properties. Glass is an effective barrier to heat radiation, but is transparent to light radiation. Parking areas cannot be eliminated. However, relocation of parking area may benefit the energy demand and comfort of the building. Parking areas can be sheltered from sun and wind or shaded by trees.

☐ Introduce the landscaper into the project early.

☐ Conceive of hedges and trees as architectural elements.

☐ Combine deciduous and evergreen trees in both inviting in and protecting the house from the sun.

☐ Keep trees away from the foundation area.

☐ Keep trees away from the immediate area of the swimming pool.

☐ Keep the lot clean during construction.

☐ Minimize landscaping lighting, except for safety.

☐ Screen off a portion of a large lot.

☐ Favor hedges over walls and fences for windbreaks.

☐ Plan to use a shape that resists unwanted heat gains or losses.

To minimize heat transmission for a given enclosed volume, a building should be constructed with a minimum exposed surface area. A round building has less surface, hence, less heat gain or loss than any other shape for an equal amount of total floor space. A square building has less surface than a rectangular building of equal area per floor, and so experiences less thermal transmission loss or heat gain. However, the number of stories modifies this relationship for the building as a whole.

A tall building has a proportionately smaller roof and is less affected by solar gains on that surface. On the other hand, tall buildings generally are subjected to greater wind velocities which increase infiltration and heat losses. Tall buildings are less likely to be shaded or protected from winds by surrounding buildings and trees. They require more mechanical support systems, including longer exhaust duct systems. The stack induction action in tall buildings increases infiltration, thus requiring special measures to reduce its influence on heat gain and heat loss.

The ceiling thickness, the floor thickness, and the floor-to-ceiling height, together constitute the floor-to-floor height. The floor thickness is usually determined by construction and structural considerations. The floor-to-floor dimension most directly affects energy conservation, in that it affects the area of the exterior building skin exposed to the weather. It also increases the amount of raw materials (and therefore energy consumed) which go into the construction of the building, especially the skin.

The effect of added skin area on energy consumption reduces as the skin "U" value increases and the climate becomes more temperate.

Greater ceiling heights improve environmental conditions in the summertime by permitting warm air to rise. However, greater ceiling heights increase the perimeter areas, thus increasing heat transmissions through the walls.

Floor-to-ceiling height is determined by physiological comfort, height of light fixtures for proper light distribution, and height of windows necessary for good natural lighting.

In general, increases in ceiling height need increase only the exposed wall surface (not window surface). The effects of greater heights on energy consumption may be rather small, depending on the thermal characteristics of the wall.

Reduced ceiling heights reduce the exposed exterior wall surface area and the enclosed volume. A reduced ceiling height can also increase illumination effectiveness.

In general, if overhead light is used, and if the lighting is an integral part of the ceiling, the ceiling height could be decreased to make it possible to save lighting wattage by bringing the fixture closer to the task. Less lighting wattage may be needed if the ceiling is lowered (perhaps independently of the suspended lighting fixtures). If task lighting, rather than general overhead lighting, is used, it becomes possible to take advantage of the light reflected off of the ceiling surface.

☐ Consider the advantages of a thicker ceiling plenum, especially in commercial builidngs. With a constant floor-to-floor height, a decreased floor-to-ceiling height will provide for a larger ceiling plenum, resulting in possible savings in the mechanical air distribution system.

Deep ceiling voids allow the use of larger duct sizes with low pressure drop and reduced HVAC air handler and fan requirements.

The dimension of the ceiling plenum can greatly affect the efficiency of the mechanical equipment. For example, floor-to-floor heights are typically 12 to 12½ feet in commercial buildings. If this were increased to 13 feet (through an increase in the size of the ceiling plenum), there could be significant savings resulting from re-design of the mechanical system. Ducts could be larger, allowing greater volumes of air to be moved with smaller pressure drops, permitting reduced fan horsepower. Duct aspect ratios could also be reduced to approach square or round sections, resulting in significant savings in sheet metal and insulation in construction, and subsequent reduced friction and reduced heat transmission losses through the duct. Larger ceiling plenums may also permit the use of more effective energy conservation systems, such as variable volume and heat-of-light.

☐ Select a building configuration and wall arrangement (horizontal and vertical sloping walls) to provide self shading wherever possible.

☐ Consider exotic shapes for special situations.

Zig-zag exterior wall configurations, rhomboid shaped buildings, and other forms can all be used to control heating, cooling and lighting.

Zig-zag configuration of east and west walls provides self-shading to reduce summer solar loads, and provides natural wind breaks. South facing zig-zag walls permit low rays to enter the building in the winter to supplement the heating system. Face the windows north in the zig-zag in a southern location to reduce heat gain year round. This way in both summer and winter natural lighting and a good view are available at both east and west facades without the penalty of increased summer heat gains. However, the energy requirements due to the additional wall surface for the zig-zag form must be weighed against the other energy benefits. The zig-zag configuration is only one example of manipulating form to achieve maximum energy benefits.

☐ Avoid overhanging floors. Buildings that are elevated on posts or have overhanging upper floors increase heat loss and heat gain due to the extra exposed floor surfaces. While this may be of slight advantage all year in the southern regions, or anywhere in the summertime, it will result in increased heat loss in colder climates.

Orient for Interior Lighting

Make maximum use of sunlight for interior lighting. In many cases, energy can be saved by using sunlight for lighting if the building perimeter can be increased and its interior space proportionately decreased. This will result in different building forms, such as multiple courtyards, atriums, light wells, skylights, etc. However, if more energy is conserved by using reduced window areas with artificial lighting systems, then a reduction of the perimeter exposure should be considered.

☐ Use of reflective surfaces such as sloping white ceilings to enhance the effect of natural lighting and increase the yearly energy saved.

☐ Windows placed to use winter sunshine should be positioned to allow occupants the opportunity to avoid the sun's direct radiation by moving or using shading devices.

Wind Control

☐ Orient the building to use cooling breezes in summer and avoid cold winds in winter. Wind velocities are greatest in cold climates on the north and west facades of the building so that each surface is subjected to different environmental influences, even for two buildings located in the same latitude in the United States.

In climate zones where outdoor air conditions are close to desired indoor conditions for a major portion of the year, consider the following:

☐ Adjust the building orientation and configuration to take advantage of prevailing winds.

☐ Use operable windows to control air flow through the building.

☐ Adjust the configuration of the building to allow natural cross ventilation through occupied spaces.

☐ Utilize stack effect in vertical shafts, stairwells, etc., to promote natural air flow through the building.

☐ Orient operable windows, intakes or exhaust outlets to take advantage of prevailing winds.

☐ Use wall textures, vines, fins or recesses on the building to help maintain a still air film on the walls and roof.

Building Interiors

- [ ] Favor two-story houses for minimizing heating and cooling.

- [ ] Evaluate split-level houses critically.

- [ ] Plan rooms so they can be closed off.

- [ ] Try to arrange an entry so that it can be closed off.

- [ ] See that there is plenty of natural light in the entry.

- [ ] Halls should receive natural light.

- [ ] The powder room should have proper noise separation.

- [ ] Consider an exhaust fan for the powder room.

- [ ] It should be possible to close off the dining room.

- [ ] The family room should have its own fireplace with heat circulation and outside combustion air intake.

- [ ] Be able to close off the living room and family room.

- [ ] Try to get morning sun in the breakfast area.

- [ ] Install specific light for reading.

- [ ] Emphasize natural light in bedrooms.

- [ ] Heat lamps can save energy in dressing areas.

- [ ] Locate switches to promote turning light off when not in use.

- [ ] Favor efficient appliance and plumbing fixtures.

- [ ] Avoid aluminum wiring.

- [ ] Plan enough electrical circuits to avoid overloading.

- [ ] Use low voltage switching of lighting fixutres.

- [ ] Use a jamb switch or pilot lite when lighting remote areas.

- [ ] See that the master bath has a stall shower.

- [ ] Design Roman tubs so they do not waste water.

- [ ] Consider the half-tank flush valve for toilets.

- [ ] See that bathroom windows are large.

- [ ] Place heat lamps where they do the most good.

- [ ] Compartmentalize the master bath for noise control.

☐ Favor carpeting for bathroom flooring.

☐ Favor fluorescent lighting in kitchen and utility areas.

☐ Locate the laundry near the bedrooms.

☐ Plan a drip-dry hanging and drainage area.

☐ Favor a natural gas dryer.

☐ Create alternate natural drying areas.

☐ Plan a floor drain and an exhaust fan for the laundry.

☐ Plan for storage of fireplace wood.

☐ The basement should have some natural light.

☐ The garage should have some natural light.

☐ Develop the garage as a proper usable room.

☐ The apparent temperature of spaces is also affected by color. Interior rooms and basements, in particular, "feel" warmer or cooler depending upon the colors used in them. Light colored walls, floors, and ceilings, for example, have greater reflectance than dark colors, resulting in more effective use of available light.

☐ Dark colored surfaces absorb light. Light colored finishes may cause glare. In general, ceilings should be finished in white (80-90% reflectance); walls, except for small accent areas, should be medium to light (50-80%); and floors should be light medium to medium (20-50%). Avoid the use of highly reflective surfaces within the normal visual field. Larger rooms are more efficient than smaller rooms because there is less wall surface to intersect and to absorb the light. Small rooms with darker finishes can require more than double the lighting per square foot as large rooms with lighter room finishes.

☐ Use open planned design when possible. Open planned design allows excess heat from interior spaces to be transferred to the perimeter spaces to offset heat losses. Open planning also allows more effective use of lighting fixtures. The reduced area of partitioned walls decreases the light absorption and less lamp lumens are required for the same level of illumination. Also, increasing the percentage of usable area to gross area can result in small buildings with a corresponding conservation of energy.

☐ Group spaces or rooms with similar functions. Grouping spaces that have similar water, waste, exhaust and power needs can reduce the extent and complexity of the mechanical systems and permit heating, cooling, ventilation, and lighting to be concentrated in areas that have maximum requirements. Thus, it is not necessary to provide the same degree of environmental comfort throughout the entire floor area.

Grouping bathrooms back to back or one above the other simplifies the exhaust systems and the plumbing systems, and generally requires less energy for the distribution systems.

☐ Use low temperature sensitivity areas as buffer zones.

The building plan can have a major effect on the energy required to maintain comfort conditions in both summer and winter. In both northern and southern climates, corridors, equipment spaces, closets, bathrooms, garages, and other areas which do not require close temperature control can be located to act as buffer spaces. They can protect best against the cold in northern climates when located on a north wall, or they can protect against excessive thermal loads in southern climates when located on east, west, or south walls.

Areas which have high internal heat gains are best located adjacent to exterior surfaces in cold climates to permit dissipation of excess heat without mechanical assistance.

Rooms with high heat gain can be placed against outside surfaces that have the highest exposure loss.

Windows and Doors

Heat transmission is much greater through glass than through most walls. "U" values for walls can be reduced to 0.06 or less, but single glass has a "U" value of about 1.13, double glass of 0.58 to 0.69, and triple glass of 0.36 to 0.47.

☐ Manipulate east and west walls so that glass walls and windows face south.

☐ Allow direct sun radiation on windows from November through March.

☐ Avoid window frames that form a thermal heat transfer bridge between interior and exterior.

☐ Use operable thermal shutters which can decrease the composite "U" value to 0.1.

☐ Shade windows from direct sun from April through October.

☐ Use tinted glass or films when appropriate. Reflective and heat-absorbing glass intercepts up to 80% of the radiant energy. It can be very beneficial for cooling in summer, but results in a loss of useful heat in winter. Natural light will be lost as well. Once again, the effects on yearly energy consumption must be considered before a choice is made to use special purpose glass.

☐ Where the heating season is 7500 degree days or greater, use triple glazing:

  ☐ Remove existing single window and frame and replace with triple glazing.

  ☐ Add double glazed storm window to existing single glazed window.

☐ Where heating season is 4500 degree days or greater, install a storm window to reduce both conduction loss and infiltration. Where the window is tight, remove glazing from the window frame and install double glazing unit.

☐ Where the heating season is between 1500 degree and 4500 degree days, use double glazing. Where the heating season is less than 1500 degree days, double glazing cannot be justified by heating energy saving alone, but may be desirable to reduce noise.

☐ When considering storm windows or other options listed above, north facing windows should be given priority followed by east or west windows, whichever is on the prevailing wind side of the building or most heavily shaded. Storm windows may be applied either to the outside or inside of the existing window. In an existing building, determine the most suitable location for the storm window, taking into account the building construction (is there enough space within the window reveal to fit a storm window) and the change in window appearance from inside or outside the building. If existing windows and frames are of poor construction and allow a high rate of infiltration, the storm windows should be fitted on the outside where possible. This will reduce infiltration without incurring the extra cost of caulking the window. The space between the storm window and the existing window should be vented to the outdoors and provided with drainage weepholes to prevent moisture build-up. If storm windows are added to the existing windows, consider the use of reflective or tinted glass to reduce solar gain and glare in summer.

☐ Minimize the heat loss through windows by using small windows on north exposures.

Heat loss through windows is highest in high degree day areas. For any one geographic location heat loss is greatest through windows of north exposure and least in windows of south exposure due to the beneficial heating effect of the sun. This modifying effect of the sun is greater in cold climates where sun altitudes are low.

☐ Install plastic film over windows to cut heat loss on a temporary basis. Where natural lighting is desirable but appearance and visibility through the window are not important, a low cost interim solution which will provide double glazing is to use clear plastic film attached to a simple frame. This will not provide a durable storm window but should be considered as a temporary means to save heating energy where low cost is essential. This could be done for about $6 per window including both labor and materials.

☐ Have windows as high as possible for light penetration.

☐ Have windows on more than one wall, if possible.

☐ When replacing or adding glazed surfaces, use one layer of reflective glass or reflective coatings to reduce solar heat gains, if windows are in direct sunlight for more than three hours per day during the cooling season.

☐ Where windows are subjected to high winds for a long duration of time in the winter and to sunlight in the summer, use prefabricated sunscreen on the exterior of the window to serve a dual purpose: Minimize the effect of heat loss due to wind, reduce solar heat gains in the summer.

Install thermal barriers whenever the heating period exceeds 70 hours per week and heating degree days exceed 4500 if existing windows are single glazed, and 6500 or greater if double glazed. Consider thermal barriers also in areas with fewer degree days, particularly in windy areas.

☐ Operate thermal barriers in the same manner as conventional drapes. Close them even in occupied hours whenever daylight cannot be used and when vision through the window is not required. Do not close thermal shutters at night in the cooling season except on the west side when there is considerable sunshine after the work day ends.

☐ Install storm doors in all locations where degree days exceed 3000 and provide not more than 50% glass area in the storm door. Storm doors should be wood rather than metal, unless a thermal break is provided.

☐ Where exterior doors are not used during the heating season and are not required as fire exits, caulk the doors or seal them with removable strips, or insulate the areas between the storm door and the existing door. Double windows or storm doors are not cost effective to reduce cooling loads alone, and are not recommended for that purpose alone. But when installed to reduce heat loss, they will also reduce heat gain to a smaller extent in the summer.

☐ Where operable storm sash is desired, provide hopper type windows with 25% of the total sash operable, or sliding windows, casement windows, or double hung windows to most nearly match existing windows.

☐ Where energy for cooling exceeds the amount of energy required for heating on a seasonal basis, minimize the amount of glazing in the west first, then east, south, and north exposures in that order.

☐ Where the outdoor air conditions are close to desired indoor conditions for a major portion of the year, do not caulk or install double glazing. Provide the greatest amount of operable windows to permit natural ventilation and cooling.

☐ Install insulating draperies to reduce heat loss through windows.

Use Skylights

☐ Use skylights to provide daylight to supplement electric lighting without glare or excessive heat.

The amount of illumination available from skylights varies with the following factors:

-The duration and intensity of available daylight which is affected by amount of sunlight, shading, and ground reflectances.

-Area and location of the skylights.

-The distance from floor to skylight.

-The transmission properties of the skylight.

-The construction of the skylight in regard to orientation of transparent or translucent surfaces.

-The reflectance of the interior surface of the skylight well.

If electric lighting is turned off when daylight from skylights is available, as much as 40 watts of electric power can be saved per square foot of skylight area. The amount of energy saved for lighting using skylights must be analyzed in comparison to the increased amount of energy required for heating and the increase or reduction in heat gain and cooling load in order to determine the net yearly increase or reduction in energy due to skylights.

☐ Paint skylights with white or light colored paint.

☐ Add prismatic lighting lens below the skylights to reduce glare.

☐ Provide an external louver above the skylight to reduce solar heat gain.

☐ Add louvers above the skylights and lens below to reduce glare, heat loss, and heat gain.

☐ Install a movable shutter above the skylight to reduce heat gain and glare in summer, but allow solar radiation to be used to offset heat loss in the winter.

☐ Paint the interior of the light well with a light color to increase illumination.

☐ Use double or triple glazing when heat gain or loss is important.

☐ The order of priority for treating skylights should follow treatment of glazing: first on the north wall in cold climates, and the west, east, and south wall in warm climates.

Sun Control

Solar controls (such as internal or external shading devices for glazed areas) can manipulate the effect of the sun's rays on the building. The extent and type of control should be determined by the intensity and duration of sunlight. Heat gain due to transmission and radiation can vary between two building locations at the same latitude, greatly modifying the requirements for heating and cooling.

☐ Use shading devices. Sun shades can reduce heat gain in the summer and are most effective when located on the exterior of the building. They are particularly effective when movable. Fixed solar fins and overhangs can eliminate direct solar penetration in the summertime but also would block out some of the solar rays in the late spring and early fall when rays could be useful for heating.

☐ Design each side of the building with sun control in mind.

Solar control is most effective when designed specifically for each building since time and duration of solar radiation varies with the sun's altitude and azimuth. Horizontal shading is most effective on southern exposures. But if it is not extended far enough beyond the edges of the windows, it will permit direct sunlight to enter the building at certain times of the day. In hot climates, south-facing glass with horizontal operable overhang for summer control is an effective way to reduce solar heat gain. On the east and west walls, a combination of vertical and horizontal sun baffles is required.

Solar Heat Gain

☐ Exterior solar control devices are the most effective. Install horizontal fixed or movable eyebrows over south facing glass. Install fin sun screens on the exterior of east, west, and south facing windows to reduce solar heat gain and wind loads in the winter. In locations where winds are minimum in the winter or existing construction and aesthetics preclude locating the sun screen on the exterior, install them in the interior surface of the window. Screens can be hinged to permit easy access to operable windows. Sun screens reduce the available day lighting for illumination. All exterior solar control devices should provide shading from May 1 through October 31.

☐ Install awnings over windows to block out summer sun. Awnings are particularly suitable to shade large display windows in commercial stores.

☐ Replace single clear glass on the east, west, and south facades with reflective glass when replacing broken windows if the windows are in direct sunlight 200 hours or more during the cooling season. Replace all single glass on west, east, south facade if windows are in direct sunlight 500 or more hours per year during the cooling season. Reflective glass is more effective in reducing heat gain than heat absorbing glass.

☐ If double windows are added to reduce heat loss in the winter time, provide the inner layers with reflective glass to reduce transmission at peak conditions to 50% of maximum.

☐ Use a zig-zag wall with the glazing in the west wall and east wall facing north in the southern climates and south in the northern climates. The wall will be self-shading in the summer, while permitting the sun to penetrate through the glass during the heating season.

☐ Install lined drapes, venetian blinds, or shutters on the inside of all south, east, and west facing windows which are subject to direct sunlight in the cooling season or exposed to a large expanse of sky. These devices are not as effective as external shading devices or sun screen, but are least expensive to install.

☐ Where the materials and aesthetics are not jeopardized, paint exterior sun walls with white reflective paint to reduce the absorption coefficient and the radiation heat gain.

☐ Cant the glass at an angle to affect the amount of transmittance through the glass and also reduce solar radiation loads.

☐ Color is important in all window treatments. Where cooling is a problem, venetian blinds and the inside and outside of shutters should be light in color to reflect heat and light away from the building. Where heating and light restriction are desired, the use of dark drapery or dark shades makes sense.

☐ Windows planned to make beneficial use of winter sunshine should be positioned to allow occupants the opportunity of moving out of the direct sun radiation.

☐ Judicious use of reflective surfaces, such as sloping white ceilings, can enhance the effect of natural lighting and increase the yearly energy saved.

Heating, Cooling and Ventilating

☐ Select equipment that has a high energy efficiency rating.

☐ Most equipment has the highest energy efficiency at full load, and therefore should be sized to match the requirements without excess safety factors.

☐ Air handling systems should be sized to operate at lowest pressure possible consistent with available space.

☐ Increasing pipe sizes to reduce pressure drop can result in reduced pump sizes which will save energy and may not increase the initial cost.

☐ Use a combination of two or more systems for the same building--each system having the best energy utilization for its particular area. For instance, fan-coil systems in conjunction with variable air volume; low velocity air for interior spaces with fan-coil units on the perimeter; or, a heat pump in conjunction with any of the above.

☐ Some variable air volume systems use less energy than constant volume systems for the same system static pressure.

☐ Dual duct and multi-zone systems mix hot and cold air and are therefore not energy efficient.

☐ Electric heating, generally in the form of electric radiation or electric reheat coils, consumes more raw source energy than well-adjusted fossil fuel systems. However, heat pumps, particularly air-to-air or water-to-water units use ½ to ⅓ the amount of electricity as electric heating equipment to produce the same number of BTU's.

☐ Passing contaminated air through charcoal filters to remove odors and then recycling the clean air can reduce exhaust air quantities and thus reduce ventilation and infiltration.

☐ Care should be taken in locating outdoor intakes so that they do not pick up unwanted radiant heat reflected from adjacent roofs or wall surfaces.

☐ Outdoor air which is used as makeup to replace air exhaust through a kitchen hood creates a heating and cooling load which can be reduced by supplying outside air to the hood.

☐ The energy required to operate air circulating fans in a building may be greater than the energy required to operate the refrigeration equipment.

☐ To minimize this fan horsepower, ductwork should be designed for the lowest practical total pressure drop. This is done by using larger nearly square or round ducts with a minimum number of turns and offsets. Larger ductwork may require increasing the depth of the ceiling plenum which, in turn, increases the total area of the building envelope.

☐ Consider solar heating to carry about 50% of the maximum heating requirement.

☐ Favor a perimeter duct forced air heating system in cold climates.

☐ Locate heating and cooling equipment near the center of the building.

☐ Locate thermostats at about shoulder height on the interior wall of a well-used room.

☐ Make sure the unit selected will not be too large for the reduced load of a snug home.

☐ Install an automatic setback thermostat.

☐ Don't locate registers directly under or over windows or doors.

☐ Consider some way to zone the heating and cooling of the building.

☐ Fireplaces should be the warm air circulating type and should have an external air intake.

Heat Pumps and Air Conditioners

☐ Where possible, direct the warm exhaust air from the building to the inlet of air-to-air heat pumps to raise their coefficient of performance.

☐ Replace air-to-air heat pumps with water-to-air heat pumps where there is a source of heat such as ground water with temperatures above average winter air temperatures.

☐ Install a timer to control operation of compressors in accordance with day and night temperature requirements.

☐ When replacing incremental air conditioning units which are equipped with electric heating coils, install a heat pump model instead.

☐ Replacement compressors should have an EER rating of 9 or better during the cooling cycle. This is applicable also to window air conditioning units.

☐ Some cooling without refrigeration can be accomplished when the total heat content of the outside air is less than the total heat content of air at the inside design conditions.

☐ All of cooling can be accomplished without refrigeration when the dewpoint of the outside air is at or below the dewpoint of air required to offset the internal heat loads.

☐ The basic system for free cooling is to provide for variable outdoor air inlet and variable return air disposal up to the full capacity of the air circulation system. Through the use of a proper control sequence, the return and outdoor air are mixed to produce the required supply air temperature.

☐ The amount of pollution in the outdoor air will affect the decision to utilize this free cooling cycle.

☐ For areas requiring constant high humidity, it may be impractical and energy wasteful to add water vapor to large quantities of outdoor air, and a system energy analysis would show a better energy profile using mechanical refrigeration to maintain indoor temperature.

☐ Install dampers in the fresh air duct and the return air duct at air handling units and interlock dampers, so that one opens when the other closes. Provide control to open the outdoor air damper when the outdoor temperatures are 5° or more below indoor conditions.

☐ Install an enthalpy control to open outside air damper during occupied periods with the refrigeration equipment in operation when the outdoor wet bulb temperature is below 65°F and the dry bulb temperature is below 85°F.

Heating Commercial Buildings

☐ Install a seven-day dual stat to operate the oil, gas, stoker, or electric heating elements. The stat should be set to maintain the temperature levels during unoccupied periods, and to reduce levels when the building is unoccupied at nights, weekends and holidays.

☐ Install a seven-day stat to control the operation of pumps for forced circulation hot water systems, automatic control valves for hot water or steam systems when boilers are operated by aquastat or pressure-trol.

☐ Install a seven-day timer control to reset operating aquastat or pressure-trol for dual level settings.

☐ Install additional thermostats for individual zones where duct or piping systems permit control of individual zones and where necessary at zone control valves. Operate controls on a seven-day cycle.

☐ Provide room stat and automatic damper controls and dampers in supply air duct systems for additional zoning to permit further reduction of temperature levels in non-critical areas.

- ☐ Where missing, install manually operated radiator valves, or duct dampers to control or shut off heat supply to non-critical areas in portions of the building.

- ☐ Install occupied/unoccupied, on-off switch to control water supply to humidifiers to permit shutdown at night.

- ☐ Remove and relocate any central humidifier serving the entire building and install a duct type of package room humidifier to serve only those zones which require humidification.

- ☐ Where supply duct dampers are adjusted to reduce air flow into the space during the heating season, provide a damper to reduce return air from the space.

- ☐ Relocate room stats to the most critical area and rebalance the air or water system to reduce temperature and humidity levels in the other less critical areas.

- ☐ Where window air conditioner units or through-the-wall units provide heating as well as cooling, provide seven-day temperature control stats to operate the heating elements.

- ☐ Do not operate refrigeration systems or introduce outdoor air for the purpose of cooling in winter to reduce indoor temperature levels to the heating set point of 68°F. If gains exceed losses, allow the space temperature to rise to 78°F.

- ☐ Where room stats control both heating and cooling systems, exchange them for stats with a dead band level.

- ☐ Provide locking devices on all room stats to prevent tampering.

Cooling Commercial Buildings

- ☐ Install charcoal filters or other air treatment devices in the exhaust air systems and circulate treated air back into the space to reduce the amount of outdoor air required for make up for all systems handling 2,000 CFM or more. Supply slightly more outdoor air than exhaust air to pressurize the conditioned space. It is necessary to obtain approval of code administrating agencies having jurisdiction in the location of the building when reducing outside air quantities below code requirements.

- ☐ Install damper and controls in commercial buildings to permit the ventilation system to delay the introduction of outdoor air for one hour in the morning and shut it off ½ hour before closing time. A seven-day timer can be used in department stores to reduce or shut off ventilation automatically for periods during the day with light occupancy.

- ☐ Modify duct systems and hoods and introduce untreated outdoor air directly to the exhaust hood. Weigh this against changing hoods to new high velocity hoods which require less make up air.

- ☐ Wherever possible, relocate all equipment and processes that emit heat near windows on the north, or east exposures to facilitate transfer of heat from indoors to outdoors.

- [ ] Insulate hot surfaces on tanks, pipes, and ductwork which are located in air conditioned spaces.

- [ ] Install an automatic control to de-energize dry type transformers which are located in air conditioned spaces when there is no operating load.

- [ ] Locate vending machines, office duplicating equipment and other equipment and appliances out of air conditioned areas. (It may be possible to relocate them back into areas requiring heat in the winter time).

- [ ] Install hoods, baffles, and insulated panels to minimize heat gain to the space from equipment of high heat emission characteristics.

- [ ] If exhaust is used, analyze the trade-off between exhausting air from heat releasing equipment vs. returning it to the system based on enthalpy of make up air required.

- [ ] Reduce the temperature of incoming outdoor air by using evaporative coolers in geographical areas with high dry bulb temperatures coincident with low wet bulb temperatures (65°F or less).

Domestic Water Consumption

- [ ] Reduce the cold water pressure with an automatic control valve, but do not set it lower than pressure needed to flush toilets or for pressures required for fire protection.

- [ ] Install flow restrictors on taps when existing faucets have flow rates greater than 1½ GPM or showers have flow rates in excess of 3 GPM.

- [ ] Install spray type faucets that use only ¼ GPM instead of 2 or 3 GPM.

- [ ] Install self-closing faucets on hot water taps.

- [ ] Avoid obsolete high water volume dishwashers and clothes washers. Favor new types that have minimal water requirements.

- [ ] Insulate hot water tanks when insulation is less than the equivalent of 3'' fiberglass or when insulation is in need of repair.

- [ ] De-energize hot water circulating pumps to reduce heat loss from piping within the building. Where extremely long runs require that a circulator be in operation during occupied periods, install a timer to automatically shut off the pump during periods of no use.

- [ ] Insulate the exterior jacket of tankless or tank heaters which are not immersed in the hot water boiler or hot water tank.

- [ ] Insulate long runs of exposed hot water piping whenever there is less than the equivalent of 1'' fiberglass.

Water Heating Equipment

☐ Replace gas pilots with electrical ignition.

☐ Install a storage water heater for summer use when the existing space heating boiler is used for hot water generation.

☐ Replace electric hot water heaters with heat pumps to improve the coefficient of performance from 1 to approximately 3. Use hot drain water as a heat source for the heat pump, or use an air-to-water heat pump.

☐ Repipe hot water storage tanks if the cold water make-up supply is connected to the upper half of the tank or if the hot water outlet from the tank is in the lower portion of the tank.

☐ Provide either oil- or gas-fired water heaters or heat pumps rather than electric resistance heating. If the heating boiler has sufficient capacity and is in operation year-round for air conditioning as well, install a tank or tankless heater in place of a separate hot water generator. If the additional requirements for hot water are to serve facilities remote from the boiler and usage is small, install a separate heater in the cold water line directly at the fixtures rather than serving them from a central system.

☐ Install local hot water heating units when domestic hot water usage points are concentrated in areas distant from the generation point.

☐ Install a solar water heater to supplement conventional equipment.

Ventilating Commercial Buildings

☐ Provide a seven-day timer to operate automatic fresh air damper control (install controller where missing), or to shut off all outdoor air for ventilation during unoccupied periods where separate outdoor air supply fans exist.

☐ Install automatic damper control where missing, for operation with seven-day timer.

☐ Add separate ventilation fan for zones requiring outdoor air and shutoff damper to separate unit serving the entire building.

☐ Reduce operating time of exhaust systems. Where interlocks with outdoor air makeup systems have been or will be installed, control the exhaust-outdoor air makeup unit or damper with seven-day stats.

☐ Utilize waste heat or recovered heat from exhaust systems and other equipment to temper the outdoor air supply to reduce the heating load.

☐ Install charcoal filters or other devices to control supply air quality and reduce the amount of outdoor air for ventilation. Check with Code Authorities before making the change.

☐ Modify exhaust hoods to reduce the ventilation as follows:

☐ By inspection, determine whether the existing exhaust hood is of the simple open type and by measurement, determine the quantity of air exhausted. If the exhaust hood is of the open type, install baffles to allow reduction of exhaust air quantity without reducing the face velocity at the edge of the hood.

☐ If baffles are installed, reduce the rate of exhaust and by measurement determine the new quantity.

☐ Install a make up air system to introduce outdoor air equal in quantity to that exhausted.

☐ Do not heat make up air to more than 55°F and introduce as close as possible to the hood in several positions around the perimeter to promote even air flow.

☐ Consider using reclaimed hood exhaust heat or solar heat as the energy source for make up air.

☐ Do not cool or dehumidify make up air.

Insulation

☐ If possible, insulation should be located not only on the outside of a wall section, but also on the outside of the structure itself. This will help reduce air leakage through construction joints and reduce heat loss by eliminating the effect of thermal bridging through structural wall members.

☐ Consider insulation types which will be both effective and easy to use correctly. For example, some types of insulation are difficult to install without voids or shrinkage.

☐ Increasing the thickness of insulation provides diminishing returns. Considering insulation alone, doubling the original thickness reduces the heat flow by 50%; tripling the thickness reduces the heat flow by another 17%; and quadrupling the thickness reduces the heat flow only by an additional 8%.

Infiltration

☐ Instead of caulking, add tight fitting storm windows.

☐ Weatherstrip all doors with a copper interlocking type weatherstrip. In buildings where carpeting extends to the doors, use a compression type weatherstrip attached to the bottom of the door to clear the carpeting.

☐ In locations where strong winds occur for long durations, use external wind baffles to shield windows and doors.

☐ In areas where operable windows are not required, close them permanently and caulk cracks. Block off windows entirely with masonry or insulated wall panels. Where insulated wall panels are used, fit them to effectively block infiltration.

- [ ] Where wall construction is particularly porous (cinder block walls or other similar porous materials), cover the exterior surface with epoxy paint.

- [ ] Install vestibules in stores and other buildings where doors are open frequently throughout the day.

- [ ] Install revolving doors where exceptionally heavy traffic occurs and infiltrated air circulates freely to occupied spaces. When installing revolving doors, maintain a sufficient number of operable single or double doors to meet Code requirements for safety exit. Where operable windows are not used during the winter, removable tapes can be used to seal cracks.

- [ ] Caulk cracks around window air conditioning units or through-the-wall units which remain permanently installed year round, and cover window air conditioning units with plastic covers outside.

- [ ] Install automatic door closers on exterior doors.

- [ ] To reduce infiltration through leaky or jalousie windows where operable sash is not required in the winter, cover the windows with a 5-mil plastic sheet, tacked in place to the exterior of the building. Makes sure that the plastic shield extends to cover cracks around the window frames. Covers can be taken down in the summer.

- [ ] When installing new screens on windows and doors, select units which are rated to limit air leakage to 0.5 CFM per foot of crack when subjected to a wind pressure of 25 miles per hour.

- [ ] Seal off large openings in stair towers with masonry partition or with a tight fitting door.

- [ ] Pressurize the building with outdoor air, properly controlled and treated, to reduce uncontrolled infiltration.

- [ ] Reduce air volume to bathrooms to 1 CFM per square foot.

- [ ] Verify the presence of a vapor barrier on all outside walls.

- [ ] All wood doors and windows must be weatherstripped.

- [ ] Caulk around windows, doors, sills and all breaks in the wall that could admit outside air.

- [ ] Operable windows should have sealing gaskets and latches.

- [ ] Locate building entrances on the downwind side and provide wind breaks.

- [ ] Seal all vertical shafts.

- [ ] Locate ventilation louvers on the downwind side of the building and provide wind breaks.

☐ Insulate the roof well. On a square foot basis, insulation for the roof should be considered immediately after that for the north facing walls. Since the greatest heat gain in the summer time per square foot due to solar radiation is on the roof, the energy and economic benefit of insulating the roof will be most favorable on a year-round basis.

The following table shows the minimum acceptable "U" value for roofs in various heating degree day zones. Every existing roof below this standard should be insulated.

Heating Degree Days	Minimum Acceptable "U" value
1,000	0.3
2,000	0.2
3,000	0.2
4,000	0.15
5,000	0.15
6.000	0.1
7,000	0.1
8,000 and above	0.06

The cost of insulation materials is small in comparison to the labor costs for installation. Once the decision is made to insulate the roof, recommend at least enough insulation to improve the "U" value to better than 0.05. This is nearly equivalent to R19 or 6 inches of fiberglass.

☐ If priorities must be considered in insulating the roof, insulate a 15'-0" wide band around the perimeter, rather than the entire roof. The roof area over the perimeter zones experience the greatest heat loss.

☐ When adding insulation to the roof surface, select a finish with a high absorption coefficient (light color) in areas where the yearly heating load exceeds the yearly cooling load. Select a low absorption coefficient in areas where the yearly cooling load exceeds the yearly heating load.

☐ If the ceiling void is used as a return air plenum, insulation applied to the underside of the roof should be bonded or sealed to prevent migration of fibers and should not extend over the lighting fixtures.

☐ If possible, include an air space between insulation boards and the underside of the roof to gain added insulating effect.

☐ Insulate all pipes and hot ducts in an attic space if insulation is added on top of the ceiling below (attic, floor), as the attic temperature will tend to approach outdoor temperatures.

☐ When adding insulation, provide vapor barriers on the interior surface of the roof of sufficient impermeability to prevent condensation.

☐ Seal all corners to prevent infiltration.

☐ Do not resurface the roof with a special black material to absorb more radiation in the winter time. It is relatively ineffective to do so, especially with good insulation.

☐ Where an unheated room or pipe space occurs directly under the roof, do not add additional insulation above the ceiling.

☐ If solar collectors are being considered for present or future insulation on the roof, the amount and type of insulation must be taken into account. Where the existing roof is in good condition, consideration should be given to insulating the underside rather than exterior or the void between the ceiling and the roof.

☐ If reflective insulation is used, it should be selected to have an equivalent R value of not less than four and should be installed so that the shiny surface faces an air space at least ¾ inch in thickness. Where possible, use board, batt, or fill type insulation instead of reflective insulation to reduce heat loss.

☐ Provide insulation on top of the roof, or below the roof and above the ceiling whenever the interior surface temperature of the ceiling (roof if there is no ceiling) is above 82°F on clear days with 60% or more possible sunshine.

☐ Cover the exterior surface of the roof with white pebbles, light colored tiles, or other durable materials to reduce the absorption coefficient in direct sunlight to 0.3 or less.

☐ Install a roof spray system to reduce the temperature of the exterior surface of the roof, if calculations indicate that air temperatures exceed 100°F for 250 hours or more. If the roof is insulated to a "U" value of 0.2 or better, and has a mass of 50 pounds per square foot or more, do not consider roof sprays.

☐ Note the special importance of a south facing roof. This is the ideal location for a solar collector but is otherwise undesirable in most climates. A sloping roof facing south will be subjected to more solar radiation in any climate in the United States than a roof facing north or even east or west. Therefore, select a building configuration to give minimum south roof and wall (which receives maximum solar radiation) to reduce cooling load where applicable. Similarly, select a building configuration to give minimum north wall (which receives minimum solar radiation) to reduce heat losses in cool climates.

☐ Insulate the attic door.

☐ Use unfaced (no vapor barrier) insulation when adding insulation over a ceiling with an existing vapor barrier.

☐ Do not let insulation in the attic touch the underside of the roof.

☐ Determine the "U" value of existing walls by inspection, measurement and calculation. The table below shows the minimum acceptable "U" value for walls in various heating degree day zones. Every wall below this standard should be insulated.

Heating Degree Days	Minimum Acceptance "U" Value
1,000	0.40
2,000	0.30
3,000	0.30
4,000	0.20
5,000	0.20
6,000	0.15
7,000	0.15
8,000	0.10
9,000	0.10

☐ The cost of materials to insulate a wall is small in comparison to labor costs. Once the decision is made to insulate a wall add at least enough insulation to improve the "U" value to 0.1 or R11, 3½ inches of fiberglass.

☐ Insulation is most effective on the north walls. These should be given priority, followed by east or west walls, whichever face into the winter prevailing wind, then the south wall.

☐ If any exposure is shaded, its priority for insulation should be modified according to the hours of shading experienced on an average winter day.

☐ Give priority to spaces that are continuously occupied for the greatest length of time. Corridors, bathrooms, storage rooms, etc. should be assigned a lower priority regardless of wall orientation.

☐ Reflective insulation is more effective on the walls than on the roof, but is not as effective as other types of insulation with higher "R" values.

☐ Use 2" x 6" studs spaced at 24" centers rather than 2" x 4" studs at 16" centers.

☐ Tuck insulation into all wall voids so that all wall area not consisting of structural members or wall openings are insulated.

☐ Where possible, install insulation on the exterior surface of masonry walls. For other types of construction, provide insulation on the interior surface or in the cavity, if there is one.

☐ Check all codes before installing insulation on the interior surface of the building. Some insulation materials are not acceptable due to low ignition temperatures or toxic or poisonous fumes when burned.

☐ When blowing insulation into a masonry wall cavity or stud space, the cavity should be completely filled under slight pressure, since fill insulation often settles with time.

☐ Provide vapor seal on the exterior surface of insulation when it is applied to the exterior surface of the wall. Provide a vapor barrier on the room side of the insulation when the insulation is applied to the interior surface of exterior walls.

☐ The combined "U" factor for a wall and glazing should not exceed the "U" values listed in the table above by more than 0.05. This can be accomplished by a combination of insulation and double or triple glazing in correct proportions. In retail stores with display windows, the space between the show window and the sales area should be blocked off by an insulated partition with a "U" value not less than 0.20.

☐ Use wall color to control heat gain. In most cases, a dark-colored north wall and a light-colored east and west wall will be the most energy conserving. In hot climates, all walls (and roofs) of light color and high reflectivity are best. The color of the wall has relatively little effect on energy consumption when used on exterior walls of low "U" values and high thermal mass.

Floors

☐ The following table shows the minimum acceptable "U" value for floors with exposed undersides in various degree day zones. Every floor below these standards should be insulated.

Heating Degree Days	Minimum Acceptable "U" value
1,000	0.40
2,000	0.35
3,000	0.30
4,000	0.22
5,000	0.22
6,000	0.18
7,000	0.18
8,000 and above	0.12

☐ If insulation is added, improve the "U" value to 0.08 or better. This is equivalent to R12 or 4 inches of fiberglass.

☐ Insulate slab-on-grade floors that are subject to condensation or that have low surface temperatures.

☐ Insulate slab-on-grade floors with edge insulation and protect insulation with a waterproof seal.

☐ Where suspended floors are over a closed-in but unused space, apply insulation to the underside of the floor. If there may be some future use for the space, or if it contains pipes and ducts, apply insulation to the inside walls of the space, leaving the floor uninsulated.

Distribution Losses

☐ Heat loss from boilers and furnaces may comprise as much as 15% of the total heating energy used in the building. While some of the heat loss from the boiler may seve to reduce heat loss from adjacent occupied spaces, more often it is lost directly through basement walls and floors without contributing useful heat to the building. Roof top or basement units are exposed to very low temperatures with corresponding greater losses and require better insulation than the equipment located within the building. Insulation of roof top or attic units that are also used for cooling will reduce the cooling loads as well.

☐ Install, increase or replace the insulation on air ducts, hot water and steam piping. (Heat loss from piping should not exceed 0.25 BTU's per square foot per degree difference between fluid temperature and air temperature).

☐ Insulate valve bodies, fittings, and other pipe appurtenances, except steam traps and condensate legs within 5 feet of the trap.

☐ Insulate the exterior surfaces of boilers, hot air, and forced warm air furnaces, and air handling units with insulation of sufficient R value, so that exterior surface temperatures do not exceed 90°F at full load operating conditions for units located in the building.

☐ For roof top units, the R value should not be less than 20 in all areas which have fewer than 7,000 degree days and not less than 30 where degree days exceed 7,000.

☐ For hot air furnaces, insulation should be done after a forced air blower is installed since the loss will be greatly reduced with the addition of the blower.

☐ Make sure air ducts are taped to prevent air loss.

Condensation Damage

☐ A vapor barrier must be provided on the interior surface of exterior walls to prevent condensation.

☐ Insulation should be protected from moisture, both from outdoors and indoors. Its insulation value decreases greatly when wet or damp. Consider insulation with low water absorption or insulation that dries out quickly and returns to its original thermal performance. Blown and organic insulations may not do this.

☐ Discourage the excessive use of humidifiers.

☐ Use a continuous vapor barrier with a perm value of .25 or less on all walls.

☐ Barriers under slabs should have a perm value of .5 or less.

☐ Use a barrier with a perm value of 1.0 or less in crawl spaces.

☐ Provide adequate ventilation in crawl spaces and attics.

Electric Lighting

☐ Replace louvers and lenses and install lenses that give better quality, more efficient lighting, on the tasks. Lenses should be selected for low brightness and high efficiency.

☐ Provide photo-cells to shut off lights when available daylight is adequate to replace the required lighting.

☐ Install additional switches to permit shutting off lights in unoccupied areas of the building.

☐ Install time switches which automatically turn off lights after a preset time, in areas where occupancy is light or spasmodic, and requires manual switching to energize the lights again after that time.

☐ Modify existing fixtures to accommodate higher efficiency lamps; for instance, convert incandescent lamp fixtures to high intensity discharge (HID lamps) or convert existing HID lamps to newer or more efficient ones.

☐ Replace incandescent fixtures with more efficient fluorescent or mercury fixtures, depending upon application.

☐ When replacing fixtures, select that type with higher coefficient of utilization.

☐ Paint or apply light colored reflective surface on interior room surfaces to increase inter-reflectances and improve the performance of both natural and artificial illumination. Walls should be first in priority, then ceiling and floors.

☐ When undertaking alterations for other purposes, use open planning to the greatest extent possible. This will reduce the amount of lighting energy which would be absorbed by walls.

☐ Where partitions are required, install low partitions to reduce light absorption while permitting the use of "borrowed" light from adjacent spaces.

☐ When refurnishing, select lighter colored furnishings that do not have a glossy surface or give specular reflectances.

☐ When retrofitting a building, lower the fixture mounting height.

☐ Relocate existing lighting fixtures to immunize veiling reflectances. Where possible light tasks from the side rather than from the front.

☐ Install dimmers to reduce light levels in areas where lighting level requirements are constantly changing. The savings in energy will not be in proportion to the percentage of light reduction but will provide net savings of energy.

☐ Install reflectors on the exterior of the building or treat the horizontal surface below windows with light reflective materials to increase the intensity of daylight illumination at the window surface.

☐ Color selection should be carefully considered in view of the available light source (i.e., natural, incandescent, fluorescent, etc.). Where efficiency is the goal, incandescent light should be controlled with materials that absorb the minimum red and yellow; mercury light should be controlled with materials that absorb the minimum blue and green. This is not to say that the color of materials adds to the efficiency of light at the primary source, but they do have an effect on apparent intensity.

Mass

☐ Use the mass of roofs or walls to control heat transfer. Large mass gives high thermal inertia which modifies the effect of a "U" value on heat transmission by expanding the time scale. For instance, a wall of high thermal inertia, subjected to solar radiation for one hour, will absorb the heat at its outside surface but transfer it to the interior over a time period as long as 12 hours. Conversely, a wall having the same "U" value, but low thermal inertia, will transfer the heat more quickly, perhaps in two hours.

The value of adjusting the time lag period must take into account all factors, including the general climate conditions, diurnal swings, and occupancy modes. In areas subject to long cold winters or long hot summers, with extreme peak temperatures and large daily temperature swings, large thermal inertia has a high priority for energy conservation. Heavy construction (up to 100 pounds per square foot) can be very effective in reducing energy consumption. The priority would be low in areas subject to small temperature swings from day to night. Where diurnal variations are greatest (deserts, northern climates), large mass is more important. Use clay tile, slate or concrete roof decks and masonry or stucco walls rather than lighter materials.

☐ Locate insulation outside of the mass for best results.

The location of insulation in a wall section can affect energy consumption, but usually not as much as the thermal value of that insulation. Studies show that the best location for insulation is outside of the mass of the building, making it poissible for the mass of the building to act as thermal storage and thus dampen the effects of daily temperature variations and indoor occupied-unoccupied temperature cycles. Insulation location to the exterior of the wall is more important in heavy construction than for low mass walls.

Pools

☐ Locate the pool so that it is out of prevailing winds but receives a maximum of sunlight.

☐ If a heater is planned, make sure it is adequate for the purpose.

☐ Always consider a solar heater.

☐ Control water evaporation with a cover.

☐ Control the water alkalinity to between 7.2 and 7.4.

Appendix 2

Cost Estimates For Energy Saving Improvements

Most energy conservation measures in new construction involve conventional methods and materials that present no particular cost estimating problems. The cost of bringing existing homes and commercial buildings up to modern standards may be much more difficult to estimate. The estimating data in this appendix is intended to provide guidance to the cost of many common energy conservation improvements in existing buildings. The costs are current as of 1977 and include only direct labor and material costs for typical residential and commercial jobs. Add the cost of supervision when it is required, overhead and profit to arrive at a reasonable bid figure. Naturally, small jobs, work performed under poor working conditions or where access is difficult, exceptionally high quality workmanship, and jobs that require reuse or matching of materials will cost more. Most of the costs are based on quantities that would be typical of a small to medium size commercial job. Modify the figures for smaller or larger quantities of work.

Costs for Supplying Plastic Film Tint to Windows Standard Cool Quality

1. Costs are complete and include supply and installation.

Area of window	Per 10 windows		Per 200 windows		Per 400 windows	
	12 SF	30 SF	12 SF	30 SF	12 SF	30 SF
Cost of SF	2.00	2.00	1.70	1.60	1.40	1.35
Cost per window	24.00	60.00	20.00	48.00	17.00	41.00

Cost for Installation of Venetian Blinds or Vertical Louver Blinds to Windows in Existing Masonry Building

1. Costs exclude:
   (a) Removal of any existing blinds or drapes.
   (b) Adapting or fitting blinds around existing window mounted air conditioners, louvers or fans, etc.
   (c) Any interior redecoration.

2. Costs are for supply and installation by a specialist contractor dealing in venetian and louver blind work.

Venetian Blinds

For quantities of: Approx. window area	10 windows		50-200 windows		Over 400 windows	
	12 SF	30 SF	12 SF	30 SF	12 SF	30 SF
2" venetian blind including all hardware, supplied and installed in existing building	$9.75	21.72	8.68	19.34	8.33	18.36

P.V.C. vertical louver drapes

For quantities of: Approx. window area	10 windows		200 windows		400 windows	
	12 SF	30 SF	12 SF	30 SF	12 SF	30 SF
Vertical P.V.C. louver drapes including all hardware, supplied and installed in existing building	$48.00	75.00	30.00	45.00	30.00	45.00

Cost Study for Removal of Glazing

1. Costs exclude:
   (a) Scaffolding costs.
   (b) Moving of internal furniture, etc.
   (c) Repainting walls internally around affected window openings.

2. Costs are:
   (a) Based on a quantity of 10 windows each size 3' x 4'.
   (b) Presume windows accessible at ground level.

3. Escalation:
   The materials included in this cost study have not been subject to the excessive increases in costs prevalent in materials with petro-chemical content. It is suggested that a rate of 8% per annum be used when updating costs listed here.

Example 1 - Masonry Structures

Costs exclude specifically unusual or difficult to match brick.
   (a) Removing aluminum windows and filling opening with masonry. **$170.00 per opening.**
   (b) Removing aluminum windows and filling opening with insulated sandwich panel and backup. **$198.00 per opening.**

Example 2 - Light Frame Construction

Costs exclude specifically repainted or restaining to achieve closer match, or repainting whole wall.
   (a) Removing window and filling opening with matching wall construction. **$165.00 per opening.**
   (b) Removing window and replacing with sash for 50% of area and filling balance of opening with matching wall construction. **$156.00 per opening.**

1. Costs exclude removal of interior furniture and fixtures including drapes and blinds.

Skylights

Provision of 48" x 48" acrylic double glazed domes based on a quantity of 6 to be installed and **excluding** (a) any major structural alterations (b) electrical and mechanical work and (c) redecoration internally. **Cost $500.00 per unit.**

Improve Caulking and Seals

1. Costs presume that:
    (a) Ladders can be used on jobs involving 10 windows.
    (b) For all other examples, stage hoists are used on exterior face of building.

Cost Study for Raking Existing Caulking and Re-caulking Around Windows

(Preformed closure costs not included in these costs.)

Caulking
Rake out old caulking and recaulk: $1.22/L.F.

Premoulded Seal
Assumed all work done in conjunction with caulking windows, etc., therefore additional scaffolding, etc., not required (or work can be accomplished by ladder to 30' height).

Rake out old caulking and recaulk using ½" x ½" premoulded polyfoam material: $2.03/L.F.

The same as above but using 1" x 1" premoulded polyfoam material: $2.80/L.F.

	Costs Per Window					
	10 Windows		50-200 Windows		Over 400 Windows	
	Window 12 SF	Window 30 SF	Window 12 SF	Window 30 SF	Window 12 SF	Window 30 SF
Rake out old caulking and recaulk around edges of windows	$18.00	25.00	17.00	27.00	18.00	27.00

Weatherstrip Doors, Windows and Other Openings to Prevent Infiltration

1. Costs exclude:
    (a) Removal of any blinds, drapes, etc.
    (b) Fitting weatherstripping around any existing windows, mounted air conditioners, fans, etc.
    (c) Any adjustment to frame, new threshold or sill which might be necessary.
    (d) Redecoration of the door or window frames.

2. Costs presume that:
    (a) No field foreman would be required for up to 50 windows, but that foreman (non-working) would be required for over 50 windows.
    (b) This work would be undertaken by an outside contractor.

	Costs Per Door	
	3' x 7' Door	Pair 6' x 7' Doors
Weatherstrip door with wood frame	$51.00	$ 74.00
Weatherstrip door with metal frame, with aluminum and rubber	96.00	138.00

	Costs Per Window					
	10 Windows		50-200 Windows		Over 400 Windows	
	Window 12 SF	Window 30 SF	Window 12 SF	Window 30 SF	Window 12 SF	Window 30 SF
Weatherstrip double hung window	$33.00	47.00	26.00	39.00	23.00	35.00

Cost Study for Surface Mounted Door Closers to Single Doors

1. Costs exclude:
   (a) Any necessary redecoration to door or frame.

2. Costs presume that:
   (a) Door is capable of receiving closer without any additional blocking, cutting, etc., being required.
   (b) Work is undertaken by general contractor in conjunction with other work on the building.

Cost of supplying and fixing door closers to single doors based on a quantity of about 10 doors = **$91.00 per door.**

Costs For Installing Revolving Doors

1. Costs exclude:
   (a) Any readjustment necessary to existing electrical and mechanical installation.
   (b) Additional swinging or hinged doors for use by handicapped, etc.

2. For installing the door in a new opening it is presumed that:
   (a) The external wall is masonry.
   (b) The street and ground floor levels are compatible.
   (c) The new opening leads directly into an entrance hall area.

Provide revolving door and install it in an existing opening:
Including removing existing aluminum tube section doorway and sidelights, finished opening 8' x 8' high. Installing new 7' diameter aluminum revolving door and trim opening. **Cost per unit installed: $10,300.00**

Provide revolving door and install it in a new opening:
Form new opening in external wall and install a new 7' diameter aluminum revolving door. **Cost per unit installed: $13,000.00**

Add Vestibule to Building Entry

1. Costs exclude:
   (a) Modification to existing doors.
   (b) Heating and cooling of vestibule.

2. Costs include black anodized aluminum tube section, gray tinted glass, concealed head door closers and light roof. **Cost per unit installed complete: $3,105.00.**

Epoxy Resin Insulation Coating on Exterior Walls

1. Costs presume that:
   (a) Building to be treated is a 100' x 50' three-story office building 10'-0" floor to floor.
   (b) An area of 10,000 S.F. will be treated.
   (c) Exterior wall construction is brickwork or blockwork.
   (d) Resin will be applied in two coats, total 4 mm. thick.
   (e) Swing staging will be required for application of resin.

4 mm. epoxy resin on external walls: **$0.42 per S.F.**

Add Rigid Insulation to Outside of Exterior Walls

1. Costs presume that:
   (a) Building to be insulated is a 100' x 50' 3 story office building with 10' floor to floor height.
   (b) An area of 10,000 S.F. will be insulated.
   (c) No external trim, fixtures or paint are to be removed nor will there be complications with windows, other openings or fascias.

2. Escalation: Cement costs are increasing on the order of 5% per year.

Rigid insulation and stucco to outside of exterior walls.
   (a) Using 1½" rigid insulation: **$3.12 S.F.**
   (b) Using 2" rigid insulation: **$3.24 S.F.**

Add Insulation to Core of Exterior Walls

All as described using blown insulation (**not** batt type) of fiberglass, perlite and urea formaldehyde.

1. Costs exclude:
   (a) Any special guarantees which may be called for.
   (b) Movement of furniture and occupant relocation.
   (c) Major patchwork.

2. Costs cover:
   (a) Start up through clean up.
   (b) Reasonably good accessibility to wall space.
   (c) A well planned operation (one-trip job with no delays and no premium time).

3. Escalation: Urethane material costs in the past have increased by as much as 15% per year. Urea-formaldehyde material costs in the past have increased by 10% per year. Fiberglass and perlite have shown similar cost increases.

4. Costs:
   (a) Blown insulation (from interior of building)
       Fiberglass $1.45 S.F.
       Perlite $1.83 S.F.
       Urea formaldehyde from 75-80 cents S.F.
   (b) Blown insulation (from exterior of building)
       Fiberglass $1.24 S.F.
       Perlite $1.61 S.F.
       Urea formaldehyde from 65-75 cents S.F.

Add Insulation to Inside of Exterior Walls

1. Costs presume that:
   (a) Building to be insulated is a 100' x 50' three story office building with 10' floor to floor height.
   (b) An area of 10,000 S.F. to be insulated.

2. Costs exclude:
   (a) Resetting electrical and mechanical equipment.

   (b) Framing out to door and window openings and setting door and window trim and cover base.

Costs per square foot
Insulate interior faces of exterior walls with 1½" rigid insulation: **$2.03 S.F.**

Apply Spray-On Insulation to Exterior of Roofs

1. Costs exclude:
   (a) Any special guarantees or roof bonds which may be called for.
   (b) Extra masking, any unusual edge or flashing condition.
   (c) Any new flashings or expansion joints required.

2. Costs include:
   (a) Start up through clean up.

   (b) Work on flat relatively unobstructed roof.

3. Costs are based on a roof of 10,000 S.F.
   (a) Cost using 2" polystyrene insulation and butyl roofing - **$2.08 S.F.**
   (b) Cost using 2" urethane and elastomeric roofing - **$2.15 S.F.**
   (c) Additional cost to be added to (a) or (b) above for spraying elastomeric roofing with aluminum spray (3 mils thick) - **$0.30 S.F.**

Apply Rigid Insulation to Exterior of Flat Roof

1. Costs exclude unusual roof conditions, catwalks or walkways.

2. Costs include:
   (a) Start up through clean up.
   (b) Work on flat relatively unobstructed roof.

3. Costs are based on a roof of 10,000 S.F. at a height above ground level of 4 to 8 stories. For tall buildings costs would not increase a great deal providing easy access was available to a suitable elevator.

4. Costs using 4 ply tar and gravel 20 year bonded roof and the following insulation materials.
   (a) 2" rigid urethane   = **$2.61 S.F.**
   (b) 2" fiberglass   = **$2.16 S.F.**
   (c) 2" fiberboard   = **$2.35 S.F.**
   (d) 2" cellular glass   = **$2.38 S.F.**
   (e) 2" perlite   = **$2.35 S.F.**

Apply Rigid Insulation and Shingles to Exterior of Sloping Roof

1. Costs exclude any special guarantees which might be called for.

2. Costs:
   (a) Are for roofing a 10,000 S.F. pitched surface of a 4-story building.
   (b) Include scaffolding up to eave level on all faces and a materials hoist.

3. Costs:
   (a) Using 265# asphalt shingles and 2" insulation - **$1.79 S.F.**
   (b) **Alternative** using 260# fiberglass shingles and 2" insulation - **$1.70 S.F.**

Apply Spray-On Insulation to Underside of Roof

1. Costs exclude:
   (a) Any special guarantees which might be called for.
   (b) Moving furniture.
   (c) Protection of sensitive equipment.

2. Costs include:
   (a) All work to be done at night on double-time wages.
   (b) Removal of existing 2' x 4' ceiling and suspension system and **replacement** with a new suspended ceiling.
   (c) Cleaning surface and masking ducts prior to application of spray.
   (d) Final clean up.

3. Costs are based on a ceiling of 10,000 S.F. as might be encountered in a large supermarket.
   (a) Cost using 1" mineral fiber spray - **$2.65 S.F.**
   (b) Cost using 1" urethane plastic spray - **$3.14 S.F.**

Apply Rigid or Batt Insulation Below a Roof

1. Costs exclude:
   (a) Any special guarantees which might be called for.
   (b) Moving furniture.
   (c) Protection of sensitive equipment.

2. Costs include:
   (a) All work to be done at night on double-time wages.
   (b) Removal of existing 2' x 4' ceiling and suspension system and **replacement** with a new suspended ceiling.
   (c) Cleaning surfaces and masking ducts prior to installation of insulation materials.
   (d) Final clean up.

3. Costs are based on an area of 10,000 S.F.

4. Alternative (A) using rigid insulation board.
   (a) 2" styrofoam   = $2.78 S.F.
   (b) 2" fiberboard   = $3.12 S.F.
   (c) 2" fiberglass   = $2.95 S.F.
   (d) 2" expanded glass   = $2.98 S.F.
   (e) 2" perlite   = $3.12 S.F.

5. Alternative (B) using batt insulation.
   (a) 3" fiberglass   = $2.24 S.F.
   (b) 3" mineral fiber   = $2.22 S.F.

Protect Insulation with Vapor Barrier

1. Costs exclude:
   (a) Removal of existing ceiling and replacement with a new ceiling.
   (b) Replacement of any deteriorated insulation.

2. Costs include:
   (a) Work to underside of flat relatively unobstructed roof.

   (b) Start up through clean up.

3. Costs are based on an area of 10,000 S.F. Application of sheet vapor barrier by stapling including lapping and gluing = **$0.14 S.F.**

Cost Study for Repainting Existing Walls and Ceilings

1. Costs exclude removal of interior furniture and fixtures, including drapes and blinds.

2. Costs presume that:
   (a) Work would be completed in sections.
   (b) Paint would be roller applied.
   (c) Walls are in good condition and do not need excessive scraping or filling of cracks.
   (d) No field foreman would be required for areas of approximately 10,000 S.F., but that foreman (non-painting) would be required for greater areas.

3. Costs:
   (a) Wash, touch up, and apply two coats gloss paint on smooth finish plaster: Areas of approximately: 10,000 SF = $0.27 SF; 20,000 SF = $0.24 SF; 50,000 SF = $0.23 SF; 100,000 SF = $0.23 SF.
   (b) Clean down and apply two coats flat finish on concrete block walls: Areas of approximately: 10,000 SF = $0.34 SF; 20,000 SF = $0.32 SF; 50,000 SF = $0.31 SF; 100,000 SF = $0.29 SF.
   (c) Wash, touch up, and apply one coat gloss paint on smooth finish plaster: Areas of approximately: 10,000 SF = $0.20 SF; 20,000 SF = $0.17 SF; 50,000 SF = $0.16 SF; 100,000 SF = $0.16 SF.
   (d) Clean down and apply one coat flat finish on concrete block walls: Areas of approximately: 10,000 SF = $0.24 SF; 20,000 SF = $0.23 SF; 50,000 SF = $0.20 SF; 100,000 SF = $0.20 SF.

Change Color or Texture of Interior Walls

1. Costs exclude removal of interior furniture and fixtures.

2. Costs presume that:
   (a) Work would be completed in sections.
   (b) Paint would be roller applied.
   (c) No field foreman would be required for areas of approximately 10,000 S.F. but that foreman would be required for greater areas.

3. Costs:

   (a) Apply 3/8" gypsum board on furring strips taped and spackled and painted with **two** coats of latex paint. Areas of approximately: 10,000 SF = $0.88 SF; 20,000 SF = $0.86 SF; 50,000 SF = $0.86 SF; 100,000 SF = $0.85 SF.
   (b) Apply 3/8" gypsum board on furring strips taped and spackled and painted with **one** coat of latex paint. Areas of approximately: 10,000 SF = $0.81 SF; 20,000 SF = $0.80 SF; 50,000 SF = $0.79 SF; 100,000 SF = $0.79 SF.

Cost Studies in Connection with Plumbing Work

1. Costs presume that work would be undertaken by a plumbing subcontractor. The examples given cannot be taken in isolation and may be much higher if only a small volume of work is undertaken.

2. Costs:
   (a) Replacing screw-down type faucet with spring operated, self-closing type faucet, ½" iron pipe size including all accessories. **Cost per faucet = $51.00.**
   (b) Insulating hot or cold water tanks with 3# density glass fiber with foil scrim kraft facing, finished with pre-sized glass cloth jacket.

Material Thickness	Cost per S.F. of surface area
1"	$2.60
1½"	2.70
2"	2.95
3"	3.60

   (c) Insulating hot and cold water pipes with pre-sized glass fiber material with a standard jacket.

Pipe Sizes	Price per L.F. Installed Insulation Thickness	
	1"	1½"
½"	$1.35	$2.05
¾"	1.40	2.10
1"	1.45	2.15
1¼"	1.50	2.20
1½"	1.55	2.25
2"	1.60	2.35
2½"	1.65	2.45
3"	1.70	2.50
4"	2.00	3.05
5"	2.25	3.15
6"	2.55	3.30
8"	3.15	4.20
10"	3.85	5.00
12"	4.50	5.60
14"	5.20	6.45
16"	6.00	7.20
18"	6.70	7.60
20"	8.25	8.50
24"	9.00	9.70

For costing purposes, add to total lineal feet of piping three linear feet for each fitting or pair of flanges to be insulated.

Appendix 3
Glossary

Absorption   A process whereby heat extracts one or more substances present in an atmosphere or mixture of gases or liquids, accompanied by physical change, chemical change, or both changes of the material.

Absorption Chiller   A refrigeration unit based upon absorption refrigeration.

Absorption refrigeration   Cooling which is effected by the expansion of liquid ammonia into gas by water. Heat is the primary source of energy.

Active   When applied to building design, it refers to the mechanical movement of energy by the use of an external force of energy.

Aerobic   Requiring the presence of oxygen.

Air change   The movement of a volume of air in a given period of time; if a house has one air change per hour, it means that all the air in the house will be replaced in a one-hour period. Air changes are expressed in cubic feet per minute.

Air conditioning   The process of treating air to control its temperature, humidity, flow, and odor.

Altitude   The measurement in degrees of the difference in vertical direction on perpendicular to the earth's surface and a given object.

Ambient temperature   Temperature of the outside air.

Anaerobic   The absence of oxygen which prevents normal life for organisms that depend on oxygen.

Attic ventilation   In houses, screened openings provided to ventilate an attic space. They are located in the soffit area as inlet ventilators and in the gable end or along the ridge as outlet ventilators. They can also consist of power-driven fans used as an exhaust system.

Azimuth   The measurement in degrees of the difference in the south horizontal direction on the earth's surface and a given object.

Berm   A mound or small hill of earth, man-made.

Boiler   A device used to heat water or produce steam. It includes burner, heat exchanger, flue, and container and controls; may be fueled by oil, gas, or electricity.

British Thermal Unit (BTU)   The amount of heat necessary to raise the temperature of one pound of water one degree Fahrenheit; a unit of heat roughly equal to the amount of heat given off by burning a kitchen match.

Building skin   The physical structure which encloses a building.

Bypass loop   A piping arrangement which bypasses or circles the flow of a heat absorbing medium around rather than through a piece of mechanical equipment.

CFM An abbreviation for cubic feet per minute.

Capacity The usable output of a system.

Centrifugal fan A machine for moving a gas, such as air, by accelerating it rapidly outward in an impeller to a surrounding casing; generally of a scroll shape.

Change of state (*phase change*) The change from solid, liquid, or gas to either of the other two.

Chimney effect The tendency of air or gas in a duct or other vertical passage to rise when heated due to its lower density compared with that of the surrounding air or gas. In buildings, the tendency toward displacement (caused by the difference in temperature) of internal heated air by unheated outside air due to the difference in density of outside and inside air.

Coil A cooling or heating element made of pipe or tubing.

Comfort zone The ranges of indoor temperature, humidity, and air movement under which most persons enjoy mental and physical well-being.

Compression In a compression refrigeration system, a process by which the pressure and temperature of the refrigerant is increased to allow for greater heat transfer.

Conduction A process of heat transfer whereby heat moves through a material.

Control logic The sequence of steps required to perform a specific function.

Convection Transfer of heat by movement of a fluid or gas.

Crack method A method used in the calculation of air movement from the outside into an enclosed space. The method is based on the rate through one foot of crack between sash and frame or between door and frame.

Cursor A movable, clear scale which can be used to read a value on a stationary scale accurately.

DHW tank Abbreviated form for Domestic Hot Water tank.

Damper A device used to vary the volume of air passing through an air outlet, inlet or duct.

Dehumidification The condensation of water vapor from air by cooling below the dew point or removal of water vapor from air by chemical or physical methods.

Density The weight per unit volume.

Desalination Removal of salt, as from water or soil.

Dew point The temperature at which water vapor begins to condense.

Diurnal cycle The day-to-night change or cycle of natural phenomenon. An example is the variation of outdoor temperature throughout a twenty-four hour period.

Dry bulb temperature A measure of the sensible temperature of air (the one with which we are most familiar).

Economizer cycle A cooling mode which uses cool outdoor air to offset heat gains in buildings rather than using an energy consuming cooling device.

Electronic air filter The use of electricity to set up a static charge which can remove dust and other particulate matter.

Energy The capacity for doing work; taking a number of forms which may be transformed from one into another, such as thermal, (heat), mechanical (work), electrical and chemical; in customary units, measured in kilowatt hours (KWH) or British Thermal Units (BTU); in SI units, measured in joules (J), where 1 joule = 1 watt-second.

Enthalpy A measurement of the total energy content of the air. The total energy content is composed of both sensible and latent heat as measured by the dry bulb and wet bulb temperatures.

Equinox Occurring in Fall about September 23rd and in Spring about March 21st, it is the time at which light falls equally on the Northern and Southern Hemispheres, day and night are of equal duration everywhere on earth.

Evacuated tube collector A solar collector composed of air evacuated cylindrical tubes.

Evaporative cooling Lowering the temperature of a large mass of liquid by utilizing the latent heat of vaporization of a portion of the liquid; cooling air by evaporating water into it.

Flame spread The rate at which combustion will occur.

Flat-plate collector A solar collector composed of sheet materials for the glazing and absorber plate.

Flow rate Velocity at which a fluid travels, usually through an opening or duct.

Frequency of occurrence The number of times a given event will occur during a given period of time.

GPM An abbreviation for gallons per minute.

Greenhouse effect The effect of the earth's atmosphere in trapping heat from the sun. The atmosphere acts like a greenhouse by admitting the sun's shortwave radiation but blocking the exit of long wavelength radiation re-emitted by the earth or other warmed objects.

Heat capacity Sometimes called the thermal capacity, a measure of how much heat is required to raise the temperature of a specific quantity of material by a given amount.

Heat dissipator The method of transmitting energy or power out of a system in the form of heat.

Heat exchanger A device used to transfer heat from one medium to the other.

Heat gain An increase in the amount of heat contained in a space, resulting from direct solar radiation and the heat given off by people, lights, equipment, machinery, and other sources.

Heat loss A decrease in the amount of heat contained in a space, resulting from heat flow through walls, windows, roof, and other building envelope components.

Heat pump A reversible refrigeration system that delivers more heat energy to the end use than is put in to the compressor. The additional energy input results from the absorption of heat from a low temperature source--the combination heating and cooling unit. It operates like a normal air conditioner in summer, and in winter operates in reverse, ejecting warm air indoors and cool air (or water) outdoors.

Heat wheel A device used in ventilating systems which tends to bring incoming air into thermal equilibrium with exiting air. As a result, hot summer air is cooled and cold winter air is warmed.

Humidifier A device to add moisture to air.

In-line pump A pump which is supported by the piping system.

Incident Usually used in the term "incident radiation" which is the amount of energy striking a collector surface before entering the collector.

Infiltration The uncontrolled flow of air into and out of a building through cracks, openings, doors, or other areas which allow air to penetrate.

Initial cost The original price of an item or system.

Insolation The exposure of an object to the sun; solar energy received, often expressed as a rate of energy per unit horizontal surface.

Insulation, thermal Any material high in resistance to heat transmission that, when placed in the walls, ceilings, or floors of a structure, will reduce the rate of heat flow.

Kilowatt Hour (KWH) Unit of electrical energy consumption which equals about 3,400 BTU.

Latent heat A change in heat content that

occurs without a corresponding change in temperature, usually accompanied by a change of state.

Latitude   The measurement in degrees of a given position on the earth perpendicular to the equator.

Life-cycle cost   The total cost of a system calculated over its anticipated operational life span.

Longitude   The measurement in degrees of a given position on the earth and perpendicular with the meridian of Greenwich, England.

Longwave radiation   Energy radiation in the infra-red portion of the spectrum; normal window glass is opaque to longwave radiation, hence forming a heat trap.

MBTU   A thousand British Thermal Units.

Masonry   Stone, brick, concrete, hollow tile, concrete block, gypsum block, or other similar building units or materials, or a combination of the same, bonded together with mortar to form a wall, piers, buttress, or similar mass.

Mass   The property of density of a material. The use of mass by itself or in combination with insulation gives building structures the capacity to store energy or heat.

Mean   The average or expected value.

Mechanical system   The use of mechanical methods to provide comfort for occupants.

Mode   One of several alternative conditions or methods of operation of a device or system.

Moisture content   The quantity of water in a volume of air expressed in grains of moisture; a grain of moisture is one seven thousandths of a pound.

Operating cost   The cost in money to operate a system for a given period of time. Its greatest use is in the comparison of different systems.

Overheated period   The times during a day, or year, in which the interior of an enclosure is above the comfort zone.

PSIG   Abbreviation for Pounds Per Square Inch Gauge.

Passive   The use of the natural movements of energy such as convection or conduction through fluids and gases to provide human comfort.

Peak load   Maximum predicted energy demand of a system.

Perms-permeance   The ratio of water vapor flow to the vapor pressure difference of the surfaces; permeance is expressed in perms or (grains)/(Sq.Ft.)(Hr.), and of mercury vapor pressure difference.

Potable water   The drinking water for the house. In solar water heating systems where anti-freeze is used, this must be kept separate by use of a heat exchanger.

Psychrometric   Pertaining to the device comprising two thermometers, one a dry bulb, the other a wet bulb or wick-covered bulb, used in determining the moisture content or relative humidity of air or other gases.

R-Value resistance   The resistance of a material to the flow of heat or energy.

Reflectance   A property of a material indicating the percentage of light that is reflected when a certain amount of light strikes the surface of the material or is transmitted through it.

Relative humidity   The ratio of the amount of water vapor at a given temperature to the maximum amount of water vapor that could be held as vapor.

Roll roofing   Roofing material composed of fiber and saturated with asphalt that is supplied in rolls, each containing 108 square feet in 36-inch widths with a weight of 45 to 90 pounds per roll.

Roof sheathing   The boards or sheet material fastened to the roof rafters on which the shingle or other roof covering is laid.

SHW tank   Abbreviation for Solar Hot Water tank.

Sensible heat   Heat that results in a temperature change.

Set back   The lowering of the thermostat setting. The technique is used to reduce the amount of heat required to heat a space.

Set up   The raising of the thermostat setting. The technique is used to reduce the amount of cooling required to cool a space.

Shading coefficient   The effectiveness of any shading device can be expressed by its shading coefficient which describes the fraction of the incident solar energy which is transmitted through a window.

Shading device   A covering which blocks the passage of solar radiation. Common shading devices consist of awnings, overhangs, or trees.

Shortwave radiation   A term used loosely to distinguish radiation in the visible and near-visible portions of the electromagnetic spectrum (roughly 0.4 to 1.0 micrometers in wavelength) from longwave radiation (infra-red radiation).

Sky vault   All of the sky from the horizon in all directions, upward.

Sling psychrometer   A psychrometer in which the wet and dry bulb thermometers are mounted upon a frame and connected to a handle at one end by means of a bearing or a length of chain. It may be whirled in the air for the simultaneous measurement of wet and dry bulb temperatures.

Solar intensity   The amount of solar radiation.

Solenoid valve   A valve actuated by a solenoid or an electronic impulse for controlling the flow of gases or liquids in pipes.

Solstice   The two days (actually instants) during the year when the earth is so located in its orbit that the inclination (about 23½°) of the polar axis is toward the sun. The days are June 21st for the North Pole and December 22nd for the South Pole; because of Leap Years, the dates vary slightly.

Space heating   Interior heating of a building or room.

Stagnation   The condition of a fluid or gas unstirred by a current or flow.

Thermal comfort   The zone in which a majority of the human population would not feel too hot or too cold.

Thermal lag   The ability of materials to delay the transmission of heat; can be used interchangeably with time lag.

Thermal sensation   The ability of the body to sense the temperature as being too hot or too cold.

Time lag   The time between a cause and a resultant effect, as between occurrence of heat input on an exterior surface of a wall and the time until the heat is transmitted to the interior wall surface.

Ton (of air conditioning)   The thermal refrigeration energy required to melt one ton of ice (2,000 pounds); equals 12,000 BTU.

"U" value   A coefficient which indicates the energy (BTU) which passes through a component for every degree (Fahrenheit) of temperature difference from one side to the other under steady state conditions.

Vapor barrier   A component of construction which is impervious to the flow of moisture or air.

Vapor pressure   The force exerted when moist air attempts to seek equilibrium by migrating to areas with less water vapor.

Velcro   Trade name denoting a fabric composed of two pieces which join together or adhere by means of interlocking synthetic fibers.

Ventilation air   Outside air that is intentionally allowed to enter an interior space.

Weatherstripping   Foam, metal, or rubber strips used to form a seal around windows, doors, or openings to reduce infiltration.

Wet bulb temperature   The lowest temperature attainable by evaporating water into the air, without altering the energy content.

Index

Practical References For Builders

Roofers Handbook

The journeyman roofer's complete guide to wood and asphalt shingle application on both new construction and reroofing jobs: When and how to use shakes, shingles, and T-locks to full advantage. How professional roofers make smooth tie-ins on any job. The right way to cover valleys and ridges. An excellent chapter on handling and preventing leaks is by itself worth the price of the book. Chapters 12 and 13 show you how to prepare an estimate (including man hour requirements), how to set up and run your own roofing business and how to sell your services as a professional roofer. A sample roofing contract is included. It's all here with easy-to-follow explanations, over 250 illustrations and hundreds of inside-trade tips available nowhere else. If you install shingle roofing this will be your most valuable working reference.

| 192 pages | 8½ x 11 | $7.25 |

Practical Rafter Calculator

Cut every rafter right the first time and know it is perfect. This book gives you rapid, accurate, 100% error-free answers . . . the exact, actual lengths for common, hip, valley and jack rafters for every span up to 50 feet and for every rise from 1/2 in 12 to 30 in 12. Everything is worked out to give you the correct rafter length at a glance—to the nearest 1/16 inch! Angle, plumb and level cuts are included so that you have all the information you need to do the job right the first time—everytime. If you know the pitch and you know the roof span, this practical reference will give you everything else. Every framing professional needs this time-saver.

| 124 pages | 3 x 7 | $3.00 |

Remodelers Handbook

The complete "How to . . ." of home improvement contracting: planning the job, estimating costs, doing the work, running your company and making profits in home improvement. Pages of sample forms, contracts, documents, clear illustrations and examples make this your most practical reference if you do any remodeling or home improvement work. Complete chapters on evaluating the work necessary, rehabilitation, remodeling kitchens, remodeling bathrooms, finding and adding living area, re-flooring, re-siding and adding soffits, re-roofing and installing gutters, replacing windows and doors, installing new wall and ceiling covers, re-painting, upgrading insulation (with rolls, batts and blown materials), adding ventilation and combating moisture damage, installing modern fireplaces and chimneys, repairing porches and building modern exposed wood decks, estimating and controlling costs, simple but adequate money management (including a complete bookkeeping system for remodelers), handling production and bringing in the sales needed to keep your crews busy and profits up. You'll be surprised at how much of this good, practical information you can put to use right away. In fact, you're missing a good bet· if you try to run a home improvement operation without this new reference.

| 416 pages | 8½ x 11 | $12.00 |

Finish Carpentry

Money-making know-how for the carpentry "pro". Sure answers to practical carpentry problems. This new handbook has the time-saving methods, inside trade information and proven shortcuts you need to do first class finish carpentry work on any job: cornices and rakes, gutters and downspouts, wood shingle roofing, asphalt, asbestos and built-up roofing, prefabricated windows, door bucks and frames, door trim, siding, wallboard, lath and plaster, stairs and railings, cabinets, joinery, and wood flooring. Here you have all the information you need to figure the materials and labor required, lay out the work and cut, fit and install the items required. Over 350 man-hour tables, charts and clear illustrations make this the practical, step by step handbook every carpentry "pro" needs.

| 192 pages | 8½ x 11 | $5.25 |

Wood Frame House Construction

From the layout of the outer walls, excavation and formwork, to finish carpentry, sheet metal and painting, every step of construction is covered in detail with clear illustrations and explanations. Here the builder will find everything he needs to know about framing, roofing, siding, plumbing, heating, insulation and vapor barrier, interior finishing, floor coverings, millwork and cabinets, stairs, chimneys, driveways, walks . . . complete step by step "how to" information on everything that goes into building a frame house. Many valuable tips are included: What you should know about building codes; ways to reduce costs without cutting quality; when concrete block should be used; the advantages of slabs; how to use reinforcing properly. This new book is carefully written, well illustrated and worth several times the price.

| 240 pages | 8 x 10 | $3.25 |

The Successful Construction Contractor

Can you succeed at construction contracting? Thousands do every year and these two volumes are filled with the working knowledge contractors need and use to succeed.

Volume I covers plan reading, working with specifications and practical construction. It is written to solve problems and answer practical questions: How to understand working drawings and specifications (actual plans and complete specifications are included for residential, commercial and industrial structures). How to work with concrete and steel. Selecting the right lumber grades and framing system for your job. How to handle masonry, drywall, lath and plaster to best advantage. Over 100 practical pages on carpentry alone will help you ensure that carpentry work on your jobs is professional and efficient. With over 450 pages and more than 600 illustrations, tables and charts, this volume puts at your fingertips the time and money saving construction knowledge you need on your next job.

Volume II has the essential estimating, selling and mangement information contractors need: A complete estimating system for excavation, concrete, reinforcing steel, carpentry, masonry, lath and plaster and much more. How to take off materials and compile an estimate including profit, contingency and overhead. How to be sure your estimate is correct and control costs once work is started. Hundreds of actual man-hour estimates are included (important reference material you will use again and again). One chapter examines actual case histories of contractors who made it and contractors who didn't and isolates 8 key elements that you can use to build your own operation. Another chapter shows you how to get started—licensing requirements and permits. How to incorporate or form a partnership (complete with forms) and meet state and Federal tax requirements. How you can make sure you get the loan you request (including 26 Federal loan sources for builders). How to plan and schedule your job (using modern CPM techniques). The chapter on selling has a complete sales plan for remodelers and custom builders, from initial advertising to closing the sale. A very important section shows you how to check the financial health of your company, whether large or small, and protect it so that it can grow and prosper. A final chapter covers construction law and builders insurance and includes important information on how to get the bonds you need to move into more profitable types of work. If you want to develop a strong, money-making construction business, you should have these practical manuals.

| Volume 1 | 8½ x 11 | 452 pages | $11.75 |
| Volume 2 | 8½ x 11 | 496 pages | $12.50 |

Rough Carpentry

Modern construction methods, labor and material saving tips, the facts you need to select the right lumber grade and dimension for every framing problem. All rough carpentry is covered in detai: sills, girders, columns, joists, sheathing, ceiling, roof and wall framing (over 60 pages on roofs alone), roof trusses, dormers, bay windows, furring and grounds, stairs (42 illustrations of stair work) and insulation (including how much is needed for your area). Many of the 24 chapters explain practical code approved methods for saving lumber and time without sacrificing quality . . . important information every cost conscious builder should have. Chapters on columns, headers, rafters, joists and girders show you how to use simple engineering principles to select the right lumber dimension for whatever species and grade you are using. This new handbook will open your eyes to faster, money-saving, more professional ways to handle framing, sheathing, and insulating and will be the most useful carpentry reference in your library.

| 288 pages | 8½ x 11 | $6.75 |

Home Builder's Guide

The "how to" of custom home contracting explained by a successful professional builder. Clearly explains what you should be doing, avoiding and watching out for during each phase of the job. How to anticipate problems, eliminate bottlenecks, keep the work going smoothly, and end up with a finished home that puts profits in your pocket and pleases your customers. Includes what you need to know about working with subcontractors, lenders, architects, municipal authorities, building inspectors, tradesmen and suppliers. Here you will find simple but effective ways of avoiding design problems, getting the right kind of financing, making sure your building permit is issued promptly, avoiding excavation mistakes, preventing delays if a subcontractor's work doesn't pass inspection, coordinating framing with the other trades, developing a flexible but effective construction schedule, and getting the work done without the hundreds of problems that often delay even highly experienced builders.

| 359 pages | 8½ x 5½ | $7.00 |

Stair Builders Handbook

Modern methods, proven techniques and precise tables that guarantee professional results on every stairway you build. If you know the floor to floor rise, this handbook will give you everything else: the number and dimension of treads and risers, the total run, the correct well hole opening, the angle of incline, the quantity of materials and settings for your framing square. Accurate tables give you over 3,500 code approved rise and run combinations—several for each 1/8 inch interval from a 3 foot to a 12 foot floor to floor rise. Simple step by step instruction with big, clear illustrations help you build the right stairway for your job. Anyone who designs, lays out or builds stairways needs this time-saving, money-making handbook. There is nothing else like it available. It's your key to perfect stairs—the first time, every time—from now on.

413 pages   8½ x 5½ $5.95

Structures Cost Manual

Square foot costs for over 60 types of residential, commercial, industrial and agricultural buildings...whether of reinforced concrete, masonry or wood frame. In a few minutes you work up a reliable budget estimate or replacement cost based on the actual materials, design features, area, shape, wall height, number of floors and support requirements. Most important, **Structures Cost Manual** covers all the important variables that can make any building unique from a cost standpoint. Nearly all the figures you need for each building are brought together on a single page. You get a reliable total cost for the building you have in mind and location you select. If you have to develop building estimates, values or replacement costs, you should get the current edition of this practical manual on your desk as soon as possible. Revised annually.

240 pages   8½ x11 $10.00

Carpentry by H. H. Siegele

This book illustrates all the essentials of residential work: layout, form building, simplified timber engineering, corners, joists and flooring, rough framing, sheathing, cornices, columns, lattice, building paper, siding, doors and windows, roofing, joints and more. One chapter demonstrates how the steel square is used in modern carpentry. A whole generation of journeymen and apprentices have learned carpentry from H. H. Siegele. This reference has the essential knowledge you need to become a skilled professional carpenter.

219 pages   8½ x 11 $6.95

National Construction Estimator

Accurate building costs in dollars and cents for residential, commercial and industrial construction. Prices for every commonly used building material, the proper labor cost associated with installation of the material. Everything figured out to give you the "in place" cost in seconds. Many time saving rules of thumb, waste and coverage factors and estimating tables are included.

Thousands of copies are in daily use by estimators, tradesmen, builders, appraisers, adjusters, architects, engineers, lenders, and students of building. Revised annually.

288 pages   8½ x 11 $7.50

National Repair And Remodeling Estimator

The complete pricing guide for dwelling reconstruction costs. Reliable, specific data you can apply on every remodeling job. Up-to-date material costs and labor figures based on thousands of repair and remodeling jobs across the country. Professional estimating techniques to help determine the material needed, the quantity to order, the labor required, the correct crew size and the actual labor cost for your area. This new volume is a complete file of repair and remodeling costs and will become your working file for all pricing. Revised annually.

160 pages   11 x 8½ $8.50

Concrete And Formwork

All the information you need to select and pour the right mix for the job, lay out the structure, select the right form materials, design and build the forms and finish and cure the concrete. This is the handbook for the man on the job who needs sure answers to practical problems: What type of mix is best? What admixtures are needed? How deep should the footing be? What is the best way to lay out and design the forms? How much concrete and form material are needed? Nearly 100 pages of step-by-step instructions cover the actual construction and erecting of all forms in common use. The most useful single volume for anyone working with site fabricated wood concrete forms.

176 pages   8½ x 11 $4.25

Practical Lumber Computer

This handy book quickly and easily gives board footage for all standard sizes and lengths of lumber from 1 to 1,000 pieces. It reads directly in board feet. All the work is done for you! You arrive at the precise answer without any mathematics or calculations. The footage content of one piece of any number of pieces is calculated and tabulated for your ready reference. A table is also included which will allow you to quickly determine the board feet per linear foot of lumber. This is the most popular lumber book because it is complete, accurate and easy to use. Everyone buying, selling or using lumber needs this handy time-saver. It pays for itself the first time you use it.

124 pages   5½ x 8½ $2.50

The Minimum Energy Dwelling

This timely reference explains how to design and build a conventional residence that will cut gas, oil and electric costs by as much as 50%. It shows how to plan for proper insulation and ventilation, correct shading, both passive and active solar heating, good orientation and land use, significant temperature moderation by use of the building mass, reduced infiltration, efficient mechanical and electrical systems and much more. The last chapter shows how these design principles were actually used by a major builder to construct the home shown on the book cover. This isn't a "21st century" home. The Minimum Energy Dwelling uses conventional materials you are familiar with, yet incorporates a number of real advances that are going to appear on many of the homes built in the next few years.

280 pages   8½ x 11 $8.00
